THE POLITICAL ECONOMY
OF
AMERICAN FOREIGN POLICY

THE POLITICAL ECONOMY

OF

AMERICAN FOREIGN POLICY

★★★

Its Concepts, Strategy, and Limits

REPORT OF A STUDY GROUP SPONSORED BY
THE WOODROW WILSON FOUNDATION
AND
THE NATIONAL PLANNING ASSOCIATION

HENRY HOLT AND COMPANY · NEW YORK

Copyright 1955
By Henry Holt and Company, Inc.

Library of Congress Catalog Card Number: 55-6125

20359-0115

Printed in the United States of America

Foreword

by
WILLIAM Y. ELLIOTT
Chairman of the Study Group

The present volume on the foreign economic policy of the United States was originally conceived by the Woodrow Wilson Foundation as a logical successor to an earlier report prepared for it by a previous Study Group and published under the title *United States Foreign Policy: Its Organization and Control*.[1] Although three members of the present Study Group also participated in the earlier one—Messrs. Gideonse and Price, and myself—the two volumes are neither complementary nor supplementary, and each stands independently on its own merits.

When plans were being made for a second Study Group, Mr. Frank Altschul was President of the Woodrow Wilson Foundation. For many years he has also been—and still is—a Vice Chairman of the National Planning Association and Chairman of NPA's Committee on International Policy. In this dual capacity, Mr. Altschul became aware that both organizations were considering the initiation of studies of American foreign economic policy, and he proposed that their separate efforts be combined into a single venture to be sponsored jointly by the Woodrow

---

[1] *United States Foreign Policy: Its Organization and Control*, Report of a Study Group for the Woodrow Wilson Foundation. Chairman of the Study Group: William Yandell Elliott (New York: Columbia University Press, 1952).

Wilson Foundation and the National Planning Association. This suggestion met with immediate approval, and the two organizations soon agreed upon a list of persons to be invited to become members of the new Study Group and upon a Chairman for the Group. The Woodrow Wilson Foundation assumed responsibility for financing the work of the Study Group, for arranging meetings, and for mimeographing, printing and publishing. The National Planning Association contributed the services of Mr. Theodore Geiger, its Chief of International Studies, and of Miss Dora M. Grabfield, one of its research assistants, to carry on the staff work of the Study Group on a part-time basis.

It is difficult to say whether the initial choice of subject for the Study Group determined those invited to become members, or whether the collaboration of a group of like-minded and knowledgeable men—with considerable practical experience of foreign economic policy-making and execution—dictated the nature and limits of the study. No doubt the relation was, as is often the case, reciprocal. In any event, all persons invited to become members of the Study Group at once accepted the invitations. The backgrounds of the members may be indicated by a short listing of some of their relevant current and previous connections:

Frank Altschul—Chairman of the Board, General American Investors Co. Inc.; Vice President and Secretary, Council on Foreign Relations; Vice-Chairman, National Planning Association and Chairman of its Committee on International Policy; past President (two terms) of the Woodrow Wilson Foundation.

Richard M. Bissell, Jr.—Economic Consultant, Washington, D.C.; formerly Deputy Administrator of the Economic Cooperation Administration and Deputy Director of the Mutual Security Agency; Staff Director of the President's Committee on the Foreign Aid Program (Harriman Committee); Deputy Director of the Office of War Mobilization and Reconversion; and Professor of Economics at Massachusetts Institute of Technology and Yale University.

Courtney C. Brown—Dean of the Graduate School of Business at Columbia University; formerly Assistant to the Chairman of the Board, Standard Oil Company (N.J.); during World War II, Chief of the Division of War Supply and Resources, Department of State, and Vice President in Charge of Foreign Operations of the United States Commodity Credit Corporation.

H. van B. Cleveland—International Economist of the Committee for

Economic Development; formerly Deputy Director of the European
Program Division of the Economic Cooperation Administration;
served in various United States Government agencies, including the
Department of State, the Office of Strategic Services and the Foreign Economic Administration.

William Y. Elliott—Professor of Government, Harvard University, and
Special Assistant to the Director of the Office of Defense Mobilization; formerly Staff Director of the Foreign Affairs Committee of
the House of Representatives and of the House Select Committee
on Foreign Aid (Herter Committee); Vice-Chairman of the War
Production Board (Civilian Requirements and Stockpiling).

Theodore Geiger—Chief of International Studies, National Planning
Association; formerly Special Assistant to the Deputy Administrator, Economic Cooperation Administration; staff consultant to
the Herter Committee; served in various United States Government
agencies, including the Department of State and the War Production
Board; and taught history and economics at Columbia University
and the City Colleges of New York.

Harry D. Gideonse—President of Brooklyn College of the City of New
York; past President (one term) and member of the Board of Di-
rectors, Woodrow Wilson Foundation; formerly Professor of Eco-
nomics, Columbia University; Chairman of the Department of
Economics, Barnard College; Associate Professor of Economics,
University of Chicago.

Edward S. Mason—Dean of the Graduate School of Public Administration, Harvard University; formerly member of various Presidential
Commissions, including the President's Materials Policy Commission (Paley Commission), the Committee on the Foreign Aid Program (Harriman Committee) and Deputy to the President's Special Assistant (Gordon Gray) in preparing the (Gray) Report on
Foreign Economic Policies; served during World War II in the
Department of State and the Office of Strategic Services; and Professor of Economics at Harvard University.

Don K. Price—Vice President, The Ford Foundation; formerly Deputy
Chairman of the Research and Development Board, Department of
Defense; Associate Director of the Public Administration Clearing
House; member of the Board of Directors of the Social Science Re-
search Council; assistant to former President Hoover for the study
of the Presidency by the Commission on Organization of the Exec-

utive Branch of the Government; and served in the   United States
Bureau of the Budget.

It can readily be noted from these summaries that most of the members of the Study Group have at various times and in various capacities
served in Executive Agencies, on Executive Commissions, or on the staffs
of Congressional Committees, dealing with a variety of aspects of American foreign policy in general and of foreign economic policy in particular.

There was early agreement within the Group that it would be of relatively small value to study once again, within the conventional framework, the familiar specific issues of substantive economic policy already
amply covered by the House Special Committee on Post-War Economic
Policy and Planning (Colmer Committee); the House Select Committee
on Foreign Aid (Herter Committee), the Gordon Gray Report on
Foreign Economic Policies, the President's Materials Policy Commission
(Paley Commission), the Public Advisory Board for Mutual Security
(Bell Report), and the Commission on Foreign Economic Policy (Randall Commission). Instead, the Study Group felt that its combined experience might be brought to bear more usefully on those broader aspects
of policy in which the older tradition of *political economy* rather than
the more limited discipline of *economics* might once more be fruitfully
employed. The title *The Political Economy of American Foreign Policy*
is intended to suggest the inextricable interrelationships of all aspects
of public policy, including economic policy. The Study Group felt especially that the context and the limits of our foreign economic policy ought
to be better recognized by the American public and by American scholars, if our foreign economic policy were to be rightly made, broadly
understood, and publicly supported.

Indeed, at one time the Group was tempted to call its work "The
Limits of Foreign Economic Policy," implying not only the limits imposed on economic policy-makers by historical and political conditions
but also the limitations of what economic policy alone could be expected
to accomplish. But that seemed on reflection too negative a title and too
little suggestive of the real focus of the study, which was aimed at show-
ing the way in which the total policy and the responsibilities of the
United States were affected by, and in turn influenced, the economic
prospects of the free world in a period of "cold war." The present title
was chosen to suggest a constructive range of national adjustments to
the larger setting of our economic policies in the world. The foreign

economic policy of this country, in short, must necessarily be fitted into the world we live in. It must serve our total policy—our national security and our high diplomatic and strategic objectives. In particular, the challenge to the free world from the Soviet system and its satellites could in itself occupy the entirety of this volume and has in practice resulted in keying economic policies to the defense measures necessary in a period of cold war. We have, therefore, assumed—what in a "nuclear" world is necessarily set as the frame for all national policy—the greater likelihood of a period of long sustained tension than of a catastrophic showdown. During such drawn-out testing, American concern for the security of the free world must be a major consideration. This background of cold war means that the successful meeting of the challenge to the United States requires a maturity and a political sagacity which will test not only the political leadership of our country but the ability of our institutions—conceived in the 18th century for a small and struggling group of colonies newly freed from Britain—to adjust themselves to the role of leadership which has today been thrust upon the United States. As Woodrow Wilson once said, "In government, as in virtue, the hardest of hard things is to make progress."

The existence of a study which went into as much detail on the organization and control of general foreign policy as had the report of the first Woodrow Wilson Foundation Study Group seemed to the present Group to make unnecessary further elaboration of the same theme, important as it is. Nevertheless, we have included in this study a short chapter composed in the main of excerpts from a memorandum which the Chairman originally prepared at the request of the Randall Commission. Thus, Chapter 10 is the only bow which the present Study Group has made to the organizational aspects of the making and execution of foreign economic policy, though it has throughout attempted to recognize the closely related connections between American foreign policy, domestic politics, and the resolution of pressures which we attempt to achieve under our separation of powers and through our party system.

It is gratifying for me as Chairman to report that all members of the Group were active, hard-working participants in its activities and that attendance was unusually regular at all of our twenty sessions—three of which lasted for two days. Each member of the Group has written at least one working paper; others were prepared by the staff, and a few by outside experts. These working papers, covering the various conventional divisions of the subject matter of foreign economic policy, formed the basis of discussion during the first dozen or so meetings. The working papers, plus extracts from the verbatim transcripts of the Study Group's recorded discussions, were then fitted together and extensively supplemented with newly written material to form a first draft of the present volume. This exacting task was performed by Messrs. Cleveland and Geiger who, in addition to being members of the Group, also acted as draftsmen of the final report. This report has been through three complete revisions, each of which has been considered—page by page—by the Study Group as a whole. In addition, individual members possessing special competence on particular subjects have redrafted certain passages, especially in Chapter 9, along lines discussed and approved at the meetings. Insofar as any report can be, the present volume is a joint product.

A word should be said about the absence of personal dissents (either as footnotes or as appended statements) in a volume that covers such controversial ground and was prepared by a group of people whose initial views were often at considerable variance. It may fairly be said that the final report represents an unusual degree of consensus for such a group, particularly since we made a special effort not to water down real differences of opinion by compromises which took the essential meaning out of the policies advocated, nor to enter many tedious individual footnotes or longer dissents "for the record." At the same time, the individual responsibility of members of the Group is limited, for each—most of all the Chairman himself—could point to many statements or particular emphases with which he, personally, is not in full agreement.

A great deal of credit is due to the skillful draftsmanship and tireless labors of our two reportorial members, Messrs. Cleveland and Geiger. Their own conceptual contributions and their painstaking efforts to express accurately and to weave into a logical sequence the many substantive points agreed upon after long discussion at each of our sessions are in no small measure responsible for such merit as this report possesses. Particular thanks must go to those who did the staff work of the Group—to Mr. Geiger who, despite the pressure of his regular duties at the National Planning Association, made certain that we always had a worthwhile agenda and a set of documents of uniformly high quality to consider at every session; and to Miss Dora M. Grabfield for her accurate and helpful summaries of the policy agreements and disagreements reached at each meeting and for the long hours spent in preparing her conscientious transcriptions and editing of the verbatim recordings of our discussions. It is a pleasure to express our obligation to Mrs. Julie d'Estournelles and her assistant, Miss Mabel Austin, of the Woodrow Wilson Foundation for their remarkable efficiency in arranging the meetings and in getting out the papers and drafts so promptly. We wish also to acknowledge the useful background papers and research memoranda prepared for us on various subjects by Messrs. Laurin L. Henry, Klaus Knorr, John Lindeman and Howard S. Piquet. To the extent to which we have used portions of their findings in this volume, we naturally assume responsibility for their work.

An early draft of our study was read by four eminent consultants who spent two days going over their reactions and criticisms with us. We profited greatly from our sessions with Messrs. Max F. Millikan, Paul Nitze, Frank A. Southard and Jacob Viner, who were helpful not only because of their positive contributions but also because of their dissents —sometimes quite fundamental—from our analyses and conclusions. We also benefitted from the participation in several of our meetings of Messrs. Gerhard Colm, John Miller and H. Christian Sonne of the National Planning Association and from their comments on our final report. Various drafts of our study, or portions of it, were read by a number of other people, many of whom were kind enough to send us their comments. Messrs. Cleveland and Geiger wish to express their particular thanks to Messrs. John C. L. Hulley, John P. Lewis, Samuel Lubell, Benjamin N. Nelson and Robert Tufts for their extensive and very useful oral and written suggestions, many of which we adopted. However, while acknowledging our indebtedness both to those who met with us and to those who sent us comments, we assume responsibility for our own report and for the views expressed therein.

Finally, none of us will soon forget the gracious hospitality of Mr. and Mrs. Frank Altschul during the two memorable and creative weekend sessions held at their delightful home, Overbrook Farm.

Contents

Part II—Prescription

THE POLITICAL ECONOMY
OF
AMERICAN FOREIGN POLICY

Introduction

In the mid-20th century, the nations of the West are confronted with three fundamental challenges to the values and institutions which characterize their distinctive way of life.

The first is the unmistakable challenge of communist imperialism which seeks the revolutionary overthrow of the existing world political and economic order and its reconstitution on a totalitarian, collectivist basis. The communist threat is pervasive, menacing in one form or another virtually all of the non-Soviet countries. It aggravates their other problems and makes resolution of them much more difficult and urgent.

The second is the challenge of what Toynbee has called the "as yet uncommitted nations" of Asia, Africa and Latin America. Many of these countries are now passing through profound social transformations whose outcome is still uncertain—transformations largely induced by their encounter with the West over the past century or more. The present efforts of the underdeveloped countries to work out their own destinies are important to the West not only because of their influence on the relative power positions of the free nations and the communist bloc. More fundamentally, the profound social transformation of these countries provides a moral challenge both to their own capacity and to that of the West for building a wider and more stable community among many diverse nations and cultures despite the resentments engendered by past relationships and present conflicts of interest.

Third, and in some ways most serious of all, the West faces the challenge of its own internal problems. At bottom, many of these difficulties are moral and spiritual. A characteristic manifestation of them may be seen in the slowness of Western society to adapt constructively certain of its inherited institutions to 20th-century changes of unparalleled rapidity in social values and in political and economic conditions. Thus, for example, in a world made small and highly interdependent by technological advance, industrialism and urbanization, the sovereign nation-state system seems for many countries to be increasingly inconsistent not only with the satisfaction of contemporary aspirations for personal fulfillment and a more ample living standard but even with the survival of constitutional government and liberal forms of economic organization.

The slowness of creative adaptation is in the main a consequence of insufficient understanding, vigor and moral inspiration. In some Western countries, it reflects a decline of confidence in the basic liberal values of our civilization and of the courage necessary for innovation and enterprise. In others, their very success in realizing so adequately the material goals of Western society has made them complacent, and hence reluctant to muster the will and the creative imagination required to meet new dangers and mounting uncertainties. Nor is it a coincidence that the most acute manifestations of all three challenges have appeared in a few Western countries where the process of creative adaptation has encountered the most intractable difficulties. Today in the West there is increasing understanding of the complex and many-sided character of these challenges. In a few Western countries various circumstances have fortunately combined to preserve a sufficient degree of vigor and moral inspiration to enable them to find new strength for meeting the challenges of our times. In most Western countries, however, the response to date has been far short of assuring that these challenges will in time be surmounted effectively and by morally valid means.

Even had the West's response to its own shortcomings been more successful, it is still likely that the two external challenges would nevertheless have arisen and would now make the West's own problems so much more difficult and urgent than they would otherwise be. In turn, the internal difficulties of the West hamper every effort to grapple more effectively with the pressing danger of communist imperialism and with the subtler challenge of the new Asia and of the changing societies of Latin America and Africa. Thus, it is the conjunction and mutual exacerbation of these three sets of fundamental problems which make our period of Western history one of profound crisis. These challenges have been both cause and consequence of two world wars of unprecedented scope and violence and of the imminence of a third of vastly greater destructive potential. In our generation, they have been threatening to overwhelm men's rational hopes and moral restraints with collective megalomanias, mass irrationalities and apocalyptic myths of utopia.

One set of complex interactions among these three challenges is of central importance for a study of international economic problems. Over the past generation, changing social values have resulted in an unprecedented expansion of economic expectations—of the size and variety of material satisfactions which people believe their economic systems should fulfill. As the industrial economies of the West have become enormously more productive, people's consumption expectations have also increased, and so too has their conviction that economic and political institutions could be easily and quickly adapted to satisfying these new aspirations for economic security and rising living standards. This has been true not only in the West but to some extent also in the underdeveloped countries. In itself, the meeting in reasonable degree of these expanding desires for consumption would not be impossible, though it could certainly not be done easily or quickly. What makes it so much more difficult and urgent are the deliberately disruptive tactics of the worldwide communist movement and the unintended effects of the growing familiarity of the rest of the world with the American standard of living. More important, increasingly heavy burdens for defense against Soviet and Red Chinese aggression have been superimposed upon these expanding consumption claims. Today, communist aggression takes two forms—the conventional threat of attack across national boundaries, and the novel and less easily recognized tactic of internal aggression through sabotage, guerrilla activities and, eventually, civil war. Nor have the burdens of rearmament been solely for the defense of the West. The underdeveloped countries have proved, if anything, even more fruitful fields for communist interest than Western Europe and have thereby magnified the defense requirements of the West. At the same time, communist propaganda and subversion within the underdeveloped countries, combined with their own political and economic nationalism, have reduced their willingness and ability to contribute to their own defense, and have inhibited the growth of those mutually beneficial economic relations between the industrial and the primary-producing countries which would help to make the expanding economic claims and defense requirements of the mid-20th century easier to meet.

For the United States, as for certain other Western countries, these developments have not created insuperable difficulties. The United States has not been harmfully affected by adverse changes in economic and political conditions because its natural resources are abundant and its economy is sufficiently large, well-balanced and dynamic. With a population only half the size of that of the other Western countries combined, the United States has achieved an industrial production 60 percent greater than the total of theirs; its per capita consumption is three times as large; and its average productivity per worker is at least twice that of any other nation except Canada. The citizens of the United States are numerous, energetic and still basically united in their devotion to the traditional democratic values of the West and in their active support of the particular institutional forms by which contemporary American society expresses these ideals. Though newer weapons are greatly reducing the geographical security of the United States, our location in the New World still gives us significantly more protection than Western Europe now has with respect to the Soviet threat. The United States does not have the handicap of past or present colonial involvements in its dealings with the new Asia. In consequence of these advantages, the United States is now—and has been since World War I —by a very wide margin the largest, wealthiest and strongest country in the Western world.

Inevitably, this preponderance has thrust responsibilities upon the United States which—even had Americans so wished—they would be unable to escape. Since 1914 other friendly countries have increasingly looked to the United States to provide the decisive increments of human and material resources, of effort and sacrifice, necessary to preserve the Western way of life in the face of successive challenges and crises. Relative to their own resources and populations, the sacrifices and sufferings of other Western nations have been much greater over the past generation than have those of the United States. But this has, in effect, provided an additional cause of the growing dependence of these countries upon American leadership and support. Thus, history itself is responsible for the present position and compelling obligations of the United States.

Explicit recognition of this situation was naturally slow to develop—both here and abroad. Until World War II, it was hesitant and sporadic; since Pearl Harbor, it has been growing. But it is not yet adequate. The United States is still learning painfully to live up to the insistent demands of its new position and responsibilities, just as the other nations of the West are now going through the equally difficult process of learning to reconcile themselves to major changes in theirs.

However disappointing to many Americans and Europeans, the extent to which the United States has progressed in this task over the past decade is nonetheless remarkable if viewed in the perspective of history. Other great world leaders in the Western tradition—Rome and England—took generations to comprehend their responsibilities sufficiently to be able to evolve means effective for discharging them. American shortcomings are understandable enough when one considers not only the magnitude of the task, but also our nostalgia for a comfortable isolationist past, our democratic inhibitions, and our frequently exaggerated faith in human rationality and in social perfectibility. Notable as our progress has been, however, it provides no ground for complacency. Objectively, the urgency and intensity of the challenges confronting the Western nations are too great to permit Americans to be satisfied with the very partial successes of recent years; at best, these have only arrested precariously the deteriorating situation of the West. Subjectively, the frustration of earlier unrealistic expectations about the ease and rapidity with which the critical problems of world economic and political order could be solved has contributed—both here and abroad—to equally unrealistic disillusionment, neurotic resentments, and potentially suicidal attempts to escape responsibilities.

In the circumstances, improving the quality of American leadership is of vital importance not only to the United States but to the other nations of the West as well. This is not solely a task of devising more adequate means for grappling with world political, social and economic problems—difficult as that may be. Before questions of means can be settled, it is essential that we understand better than we have what can and should be accomplished in the peculiar conditions of the mid-20th century. Nor is better intellectual grasp of problems and objectives alone sufficient. In the absence of creative inspiration and of the moral energy and courage indispensible for successful leadership and action, intellectual understanding can merely prophesy ineffectually about the significance of events.

One lesson we are beginning to learn is that, in the conditions of the mid-20th century, foreign policy—like war—is total. However great our nostalgia for the limited political diplomacy of the 19th century, however strongly some Americans may feel that economics, ideology and even morality are irrelevant to the proper conduct of international relations, we cannot ignore the new facts of contemporary life, the revolutionary goals and practices of our opponents, and the changing values of our own citizens and those of our allies and friends abroad. Domestic politics and economics played a much smaller role in 19th-century foreign policy-making than they do in the 20th century. In the Western democratic nations today—with their highly interdependent and complex economies and their politically active populations and interest groups—foreign and domestic policies are inextricably intertwined. From this new relationship arises a serious contradiction and a great danger. The total character of the challenge to national security makes it necessary for our foreign policy to be concerned with every aspect of the relations among nations and to possess great capacity for flexibility, initiative and freedom of action. Yet, at the same time, the conduct of American foreign policy is being increasingly hampered and warped by the domestic political rivalries, economic limitations, and short-sighted group interests with which it is now so directly involved.

In consequence of the total character of contemporary diplomacy, foreign *economic* policy is neither a separate nor a subordinate compartment of foreign policy. Rather, it is an intrinsic aspect or dimension of foreign policy whose importance depends upon the particular goals which foreign policy seeks to achieve, the problems blocking progress toward these objectives, and the methods appropriate for overcoming them. Economic arrangements, like political ones, are ultimately means for the realization of individual, group and national goals. Today, the ineffectiveness of many international economic institutions and relationships is widely felt to be a major obstacle blocking more adequate realization of Western ideals. Hence, the economic aspect of contemporary foreign policy assumes major importance in the present period. But the economic aspect can be neither understood nor effectively dealt with when considered in isolation from political, strategic and psychological factors, domestic and international. The fact that, to undertake any study of foreign economic policy, it is necessary to make assumptions about the political, military and psychological future of the "cold war" is only one way—though a vitally important one—of demonstrating this basic interdependence. To emphasize it, we have entitled our study *The Political Economy of American Foreign Policy*.

Thus, our conception of the nature and proximate purpose of foreign economic policy is a broad one. The Study Group believes that, within the limits set by domestic American economic and political capabilities and national and group interests, the United States must strive in its foreign economic policy to improve the functioning of the international economic system and of the individual national economies which compose it. This means that the United States must be willing at times to forego certain short-term direct economic advantages in favor of the more substantial and enduring benefits to the United States, to the West, and to the rest of the non-Soviet world, which improvements in the functioning of the international economy can bring. Such long-term benefits are not merely economic, but political, social and psychological as well.

The problems which American foreign economic policy must overcome to achieve this proximate objective are familiar enough. The contemporary economy of the non-Soviet world is not, as was its predecessor of the 19th century, highly integrated across national boundaries. Instead, it is divided by various types of economic barriers into a large and still growing number of independent national economies. In consequence, the efficiency of the international economic system is very much reduced and it no longer provides opportunities and incentives for growth to the degree needed by many of its member national economies for maintaining their economic health. We shall define in Chapter 1 the meanings we attach to such concepts as "economic efficiency" and "economic health." Here it is sufficient to note that the incalculability and ineffectiveness of the existing international economy are especially serious problems for the advanced, industrialized economies highly dependent upon foreign trade—Britain, Japan and many of the continental West European countries—and somewhat less serious problems for those underdeveloped countries now striving to accelerate their rates of economic growth. For the nations of the West, this situation presents not merely an economic problem; it drastically reduces their capacity for meeting more adequately all of the fundamental challenges they now face. Similarly, for the non-Soviet underdeveloped countries, it hampers their social transformation. It helps to warp that transformation in directions inimical to the future possibility of building enduring community between these emerging new societies and the West.

The central objective, then, of American foreign economic policy is to foster the construction of a better integrated and more effectively functioning international economic system. We believe, however, that this cannot be done merely by imitating or attempting to rebuild the particular institutions and relationships which characterized the integrated world economy of the 19th century. The task today is to find new institutions consistent with contemporary attitudes and political realities which can perform in different ways the same integrating functions as those of the past.

This is the aspect of foreign economic policy upon which the Study Group decided to focus its main attention. In the chapters which follow, we present the results of our search for more relevant ways of thinking about the nature and problems of world economic order in the peculiar conditions—political, social and moral—of the second half of the 20th century. The particular perspective upon which we agreed in the course of our discussions is certainly not the only way in which these questions can be approached. It seemed to us, however, the most fruitful way both in explaining the inadequacies of the conventional approach to foreign economic policy and in suggesting specific means by which existing policies and programs could be improved. Our intention is not to insist dogmatically upon the perspective we have employed. Rather it is to provoke others to appraise its merits objectively, to attempt answers to many of its admittedly unexplored implications, or —if they find it without validity—to seek other new or different ways of thinking about the problems of world economic order. For of only one thing are we thoroughly convinced: the conventional approach to the critical problems of foreign economic policy has outlived its capacity to provide a solution of contemporary economic difficulties within the limits of existing political and social requirements and attitudes. This failure is owed in the main to its implicit assumptions about the nature of an international economy, the prerequisites for international economic integration, and the means whereby integration might be achieved today—assumptions which are no longer as relevant to the actual conditions of life as they were before 1914.

Consideration of these problems occupies the major portion of our study, but certain of our general conclusions regarding them may be briefly summarized here. In the view of the Study Group, much contemporary thinking about the problems of world economic order has rested upon an inadequate analysis of the essential features of the 19th-century system and of the qualitative changes which have occurred over the past half century. Indeed, the neglected characteristics of the 19th-century world economy were among those fundamental to its existence. Before World War I, the relative calculability of economic conditions and policies over the whole trading world, and the automaticity of world economic adjustments, could both be taken for granted. They were assured by certain institutional features of the 19th-century system—the ideology and practice of *laissez-faire,* the domination of vast raw material producing areas by the European imperial powers, the central position of Britain, and the subtle instruments of international economic authority operated from London. In turn, the effectiveness of these institutional features depended upon the absence of any serious revolutionary threat, external or internal, to the political, military and ideological bases of the 19th-century world. Indeed, the political revolutions in Western society during the 19th century were largely attempts to establish more adequately the values and institutions of a more liberal political and economic order.

In consequence of these 19th-century attitudes and institutions, the economic balance among national economies and within them could be determined in the main by the workings of private markets. Markets were then much less subject to the exercise of public and private economic power than now, and national economic structures were consequently more elastic and responsive to market forces than they are in most countries today. Likewise, the task of distributing the gains from trade and the opportunities for growth among national economies was substantially left to the world market, except for protective tariffs. This task was made easy by the fact that the world market was expanding. Until late in the century, the number of rival industrial centers was small and the extent of their rivalry limited. Moreover, social groups were generally willing to accept the dictates of the market as the "automatic" work of impersonal forces governed by "inexorable laws." This willingness was owed in part to the ideology of economic liberalism and to the lack of economic or political power in the hands of the groups most likely to resist these forces. It was owed also to the fact that market forces were, indeed, far less personal and conscious than they are now. In short, the main present-day causes of economic nationalism were, before World War I, either absent or still unable to find effective means of expression.

Today, all this has changed. The main social, ideological and political supports of the 19th-century system no longer stand. In the 20th century, the seamless world economy has been "nationalized" in three senses of the term. It has been compartmentalized into an ever-growing number of new and fully sovereign national economies as a result of the breakup of the European empires and the ending of indirect forms of economic and political domination. At the same time, national governments have intervened increasingly in the economic process under the impact of profound changes in social values, group relationships and world conditions. Their intervention, too, has been increasingly motivated by considerations of direct and immediate national advantage and their concern for the effective functioning of the international economy as a whole has dwindled markedly. This threefold "nationalization" of the world economy has been occurring precisely at a time when the advance of Soviet power has restricted the total area of the international market and has presented the non-communist countries with a relentless opponent whose ultimate purpose is the revolutionary overthrow of their entire political and economic system.

An attempt to re-integrate the international economy by the 19th-century method would necessarily imply that national governments would have to reduce very drastically the scope of their interventions in the economic process, both internal and external. This would mean, in turn, that national governments would have to abandon in large part the group and national interests they now seek to achieve through the active exercise of economic sovereignty over domestic and foreign economic life. The 19th-century method of world economic integration relied principally upon the automatic forces of private markets, supplemented by inconspicuous and largely informal central authority exercised from London. This method depended for its success upon a system of values and a world polity significantly different from those existing today. There is little doubt in our minds that many governments have carried the practice of economic intervention beyond the point where it contributes either to economic efficiency or to a workable conception of economic equity. Nonetheless, it is quite futile to advocate any general return to the *laissez-faire* model of classical liberalism in the face of contemporary attitudes toward economic security, income distribution and material consumption, and of the major problems created by the menace of Soviet imperialism and the transformation of the underdeveloped countries. Yet, in essence, this is what is proposed by those who today seek to re-integrate the "nationalized" world economy by 19th-century methods.

In contrast, the alternative approach suggested in this study would seek to achieve what degree of international economic re-integration may now be politically feasible by methods which seem to be more consistent with the goals and requirements of the mid-20th century. This alternative accepts the fact that, since national governments have assumed, and will continue to discharge, a wide range of new economic responsibilities, the maintenance of an effectively functioning international economy depends today—to a degree inconceivable in the 19th century—upon the continuous and conscious exercise of initiative and leadership by responsible governments. The alternative approach also accepts the fact that the present-day feasibility of the easy "automatic" adaptation of national economies to each other through private market processes has been seriously qualified. In consequence, the achievement of an adequate degree of economic integration in the contemporary world depends on a deliberate coordination of national economic policies either by cooperation among national governments or—more effectively and reliably—by supranational authorities. But, the alternative approach recognizes that effective economic cooperation among fully sovereign national governments, no less than the willingness to subordinate important elements of national economic policies to supranational authorities, require not simply the absence of deep conflicts of interest but also a positive sense of moral and historical community among the countries concerned. The requisite similarity of culture and social values and consistency of political and economic capabilities and needs do not now exist in the non-Soviet world as a whole and are likely to be soon attained only on a regional basis. For all of these reasons, the alternative approach proposes that key economic policies be cooperatively or jointly made and applied by reasonably homogeneous groups of countries, which would be relieved—to that extent at least—of the necessity to achieve narrower national objectives by undue restrictions at national boundaries.

To our minds, this second method is today the only practicable way by which a sufficient degree of order and security can be restored to international economic relations to make possible preservation of the benefits of private, decentralized decision-making and enterprise in a manner consistent with the values and requirements of contemporary life. Indeed, the evidence strongly suggests that postwar attempts at international economic re-integration have been successful only to the extent that they have involved effective coordination of national economic policies. Conversely, they have been unsuccessful to the extent that they have tried to approximate worldwide free-trade models.

In the course of its work, the Study Group made certain assumptions about future developments in the relations between the West and the Soviet bloc, and about the general character of national policies, particularly those of the United States. These assumptions may be briefly described here.

Although extensive discussion of relations between the West and the communist countries lay outside the Study Group's subject matter and available time, we inevitably devoted considerable attention to the main possibilities and probabilities. Suffice it to say here that none of us believe it likely that in the foreseeable future the nature of Soviet society will be so radically transformed as to make communist imperialism no longer a serious threat to the Western way of life or to the independence of other non-communist countries. In such circumstances, the Group has assumed that the cold war will continue, though with varying intensity and in different forms, throughout the period for which this study may be relevant—roughly the next decade. Soviet tactics will certainly change, as they have in the past, but the Soviet regime will continue to exploit, by all available means short of full-scale war, any symptoms of weakness, disunity or economic deterioration in the West. Thus the Group, in effect, assumed that continuation of the cold war is more likely than a third world war within the medium-term future. It assumed that we shall successfully avoid nuclear war without being "nibbled to death" at vital points or cowed into submission. Admittedly, these are large assumptions. But contrary expectations—though they might turn out to be validated by history—would entail radical revisions of policies, foreign and domestic, whose discussion would be outside this Study Group's terms of reference.

The foregoing assumption has certain implications for the defense policies of the West, and particularly for those of the United States, which are among the most important prerequisites of any effective foreign economic policy. Clearly, the total of our defense commitments must be determined primarily by the nature and magnitude of the threats to our security, including those involved in recurring local communist military actions. The evidence accessible to private citizens like ourselves suggests that the direction of our fiscal policies and the scale of our military planning should be kept under constant review. For, together, they must at all times be adequate to provide the United States not only with the basic requisite of global striking power but also with the ability to fight local wars at need. In addition, they should enable as satisfactory a defensive system as possible to be constructed for the continental United States, and continued help to be extended to our allies and friends abroad in their own rearmament efforts.

To be sound, however, this reappraisal must not be dominated by the well-intentioned, but mistaken, fear that the American economy cannot afford—either temporarily or indefinitely—the required level of defense expenditures. At no time since the peak of World War II has the United States been seriously strained by the scale of its military effort. The dynamic growth of the American economy over the past decade has substantially raised the limits of the military and civilian defense programs which the United States could assume without detriment to a necessary rate of productive investment or even to further increases in the standard of living.[1] It would be ironic if the richest nation on earth—indeed, the richest in all history—should nevertheless decide that it could not afford the cost of its own survival. Such a decision would be especially perverse in a period when the manpower and productive resources of the country are not being fully employed.

It has been one of the misfortunes of our times that defense against communist imperialism, rather than constructive works of peace, has come to play so important a part in maintaining the rapid rate of economic growth which the United States has enjoyed until recently. In any dynamic free enterprise economy, there will necessarily be variations in the magnitude of capital requirements and in the level of consumer demand. If this were not the case, the economy would be neither free nor dynamic. If the volume of savings seeking investment in such an economy is large at full employment levels of national income— and this has been conspicuously true of the United States even with present tax structures and rates—variations in the magnitude of capital requirements and consumer demand will inevitably generate fluctua-

---

[1] See, e.g. Gerhard Colm with the assistance of Marilyn Young, *Can We Afford Additional Programs for National Security?* Planning Pamphlets No. 84 (Washington: National Planning Association, October 1953).

tions in the rate of growth and the level of production that, in the absence of adequate government counteractions, could become more serious. Conditions conducive to instability of this sort have been largely absent from the American economy since the end of World War II. However, it would be a great mistake, we believe, to base an estimate of the character of impending international economic problems on the assumption that the favorable domestic economic conditions with which we have lived for most of the past decade will continue indefinitely in the absence of effective government policies and programs. For, even if defense expenditures should be significantly increased above present levels, it would not necessarily follow that productive resources would continue indefinitely to be fully employed. The labor force will soon again be growing by more than one million workers annually and the rate of growth of output per manhour seems to have risen above the customary 2 percent per annum of recent decades. In these circumstances, positive action by government, business and consumers will periodically be necessary to ensure that the forces responsible for aggregate demand are collectively capable of sustaining a socially desirable rate of growth and level of employment.

While corrective interludes may be a normal and desirable characteristic of a free and dynamic economy, they have a way of getting out of hand and of going to extremes which are unnecessary and which in present circumstances might prove disastrous. A setback of major proportions in the American economy could have a ruinous impact on Western Europe and on much of the rest of the non-Soviet world. Even if these countries are apparently now somewhat less vulnerable to an American recession than they were in the immediate postwar period, the political and psychological effects—both at home and abroad —of substantial and sustained unemployment in the United States would be serious indeed. This situation would furnish just the opportunity which the communists have been predicting and for which they have been waiting. Moreover, the domestic political obstacles in the way of adopting any foreign economic policy soundly conceived to promote the effectiveness of the international economy would undoubtedly increase greatly through failure to prevent moderate or serious recessions. For these reasons, the *sine qua non* of any effective foreign economic policy for the United States is the prevention in the American economy of recessions *greater* than the minimal magnitude of what could be regarded as salutary corrective interludes. Unless the

United States Government is prepared to institute, if and when necessary, positive policies and programs directed toward maintaining a desirable rate of economic growth and level of employment, there is not much use in discussing the foreign economic policies we believe to be necessary to American security and that of the whole non-Soviet world.

Admittedly, this study has the weaknesses implicit in an attempt to reconcile an ambitious choice of subject matter and a broad focus of interest with the limitations in the Study Group's time and in the scope of our final report. Though portions of our analysis have perforce had to be generalized and impressionistic, we have nevertheless tried to present in Part I a reasonably comprehensive picture, seen in a new perspective, of the chief disorders of the contemporary international economy and of its component national economies. The consequences for action which we believe follow from this analysis are then surveyed in Part II. Those familiar with the main lines of prescription in recent reports by official and private groups will recognize that our suggestions, by themselves, do not contain very much that is new. Rather, we have tried to show how many of these measures assume changed importance when viewed in the context of the analysis in Part I and how they could be modified and more effectively related to one another to make them more relevant to the purposes they are expected to achieve. The Study Group hopes that the diagnosis and prescription herein presented will prove useful to those concerned with foreign policy-making and execution, as well as to scholars and the public generally, by helping them to understand better, and to grapple more effectively with, the critical problems of world economic order in the second half of the 20th century.

PART I

Diagnosis

1

The Genesis of the Contemporary International Economy

Those who set out to survey with an open mind the problems of the contemporary international economy are at once confronted with the difference between theory and reality. On the one hand, the conventional theories of international economics are based on the model of a unified world system whose component parts trade freely with one another on private account and in accordance with the principles of international specialization and comparative advantage. On the other hand, the freedom of trade and payments in the existing international economy is greatly impaired by tariffs and import quotas, by currency regulations, and by restrictions on the movements of capital and of people. Regard for the most economical use of resources does not determine which regions specialize in agriculture and which in manufacturing. Nor are private traders free to purchase in the cheapest markets and sell in the dearest, irrespective of the national origins of the commodities and currencies involved. Indeed, a significant portion of world commerce is not conducted by private traders at all.

The general models of conventional international economic theory have not always been as divergent from economic realities as they are today. The main features of the theory were fixed during the 19th century and bore a high degree of relevance to the actual world economic relationships from which they were then extrapolated. But, as the unified and freely trading world economy of the 19th century has more and more disintegrated over the past fifty years, classical and neo-classical economic theory has had greater and greater difficulty in accounting for observable economic phenomena. Professor Viner has recently summed up the declining relevance of classical theory in a memorable passage:

> Despite my belief in its merits and its relevance during its period of dominance, I am convinced, however, that it would be a mistake to carry its rehabilitation so far as to claim for it even in its improved and modernized form, adequacy as a theory to guide policy in the present-day world. The world has changed greatly, and is now a world of planned economies, of state trading, of substantially arbitrary and inflexible national price structures, and of managed instability in exchange rates. The classical theory is not directly relevant for such a world, and it may be that for such a world there is and can be no relevant *general* theory.[1]

As Viner's remarks indicate, there are two senses in which economic theory may be relevant—descriptively and normatively. Both are important for economic analysis which, as in this study, is undertaken for the purpose of policy-making. To be relevant as a description of reality, economic analysis must grasp the essential features of the economic process in terms which reveal the causal factors at work and the kinds of deliberate human actions capable of modifying them in some degree. To be relevant in a normative sense, the analysis must accurately evaluate the nature and moral implications of the conflicting group and national interests—i.e., the human motivations and values—involved in economic problems and provide policy-makers with suggestions for reconciling these interests or with sound criteria for choosing among them. Only economic analysis which meets these two tests of relevance is capable of serving as a satisfactory guide in the choice of goals which are both desirable and possible, and of means which are both effective and morally valid.

It does not, of course, follow that every economic policy desired by a popular majority is *ipso facto* in the national interest, or even in the interest of the social groups composing the majority. As we shall have many occasions to reiterate in this study, there are situations in which satisfaction of the demands of large or powerful groups for increased consumption or economic security may be counter to the national interest,

---

[1] Jacob Viner. *International Economics* (Glencoe, Illinois: The Free Press, 1951), p. 16.

or may be self-defeating in the longer run because they seriously reduce the ability of the economic system to support itself and to grow at an adequate rate. Indeed, it has not been unusual in the interwar and postwar periods for economic policies, which in time could significantly increase the wealth of the people, to be deliberately flouted because they did not accord with majority prejudices or with popular expectations of short-run advantages. To be relevant as prescription, therefore, economic analysis must avoid opposite extremes: on the one hand, a doctrinaire insistence on applying the principles of economic theory regardless of social and political limitations or moral implications and, on the other hand, a complacent surrender to an easy expediency under the guise of "political realism." [2]

As far as the 19th century was concerned, classical economic theory was relevant both as description and as prescription. *Laissez-faire* economics largely accorded with the aspirations of the most enterprising of the politically active groups in Europe and North America not only by its attack on mercantilist doctrine but also by its positive advocacy of policies conducive to rapid economic expansion. Its increasing application in the period 1815–1914 helped to achieve a growth of output and a distribution of income which made possible an unprecedented rise of living standards in Europe and North America despite rapidly growing populations. From the perspective of the mid-20th century, there may be much to criticize in the 19th-century world economy. Social philosophies of the 20th century have increasingly questioned its concepts of social and economic justice, its trust in the automatic operation of unrestricted market forces to ensure the greatest good for the greatest number, and its underlying faith in the certainty of human progress and perfectibility. But by its own standards of liberalism, the 19th-century economy worked, and worked well.

Indeed, the efficiency with which the 19th-century system produced and distributed goods and services in furtherance of the goals of 19th-century Western society has often been acknowledged, even by some 20th-century critics of those goals and of the social consequences of the means used to realize them. Today, the economical use of resources possible in the 19th-century world economy is often regarded with nostalgia by contemporary economists perplexed by the difficulty of stretching

---

[2] For a fuller discussion of relevance in economic theory and analysis, see H. van B. Cleveland, "Economics as Theory and Ideology," *World Politics,* Vol. VI, No. 3, April 1954, pp. 289–305.

limited resources to cover the needs of growing populations, expanding consumption expectations, and mounting defense requirements. But the specific economic means by which the 19th century achieved its efficiency were consistent with the distinctive historical conditions of that period and with the particular values to which 19th-century Western society attached a high priority. Hence, we may legitimately ask: How relevant is the 19th-century prescription today in the light of the changed political, social and economic circumstances of our own times and the rather different goals and values which the mid-20th century considers of primary importance?

This question is a logical starting point for a study concerned with the political economy of contemporary American foreign policy. To answer it, we must find out what made the 19th-century prescription work; what changes have occurred in the world economy over the past half century; and to what extent they may be reversible. On this basis, we can then determine whether the specific historical forms of the 19th-century *laissez-faire* prescription for an integrated worldwide trading system are still applicable, or whether alternative means will have to be found for achieving a sufficient degree of international economic efficiency adequately to promote contemporary values in the prospective conditions of the second half of the 20th century.

Accordingly, this chapter sketches briefly the main reasons why the 19th-century system worked, and describes in broad outline the changes in institutions and values which have occurred over the past half century. This summary account of the genesis of the contemporary international economic system and of the major differences between it and the 19th-century world economy serves as an historical introduction to the more detailed analysis of current international economic problems presented in the subsequent chapters of Part I.

Why an Integrated World Economy Was Possible in the 19th Century

In considering the relationship of classical and neo-classical economic doctrine to the 19th-century world economy, it is important to remember that it was relevant as prescription long before it became relevant as description. Moreover, during the second half of the last century—when it provided a reasonably accurate model of actual economic relationships within the world trading system—its prescriptive role had already shifted from the active, crusading phase of seeking to achieve an integrated, freely trading world economy to a passive, defensive phase of merely trying to maintain it. This shift in purpose is marked by the change from the "political economy" of Adam Smith (a moral philosopher) and David Ricardo (a businessman) to the "economics" of Alfred Marshall and his professional followers to the present day. In the earlier period, the main concern was to understand, and to find effective means of fostering, the dynamic processes of economic transformation and growth. Hence, it was generally recognized that economic activities were an inseparable part of the social process and could neither be understood nor influenced in isolation from it. By the end of the century, when the main concern had shifted to maintenance of an already functioning world trading system, economists began to insist upon the autonomy of the economic process and became more and more absorbed in the study of static problems—the short-run behavior of markets, the theory of value, etc.—which lent themselves to highly abstract or mathematical analysis. Desire to share in the prestige enjoyed by the physical sciences also contributed to the tendency of economists to insist upon the autonomy of "economic laws" and upon economics as a pure or "natural" science.

This change in economic thought helps to explain the general failure of neo-classical economics to understand why the integrated world trading system of the 19th century was possible. For, the habit of believing that the economic process and economic science are both autonomous has tended to blind many analysts to the social, political and moral preconditions of a freely trading world economic system.

The economic preconditions have, of course, been well understood. Economists have long recognized that the efficiency of the 19th-century economy, and its dramatic successes in rapidly raising production and living standards, were in no small measure owed to the fact that it was integrated across national boundaries. To be sure, some parts of the planet were only slightly touched by its workings. But the whole trading world—Britain, Western Europe, North America, the European colonial empires, and parts of Latin America—was more and more involved in integrated private markets for goods and services, capital and, to a more limited extent, labor. The rapid growth of this world economic system —based on private enterprise, industrial technology, and a progressive division of labor—came to depend increasingly on its international economic integration, which in turn became ever closer as trade and commerce expanded.

Thus, the 19th century became the period *par excellence* of international commerce. In the years before World War I, the volume of goods and services purveyed across national boundaries was a significantly higher proportion of the total production of the countries participating in the world trading system than at any time since. The existence of large scale international commerce exercised a far more important influence on the pace and direction of economic development in the 19th century than it does today. For, in the relatively unrestricted 19th-century system, the pattern of economic growth in which Europe specialized on manufacturing and the other trading countries on primary production tended strongly to reinforce itself. Whether their participation in the system was owed to European settlement and investment or to their own initiative, the colonial and independent non-European areas in any case naturally found their most profitable opportunities in expanding their output of food and industrial raw materials, since these were the commodities for which European import demand was growing most rapidly and steadily throughout the century.

Private market forces were able to shape this pattern of increasing international specialization and integration because three requirements essential for their effective operation existed in sufficient degree during much of the 19th century.

First, a high degree of freedom of trade and of financial transactions from governmental restriction prevailed within the trading world. True, the free trade ideal was approximately realized only by Britain. But the tariff protection of other countries was moderate [3] and, by the mid-century, other governmental controls on trade and payments had been largely abolished or had not yet been invented.

Second, the fact that, by and large, governments did not control international trade and payments made the conditions of doing business throughout the trading world reasonably calculable. The calculability of future economic conditions abroad to the businessman, trader or investor—particularly, the stability of legal conditions and of governmental economic policies despite changes in political regimes—is a necessary condition of close economic integration across national boundaries. It is especially important for the international flow of private capital. In the

---

[3] Only a few important countries—notably the United States, France, and Germany—had protective tariffs, and until the 1880's and 90's they were quite moderate.

last century, the calculability of legal conditions and economic policies among countries could be taken for granted to a degree hard to imagine today.

Third, national economies were mutually responsive and adaptable to each other. That is, internal monetary conditions and national economic structures reacted with relative ease and rapidity to changes in the external environment, and generally in a direction consistent with these external developments. National economies could do so because the resulting domestic changes in employment, income distribution and the allocation of resources were politically acceptable. Thus, national economies did not readily get out of balance with one another. Though economic development was uneven and large areas of the planet remained stagnant for most of the century, disparities in income levels and rates of growth were not regarded as reasons for insulating the less favored countries from the rest of the world economic system. Cyclical fluctuations in market demand, temporary surpluses or shortages, and foreign exchange difficulties were permitted rapidly—and often brutally —to correct themselves.

How did the 19th century achieve and maintain this combination of economic freedom, calculability and mutual adaptability of national economic structures and monetary systems to one another? These three requirements of world economic integration depended in turn on certain political, social and psychological conditions peculiar to the 19th century.

Broadly speaking, the freedom, calculability and adaptability of the 19th-century world economy were reflections of the basic security and momentum of the political and economic institutions which Western society gradually spread over most of the planet in the years from 1815 to 1914. Within Western society, the remnants of the *ancien régime* might still delay, but could no longer prevent, the triumph of industrialism and liberal democracy. Criticism of the system and its consequences there was in plenty—from religious, romantic and socialistic standpoints. But there was no group within Western society which was conscious of its alienation from the dominant values and institutions of the 19th century and was large enough or articulate enough to constitute a serious internal threat to the system. Nor did any external rival or enemy exist capable even of restricting the growth of Western society, much less of threatening its survival. The unchallenged internal growth and external expansion of 19th-century Western society, and the self-confidence in its own future thereby engendered, provided the basic psychological assurance which underlay the businessman's willingness to trade in foreign places, to invest his capital abroad, and to face on his own the cyclical fluctuations and competitive pressures of the international market.

More concretely, the calculability and the relative freedom of international markets were to a very significant extent products of Britain's power, of its liberal ideology, and its consistent practice of *laissez-faire*. Indeed, the security of the 19th-century world polity has often been attributed to the *Pax Britannica*—to Britain's maintenance of the freedom of the seas and of the balance of power among the European states. There can be no doubt that the 19th-century economic system found its most perfect expression in the vast imperial free trade area—to which access by all other countries was freely open—created by British colonial rule and commercial policy. The British Government did not hesitate to use its unchallenged economic, political and naval power to maintain the physical security of world trade and foreign investment, to ensure commercial and financial responsibility, and to enforce freedom of international trade and payments—not only within the Empire but even outside it.

The mutual adaptability of national economies and the acceptance by national communities of the sway of the international market were likewise in part dependent upon British power and policy—in particular, on British monetary institutions and mechanisms located in, or controlled from, London. For, the Bank of England, the London money market, the sterling-gold standard system—and the anonymous authorities in London who managed them—were essential to the maintenance of a unified monetary system covering the entire trading world. The habit of regarding these institutions and mechanisms as wholly automatic and impersonal—even as "natural"—was a tribute to their extraordinary effectiveness before World War I and was, indeed, one of the reasons for their effectiveness. But this habit has obscured the fact that one of the major elements in the successful operation of the sterling-gold standard system was the possession of great discretionary power by a small number of men in London and the absence of other important competing financial centers. Commenting on the significance of central management in the 19th-century world economy, E. H. Carr has observed:

. . . the financial and economic system of the 19th century [was] operated all over the world by the organs of an anonymous authority, having no precisely defined status, but enjoying in virtue of its "non-political" services and its prestige the toleration and approval of the national governments. . . . It certainly did not seek to serve British interests in any narrow or exclusive sense; the commerce of the world was a British concern. . . . the control exercised from London was continuous, . . . autocratic, without appeal and completely effective. Nor was it, properly speaking, international, much less representative. It was at once supranational and British.[4]

Moreover, as important as the existence of this "supranational" authority was its exercise in accordance with orthodox *laissez-faire* principles of banking and financial policy which sanctified the freedom of private markets and international payments.

Because Britain's was the leading economy of the world trading system, the businessmen of continental Europe and North America desired to imitate its pattern or were constrained to conduct their affairs in a manner consistent with—though not necessarily identical to—the British way of doing business. But, quite apart from the great prestige of British economic philosophy and the compelling influence of the British economy, the business groups in other countries had motives and opportunities of their own to loosen the restraints of mercantilist policy and practice. Though never as whole-heartedly devoted to the *laissez-faire* ideal as their British counterparts, they nonetheless succeeded during the 19th century in dismantling a large part of the internal and external restrictions on industry and trade inherited from the preceding period. Even where aspects of mercantilist theory and practice survived and were gradually transformed into modern forms of restrictionism and protection, they did not usually involve active interference by governments in the economic process on anything like the scale which had existed earlier or would come into being again during and after World War I. In continental Europe and the United States, government intervention commonly took the form of active encouragement of domestic industry through subsidies of various kinds and the financing of "internal improvements" in transportation and communications. Aside from protective tariffs—quite moderate by present standards—it did

[4] E. H. Carr, *Nationalism and After* (New York: The Macmillan Company, 1945), pp. 50, 16.

not generally involve any important limitations on the freedom of private enterprise. Nor were there any counter-cyclical or economic welfare policies worthy of the name. Indeed, even in the least liberal of the West European countries, 19th-century governments had little or no economic policy in the 20th-century sense of the term.

These developments within the other leading nations of the world trading system depended, as in Britain, upon certain political, social and psychological conditions which were strongly conducive to the freedom and calculability of international trade and the mutual responsiveness of national economies. Of major importance was the character of group interests and relationships and of economic organization in Europe and North America. On the whole, existing group roles were accepted by the great bulk of the population; organized economic claimant groups—such as labor unions and farmers' organizations—had not yet emerged as politically formidable "countervailing" powers to the businessmen, except intermittently. The market power of industrial producers was still quite limited. This meant a substantially greater responsiveness of economic structures to market forces—national and international—than exists today. It meant also that economic interests were more willing than now to accept the dictates of markets—national and international —as the "automatic" work of impersonal social forces governed by "inexorable" laws. This willingness was owed in part to the prevailing belief of the business classes in economic liberalism, and to the acquiescence of the other social groups, their lack of conscious collective interest and organized economic and political power. It resulted also from the fact that market forces were, indeed, less personal and conscious than they are now when extensive government regulation and the widespread exercise of private economic power play such important and conspicuous roles. The moderate tariffs maintained by certain countries were changed only at long intervals. Unlike today, persons doing business abroad did not have to fear the effects on their investments of unforeseeable changes in the economic policies of foreign governments, for such policies as existed did not strongly affect the behavior of national and international markets.

Acceptance of the sway of the international market by the businessmen in Europe and North America was also fostered by the absence of serious competition among industrial countries until near the end of the century. With continental and American industry still small and still producing mainly for domestic markets, with British and Empire free trade policies, and with the rapid expansion of primary production and markets for manufactures overseas, there was still plenty of room for industrial expansion in Europe and America. At that stage of its industrial development, the world economy seemed to provide ample opportunity for industrial growth by all who desired, and were in a position, to undertake it. A strong motive for extreme industrial protectionism and a belief that industrial countries are inevitably economic rivals were still largely absent.

Finally, the effective working of the world market was greatly facilitated by the fact that the economies of the non-European parts of the trading world (other than the United States) were largely ruled or dominated by the European powers. European colonial policy—particularly that of the continental countries—was generally compatible with the 19th-century pattern of international specialization since it favored the growth of primary production in the dependent overseas territories and often attempted to discourage the development of local manufacturing. But, despite the claims of Marxists and native nationalists, it is likely that the actual influence of European rule on the rate and pattern of colonial economic development was more important in a negative than in a positive way. As long as they were under the direct rule or the hegemony of European powers, the colonial countries were unable to pursue economic policies which could insulate their economies from the world market or could divert their own economic development in directions in which it would not otherwise have gone. In consequence, native merchants and farmers—as well as European investors and settlers—naturally found better opportunities, greater profits, and fewer risks in specializing on the production of foodstuffs and raw materials to meet the rapidly expanding demands of the industrial countries than in the balanced internal growth of the colonial and semidependent economies. However, as the example of the United States suggests, this is probably not the way their resources would have been used had these countries been fully independent and had local enterprise existed capable of managing its own development.

There are doubtless other aspects of the political, social and psychological bases of the 19th-century world economy important enough to warrant similar attention here. But enough have perhaps been discussed to validate the conclusion that the world trading system of the 19th

century was the economic reflection or counterpart of a particular combination of moral values and political and social institutions characteristic of Western society at a particular period in its history.

Dis-Integration of the 19th-Century Economic System

It is much less difficult to summarize with reasonable accuracy the
main outlines of a period like that from 1815 to 1914 than to generalize
about the characteristics of the ensuing decades during which the distinctive 19th-century pattern of values and institutions was drastically
transformed. Though itself an epoch of unprecedentedly rapid growth,
the 19th century experienced in the main only an unfolding or expansion of potentialities inherent in, and largely consistent with, the aims
and structure of Western society as it had emerged from the Enlightenment, the French Revolution and the early stages of industrialism. The
subsequent changes in Western society during the 19th century were,
in retrospect, reasonably harmonious and logically derivative from these
antecedents, however novel they may have appeared to their contempo-
raries. Indeed, this relative prevalence of harmony over inconsistency, of
order over disorder, was a key element in the "success" of the 19th-
century world system and underlay the confidence of 19th-century liberalism in the essential harmony of human interests and the inevitability
of human progress.

In contrast, the transformation of Western society in the 20th century has been marked by major inconsistencies and conflicts. Such disorders are perennial problems of human society, but the first half of
the 20th century seems to have had more than its share of them
compared even with other periods of great social ferment and change.
This is owed not only to the fact that Western society has become so
much more complex and interdependent than any previous civilization.
Nor is it solely a consequence of the immense numbers of people now
encompassed by it or the global dimensions of the problems involved.
It has also been the result of Western society's own reluctance to abandon even yet the 19th-century positivist assumption that all human interests are intrinsically harmonious—or at least scientifically manageable—and that social progress is inevitable. In consequence, the West has
been, for the most part, intellectually unprepared to grasp the nature
of its conflicts and disorders, and morally unready to assume the re-

sponsibility for dealing with them in a creative fashion. A few examples may help to clarify this point.

Over the past generation, the impact of spreading industrialism and urban living, and the inspiration of democratic ideals and mass education have shaken the population of Europe and North America out of their acquiescence, widening their horizons and enlarging their social and economic expectations. One aspect of this now familiar "revolt of the masses" has been widespread popular rejection of 19th-century concepts of economic equity and social justice and a general unwillingness to leave the distribution of income and the level of employment to be determined by the uncontrolled operation of private market forces. In a few countries—particularly in the United States and the English-speaking Dominions—these new expectations and claims have been successfully accommodated. But in others, the effort to satisfy them within the existing constitution of the world polity and economy, and without adequate regard to the consequences of technological advance and social change, has led to two kinds of perverse responses. On the one hand, it has been largely responsible for the development of economic nationalism which, in its many contemporary forms, has so seriously impaired the efficiency of the international economy and the health of many of its component national economies. On the other hand, it has led to the rise of collectivist economic ideologies and systems which hold out the delusive promise of perpetual peace and plenty at the cost of human freedom, initiative and progress.

More fundamental, perhaps, has been the failure to find new and more satisfying ways for people to live and work together to replace the many traditional forms of human community that have been dissolved or seriously eroded by the universal solvent of a vast, impersonal, industrial and urban society. In consequence, many have sought to escape the unbearable sense of rootlessness and aimlessness—the absence of a feeling of belonging—by losing themselves in the absolute oneness of the totalitarian state.[5]

---

[5] This tendency toward the opposite extremes of excessive individualism and excessive community has been described as follows: "Since society cannot function without the presence of spirit or soul, men will insist on collectively worshipping idols rather than suffer the agonies of rootlessness and despair. Where subtle and satisfying forms of organic solidarity are unavailable, men will seek to escape chaos by adopting or imposing the yoke of mechanism. To be truly viable, the forms of association must ingeniously pattern the claims of human nature, the expectations of men in society, the underlying

Again, the impact of Western rule and of Western ideas of democracy, nationalism and economic equity has shaken the traditional societies of Asia, Africa and Latin America out of their centuries-old lethargy. But, except in the United States and English-speaking Commonwealth, Western society failed to realize while there was still time the necessity for colonialism to evolve into new voluntary forms of political and economic association consistent at each stage with the colonies' degree of readiness for self-government in an increasingly rigorous international environment. This failure left full national sovereignty as the only practicable way of meeting the demands of the colonial peoples for an equal political and economic status with the West. Desirable as the timely passing of colonialism is, it is nonetheless true that the new economic nationalism of the independent underdeveloped countries has contributed to the declining effectiveness of the international economy; their political weakness and incapacity for self-defense provide opportunities for communist subversion and aggression. Where they have not been ripe for self-rule, power vacuums have resulted.

In the sense implied by these illustrations, the slowness of creative adaptation in our times can be gauged by the severity of the three fundamental challenges to Western society today: (1) the threat to human freedom and progress presented by the imperial ambitions of collectivist totalitarianisms, today that of Soviet and Red Chinese communism; (2) the test of whether the industrial West has the wisdom and strength to work out new and mutually beneficial relationships with the independent underdeveloped countries in Asia, Africa and Latin America; and (3) the basic challenge to Western society's intellectual and moral capacity to understand and to grapple effectively with the causes of its own internal weakness and insufficient unity.

That these challenges are neither superficial nor transitory may be

---

functions of social life, and the changing requirements of culture. It is plain that a society founded on sheer egoism, a society which operates on too grand a scale, at too rapid a pace, will undergo atomization, anomic loss of a sense of belongingness. Such under-integration of the moral community and the spatial order may always be expected to generate . . . [the opposite] reactions. . . . The killing yoke of undivided oneness . . . is thrust at us because we cannot bear the ravages of total absence of community. . . . If liberal society recurrently runs the risk of under-integration and absence of compelling loyalties and coherent motivations, totalitarian society offers us no other prospect than that of over-integration, the substitution of mechanism for spirit." Benjamin N. Nelson, "The Future of Illusions," *Conflict in the Social Order,* Centennial Lecture Series, University of Minnesota, 1951, p. 43. An abbreviated version of this stimulating essay can be found in *Psychoanalysis,* Vol. 2, No. 4, Spring–Summer 1954, pp. 16–37.

seen in the changed character of world politics in the 20th century. To-day, the major political and economic issues confronting the nations are not, as in the 19th century, marginal adjustments in relative power positions or in the distribution of world resources. Instead, they touch the very constitution of the existing world polity and economy. Unlike the limited conflicts of the 19th century, the wars—hot and cold—of the 20th century have been increasingly "total" wars of unparalleled scope and intensity. They have this character not simply because modern science and technology have been capable of providing new weapons of almost unimaginable destructiveness. Equally important is the fact that the 20th century has been willing to use its science and technology for purposes and in ways from which the 19th century—for all its self-righteous indifference to mass poverty and hunger—would have recoiled in utter horror. Despite moral qualms, the 20th century has been willing to do so because its conflicts have been, since 1917, more and more revolutionary in nature, aimed at the overthrow or preservation of the whole system of world political and economic order. Indeed, in their ideological zeal and unconditional aims, the wars of the 20th century are now like civil wars.

We cannot begin to suggest here the many specific ways in which major transformations in Western society's aims, structure and conditions of life in the 20th century have shaped the political and economic problems of our times. The magnitude and baffling complexity of these changes and the general slowness of creative adaptation to them have been responsible over the past fifty years for a serious decline in many Western countries' confidence in their own future and in that of Western society as a whole. Today, a sense of increasing insecurity and uncertainty pervades all aspects of their national life—economic, political and social. This, in turn, is reflected throughout Western society in the growing incalculability of international economic relationships, in the expanding obstacles to foreign trade and investment, in the increasing reluctance of private businessmen to risk their capital abroad and to face unaided the difficulties of doing business beyond their own national frontiers. One implication of these developments is that, in a study dealing with foreign economic policy, it is necessary to analyze briefly some of the ways in which the transformation of Western society in the 20th century has contributed to this dis-integration of the unified world trading system inherited from the 19th century.

First, we have already noted the fundamental importance of the changes in social values and popular expectations which have come to be described by the phrases "the revolt of the masses" and the "revolution of rising expectations." This central phenomenon of Western society in the 20th century has had effects which ramify through every aspect of contemporary life. For our purpose here, its most significant consequence has been the rise of new organized interests or claimant groups—particularly the trade unions and the farmers' organizations —which, with increasing success as their political power has grown, have been competing with the formerly dominant business groups for a larger and more secure share of national incomes.

The advent of such organized labor and farmers' groups on the national scene in most Western countries—and the increasing group-consciousness and more effective organization of the businessmen in response to their competition—have been major elements in the growth of economic nationalism since World War I. Such organized business, labor and farmers' groups have extended their power not only in the political arena but directly in the market as well. Explicitly or unconsciously rejecting the *laissez-faire* ideal, especially in Europe, organized claimant groups of these kinds have been increasingly unwilling to accept the sway of national and international markets over their economic fortunes. With respect to the international market, these groups have come to demand active protection by the national state—as well as by private combinations and cartels—against the increasing incalculability of the external economic environment, the more strongly as their national economies have become more dependent on foreign trade. In particular, protection has been demanded against the threat of deflation or inflation from abroad and the effects of foreign competition.

The means used by national governments for this insulating purpose have gone far beyond such techniques as the 19th-century's protective tariff, subsidy or even private international cartel. The preferred means more and more employed since 1914 have been quantitative trade controls (quotas), exchange controls, bilateral trade agreements and, above all, the "nationalization of money"—the divorce of the domestic banking system from traditional international monetary mechanisms and the centralization of its control in the hands of national treasuries and legislatures. Thus, the anonymous central monetary authorities in London have been overthrown and their power dispersed among many independent national central banks and national governments, highly susceptible to popular pressures. The "power of money," which had symbolized the apparent autonomy of the economic process in the 19th century, was dethroned by the political power, as universal suffrage won the day.

A parallel and mutually reinforcing process has at the same time been taking place within the domestic economies of most Western countries. Under pressure of the same claimant groups, governments have been increasingly asserting active sovereignty over the workings of the internal market for such purposes as raising the level of employment, altering the pattern of income distribution, allocating limited economic opportunities, and restricting competition. These domestic policies and practices have helped to reduce the adaptability of national economies —that is, their capacity to respond in consistent ways to one another— and have thereby hastened the dis-integration of the unified world economy.

Second, by the turn of the century, powerful new industrial producers were already active in the international market, challenging in many branches of world trade the supremacy of the older industrial nations, especially Britain. German, Japanese and American industry, in particular, rapidly expanded their shares of world trade during the first four decades of the 20th century while the total volume of international commerce grew much more slowly, for reasons to be presently examined.[6] In these increasingly competitive circumstances, an idea radically opposed to 19th-century economic liberalism took hold among the businessmen of the industrial nations. This idea was that international competition, unlike the domestic variety, was not merely competition among firms but among whole national industries or economies. National business communities came to feel a collective interest in greatly increased tariff protection. Industries sought the help of the national state in setting up private agreements to protect their domestic markets and to stabilize their shares of export markets. This new protectionism—which began to be strong as early as the 1880's and 1890's (particularly in France, Germany and the United States) and was well developed by 1914—was another major step in the dis-integration of the 19th-century world economy.

Third, the rise of powerful new industrial and financial centers, and the general tendency to "nationalize" monetary policy led to the decline of Britain's "supranational" economic authority on which so much of

---

[6] See below Chapter 2, pp. 78–79.

the freedom and calculability of the 19th-century world economy depended. The diminishing effectiveness of Britain's central authority was a major element in the gradual breakdown of the sterling-gold standard system. World War I dealt an irreparable blow to Britain's capacity to manage the world monetary system and Britain's efforts to maintain its monetary leadership during the interwar period proved well nigh disastrous to the weakened British economy. The strains of the great depression of the 1930's gave the *coup de grace* to a system of worldwide currency convertibility based upon the unrestricted exchange of sterling for gold.

Fourth, the advent of rival industrial powers and the relative decline of British power had serious implications as well for the world trading system in consequence of their political and military effects. They created the economic and technological conditions for the collapse of the 19th-century security system—the "balance of power"—which the predominance of the British navy and Britain's "supranational" economic authority had helped to maintain. With the passing of the 19th-century security system, the pressures of national defense—or the preparations for imperialist aggression—added another major dimension to economic nationalism. Nations sought to free themselves from dependence on imported raw materials and foodstuffs by subsidizing or protecting higher-cost domestic sources of supply. Armament expenditures began more and more to compete with other important claims on national resources, particularly with the investment needed for economic growth and the consumers goods required to meet politically effective demands for rising living standards. In effect, the nature of world politics in the 20th century has made national autarky—the apogee of economic nationalism—the ideal of national military strength.

The impulse toward economic nationalism resulting from the collapse of the 19th-century security system has, moreover, been intensified by political and ideological developments which accompanied the advent of mass participation in politics. The relatively restrained national patriotism of the 19th-century European middle classes was transformed into the mass nationalism of the 20th century, with its tendencies to fanaticism and collective megalomania. Mass participation in national politics meant, in these circumstances, a much more absolute and uncompromising definition of the national political interest, just as mass participation in economic power has meant a new, nationalistic definition of economic interest.

Fifth, the direct effects of two world wars and of the intervening great depression must also be stressed. In part, these events have been both cause and consequence of the dis-integration of the 19th-century economic and political system. Quite apart from the autarkic policies and practices generated by 20th-century wars and depressions, they have accelerated the process of dis-integration in a multitude of direct ways too familiar to require discussion here. Suffice it to mention the vast destruction of people and of capital, the recurrent disruption of established trade patterns, the liquidation of foreign investments, and the major changes in economic and political power. Today, the cold war has similar adverse effects upon the security and calculability of international economic relations.

Sixth, the achievement of political independence by many primary producing countries formerly subject to European colonial control has hastened world economic dis-integration. National political independence has come to mean for these countries the opportunity to break out of the 19th-century pattern of specialization on primary production and complementary trade with Europe and North America, to reduce their dependence on foreign trade, and to industrialize. Their pursuit of "national economic independence" is today carried on with an ideological zeal borrowed from their earlier struggle for political independence.

Finally, we must recognize that the national state itself has come to have a strong interest opposed to international economic integration. This is most obvious in military matters, as already observed. But it is true also in the state's economic concerns. For, success in the exercise of its economic regulations and controls depends for the state, as it does for a private firm, on the calculability of the future conditions of success. Economic influences coming from outside the national territory are inherently much less calculable than those from inside, because knowledge of them is unavoidably less complete and—more important— because the policies of other national states often cannot be foreseen. Inevitably, therefore, national economic authorities have come to have a strong bias in favor of trying to limit the degree of dependence of the national economy on foreign trade and of "stabilizing" (i.e., controlling tightly) its foreign economic relations. This bias is the stronger as the scope of state participation in the economy is larger and the dependence of the national economy on foreign trade is greater. Thus, the growth of state intervention—under the pressure of group interests, changing social values and increasingly unfavorable world political and economic conditions—has been another potent re-enforcement of economic nationalism.

Once set in motion by changes of these kinds, the process of international economic dis-integration has fed—and continues to feed—on itself. Each new act of economic nationalism taken by one country increases the incentive for others to control their trade and payments more tightly—in order to protect their terms of trade, their level of employment, their domestic distribution of income, or their reserves of hard currencies; and to reduce the vulnerability of their national economies to similar acts in the future. Moreover, the reduced calculability and the rigidities created by each new restriction on trade or payments render national economies the less able to adapt spontaneously to economic changes at home and abroad—thereby making further insulation of them necessary. Thus, restriction has led to restriction in a complex vicious circle.

The Consequences of the Nationalization of the World Economy

The significance of the dis-integration of the unified 19th-century world trading system may be seen more clearly when it is viewed as a process of "nationalization." Over the past half century, the world economy has been "nationalized" in three ways. First, the number of independent national states has been greatly increased, thereby dividing the unified world market into more, and relatively smaller, sovereign economic units. Second, larger and larger portions of the economic process have been brought under the conscious control of national governments, thereby substituting national economic decisions for private ones. Finally, the policies followed by national economic authorities have expressed narrower and more immediate national interests and have shown less and less concern for the broader and longer-run need to maintain world economic integration. Thus, the international economy has come to consist today of a large—and still growing—number of sovereign national economies of widely disparate sizes, endowments of natural resources, and economic and political effectiveness, following divergent economic policies and practices, and more or less insulated from one another by deliberate trade and payments barriers and by the general insecurity and incalculability of contemporary international economic relations.

In consequence of this process of nationalization, there is now an important qualitative difference between the 19th-century world economy and that of the 20th century. Over much of the period before 1914, the difference between doing business at home or abroad was not generally decisive in economic decisions, private or public. For, the freedom, security, and calculability of economic conditions behind national frontiers were rarely sufficiently greater than those beyond the national frontiers to matter very much. Today, this is no longer true. The difference between the relative freedom, security, and calculability of domestic conditions and the relative restriction, insecurity, and incalculability of the external economic environment is often crucial. This difference between the two periods will be expressed by using the term *world economy* for the system of world economic relationships before 1914 and the term *international economy* for the system which has existed since then. Use of these terms will help to emphasize the distinctive characteristic of each system—the seamless, integrated economy of the 19th century; and the nationalized, compartmented economy of the 20th century.[7]

By its nature, an international economy is significantly less efficient than a world economy because it cannot provide in as large a measure the pressures and incentives conducive to an economical use of resources. The efficiency of any economic system—national, regional or global—depends upon the continuous mutual adaptation of its component units

---

[7] Contemporary economic nationalism has had its counterparts in other times, though its degree, significance and specific forms have varied widely from one historical period to another. Except for much of the 19th century, it has generally been a characteristic of economic relationships among sovereign political entities. In the middle ages and throughout the mercantilist period, restrictions on the freedom of private trade were normal and largely unquestioned features of the economic environment—not only among sovereign political communities but also within them—to which private producers and traders had to adjust their activities. For a relatively brief period from about 1830 to 1914, the degree and importance of economic nationalism was very much reduced, though it did not disappear. In consequence, the extent of international economic integration across national boundaries was so substantial that a true world economy can be said to have existed during that period. Since World War I, economic nationalism has again become a paramount consideration both for governments and for private traders. Thus, in the long perspective of civilized history, it would not be unreasonable to regard the 19th century as an exceptional case and not, as does conventional economic doctrine, as the typical one.

in such a way as to bring about the most economical use of resources (in both a short-run and a dynamic sense) in achieving the various goals of the national, regional or international community involved. In the fully developed 19th-century system, this task of adaptation was left mainly, if not entirely, to market forces. Moreover, we often overlook the fact that the 19th-century way of organizing a world economy left to the market not only the task of determining the use of resources but also, to a large extent, the choice of proximate goals of economic activity—for example, the pattern of income distribution, the degree of individual and national economic security, and the allocation of economic opportunities among social groups and nations. There were exceptions, of course, particularly the use of colonial control to channel trade and investment to the advantage of the metropolitan power.

Today in contrast, the multitude of powerful claimants—including national governments themselves—presses on the international economy many different and consciously formulated conceptions of the proper goals of economic activity—conceptions which are often totally incompatible. Claimant groups and nations are no longer willing to leave to the market the final determination of such matters as income distribution, employment levels, or opportunities for economic growth among and within national communities. The power wielded by claimant groups and governments over the economic process and the methods of its use often preclude an efficient use of resources.

Within certain national economies, however, this new situation can work out satisfactorily for economic health, though in many cases it does not. For there is still within some national communities—particularly in the largest or fastest growing—a sufficient agreement on goals, and political machinery still exists which is adequate to reconcile conflicting claims to the capacity of the national economy. In these national communities, there is usually a sufficient common concern for the efficiency of the national economy, and a sufficient rationality about the choice of economic policies, to assure a reasonably efficient use of national resources for national ends. Unfortunately, this situation is by no means uniformly true in the free world today.[8]

For the contemporary international economy, however, the situation is more serious. The economic interest of most national communities

---

[8] As we shall see in Chapter 3, political morale and social cohesion are now so reduced in some national communities that effective claims are hardly reconcilable through existing political institutions.

and of their governments in the efficiency of the international economy as a whole has become remote and indirect. There is no international consensus about the ends which the international economy is supposed to serve. There are, for example, no agreed standards for determining "equitable" terms of trade between industrial and agricultural countries; the mutual "responsibilities" of surplus and deficit countries to correct international payments imbalances; the "rights" and "obligations" of foreign capital; the "proper" rate of growth for underdeveloped countries; the "desirable" volume of international loans or grants; or the "appropriate" shares of limited foreign market opportunities. These questions were once decided largely by tradition, by British power and authority, and by the impersonal workings of the market. But today, traditional values are changed, British power and authority are much reduced, and no national community can allow its interest in these issues to be determined by market forces which are now so largely shaped by the uncoordinated interventions of other national governments. Nor is there any authoritative central machinery by which common standards on these questions, and agreed means for achieving them, could be decided and enforced. Rather, national states intervene anarchically in the international economy, each trying to achieve its own ends with little regard for the interests of other countries and with slight concern for the efficiency of the system as a whole.[9]

In such an international economy, the mutual adaptability of national economies is greatly reduced. With the exception of a few countries, necessary adaptations can be accomplished neither by market forces nor by intergovernmental coordination (voluntary or enforced) of national economic policies. This is not of great importance for the economic health of a few countries relatively independent of the international economy—for example, the United States. But for many other non-Soviet countries, whose economies are unavoidably dependent upon the international economy however tightly they may control their external trade and payments, the result has been a grave impairment of their economic efficiency and capacity for economic growth. The following chapters will examine more concretely the most important ways in which their economic efficiency and health have been damaged through the failure of mutual adaptation of national economies.

---

[9] Postwar efforts to harmonize divergent national economic policies by means of various kinds of international and intergovernmental agreements and organizations will be discussed in Part II.

These characteristic disorders of a nationalized world economic system are intensified at many points by the present character of Soviet-Western relations. Today, the Soviet and Red Chinese threat adds another source of incalculability in international economic relations. The Soviet threat is total—military, political, economic and ideological. Four of its specific aspects are important for an understanding of present and prospective international economic problems. It has meant:

(1) A serious reduction of the potential resource base and market opportunities of the West owing to the subtraction of the communist areas from the international economy and their economic transformation in ways which reduce their willingness and ability to complement the industrial economies of the West;

(2) A planned disruption of the free world economies by means of Soviet foreign economic policy and subversive communist movements;

(3) A long-term challenge to the economic pre-eminence of the West arising from the much higher current rates of economic growth (particularly of heavy industry) in the Soviet system;

(4) A source of major insecurity in the international economy due to the fact that Soviet communism threatens not merely the political and economic institutions of the West but the continued existence of human freedom and humane society everywhere.

These aspects of the cold war have hastened the disintegration of the unified world economy and have magnified the contemporary economic difficulties of the non-Soviet countries. In turn, the inefficiency of the international economy and the poor economic health of many free countries reduce the ability of the Western nations to meet the Soviet challenge in the cold war. The reciprocal relationship between these two dangerous tendencies is one of the most perplexing problems with which contemporary Western policy must grapple. This problem would be difficult enough in an efficiently functioning world economy; today, in the circumstances of cold war, the inefficiency of a nationalized world trading system makes it even more difficult.

19th-Century Britain and 20th-Century America

The disintegration of the 19th-century world economy cannot simply be reversed to re-create an integrated worldwide trading system once again. The causes of disintegration have not been adequately appreciated, as we have seen, by conventional economic theory, most of which still attributes to classical models of an autonomous economic system a greater degree of relevance and utility than they actually possess. As a result, the traditional explanations for the breakdown of international economic integration in the 20th century have tended to be superficial, for they have tried to find the causes largely, if not exclusively, within the economic system itself and have generally overlooked what was happening to the social, political and moral supports on which any existing economy must rest. Today, political economy rather than economics is again the discipline appropriate for understanding these relationships.

To a considerable extent also, economic policy still operates on the assumption that a sufficiently integrated world economic system could be again achieved by means essentially similar to those employed in the 19th century. For example, it has often been asserted in recent years that the major problems of the contemporary international economy would simply disappear "if only the United States would behave like a creditor nation." In support of this plausible prescription, people on both sides of the Atlantic will point to the relationships between Britain and the 19th-century world economy. Like 19th-century Britain, they claim, the United States is a "mature creditor" and must open its economy freely to imports and must commit itself annually to invest substantial amounts of capital abroad so that it can balance its exports of goods and services at a high level of trade.

This prescription overlooks the crucial differences between the world economic roles of 19th-century Britain and 20th-century America. Britain's role was that of a *leading economy,* fully integrated into the world economic system and in large measure making possible its successful functioning owing to Britain's dependence on foreign trade, the pervasive influence of its commercial and financial institutions, and the basic consistency between its national economic policies and those required for world economic integration. In contrast, the United States is a *dominant economy,* only partially integrated into the world economic system, with which it is also partly competitive, and whose accustomed mode and pace of functioning it tends periodically to disturb. No network of American commercial and financial institutions exists to bind together and to manage the day-to-day operations of the world trading system. However essential certain imports may be, foreign trade is in the aggregate not of crucial importance to the American economy. Though imports and exports are necessary to particular sectors of the American economy, the direct, short-run interest of the United States in following national economic policies conducive to world economic integration is not very large when considered in terms of the ratio of foreign trade to gross national product.

In the cases both of the British and American economies, structural characteristics which are products of their different historical developments have in large part determined the nature of their relationships, actual and potential, with the world economic system. Unlike 19th-century Britain, or any other nation in the free world today, the United States has both a national and a continental (or regional) economy—that is, it is a sovereign national state but with so large an area and population, and with such abundant and balanced resources that it is equivalent to an integrated regional grouping of many national states, a continent in itself. This dual character results not only from the size of its area and population and the diversity and abundance of its natural resources, but from the historical and sociological factors which influenced its economic development, political institutions and social attitudes. In consequence, the American economy is not simply the largest industrial producer in the world; it is also the world's largest agricultural producer.[10]

At the same time, its continental size and balance and its relatively liberal economic attitudes and institutions have made the American

---

[10] The following figures illustrate the size, balance and relative self-sufficiency of the American economy:

Dimensions of the American Economy

Area (in square miles)	3,022,387
Population (1953)	159,629,000
Civilian Labor Force (1953)	63,453,000
Nonagricultural Employment	55,245,000
Agricultural Employment	6,683,000
Unemployment	1,524,000

Domestic Production as Percent of American Consumption

Material	Percent	Period
Food	102	1946–50
Wheat	167	1948–52
Nonfood Agricultural	97	1946–50
Cotton	154	1948–52
Aluminum	88	1948–50
Coal	111	1946–50
Copper	77	1950
Forest products	93	1946–50
Iron ore	95	1948–50
Petroleum	91	1950

economy a highly dynamic one. Its propensity for technological innovation and aggressive entrepreneurship is probably the strongest in the world; over the past half century, output per manhour has tripled and the gross national product has risen fivefold (in constant dollars). This dynamic growth is in marked contrast to that of most other industrial nations of the free world, as will be explained in Chapter 3.

Finally, the American economy is still one of the freest—in the classical liberal sense of the term. True, governmental involvement in, and regulation of, the economic process has grown unprecedentedly over the past generation as a result of the changing values and conditions of the 20th century. But this has not basically compromised, nor even seriously impaired, the very large measure of private, decentralized decision making and control on the part of businessmen, farmers, workers and consumers over their own economic affairs.[11]

Today, no other industrial country enjoys the beneficial effects on its entrepreneurial vigor and rate of productivity growth of a domestic market remotely approaching that of the United States in size, balance, dynamism or competitive intensity.[12] As a result, in those sectors of the American economy characterized by mass production for mass consumption—comprising the largest and most rapidly growing portion of the American gross national product—imported commodities are generally not competitive with domestically produced goods either in price or in the equally important non-price aspects of competition (product design, styling and merchandising, sales effort, delivery, servicing, terms of payment, etc.).[13] The great bulk of American imports —nearly three quarters—consists of tropical agricultural products and of raw and semi-processed industrial materials not produced in the United States or not produced here in sufficient volume. And even these commodities are only a small fraction—varying in recent years from 2 to 3 percent—of the total goods and services of all kinds consumed by Americans. Beyond these small necessary imports, the overwhelming portion of the vast quantities of goods annually bought and sold

---

[11] However, it does not necessarily follow that the results would be the same if the degree of governmental involvement in the economy had been significantly greater, or if its purposes and means had been different than those actually employed.

[12] Except possibly for Canada, whose domestic market is in many respects an extension of the American.

[13] There are exceptions, of course, which will be noted in Chapter 2, but these are small relative both to total American imports and to total American demand for such products.

in the American market is bound to be the product of domestic factories, mines and fields. Thus, America is in the anomalous position of being, on the one hand, the world's largest importing nation in terms of the absolute value of the goods and services it buys abroad and, on the other hand, only a very minor importer relative to the total value of the goods and services it produces and consumes.

The commodity pattern and level of American imports are mainly determined by the structural characteristics of the American economy—its size, balance, dynamism and competitive ability—and the influence of legislatively or administratively imposed barriers against imports is much smaller. Depending upon their magnitude and duration, the fluctuations in national employment and income—to which any dynamic free enterprise economy is susceptible—may have a greater effect upon imports than existing tariff and quota restrictions. For its part, the American economy is not seriously affected by adverse short-term changes in the international economic environment. The levels of demand and of employment in the American economy are overwhelmingly dependent upon domestic economic developments—e.g., changes in domestic savings and investment, the nature and timing of government policies and programs, etc. Though these may be influenced by political and strategic events abroad, they are only marginally affected by deflationary or inflationary movements in other countries.[14]

The incentive for the United States to invest capital abroad is not by any means as compelling as that of Britain in the 19th century. Britain's major motives were the need to develop foreign sources of food and the many raw materials not produced at home and, after the mid-century, the growing attractiveness of overseas investment opportunities compared with domestic ones. Today, in the United States, the

---

[14] This was not always true in the past, nor may it be in the more distant future. Until about 1900, the condition of the American economy and its rate of growth were strongly affected by the level of foreign demand for its agricultural exports and by the availability of foreign investment capital, commercial credit and manufactured goods. Depletion of natural resources and increase of population will, over the long term, make the American economy more dependent than today upon foreign sources of supply, if national security and living standards are to be maintained or improved. Cf. *Resources for Freedom*, Report of the President's Materials Policy Commission (Washington, 1952). Furthermore, it is probable that American industry will eventually "outgrow" to some extent the potential expansibility of domestic markets for manufactures, as some other major industrial countries have already done. (See below Chapter 2, pp. 63–64.) But these are longer-term prospects whose implications for policy lie beyond the time horizon of this study.

chief incentive for private American capital to invest abroad is not any comparative decline in the attractiveness of domestic investment, but the desirability of opening up new lower-cost sources of a still limited number of industrial raw materials. In consequence, the export of American capital has neither the urgency nor the relative magnitude of British capital export in the 19th century.

Thus, the American economy has a one-sided, or non-complementary, relationship to the international economy, and its effects on the latter are apt to be contradictory. The rest of the free world relies upon the American economy to a much greater extent than the American economy depends upon it. Indeed, the rest of the free world could not live *without* the American economy, which is its largest single market and source of supply of goods and capital. At the same time, other countries find great difficulty in living *with* the American economy, which sets for them generally inaccessible and rising competitive and consumption standards, and generates inflationary and deflationary impulses against which they cannot insulate themselves successfully. The American economy is vital to them quantitatively, as a source of goods and capital, and qualitatively, as the most important stimulus to dynamism and growth in the international economy. But, by the same token, it exerts a disturbing influence in the international economy, particularly on those countries heavily dependent on foreign trade whose capacity for adjustment has been impaired.

The partial, one-sided integration of the American economy into the international economy and its competitive effects on the latter are in marked contrast to the relationship of Britain to the 19th-century world economy—a relationship which to some extent still persists today. The British economy was—if anything—more dependent upon the rest of the world than the latter was upon it. Britain's ratio of foreign trade to national income was—and still is—very high. While British industries outgrew their domestic markets at early stages of their development, British production of foodstuffs and industrial raw materials [15] became less and less adequate for the needs of a rapidly increasing population, rising living standards and growing industrial output. This meant not simply that Britain would inevitably become more and more dependent upon foreign trade, but also that its high rate of savings would impel it actively to seek overseas opportunities for investment.

---

[15] Except for coal and, until late in the century, iron ore.

In consequence of these relationships, Britain was—and still is—very susceptible to changes in the level of foreign demand and, in the 19th century, the complementary dependence also obtained owing to Britain's formerly much larger share of total world trade.

These structural characteristics of the British economy meant that most other trading nations had ready access to sterling in the 19th century. In contrast, the present and prospective nature of the American economy does not provide a valid basis for believing that the supply of dollars naturally available to the rest of the world will grow in a manner closely parallel to the growth of world demand for dollars. In the 19th and early 20th centuries, sterling was not only the international unit of account, the currency of ultimate international settlement, and the preferred form of national monetary reserves, as to a much lesser extent the dollar has become today. More significant, sterling was also the nearly universal medium of world trade and of international commercial credit.[16] Commercial credit was a far more important feature of international trade in the 19th century than it is now, and this crucial credit structure ultimately rested upon the financial resources of the London money market and the Bank of England. Thus, Britain was the monetary heart of the world economy, normally pumping out adequate amounts of sterling to float the major portion of the world's circulation of goods and capital. It was Britain's situation as the entrepôt of the world which inextricably linked the gold standard mechanism to sterling and made Britain's the leading economy of a unified world system.

Any expectation that, over the long term, the dollar could play the same role in the contemporary international economy that sterling did in the 19th century is in all probability illusory. Except in unusually favorable circumstances, the dollar will generally be too scarce a currency for that purpose. The United States has neither the need to import goods nor the pressure to invest capital abroad which, in the case of Britain, made sterling so readily accessible a currency before World War I. The failure of the United States "to act like a mature creditor nation" is not primarily the result of lack of understanding of the American position in the international economy or of reluctance to recognize American responsibilities. Nor was Britain's liberal import policy and lavish export of capital in the 19th century the result of inherently superior Brit-

---

[16] Even today, about 40 percent of world trade is still normally carried on in sterling.

ish judgment or higher moral sense. Both British and American choices and actions have been circumscribed by the limits of the possible—that is, by the structural characteristics of their respective economies—in turn, the consequences of deep historical processes. But both nations have also shown, each in its own day and way, how a dynamic people can enlarge those limits.

Concepts Relevant to Contemporary Problems

This historical survey of the genesis of the contemporary international economy has employed certain concepts which are rarely used in conventional economic analysis. Yet economics needs the stimulus of unconventional concepts today if it is to become a more adequate tool for understanding and for dealing with the crucial international economic problems of our times.

The central concept of classical economics is that of economic efficiency, or the most economical use of resources. Given the values and institutions of the 19th century, this concept alone was often sufficient to reveal fruitful analytical insights and acceptable policy changes. Today, its relevance is—if anything—greater than ever; but, by itself, it no longer provides an adequate guide either for understanding or for grappling with the complex problems of world economic order. The 20th century no longer believes, as did the 19th, that, left to itself, the economic system will not only maximize its efficiency but will also automatically ensure economic equity and justice. Nor, despite its admiration for technical perfection, does Western society today prefer efficiency to justice when the two conflict. Though greater efficiency in the use of resources is generally a requirement for ultimately achieving greater justice in the distribution of income, contemporary social groups and national states are all too frequently neither willing nor able to endure the present sacrifices necessary for such future benefits.

An excellent example of the inability of the principle of economic efficiency to serve as the sole guide to contemporary policy may be seen in the prescription it would dictate for overcoming the so-called "dollar shortage" and similar financial problems reflecting the disparate price levels and pressures of monetary demand among trading countries. Strict application of the principle of efficiency would seem to require the dollar-short countries to devaluate their currencies and deflate their economies to price and monetary demand levels which would eliminate their balance-of-payments deficits. There is no doubt that a balance in international payments could be restored by this method. But, there is little doubt that few, if any, of the dollar-short countries could afford to apply this remedy with sufficient rigor to make it effective, of and by itself. Today, social values and attitudes do not permit a government to acquiesce in—much less to encourage—increasing unemployment and declining incomes except in the most dire national emergencies. Even then, it takes an unusually strong sense of social cohesion and national morale for the application of this remedy with the required degree of thoroughness.

Indispensable as it still is, the concept of economic efficiency must, therefore, be supplemented by other concepts relevant to the kinds of values and institutions which exist today. Three concepts—in addition to a modified concept of economic efficiency—have proved particularly useful in this study for analyzing the problems of the contemporary international economy and for discovering effective and morally valid means of mitigating them.

The first is in reality two closely related concepts: *economic aspirations* and *economic claims*. Economic aspirations are desires for satisfactions requiring economic resources which individuals and social groups believe that their national community should fulfill either directly or by providing opportunities for self-fulfillment. When the satisfaction of particular economic aspirations is made the goal of an organized social group wielding political or economic power, it may be called an economic claim. Though they have a definable character at any given time, economic claims are the resultants of dynamic social processes—they change unconsciously over time and may also be changed by conscious action. Economic claims are usually in some degree competitive and, when they cannot be reconciled through market processes or private bargaining, must be reconciled through, or denied by, the political organs of the national community. If the claimants are unwilling to accept a reconciliation or denial, or if the political machinery is incapable of achieving or enforcing either kind of settlement, the result may be a paralysis of political processes, accompanied by bitter class and party conflict or even civil disorder. Today, the extent to which claims are competitive is substantially greater than in the 19th century, and the capacity of many national societies to reconcile or deny them has been correspondingly—and, in some cases, absolutely—reduced. To be relevant to contemporary problems, economic analysis and policy-making must neither ignore economic expectations and claims nor assume that they are fixed and therefore immutable.

The second concept is that of *economic requirements*. These are the national community's needs for economic resources to maintain military security, economic self-support, and the capacity for an adequate rate of economic growth. The definition of an adequate rate of growth is always a contingent one; it is, in effect, the rate of growth needed to satisfy minimum economic requirements (including investment requirements) and to meet a politically tolerable level of economic claims.[17] Just as economic claims are mutually competitive, so economic requirements may be inconsistent with each other and, more often, with economic claims. The interest of the national community in military security is always a direct responsibility of the state. The interest of the national community in economic self-support and in an adequate rate of economic growth is, in the first instance, left to private decision-making and the market in most Western countries. Ultimately, however, responsibility for the satisfaction of these two requirements may also have to be assumed by the state and, in the conditions of the mid-20th century, national governments have increasingly been compelled to assume it, wholly or in part. The process of reconciling economic requirements and claims is, therefore, sooner or later a political one. If the political machinery fails in this task, the result may in time be loss of national independence. Today, economic requirements, and the difficulty of meeting them, are both substantially greater than in the 19th century, and economic analysis and policy-making must take them explicitly into account.

The third concept is the familiar one of *economic efficiency,* but expressed now as a relative, and not an absolute, principle. The efficiency of an economy may be considered to be the degree of effectiveness with which it uses resources to satisfy existing requirements and claims. An economic system—whether national or international—is a means for achieving human values and, like any other means, it may be more or less efficient in accomplishing its purposes. This relationship implies that there is no absolute standard of economic efficiency. The standard depends upon the particular requirements and claims which the national community as a whole, and its economically and politically powerful

---

[17] This definition intentionally involves circular reasoning, for a satisfactory rate of growth is one which makes possible—among other things—the continued use of resources for a level of investment high enough to sustain the rate of economic growth.

social groups, are attempting to fulfill at any given time. Thus, an economy in which the satisfactions to be derived from economic growth and rising consumption are not felt to be desirable goals, and whose national security is not menaced, may be considered as efficient for its own purposes as an economy with a high rate of net capital formation and a progressive pattern of income distribution, even though the former's productivity is low and its techniques are, by the latter's standard, quite backward and wasteful of resources. In economic analysis, as in common speech, it is useful—often necessary—to consider improvements of economic means as proximate ends. But, it must not be forgotten that their value as proximate goals ultimately derives from the larger social context in which they are only means to the achievement of more important individual, social and national goals.

The fourth concept is *economic health*. An economy is healthy when it is actually satisfying economic requirements and claims in tolerable degree. The American economy, for example, is certainly capable of meeting the politically acceptable reconciliation of private economic claims as well as the minimum requirements of defense, of an active foreign policy, and of a satisfactory rate of economic growth. The economies of Britain and of many of the West European nations cannot be characterized as healthy today, for they do not seem to be capable of satisfying their requirements for defense, for self-support and for growth, and of simultaneously meeting rising consumption claims. Many of the underdeveloped economies are also failing to meet the economic requirements for their security and for making possible the social reforms and economic opportunities demanded by the politically active or economically important portions of their populations. Today, economic health is much more difficult to achieve or maintain than formerly because both claims and requirements have been greatly magnified by 20th-century changes in values and institutions and by the cold war. Nor is the achievement of economic health always possible, for claims may be too competitive and inordinate when compared with the capacity of the economy to fulfill them, or the society may allocate its resources too inefficiently to meet basic requirements. In such cases, changes in group and national values must occur, or the size and resources of the political unit within which requirements have to be satisfied must be expanded, if the result is not to be disastrous for the national community and for its people. Thus, the concept of economic health grows out of, and encompasses, the other three. As such, it is for the 20th century what the

concept of economic efficiency alone was for the 19th century—a tool
for the diagnosis of economic problems, and a criterion for national and
international economic policy prescriptions.

To summarize, the foregoing survey of the genesis of the international
economy suggests that there has never been—nor is there likely to be—
a successfully integrated international economic system whose component national units were highly interdependent and were at the same
time impelled by politically powerful claimant groups to exercise full
economic sovereignty. In the mercantilist period, there was a successful
international economy despite the active exercise of national economic
sovereignty. This was possible only because economic interdependence
was relatively unimportant and because the great mass of the population was, in any case, without effective political expression. After the
Industrial Revolution, when economic interdependence increased very
markedly, prevailing values and attitudes, and existing forms of international authority—colonialism, the sterling-gold standard system, the
hegemony of Britain—helped to limit the economic sovereignty of national governments. The historical changes which have transformed this
19th-century world economy into the contemporary international economy are largely irreversible. Economic interdependence among nations
is now greater than in the 19th century and entire populations have effective means of political expression. Changes in values and class roles
have led to the assumption by national governments of extensive control
over economic life. Conflicts of national economic interests are much
more intense than before 1914. The pressures of mounting economic
claims and requirements have magnified the difficulties of achieving and
maintaining economic health—a problem further aggravated by the
Soviet and Red Chinese challenge. Today, there is and can be no leading economy—like Britain in the 19th century—whose normal functioning ensures automatically the proper functioning of the whole system.
Instead, there is a dominant economy—that of the United States—which
creates problems for its trading partners by its one-sided relationship
with the international economy and by setting standards of economic
efficiency and satisfaction too high for most of them.

In these circumstances, the task of re-integrating the international
economy and restoring the health of many of its component national
economies is not simply a matter of agreeing upon marginal adjustments
in the economic policies and practices of national governments. The

measure of consensus among national governments on the ends and means of economic policy which is required in our times for international economic integration, and the scope of the necessary international authority, are (except in a few favored areas) much larger than was needed under 19th-century conditions. The task is structural, or constitutional, in nature. Like the problem of peace today, the problem of achieving international economic integration and national economic health goes to the very roots of the existing system of world order.

2

Western Europe and Japan

External Economic Problems

In Western Europe, the external and internal challenges to Western civilization come to a sharp focus. There, the communist challenge is most direct—for Western Europe lies in the shadow of Soviet military power—and to capture or to neutralize it has been a central aim of Soviet foreign policy. Western Europe is profoundly affected by the revolutionary transformations now occurring throughout the underdeveloped areas of the free world. It is in Western Europe that the internal conflicts, the loss of sense of direction, and the decline of moral vigor—which afflict much of the West today—are most in evidence. Our concern here is not, however, with all of these dimensions of the European crisis but only with its economic aspects insofar as they are relevant to American foreign policy.

The national economies of Western Europe, to be healthy, must be able to discharge adequately three basic tasks. They must be able to provide an effective economic base for military defense against the Soviet bloc. They must be able to satisfy the claims of their peoples for consumption—and, more broadly, for economic welfare—to the minimum set by the tolerance and political effectiveness of claimant groups, and by the capacity of political institutions to reconcile or to deny economic claims. To perform these tasks and still remain economically self-supporting, they must be able to stand up competitively to their principal commercial rival, the United States. The crux of Western Europe's economic problem is that the economic size of these three tasks has been growing more rapidly than the ability of the European economies to discharge them. For, the external and internal challenges to Western Europe accelerate the growth of economic claims and requirements and, at the same time, impair the ability of the West European economies to meet them.

In different circumstances, Western Europe's poor economic health might not be a critical problem for the United States, though it would continue to arouse our humanitarian response. In the context of the cold war, however, Western Europe's poor economic health is of direct and urgent concern to us. If it persists, it is likely to mean a continuing decline in the ability of the West to resist communist subversion and aggression. It is likely to contribute—indeed, it is already contributing —to psychological and political reactions in Europe and in this country which threaten to destroy the Western Alliance and to isolate the United States.

There are three major ways in which Europe's economic problems contribute to these military and political dangers.

The first is evident when industrial Europe's prospective economic capabilities relative to military requirements are considered. The economy controlled by the Soviet Union is already nearly as large as that of industrial Europe.[1] The economy of the U.S.S.R. itself is still inferior in important respects to that of industrial Europe, but it has been growing more rapidly. Within the next decade, the production and consumption of major industrial materials in the Soviet Union may well overtake that of industrial Europe.[2] Soviet real national income appears to have

---

[1] The phrase "industrial Europe" as used in this study includes the seven most industrialized countries of non-communist Europe: Belgium, France, Italy, Luxembourg, the Netherlands, the United Kingdom and West Germany.

[2] "With the growth of industry, the output of certain major industrial products in the Soviet Union has by now become comparable to that in seven Western European [industrial] countries, which together contain about the same population. . . . The output of coal, electricity and steel in the Soviet Union is about one-half of that in Western Europe and is increasing at a much faster rate than can be expected for Western Europe. With the planned increase in oil production, the Soviet Union will have more oil available in 1955 than Western Europe consumes at present, although the Western European rate of consumption is also rapidly rising. There are indications that, if present rates of expansion are maintained, by the end of this decade the production and consumption of major industrial raw materials in the Soviet Union will be equal or superior to that in the seven most industrialized countries of Western Europe." United Nations Economic Commission for Europe, *Economic Survey of Europe Since the War* (Geneva, 1953), pp. 49–50.

grown about 6 to 7 percent per year during the decade or so before World War II and in the post-reconstruction period.[3] The real national income of industrial Europe grew about 1½ percent a year in the period 1913–1938.[4] In the last few years, it has grown considerably faster than before the war. However, industrial Europe's economic growth rate in recent years has benefitted from temporary recovery factors and will probably decline substantially again. In such circumstances, the real national income of the Soviet Union would be increasing considerably faster than that of industrial Europe during the next decade, though the discrepancy in growth rates is not likely to be as large as before World War II. This may be true if only because it seems not unlikely that the rate of Soviet economic growth will be lower in the future than it has been.

If this judgment about the prospective growth of the Soviet and West European economies is correct, its military implications are most serious. To the extent that military potential depends on the total volume of output, Western Europe's military potential relative to that of the Soviet Union will be declining steadily over the next decade. What is true of military potential is presumably even more true of military power-in-being and of the capacity to mobilize effective forces in an emergency. To judge from post-Korea rearmament efforts, the ability of the West European countries to mobilize their economic resources in an emergency (measured, for example, as a proportion of their gross product) would be far less than that of the United States or of the Soviet Union. If industrial Europe's economic growth rate does not improve, it is doubtful if this ability will increase. It may well decline in the face of rising consumption claims and, in France and Italy, the declining effectiveness of political institutions.

The conclusion that Western Europe's military potential will decline relative to that of the Soviet Union holds true even if military capabilities come to depend on the newer weapons to a degree that makes general economic strength no longer the principal measure of military power. For, the Soviet advantage over Western Europe in the newer weapons

---

[3] See A. Bergson, ed., *Soviet Economic Growth*, (Evanston, Ill.: Row Peterson & Co., 1953), p. 9. Although much uncertainty attaches to estimates of Soviet economic growth rates, these orders of magnitude are now apparently accepted by most qualified American scholars.

[4] See Ingvar Svennilson, *Growth and Stagnation in the European Economy* (Geneva: United Nations Economic Commission for Europe, 1954), p. 58.

is, and will doubtless remain, much greater than its growing advantage in economic strength.

Equally important from an American standpoint are the possible effects on European morale and on the political cohesion of the Western Alliance of Western Europe's growing economic and military inferiority to the Soviet Union and to the United States. If the relative rise of Soviet military power continues, it will tend to raise the prestige and the morale of domestic Communist Parties in Europe. Worse, it will give strong impetus to European neutralism and pacifism. Many Europeans already feel that their countries are helpless pawns in a struggle of giants; the spreading and darkening shadow of Soviet power will tend to increase that feeling and to strengthen the desire of many Europeans to withdraw, politically and morally, from the struggle between communism and Western civilization. The fact that Russian living standards are far below those of industrial Europe and will presumably remain so for the foreseeable future does not affect this conclusion, although it may continue to make the Soviet way of life unattractive to the majority of Europeans. It is precisely the ability of the Soviet Government to resist large increases in living standards that permits the high rate of investment on which the rapid growth of the Soviet economy depends.

In short, the possibility exists that the relative growth of Soviet power will paralyze the will of free Europe to resist Soviet policy. We do not say that this will necessarily happen. There are many other factors which will affect the attitudes of West Europeans toward the East-West struggle. Much, for example, depends on the vigor and the content—political, economic and moral—of American leadership. Nonetheless, the possibility of a neutralist and defeatist reaction in Europe to declining relative power is one major reason why the United States should be deeply concerned about the rate of Western Europe's economic growth.

Second, just as the economic requirements of Western Europe's military security are expanding, so also have claims on the West European economies for consumption and economic security been expanding and finding more effective political expression. In contrast to their 19th-century attitudes, West Europeans of all classes have in this century come to regard continuing improvement in their economic lot as their right. It is beyond the scope of this study to speculate on the complex causes of this change, but one critical aspect may be noted. As traditional European values and patterns of life have disintegrated under the impact of 19th-century industrialism, urbanization and democratic ideology, personal and collective aspirations have increasingly been focussed on the desire for improved and more secure economic status. That desire has been widely substituted for other, traditional, values as the goal and meaning of individual and social life. This change of values is re-enforced by increasing knowledge of the American material standard of living. The change has not affected all West European countries or social groups equally and in no European country is the goal of rising material consumption so fully and generally accepted as in the United States. The change has gone further in Britain than in France, and further in France than in Germany and Italy. But throughout Western Europe, the new attitudes have found expression—more or less effective—in powerful claimant groups of workers and farmers demanding rising incomes and a larger, or a guaranteed, share of the national dividend for their members. It is the power of such workers' and farmers' organizations, and of the political parties they influence or control, which has translated rising economic aspirations into effective claims for income and security. Such claims are made effective in different and sometimes inconsistent ways—in rising industrial wages, in rising agricultural prices and in greatly increased social welfare payments by governments. Business groups, unable to satisfy workers' claims while maintaining their own negative attitudes toward productivity increases, have often supported expanding social welfare payments as a means of shifting the burden from themselves to the national budget.

In several of the West European countries, the power and insistence of the claimants is such that consumption tends to crowd out investment and defense in the competition for economic resources. In some, social welfare payments financed through government budgets compete directly with public investment and with defense programs for limited tax revenues; and because social welfare payments have such strong political support, they are given priority over other uses of resources. Again, in most West European countries—particularly in those which had the worst postwar inflations—the labor unions insist that wages follow upward movements of the cost of living with a minimum delay. This, too, tends to give the maintenance of consumption a priority over investment and rearmament. Thus, in Western Europe's present circumstances, the effectiveness of claims for consumption and economic security is apt to mean inadequate provision for the requirements of defense and of future economic growth.

It is difficult to see how this dilemma is to be resolved unless the national incomes of the West European countries grow more rapidly than now appears likely. We may hope that a part of the postwar pressure in Europe for rising consumption has been a temporary response to the austerity, social disintegration and political excitement of the war and the occupation. It may lessen now that more "normal" economic and political checks and balances among competing claimant groups have been in large part re-established, wartime consumption arrears have largely been made good, and recognition is beginning to spread of the utopian character of economic expectations in the earlier postwar years. To some extent, this appears to have happened in Northern Europe and may now be occurring in Britain. In France and Italy, however, there is little evidence that the pressure of economic claims will be lessened in this manner. For in these two countries, the strength of claims for consumption and economic security is a function not simply of the desire for greater material satisfactions but also of a bitter sense of social and economic injustice on the part of the urban working classes, the poorer peasants and the agricultural laborers. Income distribution in France and Italy is considerably more uneven than in Scandinavia and Britain, to the disadvantage of these groups. The sense of injustice thereby engendered among them is sharpened to a critical degree by class tensions of more ancient origin and by Marxist ideology, which seems to have a particular attraction for them. It promises such a simple and perfect "solution" for all their problems that the grim reality of Russian living standards and police rule makes little impression on them. There is small prospect that these large disaffected groups can be reconciled to existing patterns of income distribution and to their present standards of living. Yet without a more rapid growth of the national income in France and Italy, no major rise in the incomes of these groups will be economically possible and no significant change of income distribution in their favor is likely to be politically feasible.

If the West European economies fail too seriously to meet these new economic claims, dangerous psychological and political reactions are likely. In France and Italy, for example, the reaction could take the form of heightened class tensions, increasing communist and neo-fascist strength, and growing paralysis of democratic institutions. Moreover, resentments among Europeans provoked by frustration of their economic claims are quite likely to be directed in part against the United States. For, the contrast between their economic frustrations and our economic success—a contrast sharpened by our often naive pride in our material satisfactions—is too glaring not to be a source of envy and resentment. Communist propagandists know how to exploit these feelings, and seemingly to justify them, by blaming Europe's economic troubles on American foreign policy—even to the extent of alleging that our economic success is itself evidence that we are "exploiting" Europe. It is always easier to find a scapegoat than a real remedy: in the Marxist dogma, differences in living standards among classes and even among nations must, by definition, be the result of "exploitation."

Third, the industry of Western Europe—with West Germany, the Netherlands, Sweden and Belgium as partial exceptions—has difficulty in coping with competition in export markets from the more rapidly growing and technologically more progressive American economy. This problem will be more fully discussed later in this chapter. Here it may suffice to mention that this difficulty leads not merely to conflicts of interest among European and American businessmen. It leads also to more widespread and fundamental resentments which divide the Western Alliance. Many Europeans are aware of the importance to their economic welfare of expanding exports, and they sense that the competition of the United States, as well as of the other industrial countries, adds to their own economic problems.

Enough perhaps has been said to suggest the importance for American foreign policy of Western Europe's economic health and, more particularly, of its rate of economic growth. No claim is, however, intended that the rate of economic growth in Western Europe is the crucial factor which by itself will determine the future course of West European politics and foreign policy. There are many other influences—including the future policies of the United States itself, as well as stubbornly rooted European nationalism and tenacious "values"—which will also affect the psychology and politics of Western Europe over the next few years. There might, for example, be a fundamental change for the better in the nature and aims of world communism; or the character of European class expectations and economic claims might change. But these possibilities are so remote that it would be folly to base policy upon them. The probability that Western Europe's rate of economic growth could be significantly increased—difficult as that may be—is considerably greater than the probability that favorable developments along the fore-going lines would make such an increase unnecessary. For, the deter-minants of Western Europe's rate of economic advance are much more accessible to policy, European and American, than are the factors re-sponsible for Soviet economic growth, for the aims of Soviet foreign policy, or for the expansion of economic claims in Western Europe.

Accordingly in this and the following chapter, some of the principal factors limiting Western Europe's economic growth are examined. These chapters are not concerned with the causes of short-term variations in economic growth rates, but rather with persistent, underlying factors which influence the rate of economic growth over longer periods of time. An analysis of this kind is, in the main, necessarily qualitative rather than quantitative. It is concerned with underlying structural and institutional factors more than with the changes in supply and demand, and in prices and monetary conditions, which constitute the economic process as it is usually conceived. This chapter considers the main ex-ternal aspects of Western Europe's problem of economic growth; the following chapter deals with internal factors and considers the pros-pective economic health of the larger countries individually.

Because of Japan's unique industrial and strategic position in the Far East, Japan's economic growth problems are considered along with those of Western Europe. There are, to be sure, differences between Japan's economic difficulties and those of Western Europe from the standpoint of American foreign policy. Japan is not part of the Western Community and its ties with us lack the historical and ideological di-mensions of our ties with Western Europe. Nonetheless, Japan and the West have a common interest in the security of Japan; Japan's strategic role in the Far East parallels that of Western Europe, particularly West Germany and Britain, on the other side of the world; Japan's economic health, like that of Western Europe, has a direct bearing on American security. Moreover, the similarity of Japan's economic problems—at least in their external aspects—to those of Western Europe is striking.

Dependence of Western Europe's and Japan's Economic Growth on Foreign Trade

The countries of Western Europe and Japan became industrialized within the old freely trading world economy. The level of industriali-zation and real income they have achieved has depended on the pattern of international economic specialization developed within that world economy. As a result, these countries have been committed in greater or lesser degree to a pattern of economic development which depends crucially upon the expansion of their foreign trade. They cannot reverse that pattern and follow one which involves a progressive reduction of their external dependence, without sacrificing potential future gains of productivity and real income. Their economies have become so dependent on foreign trade as to make it impossible for them to adopt a policy of national autarky without sacrificing much of their future potential for economic growth—dependent both in the sense that the ratio of their trade to their national output is high [5] and in the sense that their future rate of growth will tend to be higher if that ratio rises than if it falls. They cannot find a satisfactory answer to the problem of living and growing in the present disordered international economy, and in the face of America's superior competitive power, by turning in upon themselves.

This conclusion is crucial for an understanding of the economic problems of Western Europe and Japan. For these more or less advanced industrial economies, with their relatively meager domestic endowment of natural resources, an adequate rate of economic growth depends upon a rapid expansion of industrial exports and of imports of primary products at favorable terms of trade. Given the existing structure of their economies, future gains in productivity will be greater if future additions to their capital stock and their labor force are concentrated in the export industries than if spread more evenly over a wide range of industries and agriculture producing for domestic markets. This is true partly because these economies have "outgrown" their base of natural resources, in the sense that their arable land and mineral resources are already so intensively exploited that a more intensive exploitation would, in most cases, yield real returns far smaller than could be earned in export industries, assuming favorable external conditions. It is true also because these economies have, in varying degree, "outgrown" the potentialities of their domestic markets for manufactures, in the sense that a high rate of growth of industrial productivity could be maintained only if exports of manufactures could be expanded

---

[5] For example, in 1952 the ratio of the United Kingdom's total foreign trade (imports plus exports) to gross national product was 43 percent, as compared with 7 percent for the United States. The corresponding ratio for West Germany in 1952 was 27 percent; for Italy, 22 percent; for Japan, 17 percent; and for France, 12 percent.

rapidly at favorable terms of trade—i.e., only if their output of some manufactures expands far more rapidly than the growth of domestic demand alone would permit.[6] This applies particularly to the British economy and in lesser degree to the rest of industrial Europe and Japan.[7]

Yet these things are relevant only to the extent that these countries *can* expand their industrial exports and imports of primary products rapidly and at satisfactory terms of trade. For some years, that has not been possible for most of them and a good deal of the present poor economic health of the other industrial countries of the non-Soviet world is chargeable to that fact. Since World War I, these countries have lived in an international economic environment which has been increasingly uncongenial to the rapid expansion of their industrial exports at satis-

---

[6] More precisely, the reason why (assuming a reasonably favorable external economic environment) a greater rate of increase of productivity can be realized in the other industrial countries—especially Britain—by devoting a larger proportion of labor and capital to export industries is, essentially, the potentially greater volume of foreign demand than of domestic demand for the products of those industries in which the possibilities of rapid increase in productivity with expanding output (i.e., "increasing returns") are still very great—as they are, for example, for much of the British automotive, chemical and engineering industries. If the growth of British industry, for example, were confined closely to the requirements of the domestic market, returns (productivity) would increase less rapidly because the industries in which potential productivity increases are largest (the export industries mentioned above) would grow more slowly in output relative to consumer goods industries and agriculture, where the possibilities of realizing further increases in productivity with expanding output are very much less. It is in this sense that industry in the other industrial countries may be said to have "outgrown" the potentialities of domestic markets.

In a study of postwar production trends in Western Europe, the United Nations Economic Commission for Europe suggests another important reason why the growth of West European production is peculiarly dependent on the growth of foreign demand for European exports. The study shows that, for four European industrial countries and presumably for others, the growth or stagnation of exports has been the major— even the preponderant—factor on the side of demand explaining the growth or stagnation of industrial output in the period 1948–53. The reason given by the ECE study for this dependence of production on export demand is that the "multiplier" and "accelerator" effects of rising exports seem to have been much larger than the corresponding effects of expanding domestic expenditure, especially consumers' expenditure—a fact which the study traces to structural and institutional characteristics of the West European economies. See United Nations Economic Commission for Europe, *Economic Survey of Europe in 1953* (Geneva, 1954), ch. 2.

[7] A further reason why the rate of growth of exports is a critical factor for Western Europe's economic growth is that slow-growing exports tend to cause balance-of-payments strain, which necessitates resort to tight control of imports. Such control may interfere with economic growth by removing the stimulus of foreign competition and by aggravating economic rigidities. The balance-of-payments aspect of Western Europe's and Japan's economic growth problem is considered in the final section of this chapter and in Chapter 7.

factory terms of trade. Basically, the trouble stems from the character-istics of the international economy examined in Chapter 1—above all its "nationalized" character, but also to some extent the dominant position of the American economy, and, to a small extent, the subtraction from it of the Soviet empire and China. These factors, together with other influences, impair the external economic environment of the other in-dustrial countries in three basic ways:

(1) By restricting the freedom of foreign trade and making the condi-tions of foreign trading and investment much less secure and calculable than in the 19th century;

(2) By restricting the growth of agricultural production in the trad-ing world; and

(3) By the pressure of American competition on European and Japanese industrial exports.

The adverse effects of these and other factors on the external economic environment of Western Europe and Japan are cumulative and mu-tually re-enforcing. Moreover, in combination, they give rise to Western Europe's and Japan's "dollar problem." That is, they increase the need of the other industrial countries for North American products and, at the same time, they reduce the ability of these countries to buy such products; they compel the West European countries and Japan to re-strict imports from North America and thereby to shelter their econ-omies from American competition to an unhealthy degree. The re-mainder of this chapter is devoted to an explanation of Western Eu-rope's and Japan's three basic external problems and of the dollar prob-lem which derives from them.

Against the background of the historical discussion in the preceding chapter, the first of the three basic problems is the easiest to explain. It is also, in many ways, the most important. Rapid expansion of interna-tional trade depends on the absence of governmental or private barriers to it and on the absence of serious risks that such barriers may be im-posed in the future. It depends likewise on the existence of political, legal and security conditions conducive to international trade and in-vestment and on the absence of serious risk that these conditions will deteriorate markedly. It depends, in short, on the *freedom, security,* and *calculability* of the conditions of doing business across national frontiers.

But the nationalization of the world economy and the accompanying breakdown of the 19th-century political order have seriously impaired the freedom, security, and calculability of the international economy.

Today, foreign traders and investors—even if their activities are not actively restricted by national governments—are subject to the incalculable risks of major changes in the economic policies of national governments and to the still graver risks of foreign political disorders or war. In these circumstances, the growth of foreign trade and of the international investment on which it depends is seriously inhibited, if not by actual restrictions, then by these extraordinary and incalculable risks. The restriction of trade and the fear of relying on insecure and incalculable foreign markets and sources of supply have large, though unmeasurable, effects on the direction of investment in most countries, tending to encourage an autarkic and nationalistic pattern of economic development. There is a presumption that this pattern involves a relatively uneconomical use of resources—a presumption which becomes a certainty for industrial economies which have already "outgrown" their national boundaries in the sense explained above. The insufficient freedom, security and calculability of their external environment accounts for much of the difficulty encountered by the other industrial countries since World War I in maintaining adequate rates of economic growth.

The Inadequate Growth of Agricultural Production in the Non-Soviet World

The rate of growth of primary production in, and exports from, the major primary producing countries is one of the key factors in the economic growth and health of Western Europe and Japan. These industrial economies depend on exchanging exports of manufactures for imports of primary products. For that reason, the rate of growth of their industry and of their real income is strongly influenced by the rate of expansion of overseas demand for their manufactures, and by their terms of foreign trade; and these factors are, in turn, strongly influenced by the rate of growth of overseas primary production and exports.

If world primary production [8] and exports are expanding rapidly, the world's import demand for manufactures will also grow rapidly and Western Europe's and Japan's terms of trade will tend to improve. Conversely, if world primary production lags, the terms of trade of Western

---

[8] "Primary products" include foodstuffs, non-food agricultural materials, metals, and minerals. Our concern here is largely with food and agricultural materials, for they account for the great bulk of international trade in primary products.

Europe and Japan will tend to deteriorate and the expansion of their exports of manufactures will be inhibited. Broadly speaking, during the forty years before 1914, Western Europe enjoyed the advantages of the former situation—rapidly expanding primary production overseas (except for occasional cyclical interruptions), expansive demand for exports of manufactures, and improving terms of trade. In contrast, leaving aside for a moment the interwar period, the latter situation has prevailed since 1939—total primary production and exports have grown much more slowly than before 1914, and the trend of the terms of trade has been against the industrial countries. In the following discussion we shall describe these trends briefly and try to explain their fundamental causes. The explanation is complicated by the fact that the longer-term trends in supply and demand for primary products and manufactures in world trade are overlaid, and their effects sometimes exaggerated and sometimes obscured, by shorter-run influences, such as changes in the monetary "climate" in the industrial countries, periodic agricultural overproduction, and the effects of the two world wars.

In the 19th-century trading world, industrial and agricultural production and international trade in manufactures and primary products grew together in a complementary relationship which was largely governed by market forces. The growth process was dominated by the industrial economies of Western Europe and, to a much lesser extent, the United States. The rate of growth of primary production over the whole trading world was governed by the growing demand of industry and of urban populations in Western Europe and the United States for raw materials and food.[9] It was readily responsive to the growing demand of industrial countries, owing to the freedom and calculability of international markets, the freedom of European capital and labor to move overseas, the large unexploited agricultural and mineral resources of the

---

[9] "The dynamic factor in that [the 19th] century was the growth of the industrial countries; what happened in primary producing countries, by way of increased production of primary products, and increased trade, was merely by way of reaction to disturbances originating in the industrial countries; no one can argue seriously that the original disturbances making for growth were occurring in the primary producing countries, and that the industrial countries were merely adjusting themselves to what was happening to primary producers. . . . It has been the growing demand of industrial countries for primary produce that has dispensed purchasing power to primary producers for buying manufactures, and not the growing demand of primary producers for manufactures that has dispensed purchasing power to the industrial countries with which to buy primary products." W. A. Lewis, *Economic Survey 1919–1939* (London: Allen and Unwin, 1949), p. 153.

New World, and revolutionary technological advances, particularly in transportation. Thus, in the forty years before 1914, world manufacturing and primary production grew at approximately the same average rate (3½ percent per year cumulative and both grew twice as fast as population.[10]

This close relationship between industrial and agricultural production worked out very well for the industrial countries of Western Europe. It made rapid economic growth and good economic health possible for them. The ready responsiveness of primary supply to industrial demand made possible huge increases in primary production from the Americas, Oceania, and Eastern Europe in the years before World War I at terms of trade generally improving for the industrial countries. It meant also rapidly expanding foreign markets for the industry of Europe and later of North America and Japan. The rapid expansion of foreign demand for manufactures was especially important for the continued economic growth of Britain and the continental industrial countries. Having already partly "outgrown"—in the sense explained above—their domestic resources and markets, European industry depended for continued rapid growth on an expanding exchange of manufactures for primary products from overseas.

Most of the major primary producing countries also found the pre-1914 situation reasonably satisfactory relative to the limited economic claims and requirements of that period, although there were relatively brief spells of temporary agricultural overproduction during which agricultural producers suffered reduced incomes.[11] Though the terms of trade of the agricultural countries were probably deteriorating throughout most of the period, the rapid growth of agricultural productivity nevertheless made possible a substantial growth of real per capita income in many agricultural countries, although in others the gains in real income were largely absorbed by the growth of population. It is true that today the peoples of underdeveloped countries in Latin America and Asia tend to regard the years before World War I as a time of

---

[10] *Ibid.*, pp. 153–4.

[11] It seems that in periods of rapid growth of world agricultural production, the growth of agricultural output eventually outruns demand and gives rise to a temporary overproduction crisis, even if nothing happens (such as a depression in the industrial countries) to check the regular expansion of industrial production and of the demand for agricultural products. See, e.g., W. Malenbaum, *The World Wheat Economy* (Cambridge, Mass.: Harvard University Press, 1953), pp. 214 *et seq.*

"ruthless economic exploitation" at the hands of Europeans. But this attitude is more a product of the revolutionary change in outlook which has since occurred in these countries than of historical fact. In sum, before 1914 the relationship between world primary production and world manufacturing was such as to make possible their rapid growth. The international distribution of the resulting gains in real income was particularly favorable to the industrial countries yet not, on the whole, unsatisfactory to the agricultural countries.

But this favorable, expansive relationship did not survive World War I. The whole interwar period was characterized by agricultural overproduction.[12] During World War I, there was a great expansion of agricultural output in the Americas and Oceania, induced by swollen wartime demand and reduced European output. As European production recovered after the war, total agricultural output became temporarily excessive, especially in view of the sharply reduced rate of population growth in Europe during and just after the war. This temporary imbalance was slowly correcting itself through market processes, at the cost of widespread agricultural depression, when—in 1930—the problem was intensified by general deflation originating in the industrial countries, for deflation reduced world manufacturing more than world agricultural output. Agricultural depression meant very favorable terms of trade for Western Europe throughout the interwar period. But it also reduced purchasing power in the agricultural countries so seriously that their effective demand for imports of manufactures grew but little during the interwar years. "Favorable" terms of trade for the industrial countries may, on this evidence, mean too little trade and too little industrial growth.

World War II brought a major change in the relation between world agricultural and industrial production. The problem is no longer general agricultural overproduction as in the interwar years. Rather, the growth of world agricultural production has been insufficient in relation to demand, as determined by the growth of population and industrial production. The following indexes point up this contrast between the interwar period and the first postwar years: [13]

---

[12] I.e., expansion of agricultural output more rapidly than the factors that determine demand for it: population and industrial production.

[13] From W. A. Lewis, "Food and Raw Materials," *District Bank Review,* (September 1951), pp. 4–5. These indexes refer to the whole world, including the Soviet Union.

	1913	1929	1937	1950
World output of:				
Manufactures	100	152	172	247
Agricultural materials	100	149	194	178
Foodstuffs	100	116	125	131
World population	100	113	124	138

For the whole period 1913–50, the average annual rate of growth of world primary production was only 1.2 percent (cumulative), as compared with some 3½ percent (cumulative) in the forty years before 1914.[14]

A continuation of this low rate will be detrimental to the future economic growth and health of Western Europe and Japan because of its adverse effect on their terms of trade. Lagging agricultural production and exports have already caused the prices of Western Europe's and Japan's imports of primary products [15] to rise relative to the prices of their manufactured exports as compared with prewar. For example, in 1952, the prices of Britain's imports were 30 percent higher than the prices of its exports, relative to 1938. As a result of this change in the relative prices of manufactures and primary products, the industrial countries have had to export a greatly increased volume of manufactures, as compared with prewar, in order to pay for a volume of primary imports only slightly larger than prewar. In 1952, for example, the volume of world exports of primary products was only about 5 percent above the 1937 level, while the volume of world exports of manufactures was some 50–60 percent above 1937.[16]

---

[14] *Ibid.,* pp. 3–4.

[15] World output of minerals and metals has expanded much more rapidly than world agricultural output since the war, but this increase has been forthcoming only at a large increase in prices.

[16] See The Contracting Parties to the GATT, *International Trade 1952* (Geneva, 1953), pp. 4–5. In 1951–52, the volume of world exports of foodstuffs was still 9 percent *below* the average 1934–38 level. See United Nations Food and Agriculture Organization, *The State of Food and Agriculture: Review and Outlook 1952* (Rome, 1952), p. 16. The difference between the volumes of exports of manufactures and primary products in 1952 relative to 1937 can be explained chiefly by the change in the relative prices of primary and manufactured products, due to factors limiting the supply of primary products relative to the demand of the industrial countries. This difference is also owed in part to certain war-caused changes in non-trade items in the balance of payments between the industrial and primary producing countries which have increased the latter's effective demand for imports of manufactures—e.g. the reduction (in real terms) of Europe's investment earnings.

For the United States, the postwar increase in the cost of primary imports in terms of manufactured exports is not so serious a matter. The low dependence of the American economy on foreign trade, the rapid growth of American productivity, and the fact that the United States is a large exporter of agricultural commodities (financed in part by grants of farm surpluses to other countries) make the American economy less vulnerable to this change. For other industrialized countries, however, it is a very serious problem in two ways. First, the deterioration of their terms of trade has a large adverse effect on their real income. For example, if Britain could have bought its 1952 volume of imports at 1938 terms of trade, its real national income in 1952 would have been some 6–7 percent higher than it was.[17] Second, continued deterioration of their terms of foreign trade will tend to reduce their opportunity for economic growth. For it will force them to use a larger proportion of their labor and capital in expanding agricultural and industrial production for domestic markets where, as we have seen, potential productivity gains are relatively small. In other words, the continued deterioration of their terms of trade, if it occurs, will contribute to the progressive breakdown of the international specialization on which the economic growth and health of Western Europe and Japan have depended.

In consequence, it is important to know whether the postwar lag in world agricultural production relative to demand is merely a temporary phenomenon caused by the fact that agriculture recovered more slowly than industry after the war—or whether it has a more persistent and structural character, as the low average rate of growth of world primary production since 1913 suggests. To put it another way, the question is whether it is now reasonable to suppose that, with the direct effects of the war and its aftermath on agricultural production largely overcome, the increased relative prices of agricultural products will call forth an accelerated growth of agricultural production sufficient at least to prevent a downward trend of Western Europe's and Japan's terms of foreign trade.

There are countries where agricultural production and even exports

---

[17] Moreover, if the United Kingdom, for example, attempts to avoid this impact by keeping the prices of its manufactured exports up—e.g., by means of an overvalued pound—there will be an adverse effect on the volume of its exports, because of the consequences for the United Kingdom's competitive position, and because higher British export prices would mean reduced foreign ability to buy British exports.

have expanded far above prewar levels under the stimulus of the postwar terms of trade—Turkey, the United States and Canada, for example. But on the whole, it appears that there are continuing structural conditions which block the expansion of agricultural output or exports and which make it likely that, for the foreseeable future, the growth of primary production in the non-Soviet world will be inadequate from the standpoint of Western Europe and Japan unless basic remedial action can be taken. These structural conditions are of two kinds: (1) those which tend to limit the *supply* of agricultural imports available to Western Europe and Japan from sources outside of North America; [18] and (2) those which limit the ability of Western Europe and Japan to expand their agricultural imports from the United States and Canada, where the growth of agricultural output is not limited by supply difficulties but rather by effective foreign *demand*. As will be seen, these conditions are largely traceable, directly or indirectly, to the basic changes in the international economy outlined in Chapter 1.

In the first place, the memory of agricultural overproduction in the interwar period and the growing incalculability of international market conditions have inhibited the major independent agricultural producing and exporting countries from expanding their agricultural exports. During and after World War II, there was a widespread expectation that the end of the war would bring a repetition of the interwar experience—chronic agricultural surpluses, worsened terms of trade for agricultural countries, and general deflation. Agricultural countries were anxious not to repeat that experience. Fear of it and, more generally,

---

[18] It is not, of course, suggested that supply limitations are the whole explanation of the reduced average rate of growth of world agricultural output since World War I. During the interwar period, as already suggested, demand for agricultural commodities tended to be inadequate in relation to supply, due to rapid overseas agricultural expansion during World War I and depression in the 1930's. Moreover, in the higher income countries, the rate of growth of demand for food is affected by a declining income elasticity of demand for food. Similarly, in the industrial countries, there is a tendency for the demand for some major agricultural raw materials (e.g., fibers) to grow less rapidly than total income or total industrial production—because of technological changes and shifts in the pattern of consumer demand. Despite these factors which affect the rate of growth of demand of the industrial countries for agricultural commodities, the major shift which has occurred in the relative prices of industrial and agricultural products suggests that supply limitations, such as those discussed below, are affecting significantly the rate of growth of agricultural output—particularly output for export—outside North America.

fear of excessive dependence on incalculable international markets and on the variable demand of the industrial countries for agricultural products have been potent motives for government policies restricting or neglecting the growth of agricultural output in, and exports from, Latin America, Oceania and Asia. The experience of many countries in these areas with agricultural exports during two World Wars and the interwar years was traumatic. It has permanently reduced their interest in agricultural exports and in national specialization on agriculture.

Secondly, the incalculability and insecurity of international economic conditions have greatly reduced the flow of international capital from industrial Europe into overseas primary production. Since World War I, the real volume of capital movement from the industrial countries to primary producing countries has been well below the level of the years before 1913:

> Between 1911 and 1913, the average annual capital export of Britain, France, Germany and the United States, to the rest of the world, was $1,400 million. This dropped, between 1924 and 1928, to $860 million worth, when allowance is made for changing prices, less than half as much as the figure for the earlier years. Then came the slump, and a decade in which international investment dried up altogether. The creditor countries not only did not lend in the 'thirties; they also withdrew substantial sums of capital from the rest of the world.

> Today, the United States is virtually the only country which exports capital. Her loans and gifts, to countries outside Europe, totalled only $500 million net in 1950. The U.K., in 1950, lent to countries other than Europe and the dollar area less than half as much as she borrowed from them. Her net capital inflow from these countries was £181 millions. Can anyone be surprised that world production grows so slowly in these circumstances? [19]

Moreover, most of the foreign capital that now moves to primary producing countries goes into production of petroleum and metals and into industry, services and urban construction, rather than into investment related directly or indirectly to the expansion of agricultural exports.

A third reason—also related to the nationalization of the world econ-

---

[19] W. A. Lewis, "Food and Raw Materials," *op. cit.,* p. 8.

omy—why overseas agriculture has been unresponsive to the growth of demand has been industrialization in Latin America, Oceania and Asia. Industrialization got underway in these areas during World War I and was greatly accelerated in the 1930's and during World War II. It continues unabated. Many of the Asian countries which gained political independence after World War II seem to identify dependence on primary production with their former colonial status. They now pursue the goal of "economic independence" and industrialization with the same determination which went into their earlier struggle for political independence. The priority given by national policies in many countries to industrialization as against primary production has been a major factor retarding the growth of agricultural exports to the industrial countries. Argentina and Australia are the most familiar and the most important examples. In Argentina, total agricultural output has reached —though exports are still far below—the prewar level. In Australia, total agricultural output has barely recovered to prewar levels and exports of agricultural products are well below prewar. In both countries, government policies are the principal cause of lagging agricultural production. With different policies, agricultural output in, and exports from, Argentina and Australia could by now have been far above prewar and real income in both countries could have been substantially higher than it is.

A fourth reason for the lag in agricultural supplies within the non-Soviet world is the absorption into the Soviet empire of countries in Eastern Europe which formerly supplied important tonnages of grain, timber and other agricultural products to Western Europe. The result has been a substantial decline of agricultural exports from Eastern to Western Europe as compared with prewar. One reason is the special insecurity and incalculability of the conditions of East-West trading and the political obstacles placed by both sides in the way of a larger East-West exchange. But the main trouble is that rapid industrialization, the forced collectivization of agriculture, rapid population growth in Eastern Europe and the Soviet Union, and the relative backwardness of agriculture in the Soviet Union itself, have created an imbalance between industry and agriculture within the Soviet sphere which is considerably more serious than the similar imbalance within the non-Soviet world. The decline in agricultural exports from the Soviet bloc to the free world is mainly a by-product of agricultural production failures and of the planned imbalance of industry and agriculture within the Soviet imperial economy.[20]

Fifth, the growth of world population has accelerated in recent years [21] and is particularly rapid in the underdeveloped areas of Asia and Latin America. This means that a larger part of the output of foodstuffs in these areas is being consumed locally; i.e., the proportion of their food output available for export to Western Europe and Japan tends to diminish. Indeed, there is but small likelihood that the growth of food output in the underdeveloped countries as a group will even be able to keep ahead of the growth of population.[22] This fact highlights the imperative need for population control in some underdeveloped countries for the sake of their own economic health as well as to improve the balance of agriculture and industry in the free world.

Finally, there is the quite different problem of expanding agricultural exports from North America. Here the difficulties are not on the side of supply. There is little doubt that, at existing prices, agricultural output in North America could expand rapidly if there were effective European and Japanese demand for it.[23] The problem is that Western Europe and Japan are unable to expand their earnings of dollars with sufficient rapidity to enjoy the advantages of larger international trade and more intensive international specialization with North America. They are unable to do so because of the weakness of their competitive position *vis-à-vis* the United States, the causes of which are considered in the following section of this chapter.

---

[20] The imbalance of industrial and agricultural production within the economy of the Soviet bloc has, since Stalin's death, had political repercussions serious enough to force some shift in Soviet economic policy toward increased allocation of resources to agriculture and reduced political pressure for collectivization in the Eastern European satellites.

[21] "The population of the world excluding China rose fairly steadily at a rate of about 0.95 percent per year from 1850 to 1914. Since 1940, the rate of increase has been slightly over 1.1 percent per year, which rate is expected to rise to about 1.125 percent for the period 1950–70. . . . The only serious check to the rate of growth of world population in recent times came in the decade 1910–20—not due principally to the military losses (some 10 million) of the First World War so much as to the typhus and influenza epidemics of that period, which killed far more people." Colin Clark, "The Future of the Terms of Trade," *International Social Science Bulletin*, (Spring, 1951), p. 39.

[22] See e.g., W. Malenbaum, *op. cit.*, pp. 224–7.

[23] See E. S. Mason, "An American View of Raw Materials Problems," *Journal of Industrial Economics*, (November, 1952), p. 6. Agricultural exports from the United States would not be even at their current level except for the government's surplus-disposal grants and other economic aid to foreign countries.

If all these factors persist—and their structural character suggests that they will—the future growth of agricultural supplies available for Western Europe and Japan is likely to be inadequate. There is likely to be a continuing adverse trend of these countries' terms of foreign trade, with all that it implies for the impairment of international specialization and the slow growth of their real income. The improving trend of Western Europe's and Japan's terms of trade over the last three years may seem to contradict this conclusion, but the inconsistency is apparent only. The improvement has not been due to a sustained increase in the rate of growth of agricultural output in the free world but rather to a marked slackening in the expansion of the demand of the industrial countries for primary imports. This slackening has been owed chiefly to short-term monetary causes: the end of the postwar inflation and of the Korean war boom, which left much of the industrial world in a condition of less-than-full employment of industrial capacity and labor. Unless it is assumed that this condition will be chronic in the industrial countries—as it was during the 1930's—it may be supposed that it is a relatively short-term, or cyclical, phenomenon. As demand in the industrial countries rises again and their industrial output again expands at the rate permitted by the growth of industrial investment and productivity, it is probable that the terms of trade of Western Europe and Japan will again tend to deteriorate—and that this tendency will persist so long as the structural limitations on agricultural output persist.[24] It is unlikely, however, that the rate of deterioration over the longer run will be nearly as rapid as in the period 1945-51, when industrial output in the non-Soviet world was recovering rapidly from the war and agricultural recovery was still retarded.

In conclusion, a substantial acceleration of the growth of agricultural production and of the volume of trade in agricultural products within the non-Soviet world—whether obtained by overcoming supply limitations in non-dollar countries or by expanding Europe's and Japan's dollar earnings—would be highly beneficial to the other industrial countries. It would be beneficial also to the growth of real income in

---

[24] A major assumption underlying this discussion is that shorter-run changes in the international terms of trade between manufactures and primary products are influenced mainly by changes in the *supply* (output) of primary products and in the *internal demand* of the industrial countries for manufactures. Theoretical and empirical reasons for believing that this is, generally speaking, true may be found in *International Trade 1952, op. cit.,* pp. 115-116.

the agricultural producing countries, provided serious agricultural over-production were avoided and prosperity in the industrial countries were maintained.

Competitive Superiority of American Industry

Since World War I, American industry has enjoyed a persistent superiority in competition with the industry of Western Europe and Japan in export markets and in the American domestic market. The statistical evidence of this superiority is that, for many years, the United States has been increasing its share of the world market for manufactures at the expense of many other industrial countries. The following table shows the changing percentage shares of certain countries in their combined total exports of manufactures during the period 1899–1950: [25]

	1899	*1913*	*1937*	*1950*
United States	11.2	12.6	19.6	29.1
United Kingdom	32.5	29.9	22.4	25.0
Germany	22.2	26.4	22.4	7.1 [b]
France	15.8	12.9	6.4	10.2
Belgium	5.6	4.9	5.9	5.8
Italy	3.7	3.6	3.6	3.8
Japan	1.5	2.4	7.2	3.3
Canada	0.3	0.6	5.0	6.1
Other [a]	7.2	6.7	7.5	9.6
	100.0	100.0	100.0	100.0

[a] Sweden, Switzerland and India
[b] West Germany

A part of the increase in the American share between 1937 and 1950 results from relatively temporary effects of World War II. For example, the delayed recovery of German and Japanese exports affects markedly the 1950 figures. Since 1950, there has been a considerable shift in the direction of, but by no means back to, prewar shares. For example, the share of West Germany in 1953 had increased substantially over 1950, though it remains far below Germany's prewar share. The share of

[25] Source: H. Tyszynski, "World Trade in Manufactured Commodities, 1899–1950," *The Manchester School* (September, 1951), p. 286.

Japan has increased a little but is still less than half of what it was before the war. The share of the United Kingdom has recently declined to about its size in 1937. At the same time, the share of the United States in 1953, though smaller than in 1950, remains much larger than prewar.[26] These recent changes are due principally to the recovery of production in Europe and Japan, to the end of general postwar inflation, and to the postwar revaluation of currencies in 1949. They have not gone far enough to suggest that the long-term tendency for the United States to increase its share has been, or is about to be, reversed. Indeed, as will be seen, an examination of the major causes of this tendency suggests the opposite, for many of them are still operative with undiminished, or even increased, force today.

Before causes are examined, however, the significance of this trend for Western Europe's and Japan's economic growth and health should be noted. The bare fact that the American share of world markets for manufactures has been increasing for many years does not by itself create a serious problem for the other major industrial countries. As long as total world demand for imports of manufactures was expanding rapidly—as in the years before 1914—there was plenty of opportunity for all industrial countries to increase their exports. It mattered relatively little to Britain's economic health, for example, that its share of world exports of manufactures fell from about two-thirds in 1870 to less than one-third in 1913, because world exports of manufactures were expanding so rapidly.

Since World War I, however, world demand for imports of manufactures has been growing much more slowly than before 1914, for reasons previously considered. In the forty years before 1914, the volume of world trade in manufactures was growing about $3\frac{1}{2}$ percent (cumulatively) per year. In the forty years since 1914, it has grown only about $1\frac{1}{2}$ percent (cumulatively) per year. War, the growing restriction of international trade and payments, and the increasing insecurity and incalculability of the international economy have been the most important causes. During the interwar years, the growth of international trade in manufactures was further reduced by the effects of overproduction in agricultural countries and of deflation in industrial

---

[26] Data concerning changes in shares of world exports of manufactures between 1949 and 1953 may be found in *Economic Survey 1954,* Cmd. 9108, (London, March 1954), p. 43. See also The Contracting Parties to the GATT, *International Trade 1953* (Geneva, 1954), p. 40.

countries. After World War II, world trade in manufactures recovered rapidly until 1951 but since then has tended to stagnate, as noted above. For the future, the lag of agricultural production will tend to retard the growth of world demand for imports of manufactures.

In these circumstances, the power of American competition has had —and will continue to have—adverse consequences for the volume of exports from the other industrial countries and for their terms of trade. During the interwar period, for example, American competition meant not merely a reduction in the relative position of the European countries in world export trade. It meant also that the absolute volume of their exports failed to grow. Thus Britain's and Germany's exports of manufactures never recovered their 1913 volume during the whole interwar period, while American exports of manufactures were more than double their 1913 volume in the peak years of the interwar period.[27] In the different circumstances of the first postwar years, the impact of American competition has probably affected Western Europe's and Japan's terms of trade more than their export volume, since the volume of their exports was determined in the main by limitations of domestic supply. For the future, American competition will probably affect adversely both their export volume and their terms of trade.

What causes have been mainly responsible for the persistent competitive superiority of American exports? Are the causes temporary or are they persistent and structural? These questions cannot be answered categorically; too many factors are involved. Certain among them, however, stand out.

The technological leadership of American industry is of particular importance. It works in several ways to enhance the international competitive position of American manufactures. Technological leadership

---

[27] The following figures show rather strikingly that, in the interwar period, successful American competition in an unexpansive total market meant a declining volume of exports for the United Kingdom and Germany:

Volume of Exports of Finished Manufactures

	1913	1929	1937
United States	100	269	221
United Kingdom	100	90	74
Germany	100	94	71
Total	100	124	99

Source: A. J. Brown, *Applied Economics* (London: Allen and Unwin, 1947), p. 198.

means—by definition—that American industry tends to have a comparative cost and price advantage in the production of the technologically newer products. Moreover, technological leadership also gives important competitive advantages of a non-price character. As originators and developers of many more new products than other countries, American manufacturers thereby enjoy important, if temporary, advantages over their European and Japanese competitors. These factors are important in explaining America's increasing share of world exports of manufactures because it is the technologically newer products which provide the major growth element in world trade in manufactures. World demand for them grows more rapidly than for the older types of manufactures. Therefore, as trade in manufactures grows, the United States tends to get a rising share of the total. A recent study of changes in the competitive positions of the industrial countries concludes that the competitive strength of the United States in products for which world demand has been expanding most rapidly is the principal explanation of America's growing share of world export markets for manufactures.[28]

Technological leadership has been associated with superior international competitive power since the beginning of modern industry. This was true in the case of Britain until the 1880's or 1890's. Similarly, German industry made large gains over British industry in export markets before World War I because it enjoyed technological leadership in such rapidly growing industrial fields as chemicals and the then-newer kinds of industrial equipment. Since World War I, American industry has done the same thing—to German as well as to British industry— with respect to a great many of the industrial products for which world import demand has been expanding most rapidly.[29]

The fact that the United States has gained a disproportionate share of the expanding sectors of world trade in manufactures is probably

---

[28] H. Tyszynski, *op. cit.*, pp. 288–9.

[29] The basic study on which this conclusion is based is Gerhard Colm *et al., Der deutsche Aussenhandel unter der Einwirkung Weltwirtschaftlicher Strukturwandlungen,* quoted in Eugene Staley, *World Economic Development* (Montreal: International Labour Office, 1944), p. 150 ff. This is not to say, of course, that American industry enjoys the competitive advantages of technological leadership in all fields where world import demand is expanding rapidly. There are several such fields where, for example, German and British industries are technologically equal or superior to American. In such cases, lower wages give German and British exporters a very real price advantage over their American competitors.

due also to another cause—the greater responsiveness of American industry generally than of most European industries to new foreign market opportunities. Two reasons for this greater responsiveness are of particular importance. One is the much larger size of the American domestic market and the consequently lesser dependence of American exporting industries on their foreign business. This lesser dependence makes American exporting firms less subject to the hazards of the contemporary international environment and therefore better able than British industries, for example, to expand their exports by a given percentage in response to rising foreign demand. In the international economy today, the more dependent a national economy is on foreign trade, the less capable it is of managing the continuous changes in structure necessary to preserve its competitive position in export markets in the face of changing foreign demand and competition. For, greater external dependence makes the proportionate size of necessary structural changes much larger for Europe and Japan than for the United States and, at the same time, inhibits these adjustments, because of the incalculability of international conditions.

Another reason for the greater responsiveness of American industry to foreign demand is its generally greater vigor of enterprise and the greater availability of capital it enjoys, as compared with the other industrial countries, together with the absence of many of the restrictive arrangements and other institutional obstacles to change so conspicuous in much of European industry. These matters are considered in the following chapter.

American industry has also had certain advantages of a quasi-monopolistic character over its European and Japanese rivals, especially in Western Hemisphere markets. For example, for more than a third of the time since 1913, Europe's ability to supply overseas markets has been interrupted or greatly restricted by war or by postwar reconstruction and inflation. The same was true of Japan during and after World War II. During these periods, many countries which normally bought primarily from Europe and Japan became used to American products and were afterward disinclined to return completely to their traditional suppliers. Sales methods, servicing, packaging, delivery dates, credit terms and other non-price considerations now tend with greater frequency to be more attractive in the case of American products than of European. In addition, because the United States is the leading industrial and political power of the non-Soviet world, American products frequently enjoy a prestige value—a kind of "snob appeal"—unrelated to "real" differences in quality or price. Within the Western Hemisphere, the trade of Canada and Latin America tends to be more and more oriented toward the United States in consequence of the growth of direct American investment and the proliferation of commercial, financial and managerial relationships. Likewise, the mere fact of geographical proximity and the greater military security and calculability of economic conditions within the Western Hemisphere work toward an intensification of trade between the United States and other Western Hemisphere countries.[30] Thus, the special position which American industry enjoys in the Western Hemisphere—particularly in Canada and northern Latin America—results from the cumulative advantages which naturally accrue to the leading industrial country in its own sphere of greatest economic and political influence. Britain enjoyed the same advantages in the 19th-century world economy, and even today retains a similar special position in some Commonwealth and Sterling Area markets.

It is, however, within the American domestic market that these or analogous advantages of American industry over its foreign rivals

---

[30] The following comment from a recent United Nations study testifies to the importance of non-price factors in increasing the American share of the Latin American market for manufactures: "Price advantages [of American manufactured products], however, do not tell the whole story, even when distribution costs are taken into consideration. Other factors are speed of delivery, terms of payment and credit facilities, availability of technical services and spare parts, ease of replacement, standardization of product, commercial ties and sales techniques, such as the use of advertising and representation in the field. There is some reason to believe that these factors have been as important as price advantages in stimulating demand for United States goods in the Latin American market. Lack of standardization of some European products, such as tractors and some types of industrial machinery, has restricted sales, while United States advertising, extensive representation of its firms abroad, and readily available servicing and replacement facilities have unquestionably stimulated the country's exports. The growth of United States direct investment at a time when European investments were static or declining must have contributed to the same effect. Furthermore, although the European countries taken together can probably offer as wide a range of manufactures as the United States, the types of goods they offer are different in a number of fields, such as machine tools, motor-cars and many household appliances. Strong preferences may thus develop for the types of goods of one country, not only in the industrial field, where a changeover from one type of machinery to another will normally involve considerable investment, but also in the field of durable consumption goods. These rigidities of the market, which helped to sustain European exports in the 'twenties, are now playing in favour of the United States, which in the last ten years has occupied a preponderant position in Latin American markets." United Nations, *A Study of Trade Between Latin America and Europe* (Geneva, 1953), p. 49.

are most strongly felt. And in this market their effect is re-enforced not only by the tariff but by an obstacle to imports of far greater importance —the much greater security and calculability of domestic, as compared to foreign, trading. In consequence, it does not appear that the opportunity for expanded commercial exports of manufactures from the other industrial countries to the United States is nearly as great as the size and rate of growth of the American market might lead one to suppose —even if the American tariff were to be drastically reduced.

It is perhaps surprising that the American market for manufactures, which is the largest and most rapidly growing in the free world, does not seem to offer greater opportunity to foreign exporters. But—even apart from the tariff and from non-price considerations—domestic industry tends to have a large comparative cost advantage over foreign industry in the more rapidly growing areas of American demand. These areas include not only most types of producers' goods, but virtually all of the newer forms of consumers' goods—electrical, mechanical and electronic consumer durables; synthetic products designed for a growing multitude of consumer uses; drugs and medicines, etc. The industries producing these goods have been characterized by rapid technological advance and rapidly growing demand, stimulated by national advertising and sales promotion on a colossal scale. These characteristics are mutually dependent and are ultimately derived from the size and dynamism of the American economy and from the character of American life. Obviously, the other industrial countries have, in most instances, no comparative cost advantage in American markets for products of this kind and would gain little of the American market even if tariffs, which are generally low for these products, were removed entirely.[31] The inability of European and Japanese industry to compete effectively with American industry in these rapidly growing and relatively unrestricted domestic markets is a major reason why Western Europe's problem of finding adequate export markets is unlikely to be overcome through trying greatly to expand commercial exports to the United States.

---

[31] Even in the relatively few cases where foreign products in these categories are competitive with domestic products on the basis of price, foreign products could not make large inroads into the American market unless backed by sales promotion and merchandizing facilities comparable to those behind competing domestic products. Apart from the serious risks (e.g., of upward tariff revision) involved in so doing, the undertaking of such a sales effort is something outside the experience and beyond the means of all but a very few European and Japanese manufacturers.

These comments apply also to the American competitive position in the Canadian market, though in lesser degree. The Canadian market for manufactures is so similar in structure and direction of growth to the American domestic market that American industry also enjoys a comparative cost advantage there over Western Europe and Japan in the sectors where Canadian demand is growing most rapidly. It is significant that the American share of imports of manufactures has increased more over prewar in Canada than in Latin America or in Asia and that, in Canada, the American share shows less tendency to decline to its prewar proportion.[32] This is not, of course, due solely— or even mainly—to cost advantages; American industry has also important non-price advantages in the Canadian market, as already noted.

The comparative cost advantage of European and Japanese goods in the American market lies chiefly in two areas: (1) the older forms of manufactures, where recent technological progress has been relatively slow and production methods tend to be labor-intensive rather than capital-intensive—e.g., textiles, leather goods, manufactured specialty foodstuffs, optical goods, ceramics and glassware, watches and clocks, cutlery, and various products of a semi-handicraft nature; and (2) a relatively few newer products which, for various reasons, are manufactured in the United States and abroad by much the same kind of machinery and equipment—e.g., heavy electrical equipment, some synthetic organic chemicals, rayon staple fiber, flat glass, bicycles, some kinds of machine tools, etc. Here large wage differentials give foreign

---

[32] It is significant, too, that Canada is the only country able in recent years to increase its share of the American market for manufactures. For Canada is the only other industrial country whose industry seems to have considerable areas of comparative advantage over American industry with respect to the more expansive sectors of American demand. Basically, this results from the fact that, though much smaller, the Canadian economy has many of the same characteristics as the American. In addition, the contiguity of the two countries and the relatively high security and calculability of economic relationships between them, the similarity of their economic motivations and business attitudes, and the close managerial and financial ties between Canadian and American industry, work in favor of Canadian exporters to the United States as they do for American exporters to Canada. In effect, much of the industrial sector of the Canadian economy is an extension of the American economy. Thus, over a considerable range of manufactured products, Canadian firms—often branches of American concerns—have been able to take advantage of growing market opportunities in the expansive sectors of the American economy. In contrast, Canadian efforts to export agricultural products and manufactures competitive with the non-expansive sectors of the American economy have encountered the same import barriers as do efforts by other countries.

manufacturers a competitive advantage over domestic producers. In the aggregate, however, these two categories make up a relatively small and declining component of the American consumption of manufactures. For some of them, per capita consumption has been declining.

Moreover, many of these products—particularly those in the first category—enjoy the greatest tariff protection.[33] Although these industries and specialized agricultural producers are a relatively small part of the total American economy, they are, in many cases, concentrated in certain localities where their economic importance is far out of proportion to their significance for American national income as a whole. The removal or reduction of protection would, therefore, involve a concentration of damage, small in the aggregate, but severe for the affected communities. It seems unfortunately to be true, then, that the sectors of the American economy in which European and Japanese products enjoy a comparative cost advantage are in the main the sectors where a rapid expansion of demand is not likely and where protectionism is naturally to be expected and is, therefore, most difficult to overcome.[34]

One further cause of American competitive strength in foreign and domestic markets has been important in the postwar period—greater relative inflation in Europe than in the United States. Insofar as this has been a temporary result of the war and of postwar recovery, the European currency devaluations of September 1949, and the general subsidence of inflation have now eliminated it, except in Japan. It can be argued with some force, however, that in certain industrial countries—Britain and France in particular—there is a continuing tendency for aggregate demand to expand more rapidly relative to output than in the United States—thus tending periodically to push the general level of their export prices above American export prices, until corrected by devaluation. This tendency seems to be related both to the relatively slower growth of productivity, and to the greater relative pressure of economic claims and requirements in Britain and France than in the United States. Whether it will in fact prove to be a continuing tend-

---

[33] Evidence that American tariffs on imports from Britain are highest on products for which Britain has a comparative cost advantage is given by G. D. A. MacDougall in "British and American Exports: A Study Suggested by the Theory of Comparative Costs," *Economic Journal* (December, 1951), pp. 704–5.

[34] On this subject generally, see Howard S. Piquet, *Aid, Trade and the Tariff* (New York: Thomas Y. Crowell, 1953), and Don D. Humphrey, *American Imports* (New York: Twentieth Century Fund, 1955).

ency and a chronic source of competitive weakness for Britain, France and possibly other industrial countries is impossible to forecast. Yet it is reasonable to suppose that the economy of an industrial country whose rate of productivity growth is slow, whose claimant groups are powerful and insistent on rising money incomes, and which is burdened with large military responsibilities and foreign economic commitments, will tend to be more inflated—or less deflated—than the economy of the United States (and perhaps of West Germany) on the average, though not at all times. The extreme reluctance of governments to devalue their currencies makes it all the more probable that any chronic tendency to relative inflation would have important effects on a country's competitive position in export markets.[35]

In conclusion, it appears that the causes of the competitive strength of the more rapidly growing sectors of American industry are persistent and structural in character. They are, therefore, likely—in combina-

---

[35] Since John Williams and certain British economists first argued that the higher rate of growth of American productivity might help to explain the competitive weakness of British relative to American exports, there has been considerable discussion of this issue. See John Williams' 1951 article, "International Trade Theory and Policy—Some Current Issues," reprinted in *Economic Stability in a Changing World* (New York: Oxford University Press, 1953), p. 38. This line of reasoning has been frequently criticized. Most of the criticism has been wide of the mark, however, because it has been directed to refuting the proposition that differences between economies in the rate of growth of overall (or industrial) productivity must necessarily lead to competitive trouble for the slower-growing economy. There is, of course, no *necessary* reason why countries with differing rates of productivity growth should not remain on competitively equal terms in "third" markets or in trade with each other. On the assumption that money incomes in the two economies grow in proportion to productivity—no faster and no more slowly—their average relative export prices need not change and no change in their competitive positions need result. But this assumption ignores or assumes away the possibility that the average tension of demand over a period of years (i.e., the average rate of inflation) may be higher in the slower-growing than in the faster-growing economy, because the pressure of economic claims and requirements on a slower-growing national product may tend to be greater than on a faster-growing one. And, in the case of Britain and America, the possibility that this will happen is increased by the fact that increased knowledge in Britain of the higher American standard of living tends to raise consumption claims on the British economy. In defense of the critics of this theory, however, it should be said that its proponents, by emphasizing the difference in productivity-growth rates, rather than the difference in the average pressure of economic claims and requirements on the national product, have not put their case in its most persuasive form. On this issue generally, see K. Knorr and G. Patterson, *A Critique of the Randall Commission Report* (Princeton, New Jersey: Department of Economics, Princeton University, 1954), pp. 5–12. For an interesting elaboration and development of the Williams' thesis, see J. R. Hicks, "An Inaugural Lecture," *Oxford Economic Papers,* (June, 1953), p. 117.

tion with lagging agricultural production in the non-Soviet world—to continue to restrict the expansion of Western Europe's and Japan's exports and to exert downward pressure on their terms of trade.

The Dollar Problem of Western Europe and Japan

The problems discussed in the two preceding sections of this chapter can be summarized in the following way. Industrial Europe and Japan are not now able to enjoy an adequately growing exchange of manufactures for primary products with Asia, Latin America, and Oceania, at favorable terms of trade, because of limitations on the growth of agricultural output in those areas. Nor are they able to avoid the consequences of this problem by means of a rapidly expanding exchange of manufactures for primary products with North America. For this alternative is blocked by their competitive weakness *vis-à-vis* the United States. This combination of difficulties may be said to constitute a "dollar problem" for Western Europe and Japan, not in the sense of a balance-of-payments problem, but in the sense of persistently unsatisfactory trading relations with the United States and Canada—unsatisfactory because trade between the two groups of countries does not expand fast enough to allow Western Europe and Japan an adequate rate of economic growth. We shall refer to Western Europe's and Japan's dollar problem, in this first sense, as their "structural dollar problem" or their "structural trading problem with North America."

But this is not what is usually meant when Western Europe's and Japan's dollar problem is mentioned. For these countries have also a dollar problem in a second and more obvious sense—in the sense of persistent strain on their balance of payments with the United States, Canada and other countries of the dollar area.[36] By persistent "strain" on their balance of payments is meant a persistent excess of their demand for dollar goods and services over the supply of dollars currently available to pay for them—i.e., a "shortage" of means of payment for dollar goods and services in relation to demand for them. Western Europe's and Japan's dollar problem in this second sense is thus a financial problem—a "dollar shortage." It is their dollar shortage, rather than

---

[36] The dollar area is usually defined to include the United States, Canada, the rest of North America, the independent Caribbean countries, some Northern Latin American countries and the Philippine Republic. For a brief explanation of the dollar area see page 244, footnote 9, below.

their structural dollar problem, with which we are here concerned, although, as will be seen, the two are closely related. Indeed, the dollar shortage is mainly the financial reflection or symptom of the structural dollar problem.

The concept of a persistent "strain" on a country's balance of payments —a persistent "shortage" of foreign exchange—requires explanation. According to economic theory, strain on a country's balance of payments can be temporary only, because it automatically sets in motion corrective changes in incomes and employment, in prices and wages, in international capital movements, and in the exchange rate (if the rate is determined by market forces) which bring the country's foreign payments back into balance. Therefore, a persistent balance-of-payments strain cannot occur unless these equilibrating changes are resisted, either by the action of organized claimant groups or by the national government.[37] Of course, a country's balance of payments can remain in deficit only so long as the deficit can be financed, for example, by spending its reserves or by foreign aid. Lacking such means, either the corrective equilibrating changes have to occur or payments have to be forced into balance by exchange control and restriction of imports. Therefore, when it is said that Western Europe and Japan have a dollar shortage, what is implied is that organized interest groups and the national governments in the countries concerned would rather restrict their imports of dollar goods than allow corrective changes in incomes and employment, prices or exchange rates. Western Europe's and Japan's dollar shortage is not the only contemporary example of a persistent or recurrent balance-of-payments strain, though it is much the most important from the standpoint of American foreign policy. Indeed, a tendency to balance-of-payments trouble is characteristic of international economic relations today. As suggested in Chapter 1, the incalculability of international conditions and the resistance of organized interests and national governments tend to prevent the continuous mutual adaptation of national monetary systems and economic structures necessary to keep international payments balanced without direct controls on trade and payments.

A dollar shortage, in the sense used here, must not be confused with a dollar deficit or "gap." When a country has a dollar deficit, in the

---

[37] See e.g., Joan Robinson, "The Pure Theory of International Trade," *Collected Economic Papers* (Blackwell: Oxford, 1951).

sense of a balance-of-payments deficit with the dollar area which is financed by some extraordinary means, that deficit is evidence of an underlying dollar shortage. But the reverse is not necessarily true; a dollar shortage does not necessarily produce a deficit in the country's balance of payments with the dollar area, for the shortage of dollars may be prevented from producing an actual deficit by controls on imports from, and payments to, the dollar area. For example, the fact that the "dollar gap" has disappeared since 1952, in the sense that the non-dollar world is adding to its dollar or gold holdings, does not mean that the non-dollar world's dollar shortage has disappeared. It means that, in the particular circumstances of the last few years, the non-dollar world's demand for dollar goods and services—tightly restricted in most countries by import quotas and exchange controls—has been less than its receipts of dollars, which have included some $5-6 billion a year of extraordinary United States Government expenditures abroad.[38]

Industrial Europe's and Japan's shortage of dollars is a problem for them not because restriction of their dollar imports and failure to keep their currencies convertible with the dollar are inherently bad. It is a problem because such restrictions shelter their economies from American competition to a degree which is probably damaging to economic efficiency and growth.[39] It should be said, however, that the importance of the dollar shortage as a cause of Western Europe's and Japan's poor economic health is often exaggerated. The excessive protection from American competition which it entails is a much less serious impediment to Europe's and Japan's economic growth and health than are a number of other problems—the structural trading problems examined in preceding sections of this chapter, for example, or the internal institutional obstacles to growth discussed in Chapter 3.

If, then, dollar import restrictions are damaging to economic efficiency and growth, why do the other industrial countries seem to prefer them to the economic adjustments which would make restrictions unnecessary? Because organized interests and national governments believe that the damage done by import restrictions is outweighed by the

---

[38] See Commission on Foreign Economic Policy (Randall Commission), *Staff Papers* (Washington, 1954), pp. 17–19.

[39] Western Europe's dollar shortage also tends to cause restrictions on trade and payments among non-dollar countries and to generalize the inconvertibility of currencies throughout the non-dollar world. But this consequence of the dollar shortage can be greatly mitigated by suitable payments and trading arrangements among non-dollar countries. These aspects of the dollar shortage are considered in Chapter 7.

political and economic cost of the adjustments—the cost to their terms of trade, levels of domestic employment, and rates of economic growth. Is this belief justified? Even if true for the earlier postwar period, is it still true today and for the foreseeable future? To answer these questions it is necessary to look at the dollar shortage of Western Europe and Japan in somewhat more concrete terms.

Before World War II, Western Europe financed a large bilateral current account payments deficit with North America by means of dollars and newly mined gold earned in "third countries," according to the familiar prewar triangular pattern of international settlements. The prewar pattern of Japan's international payments was similar. Today, lagging agricultural output in non-dollar areas has caused Western Europe and Japan to turn to the United States and Canada for growing quantities of food and agricultural materials to support growing consumption and industrial production.[40] But, at the same time, the competitive power of American industry, and other factors examined earlier in this chapter, have made it very difficult for Western Europe and Japan to pay for growing dollar imports by expanding their exports—either their direct exports to the United States or their exports to "third countries" where dollars or newly mined gold might be earned.

With respect to such "third country" earnings, it should be observed that Western Europe's and Japan's competitive position *vis-à-vis* the United States has been particularly weak in the areas whose dollar supplies have been increasing most rapidly (Canada and Latin America), and relatively stronger in the areas where fewer dollars have been available to be earned (the Sterling Area and the Far East). Thus, the

---

[40] The following figures of the percentage of Western Europe's imports of selected foodstuffs procured from dollar area countries, prewar and in 1950–51, show this greatly increased dependence on dollar supplies; though the dependence has declined some since 1950–51, it remains well above prewar.

	Prewar	1950–51
Bread grain	35	80
Coarse grain	8	45
Sugar	40	95
Fats and oils	7	20
Oil cake and meal	7	17

Source: United Nations Food and Agriculture Organization, *The State of Food and Agriculture: Review and Outlook* (Rome, 1952), p. 49. Japan's situation with respect to dollar imports of foodstuffs is much the same as Western Europe's. For example, in 1938 Japan imported almost no food from the United States; in 1951, Japanese food imports from the United States were $241 million.

annual current dollar receipts of Canada and Latin America in the last few years have been, in real terms, about three times their prewar level. But the annual dollar receipts of "third countries" in the Sterling Area and the Far East, where Europe's competitive position is strengthened by colonial control, traditional trading and financial connections, preferential tariffs, joint discrimination against dollar imports, or geographical proximity, have increased only a little more than 50 percent in real terms, as compared with prewar.[41]

The future geographical distribution of "third country" dollar earnings is likely to be similar. It appears that a very large part—as much as three quarters according to one estimate [42]—of the total increase in United States imports of foodstuffs and raw materials over the next 20–25 years will be obtained from Canada and Latin America—the areas where the competitive strength of American exports is at its maximum. For, as noted above, the greater security and calculability of the conditions of trade and international investment within the Western Hemisphere than between it and other areas tend to reorient the trade and the economic structures of Canada and Latin America away from Europe and toward the United States.[43] At the same time, the ability of the American economy to develop synthetic substitutes for raw materials (e.g., rubber) available only from more distant and less secure and calculable sources of supply tends to retard the growth of dollar earnings in "third countries" outside the Western Hemisphere. As a recent study concludes, "It was, of course, inevitable that the war should have enormously stimulated United States imports from the near-lying and strategically defensible countries of the Western Hemisphere, while, at the same time, giving every incentive, more powerful than any tariff, to develop substitute production for, or economies in the use of, goods previously imported from such occupied or imperilled areas as Europe and the Far East." [44]

Nevertheless, as a matter of economic logic, it is clear that these structural weaknesses in Western Europe's and Japan's trading relations with North America do not lead *inevitably* to strain on their balance of payments with North America. Balance-of-payments strain is a finan-

---

[41] See, e.g., *Economic Survey of Europe Since the War, op. cit.*, p. 17.

[42] See Henry G. Aubrey, "The Secular Increase in United States Imports and World Trade" (Federal Reserve Bank of New York, May, 1954), p. 48 (mimeographed).

[43] For a discussion of this and other examples of the increasing "regionalization" of trade since the 1930's, see *International Trade 1953, op. cit.*, pp. 19–22.

[44] *Economic Survey of Europe Since the War, op. cit.*, p. 16.

cial and monetary, not a "real," phenomenon. In principle, therefore, it can always be overcome by monetary and financial means—e.g., by some combination of deflation in, and devaluation by, the deficit countries—regardless of the "real" trading relations. But, in the case of Western Europe's and Japan's postwar dollar shortage, the economic cost of so doing would have been far too high to be politically acceptable in these countries. The reason it would be so high is, precisely, that the causes of Western Europe's and Japan's heavy dependence on North American primary products, and of their weak competitive position relative to the United States, are structural—that is, these causes are relatively unresponsive to changes in the internal monetary conditions, the export prices, and the terms of trade of the dollar-short industrial countries. Thus, the causes of lagging agricultural production outside North America will be affected relatively little by a further increase in agricultural prices and a further deterioration in Europe's and Japan's terms of trade. The most important causes of Western Europe's relatively weak competitive position (especially in Western Hemisphere markets) are in large part of a non-price and non-monetary character. They will, therefore, be offset to only a limited degree by export price-cutting (e.g., through devaluation) or by internal monetary restriction in Europe and Japan. In short, neither the rate of growth of the supply of primary products imported by Western Europe and Japan, nor the supply of their own manufactured exports, nor the demand of other countries for those exports, are likely to be sufficiently responsive to price and monetary changes.

In consequence, the dollar-short industrial countries are forced to keep their payments with North America in balance mainly by keeping down their dollar imports. To accomplish this by internal deflation and currency devaluation, unaided by exchange controls and some quantitative restriction of imports, would have been—and remains—politically unacceptable to their citizens and undesirable from the standpoint of American foreign policy. Moreover, the degree of internal monetary restriction that would be required to reduce the demand for dollar imports sufficiently would be incompatible with full utilization of their industrial capacity. It would prevent achieving the rate of domestic investment and economic expansion which limitations internal to their economies would otherwise permit.

These are the principal reasons why the dollar-short industrial countries have used direct controls to force their dollar payments into balance and why they are unwilling, or in many cases politically unable, to make their currencies convertible on current account with the dollar. To argue that this has been unnecessary—as advocates of financial and monetary correctives of the dollar shortage often do—is, then, to make a double error. For this reasoning both ignores the structural roots of the dollar shortage and overlooks the adverse effects which a purely monetary prescription would have on the economic growth and health of Western Europe and Japan.

It is sometimes said that these things may have been true in the earlier postwar years but that, since the beginning of 1952, they are true no longer—that Europe's and Japan's postwar dollar shortage has been a temporary phenomenon associated with recovery from the war and with postwar inflation and is now, or will soon be, ended. There is, of course, considerable truth in this assertion. Until 1952, the postwar inflation in Western Europe and Japan, and the slow recovery of agricultural production in Europe and Asia, greatly aggravated the dollar shortage of the industrial countries. The recovery of non-dollar agricultural production, the end of postwar inflation, coupled with the results of the drastic European currency devaluations in 1949, have lessened considerably the intensity of Western Europe's dollar shortage, as the relaxation of dollar import restrictions and the large additions to Europe's dollar reserves show. Japan's dollar shortage, however, remains serious.

Nevertheless, it appears that a good deal of the improvement in Western Europe's dollar position over the last few years has been the result of changes of doubtful permanence.[45] Only a small part of the reduction of Western Europe's dollar deficit since 1951 has been owed to the expansion of Europe's commercial dollar earnings. The major part has resulted from increases in American military expenditures in Western Europe and from a reduction of Europe's dollar imports. Only a relatively small part of the reduction of Europe's dollar imports can be attributed to increases in imports from non-dollar areas. In the main, it was the consequence of an overall reduction in Western Europe's imports—a reduction for which inadequate domestic demand, reduction of inventories and stagnating industrial output in several countries were partly responsible.[46]

---

[45] See *Economic Survey of Europe in 1953, op. cit.,* pp. 15–23.
[46] See Organization for European Economic Cooperation, *Progress and Problems of the European Economy* (Paris, 1954), pp. 24–26, 29–30.

It would be unwise, therefore, to conclude from the recent lessening of Western Europe's dollar shortage that the whole problem will soon be a thing of the past. There is little evidence that the underlying structural trading problem is being overcome. Though agricultural production in non-dollar areas has now recovered from the war, there is no evidence that its long-term rate of growth is likely to increase. Industrial Europe has not recovered its prewar share of world exports of manufactures, while the share of the United States remains well above prewar. To be sure, as long as Western Europe's dollar imports remain at present levels, or rise only slowly, Europe's dollar shortage need not worsen and may improve still more. But, as a matter of policy, the United States cannot afford to assume that Western Europe's dollar imports will rise only slowly, for that would be to assume an inadequate rate of growth of West European production· and consumption. To grow at an adequate rate, the West European economies need a rapid expansion of their foreign trade. These same considerations apply with even greater force to Japan.[47]

This is not to say that the other industrial countries are likely to be continuously and seriously short of dollars for the foreseeable future. In periods of high American prosperity and large American military expenditures in Europe and Japan, their dollar shortage may disappear entirely, even assuming that they maintain a level of internal demand adequate for industrial expansion. Yet given that assumption, and given the underlying structural trading problem, these countries are likely to have a dollar shortage whenever the conjuncture of financial and monetary conditions turns less favorable. In sum, Western Europe and Japan are likely to have a continuing *tendency* to dollar shortage, although it may be hoped that their need to restrict dollar imports will prove to be intermittent only.

This conclusion implies that the cost to the economic growth of industrial Europe and Japan of continuing or intermittent resort to re-

---

[47] In this connection, it should be noted that Western Europe and Japan have been forced—largely by their structural trading problem—to reduce considerably the ratio of their imports to their total production as compared with 1938. Thus, in 1951, the imports of 18 West European countries from other areas (i.e., excluding imports from each other) were only 89 percent of their volume in 1938, while their total production (GNP) reached 118 percent of 1938. In Japan's case, the forced reduction in dependence on imports has been even greater. In 1952, Japanese imports were only 54 percent of their 1934–36 volume, while real national income reached 119 percent of the 1934–36 level.

strictions on dollar imports is the lesser of two alternative evils.[48] The greater evil would be to follow monetary and financial policies which would assure continued payments equilibrium with the dollar area without restrictions but at the price of industrial stagnation or reduced real income in Western Europe and Japan. In short, the proper aim of economic policy in this situation is not to "solve the dollar problem," in the sense of bringing the dollar shortage to an end. It is rather to promote the economic growth and health of Western Europe and Japan, given their structural trading problem with North America. To attempt a financial and monetary cure of the dollar shortage would be to try to remedy a problem which is basically structural and institutional by treating its financial symptoms—and treating these symptoms, moreover, by means which are inconsistent with the patient's future growth and health.

The problems analyzed in this chapter are, at root, results of the constitutional characteristics of the international economy described in Chapter 1—the fact that it has been "nationalized," the dominance of the American economy, and the subtraction of the Soviet bloc and Red China. Together, these characteristics create an external economic environment for Western Europe and Japan which inhibits their economic growth in a variety of ways. Their growth is inhibited, above all, by the insecurity and incalculability of that environment and by national restrictions on international economic relations. Their growth is inhibited by unexpansive agricultural production in their traditional export market areas and by the superior competitive strength of American industry. Their opportunity for growth is reduced because they are unable to enjoy a rapidly expanding exchange of their manufactures for primary products from North America. Their growth rate is affected by their chronic shortage of dollars, which forces them to shelter their industry and agriculture from American competition to an unhealthy degree.

These economic problems do not affect Japan and the industrial countries of Western Europe equally. Nor, despite their importance, are

---

[48] This cost can be greatly reduced if the necessary restriction of dollar payments by these countries is prevented, by appropriate trade and payments arrangements, from causing generalized bilateralism in trade and payments among non-dollar countries, as will be explained in Chapter 7.

these external problems sufficient in themselves to explain the slow economic growth and poor economic health of industrial Europe and Japan. An adequate explanation requires examination of the internal situation of each country—the internal obstacles to economic growth and the character of economic claims and requirements. These matters are considered in the following chapter.

3

Western Europe and Japan

Prospects for Economic Health

To assess the prospects for Western Europe's and Japan's economic health, it is necessary to examine the countries individually. Though they share in common the external economic difficulties outlined in the preceding chapter, those problems affect some countries more seriously than others. There are also major differences among them in the nature and seriousness of the internal obstacles to economic growth. Likewise, there are marked differences among them in the pressure of economic claims and requirements on economic resources, as well as important variations in the way their peoples are likely to react psychologically and politically to the frustration of economic claims and the inability to meet economic requirements. This chapter is concerned with such differences and variations. For each of the four major West European countries and Japan, it attempts briefly to assess the prospects for economic health and to suggest the significance of those prospects for the United States.

The United Kingdom

It is appropriate to begin with the United Kingdom. For the United Kingdom is the most important European member of the Western Community from a political, economic and military point of view, and is our most important ally. Its current military expenditure and industrial output represent about 40 percent and 33 percent, respectively, of the present total of industrial Europe. On Britain's economic health and continued support of the Atlantic Alliance depend the success of that Alliance and, indeed, the political solidarity and military capability of the whole free world.

The average rate of growth of the British economy since 1913 has been remarkably slow. Colin Clark estimates that, between 1913 and 1950, real income per capita in Britain grew less than 1 percent a year (cumulatively).[1] This may be compared with a rate of about 2 percent in the United States in the same period;[2] and it was scarcely more rapid than the rate of growth of per capita real income in France and Italy. During the interwar years, the slowness of Britain's economic growth was not readily apparent because its impact on consumption was disguised by the major improvement in Britain's terms of foreign trade, as compared with 1913, during the 1920's and 1930's. But this improvement has now been wiped out and is not likely to recur. In postwar circumstances, with expanding consumption claims and military requirements, the economic health of Britain will be precarious indeed if the future rate of growth of the British national product is not markedly better than this long-term trend. Because the British economy has only recently recovered from the direct effects of the war, it is too early to tell whether its average rate of growth over the next five or ten years is likely to exceed the long-term trend to date. Without attempting a quantitative forecast, however, it is possible to describe some of the persistent obstacles to British economic growth and to suggest reasons for believing that there is serious question whether, on the basis of present prospects, the growth of British national income will be adequate in the light of expanding claims and requirements.

Intractable obstacles to Britain's economic growth arise from the extreme character of Britain's national specialization on industry and its corresponding extreme dependence on foreign trade. The extent of this dependence is shown by the fact that the ratio of the value of manufactured exports to the gross output of British manufacturing is about 46 percent. This compares with about 5 percent for the United States. The

---

[1] See "The Trend of Real Income in Britain," *Review of Economic Progress* (Brisbane, Australia, July–August, 1951), p. 5.

[2] See Solomon Fabricant, *Economic Progress and Technical Change* (National Bureau of Economic Research: New York, 1954), p. 4.

United Kingdom now grows only 22 percent of the breadgrains its people consume and produces only 55 percent of its meat consumption.

The structure of the British economy is the result of the unique character of British economic development. Because Britain was the early starter in industrialization and because, under a free trade regime, British industry developed in response to incentives and opportunities within a British-dominated, worldwide trading system, the British economy was able to assume a highly specialized structure. This pattern of growth made possible the attainment of a standard of living which is still well above that of the major continental countries and which was, until World War II, not too far below that of the United States. In contrast, France and Germany—latecomers on the industrial scene—chose, primarily for political and social reasons, to follow economic policies which initially emphasized industrial expansion for the domestic market and a "balanced" national economy. True, the logic of the industrialization process gradually increased their dependence (particularly that of Germany) on foreign trade. Nevertheless, the aim of their national economic development policies from the beginning was to limit this tendency rather than, as in Britain, to foster it. The price of this French and German policy—given the relatively limited size of their populations and of their endowments of natural resources—was a lower rate of growth of productivity and lower living standards than might have been achieved, theoretically at least, had the process of industrialization been pushed more rapidly at the expense of agricultural output.[3]

---

[3] The following quotation gives some of the historical reasons for these important differences in economic structure, in terms of a comparison of the British and German economies:

"The two countries [Britain and Germany] differ markedly in the degree of their dependence on imports as the result of developments over a long period extending back before the first World War. At that time, imports of Germany, as then constituted, were only 25% lower than those of the United Kingdom; by 1938 . . . they were only half as great; in 1951, the imports of Western Germany were only about one-third those of the United Kingdom, although the total population of the two areas is about the same and their economies show certain other similarities.

"Both historical accident and conscious policy have contributed to this difference in the degree of integration of the two countries into the world economy. The much earlier date of the industrial revolution in the United Kingdom resulted in the development of its textile production and trade to a level never reached in Germany. Despite the long term decline in the textile industry of the United Kingdom, it still imports far more textile raw materials and exports more textile manufactures than does Germany. The early depletion of the forests in the United Kingdom—to provide land for grazing, timber for ships and charcoal for iron and steel making—contrasts sharply with the present near self-sufficiency of Western Germany in forest products.

Despite the great economic advantages to Britain of pursuing a free trade policy in the pre-1914 international environment, that policy helped to create an economy so heavily dependent on foreign trade that, in the present century, its opportunity for economic growth has been seriously impaired by the external hazards and obstacles discussed in the preceding chapter. Because Britain is now more dependent on foreign trade than any other major industrial country, the incalculability of the external environment, the unexpansive character of export markets, and the prospective deterioration of the industrial countries' terms of trade are all particularly threatening to Britain's economic growth prospects. The impact of these external difficulties on the British economy would be even greater if they were not mitigated by the advantages derived from what remains of the British Empire and from the protected markets for British exports in the Commonwealth and Sterling Area.

In addition to—and interacting with—external obstacles, there are persistent internal impediments to Britain's economic growth. One of these manifests itself in a supply of capital for investment in British manufacturing industries which is inadequate to maintain a high rate of growth of output and to make possible rapid adaptation of British industry to the changing requirements of international competition. Indeed, it has been asserted that, as late as 1952, the fixed capital of British manufacturing industry was still wasting away more quickly than it was being replaced,[4] although this is probably no longer true. A part of the trouble may be charged to government policies which have apparently given investment in housing and the nationalized industries too high a priority relative to investment in domestic manufacturing. More fundamentally, however, the problem is an inadequate general rate of saving and domestic capital formation. It appears that total net domestic invest-

---

"But superimposed on these factors are the effects of deep and long established differences in policy and in ways of life which have contributed to strongly marked differences in the production and consumption patterns of the two countries. The German drive for self-sufficiency dates back to the beginning of its industrialization in the second half of the last century, at a time when the United Kingdom had abandoned tariff protection and gone in for free trade. It was further accentuated by the autarkic policies necessitated by the collapse of German exports during the great depression and espoused by the Nazi regime before the war, and by the disruptive effects of the war itself on foreign commerce. In spite of postwar developments, the structure of the United Kingdom remains essentially that of a free trade economy, whereas the pattern in Western Germany still reflects the autarky pursued for many years." *Economic Survey of Europe Since the War, op. cit.,* p. 97.

[4] See *The Economist* (London, September 13, 1952), p. 642.

ment in Britain since World War II has not yet been sufficient to make up for the wartime loss of capital due to war damage and arrears of maintenance and replacement and to restore productive capital per head in Britain to its prewar level—a level which itself reflected the disinvestment that occurred during the interwar period.[5] As the British Treasury's 1954 *Economic Survey* concludes:

> While investment in the United States, in Germany and in some other European countries has gone on rising, there has been little change in the level of productive investment in this country over the last few years. The development of basic services like fuel and power and transportation is just as important as investment in manufacturing industry but it is in the latter particularly that the United Kingdom appears to be lagging behind its main competitors.[6]

Why total domestic saving and capital formation have been inadequate to meet Britain's requirement for economic growth is reasonably clear. First, the pressure of consumption claims has been so strong and politically so effective that the amount of economic resources currently available for purposes other than consumption has thereby been restricted. The claims of organized labor for rising money incomes have been particularly effective. There has been a substantial rise in the ratio of wages and salaries to national income, and in the volume of government-financed social welfare benefits, relative to prewar years. "Successive national income 'white papers' have shown that each year wages and salaries have risen by too much, and profits and other funds available for the finance of investment by far too little, for the good of the national economy." [7] The abandonment of rationing and price control and the overcoming of war-caused arrears of consumption have brought about a welcome increase in personal savings in the United Kingdom in the last two years. It remains true, however, that—relative to the urgent requirements which the British economy also has to meet—consumption still absorbs too large a share of the national income.

Second, a large part of the resources available for purposes other than consumption in the British economy has been absorbed in overseas in-

---

[5] See A. Robinson, "British Economic Policy, 1945–50," *London and Cambridge Economic Service,* May, 1950, p. 42, and D. H. Robertson, *Britain in the World Economy* (Allen & Unwin: London, 1953), ch. i.

[6] *Economic Survey 1954,* Cmd. 9108 (London, March, 1954), p. 44.

[7] *The Economist* (London, September 13, 1952), p. 642. See also *ibid.,* April 3, 1954, p. 3.

vestment. The magnitude of British capital exports to the Commonwealth—in the forms of releases from the sterling balances and of private overseas investment—has been large. It appears that the total of sterling releases plus private capital exports to Commonwealth countries in the six years, 1947–1952, was in excess of $3.5 billion.[8] Since savings in the British economy during the same period were of the order of $16 billion, it is apparent how important capital exports have been in restricting resources available for investment at home.[9] If all or most of this overseas investment had been used efficiently from the standpoint of Britain's future growth, it would have been a desirable use of resources. A part of it has been so used and has been worthwhile. But a much larger part has unfortunately not been efficiently invested from the standpoint of Britain's economic future. Some of this investment has gone merely to increase purchases of British consumer goods by overseas Commonwealth countries. Much of the rest has helped to carry out poorly conceived programs of industrial expansion—for example, in Australia, where British capital has been contributing to an economic policy whose principal aim has been to create protected high-cost industries rather than to expand agricultural production. With its domestic shortage of capital so acute, the British economy can ill afford to export capital to the Commonwealth unless the major part of that capital is used to foster development programs which will enlarge Britain's future export markets and help its terms of trade.

Third, British military expenditures have been a large factor restricting the amount of resources available for domestic investment, especially since 1950. The extent to which military outlays reduce resources which might otherwise be available for investment is suggested by the fact that, in the three-year period 1951–53, annual military expenditures were equal to nearly two-thirds of the annual *gross* fixed investment made in the British economy.[10] Moreover, the interference of direct arms expenditure with industrial investment tends to be physical as well as financial,

---

[8] Converted at the present rate of exchange. This figure is the sum of net changes in the sterling balances of four independent sterling area (ISA) countries ($800 million) and an estimate of private capital exports from the United Kingdom to the Commonwealth ($2.8 billion) for approximately the six-year period, 1947–1952. In this estimate, increases in colonial sterling balances in this period have not been offset against reductions in ISA balances. See *Economic Survey of Europe Since the War, op. cit.,* p. 115.

[9] This $16 billion figure for British home saving (public and private) in the six years 1947–52 is based on data in D. H. Robertson, *op. cit.,* p. 30, converted at the present rate of exchange.

[10] See *Economic Survey 1954, op. cit.*

at least in periods of expanding arms production. Rising military procurement can compete directly with industrial investment (and with exports) for the not-very-elastic output of the capital equipment industries.

Britain's overseas expenditures and military outlays are large relative to its economic resources because Britain is trying to fill an exacting international role as head of the Commonwealth and as the major partner of the United States in the defense of the non-Soviet world. In contemporary conditions, the economic requirements of that role are too large for a country whose people are also demanding rising living standards and whose production is growing only slowly—too slowly to make possible the simultaneous satisfaction of these requirements and claims. In such circumstances, the investment on which future growth depends tends to be sacrificed to present consumption claims and to political and military requirements. Thus, an even more serious discrepancy between economic claims and requirements and economic resources is being laid up for the future.

A second major internal impediment to Britain's economic growth is weakness of enterprise in British industry. By "weakness of enterprise" is meant the prevalence in British industrial management of attitudes which put insufficient value on technological progress and the expansion of production. Much of British management prefers stability of output and maintenance of existing shares of a static market to expansion of output and technical advance. It is not a simple question of profit motive as such, or the lack of it. What is lacking is a set of values and attitudes which regards expansion of output and creation of better products and production techniques as akin to ends in themselves—or as direct means to social power and prestige for the business executive and for his firm. For example, the American business attitude toward economic activity and growth is characterized by the notion that the process of production is not just means, but that its continuous expansion and improvement are also felt to be ends in themselves. For much of the American business community, "the real aim of production . . . is the production itself, the means are more than means; they are felt as creations, as symbols of the infinite possibilities implied in man's productivity." [11] In Germany, industrialists in big business have typically been strongly motivated to expansion of output and technological advance for reasons of power and social prestige.

---

[11] Paul Tillich, *The Courage To Be* (New Haven, Conn.: Yale University Press, 1952), p. 108.

Though the contrast should not be overdrawn, the state of mind of much of British industrial management was well described by the Balfour Committee as early as 1929. The description is still largely true today:

> In dealing with such important factors in industrial efficiency as the rationalization of workshop practice, the standardization of products and processes, the higher training of managers and heads of business enterprises, the development and utilization of industrial research or commercial intelligence, and generally all forms of associated and combined action for the purpose of more efficient production or distribution, we have repeatedly been led to the conclusion that at present one of the most serious obstacles to progress is defective sympathy on the part of persons holding responsible positions in industrial and trading enterprises with new ideas and propositions which involve a radical change of customary practice, or a new orientation of outlook.[12]

The lack of interest in technical advance and expansion of output re-enforces an element in British managerial thinking which one writer has called "the architectural concept of industry"—that is, the belief that "every industry should hold a prescriptive right to its existing place in the economic structure and should claim that the Government ought to buttress it if the need should arise."[13]

British management's lack of vigor is not only a matter of subjective attitudes and motivations. It is also the result of objective conditions: insufficient profit opportunities and institutional restrictions on technical progress and competition. One of the most important—perhaps the most important—of these objective conditions has been British industry's excessive dependence on risky and relatively unexpansive export markets. Furthermore, in a slow-growing economy there are not the profit opportunities to evoke great vigor of enterprise even from those who might in a different environment prove most enterprising. Mention should also be made of British industrial and market organization. In most American industries—even those in which there is little price competition—most firms are still vigorously competitive from the viewpoint of costs, technical progress and sales promotion. In much of British industry,

---

[12] *Final Report of the Committee on Industry and Trade* (Balfour Committee), 1929, p. 245.

[13] G. C. Allen of London University, quoted in "Rethinking our Future," reprint of a series of articles from *The Observer* (London, 1952), p. 34.

however, a network of restrictive agreements designed to suppress competition in costs, products and sales promotion—as well as in prices —has been established, often with government support. Likewise, the process of industrial concentration in the United States has resulted, typically, in the large, highly rationalized and integrated firm. In Britain, however, industrial concentration has frequently resulted in the mere pooling of small firms without the reorganization and integration necessary to take full advantage of potential economies of scale.

In brief, the lack of vigor of much of British industrial management involves a vicious circle made up of subjective attitudes, narrowed economic opportunities and institutional obstacles. For this reason, the problem is extremely difficult to attack. Measures such as productivity programs or changes in business taxation, designed to affect this or that aspect in isolation, can have only minimal results, for the phenomenon stands or falls as a whole. This fact, true also of much of continental European industry, has important consequences for policy which have not yet been sufficiently recognized.

Even so brief and impressionistic an account of the main internal impediments to British economic growth would be incomplete without some reference to postwar British domestic economic policy. In the early postwar years, British policy was most immediately concerned with the pressing, practical problems of reconverting from war to peace, increasing exports from the low level to which they were reduced during the war, and struggling with inflation and with balance-of-payments difficulties. Despite this necessary preoccupation with immediate issues, the Labour Government in the years 1945–51 was also working toward the twin objectives for which it had received in 1945 a clear electoral mandate—"full employment" and "fair shares." The way these objectives were defined in practice owed much to the legacy of wartime "siege economics." It was also strongly influenced by the Fabian Socialism of the Labour Party, with its preoccupation with income equalization and with central direction of the economy and its lack of concern for economic growth and adjustment and for external economic relations. Thus, in practice, "full employment" came to mean an attempt to achieve a kind of absolute stability and security of employment, particularly by an easy money policy. "Fair shares" involved a major redistribution of income as compared with prewar (much of which had been accomplished during the war) by means of heavily progressive taxation, consumption subsidies, rationing and price controls. The consequences have been not only

greater equality among classes but also among workers in different industries and skill categories. Though often discussed, improvement of
productivity and the promotion of technological advance were in practice near the bottom of the agenda of British postwar economic policy in
the period 1945–51.

The effect of these policies on the British economy cannot, of course, be
disentangled from the effects of the postwar inflationary pressure and
acute balance-of-payments strain which afflicted most of the non-Soviet
world until 1951. Nevertheless, it appears that a somewhat anachronistic
fear of deflation and mass unemployment made it even more difficult for
the British Government in this period to deal with inflation and balance-
of-payments strain than it would otherwise have been. The strong
emphasis on income levelling helped to reduce personal saving in Britain
to a trickle—indeed, in some postwar years to eliminate it entirely. A
certain predilection for direct controls, as well as the familiar effects of
suppressed inflation itself, contributed to the relative rigidity of the
British industrial structure. Mention should also be made of the damaging effect on labor mobility and labor incentives of the too-great equalization of wage rates on a national basis. This practice—which persists
today—reflects the power of the British trade unions and the preoccupation of their leadership with a static, egalitarian conception of economic
equity and with an "architectural" conception of the right to work,
virtually to the exclusion of any concern for the growth of the national
product. Indeed, one can sense throughout the British economy that the
desire for an assured place in a relatively stable economic order has
greatly weakened the values of individualism and enterprise which were
inherited from the Victorian era—and which played so important a part
in Britain's economic rise. All these circumstances have tended to impair
the rate of growth of the British economy.

On the other side of the ledger, it should not be forgotten that full
employment and redistribution of income in Britain during and since
the war have done much to heal the deep wounds left by the bitter class
strife of the interwar period. They have apparently helped to create an
atmosphere for industrial relations which is more conducive than before the war to full labor effort and to acceptance by the trade unions,
as well as by management, of technological improvements. Nor should
the success of the Labour Government's attempt to channel domestic output into exports be ignored. Despite domestic inflation and raw materials shortages, this export drive helped to raise the volume of British

exports from 30 percent of 1938 at the end of the war to 180 percent in 1951.

Since 1950—perhaps even a little before—there has been a growing recognition in Britain of the one-sidedness of the earlier concern with full employment and income redistribution, and serious attempts have been made to give more emphasis to the flexibility of the economy and to its growth. With the subsidence of the general postwar inflation in the non-Soviet world and the recovery of British output and exports, it has been possible to overcome domestic inflation in Britain, to ease greatly the strain on the balance of payments, and to dismantle most of the complex apparatus of direct controls, for which inflation and balance-of-payments trouble were in part responsible. These changes are favorable, on the whole, to the adaptability of British industry to foreign demand, to Britain's competitive position in foreign markets and, more generally, to the possibilities of economic growth. At the same time, the present British Government has not been able to do much to correct the excessively egalitarian pattern of income distribution—excessive, that is, from the standpoint of savings, labor incentives and labor mobility. Even the overcoming of domestic inflation is probably not an unmixed blessing from a growth standpoint. In the slack world monetary climate which obtained in 1952 and 1953, it created a problem of maintaining sufficient demand to keep industrial output rising and in the right directions. This problem is almost certain to recur from time to time and is not easy to solve in an economy where industrial enterprise is insufficient and which is so heavily dependent on exports.

All these various factors, then, contribute to making Britain's economic growth too slow relative to the growth of claims and requirements. The essence of Britain's economic problem is that, unless these obstacles to growth can somehow be mitigated, the United Kingdom will be unable to satisfy rising consumption claims and simultaneously to carry out its role as head of the Commonwealth and major partner of the United States. In present circumstances, there is little to suggest that, over the next few years, the acuteness of this dilemma will be lessened. Such a situation is politically unstable. In the absence of an increase in the rate of British economic growth, the British people may well be forced by circumstances to choose between their claims for consumption and welfare and the desire of most of their present leaders that Britain continue to play an important and positive role in the world. And unless something happens to make the British people a good deal more willing to subordinate economic satisfactions to foreign policy ends than they have been since the war, the temptation will be very strong for them to shed more and more of the burdens of the Commonwealth and Atlantic Alliance and to retire into a "little England" role. This line of policy has not lacked spokesmen among the neutralist element in the Labour Party and elsewhere.

It would be difficult to exaggerate the danger to the United States in this possibility. For this reason, the Study Group believes that means to mitigate the obstacles to British economic growth, as well as political and psychological means to overcome the growing rift between our two countries, should occupy a very high place on the permanent agenda of American foreign policy.

France

The growth of the French economy since World War I, measured in terms of total real output, has been on the average less than 1 percent (cumulative) a year—slower than that of any other industrial country.[14] On a per capita basis, real income in France has grown at about the same low rate (less than 1 percent a year) as in Britain. External obstacles do not explain this slow growth, though the growth of the French economy is, of course, influenced to an important degree by the rate of expansion of its industrial exports and by the evolution of its terms of foreign trade. Slow growth is more directly and immediately the result of internal impediments, institutional in character and of a peculiarly intractable kind.

To understand these impediments, it is necessary to recognize that industrialism never achieved in France the exuberant expression which it had in 19th-century Britain and which it has today—in other and various forms—in the United States, Canada, Germany and the Soviet Union. In France, the dynamic of industrialism has always been qualified and partially frustrated by a surviving aristocratic spirit among the French leadership groups, by the strength of *petit bourgeois* attitudes, and by the traditional resistance of French national policy to international specialization. The survival of aristocratic values is reflected, for example, in the undynamic character of French industrial entrepreneurship. The *petit bourgeois* mentality finds expression in a resistance to economic concentration and in a desire to preserve a traditional

---

[14] See Colin Clark, "The Trend of Real National Product in France," *Review of Economic Progress* (Brisbane, Australia, December 1951), p. 2.

social and economic structure in which the small businessman, the *petit commerçant,* and the independent peasant predominate. Today, these historical factors help to re-enforce cartelism and restrictionism in the French economy, which are also responses to 20th-century economic conditions. Resistance to international specialization is to be seen in traditional French protectionism, greatly increased in the present century by the causes of economic nationalism discussed in Chapter 1. In the following brief review of impediments to economic growth in French agriculture, distribution and industry, an attempt is made to bring out the interaction of such historical factors with other causes of more recent origin.

The French economy is a "balanced" economy, self-sufficient in staple foodstuffs and with a large agricultural sector. Though France is usually considered an industrial country, nearly as many persons are employed in agriculture as in industry. This fact reflects the high tariff protection which French agriculture has traditionally enjoyed. It reflects also the low productivity of French agriculture. Though French agriculture employs nearly as many persons as industry, its net product is only half that of industry and its labor productivity is a third or more below that in Denmark, the Netherlands and Britain, where agriculture is more specialized and much more technically advanced.[15]

The importance of agriculture in the French economy makes its rate of growth a much more significant factor in the overall growth of the French economy than is true, for example, of British agriculture. But the present low productivity of French agriculture reflects the past low rate of growth and suggests that the obstacles which impede an acceleration of that rate are serious. For, though the natural conditions of French agriculture are on the whole quite favorable, there are serious obstacles to growth of output and productivity of an organizational and psychological character.

Most important among these obstacles are the excessive subdivision of agricultural holdings, and the fact that peasants' holdings are often not contiguous but are separated by considerable distances. In spite of postwar efforts of the French Government to facilitate the regrouping of holdings and their enlargement, the process of further subdivision has continued. "More than a third of French farms are worked by one person, 60 percent by less than three persons and only 8 percent by five persons or more. . . . This structure of French agriculture explains in

---

[15] See Ministry of Finance, *Statistiques et Etudes Financières, Supplement Finances Françaises, No. 18* (Paris, 1953), p. 213.

large part the low level of productivity." [16] The traditional conservatism of the French peasant, the reluctance of public authorities to interfere with his established ways, and the insufficient efforts of those authorities to teach advanced agricultural techniques—as, for example, is done so extensively in Britain, Denmark and the Netherlands—are also important obstacles to productivity growth.

Furthermore, the French Government operates a complex apparatus of agricultural price supports, subsidies and production controls whose effect is to support agriculturalists in their existing lines of production and thus to freeze the structure of output. No doubt, agricultural support arrangements in many countries tend to have this result in some degree, but in France the rigidifying effects of agricultural policies and controls seem to be unusually great—perhaps because they tend to be administered in a spirit of extreme economic and social conservatism. In any event, they interfere with the structural reorientation of French agriculture along the most economically promising lines—toward increasing production of wheat and animal products for export to other European countries.

This is the logical direction of development for French agriculture. The French population is nearly static and its per capita consumption of food is already quite high; consequently, its total demand for food will rise only slowly. Therefore, if the efficiency of use of French agricultural land and manpower is to increase more rapidly, it must involve a large expansion of French agricultural exports to other European countries which have lower per capita food consumption, more rapidly expanding populations, or large food deficits. [17] Considering Western Europe's need to economize on dollar imports, it would be good "European economics" for France to sell large tonnages of wheat, meat and dairy products to Germany, Italy and Britain. The French economy

---

[16] *Ibid*. "Even in the Loire Valley and in Normandy, the average size of farm is smaller than in other parts of northern Europe—smaller than in the Midland plain of England or in East Anglia, where conditions are not widely different. Over the whole of France, it is probable that 75–80% of all holdings are of under 25 acres; in England and Wales the corresponding percentage is about 40." PEP, "France—Some Economic Factors," *Planning* (London, May 26, 1952), p. 267.

[17] Theoretically, the growth of the productivity of French agriculture could be accelerated without much expansion of total agricultural output, provided that the flow of agricultural labor into industrial employment could also be substantially accelerated. Practically, however, the obstacles to the more rapid expansion of French industry and industrial employment are so serious that an increase in the rate of growth of French agricultural productivity will require a large expansion of French agricultural exports.

could certainly do so if the difficulties on the side of supply could be mitigated. But this would require an effectively integrated European market for major agricultural products and assurance to French agricultural producers of the continuity and stability of their new markets in other European countries.

The institutional impediments to French economic growth which are derived from the desire to maintain a large class of small, independent businessmen are especially evident in the distributive trades. This desire is reflected both in public policies and private arrangements whose purpose is to restrict competition in order to provide distributive margins sufficient to make it possible for a host of *petits commerçants*—operating tiny, inefficient establishments—to earn a very modest living. The results are a large sector of the French economy in which productivity is completely stagnant or even declining and a disproportionately heavy burden of distribution costs on the rest of the economy. Thus, distribution in France absorbs a larger share of the national income (16 percent) and a larger part of the labor force (11 percent) than in any other West European country.[18] These proportions have increased considerably since the prewar period—a fact which points to a decline in real product per person employed in distribution.[19] No doubt high costs and low labor productivity (by American standards) in distribution are general throughout Western Europe, but French distribution is in a class by itself.

In French industry, the most intractable obstacles to growth result from the weakness of enterprise, from restrictive attitudes, and from widespread restrictive practices. The growth of French industrial output and of labor productivity in industry has been slower over the past 25 or 30 years than in any other industrial country except Belgium,[20] and a large part of the cause is these institutional and psychological factors.

---

[18] See Ministry of Finance, *op. cit.*, pp. 206–208. The tiny size of most French wholesale and retail establishments is suggested by the fact that the average number of persons per establishment is less than two. The United States has four times the population of France but only two and a half times the number of retail outlets.

[19] Particularly in view of the fact that the proportion of consumption goods sold through commercial outlets to total output has fallen since the prewar period because of the greater increase of capital goods than of consumer goods production.

[20] See, e.g., United Nations Economic Commission for Europe, *Economic Survey of Europe in 1949* (Geneva, 1950), Chapter 8, and Institut National de la Statistique et des Affaires Economiques, *Quelques Aspects Fondamentaux de L'Economie Mondiale* (Paris, 1951), pp. 149–151.

Much of what has been said about the weakness of enterprise in Britain, and about its subjective and objective aspects, applies with even greater emphasis to French industrial entrepreneurship. Though there are conspicuous exceptions, the motivation of most French industrial management is deficient from the standpoint of economic growth. In French industry, the owner-proprietor and the family firm are still general. Typically, the French industrialist's motivation is not to raise output, modernize his plant, improve his product, reduce costs, or increase the size, power or reputation of his firm. It is rather to run the business so as to preserve the economic base of a middle- or upper-class social status for his family. In this, there is something surviving of the spirit of the *ancien régime*. To a considerable extent, French entrepreneurial groups do not find great personal satisfaction in actively exercising the important social responsibility of controlling industry and promoting the nation's economic growth. Nor do they generally recognize that their economic activities entail any social responsibility at all. Their personal economic ideal is that of the *rentier* or the 18th-century *haute bourgeoisie,* whose privileges were real but whose obligations were nominal. A society whose economically powerful members do not consider increasing output or higher standards of living major economic and social goals is naturally not likely to generate that general dedication to economic activity as a way of life that has marked so much of American society, particularly the business community. Moreover, the absence of such personal values and social attitudes has diminished the attractiveness of careers in business management for the most able and aggressive individuals of the French nation. Instead, they have sought careers in the army, the civil service, politics, the professions or the arts. This tendency has been re-enforced by the practice of restricting top management positions in French industry to the sons or heirs of existing owners or managers, to those who marry into established industrial families, to those possessing the leverage of a financial interest, and to the few others who can afford to acquire a degree from a university or a technical institution.

Restrictive market organization is even more typical of French, than of British, industry and its control seems to be tighter and more effective. Restrictionism in French industry reflects the values and attitudes mentioned above and the desire to preserve a large class of small independent businessmen which we have noted in the structure of French distribution. Such restrictionism goes back at least to World War I. It developed rapidly during the 1930's and was greatly strengthened during World War II by the Vichy Government's corporative conception of economic policy. The Vichy Government used existing cartels and other inter-producer arrangements as administrative arms of the state and thereby greatly strengthened their hold on industry.[21]

The spirit animating inter-producer arrangements in French industry is one of unrelieved restrictionism and protectionism; it is the "economics of organized stagnation." In general, prices and market shares are fixed at levels which provide the least efficient member firms with a comfortable profit margin. Even where productivity increases do occur in particular enterprises, the result may be neither price reductions nor production increases. Instead, the profits of these firms rise and their labor force may actually be reduced. The system of market organization provides neither the incentive nor the capital needed for increased productivity to the least efficient firms which have the smallest—but still secure—profit margins. Yet the modernization or liquidation of these many small businesses is essential to any general improvement in the rate of growth of productivity in French industry. The remarkable report of the French Finance Ministry on the basic ills of the French economy, issued in 1953, sums up the picture of restrictive agreements and practices in the following forthright fashion:

> The sclerosis of competition in the French economy is much deeper and more widespread than the precise terms of restrictive agreements, explicit or secret, would suggest. It results from a whole series of practices flowing from a state of mind which permeates the French economy. The objective sought by these practices is to assure a certain total of profit which is then divided up, by explicit or tacit understanding. The absence of competition permits a great number of obsolete economic cells to survive alongside a few efficient concerns. The consumer bears the whole burden of supporting them all, including the most backward firms. The result is that the national economy is no longer a profit economy; it tends rather to be a rent economy. The whole system leads to low productivity and high prices.[22]

---

[21] During World War II, under a series of *comités d'organization professionelle,* "industrial self-government" with strong price and production control powers was established. The *comités* were officially disbanded at the time of liberation, but in effect most of the instruments they created still exist, the main change brought about by post-liberation governments being the removal of the governmental supervision to which they were formerly subject.

[22] Ministry of Finance, *op. cit.,* p. 198. The quotation has been somewhat shortened in translation.

It should be added that French Government policy has generally supported this state of things, just as it has supported parallel restrictions on competition and enterprise in agriculture and distribution.

Another significant limitation on the growth of output and productivity in French industry is the low mobility of labor. Labor mobility in the French economy is substantially less than in Britain. Like most of the other internal obstacles to French economic growth, labor immobility is no new phenomenon of the postwar period. Both before and since the war, some areas and some industries have been short of labor while other areas have been characterized by unemployment or underemployment. The remarkable stability of the occupational distribution of the French labor force during the last thirty years reflects this low mobility, as well as the slow growth of French industry.

It is easier to point to the existence of low labor mobility in France than to be sure of its causes. The housing shortage, due to widespread destruction of housing during the war and a very low rate of housebuilding since 1945, is certainly a factor. The principle of equal treatment among industries and localities in payment of wages and social benefits to industrial workers has been applied even more consistently in France than in the United Kingdom. The high profit margins in industry, supported by restrictive arrangements, have made possible the widespread practice of keeping men on at reduced hours when output falls, thus tending to freeze the distribution of industrial labor and to create numerous pockets of hidden underemployment. Likewise, it seems that persons unable to obtain industrial work in a familiar locality often find it easier to get local employment in the already swollen distribution and service trades than to move elsewhere in search of other opportunities in industry.

Finally, industrial growth in France is limited by the special difficulty of maintaining a general level of demand in the French economy sufficient to keep industry operating near capacity, but without setting off undue price inflation. The difficulty is shown by the following facts. The periods of rapid expansion of industrial output in France since the war have also been periods of rapid increase of prices, as in 1946–49 and 1951. Conversely, periods of price stability have been periods in which industrial production has stagnated, as in September 1949–September 1950 and again in 1952–53. It has apparently not been possible to combine a sustained increase in industrial production with reasonable price stability. Postwar French Governments have thus been forced to choose between industrial stagnation and price inflation, with the serious consequences of the former for the rate of growth and of the latter for political unrest and the competitive position of French exports.

This dilemma arises essentially from two causes: the many rigidities created in the French economy by the institutional factors already described and a hypersensitivity to upward price changes (a "volatility of price expectations") which reflects a fundamental lack of confidence in the franc. This lack of confidence in the currency is not surprising in view of the long history of French inflation dating back to 1914. In the postwar years, as demand has risen, output soon presses against capacity in some sectors while in others unemployment and underutilization of equipment persists. The price rises in the fully employed sectors have tended to set off widespread sympathetic increases in other prices; speculative hoarding of materials, gold and foreign exchange; and demands for general wage increases. An inflationary spiral is soon underway despite the fact that excess capacity persists in many sectors. Thus, the French economic authorities have found it difficult to use general monetary and fiscal controls to fight inflation without bringing on stagnation; or, conversely, to move from recession to full employment without bringing on an inflationary spiral. For in any economy, the effectiveness of monetary and fiscal policy in maintaining full employment without inflation depends on a reasonable elasticity of output in most sectors—i.e., on some mobility of resources among sectors—and on confidence in the currency. Both these prerequisites have apparently been lacking in France.

In sum, the picture of the institutional structure of the French economy which emerges from this brief review is one in which motivations and economic incentives are weak and much economic activity is misdirected. It is an economy in which, in the words of *The Economist,* "economic activity is directed neither by the conscious choice of planners nor by the incentives and penalties of a free price mechanism, . . . an economy in which the perpetuation of privilege and the survival of the unfit are the unwritten principle." [23] Government policy and controls are an integral part of this structure. French economic policy has, as the Ministry of Finance Report quoted above asserts, "established a regime in which the word 'intervention' has become

---

[23] *The Economist,* "France's Economic Ills" (London, August 22, 1953).

synonymous with anarchy, in which political pressure has replaced competition in the market." [24]

This is not to say that French postwar economic policy has been generally unenlightened. Working within very narrow political limitations—much narrower than those imposed on other Western governments—some postwar French Governments have made real attempts to increase the rate of growth of the French economy. To date, the most important of these attempts has been the Plan of Modernization and Equipment—the Monnet Plan.[25] With the Monnet Plan, the French Government made a serious and fairly successful effort to use public funds to expand industrial capacity in the "basic sectors" of the economy, such as coal, steel, transportation, electric power and agricultural machinery. The theory of the Monnet Plan was that expansion and modernization of capacity in a few key sectors would eliminate actual or potential bottlenecks and reduce costs for industry generally and for agriculture, thereby permitting, and at the same time stimulating, a more rapid general expansion. By and large, the Plan has been successful, within the limitations of available financing, for the basic sectors themselves. But, unfortunately, other factors—particularly the institutional obstacles already discussed—have to a large extent prevented the Plan from having its intended effect on manufacturing industries generally and on agriculture.

Nor should it be overlooked, in any criticism of French economic policy, that it was a French Government which first seriously proposed what seems to be the only means by which the institutional obstacles to French economic growth could gradually be broken down—namely, the creation of a European political and economic union. Despite the more recent reluctance of the French Government to move ahead with this policy, many Frenchmen have recognized that it is only within a European union that it might be possible to loosen the grip on the French economy of the dense tangle of private restrictions and uneconomic public regulations which now fetter it.

It appears, then, that until radical steps of that kind can be taken, the growth of the French economy will continue to be seriously impeded by

---

[24] Ministry of Finance, *op. cit.*, p. 199.

[25] For an official account of the production and investment targets and the progress of the Monnet Plan, see Commissariat du Plan, *Cinq Ans du Plan de Modernization et d'Equipement* (Paris, 1952).

obstacles of an institutional character. What does this suggest for the prospects of French economic health?

French society is now split by class tensions which have both an economic and a traditional basis. The distribution of income in France is quite uneven by British or American standards, to the disadvantage of urban wage earners, the peasants in the poor agricultural regions, and agricultural laborers and sharecroppers. In the majority of Western countries, there has been a shift in income distribution in favor of some or all of these groups since before the war. In France, however, it appears that urban wage and salary earners receive, per capita, a slightly smaller proportion of the national income and only about the same real earnings as before the war, although their working hours are now longer and their hourly productivity is a little higher.[26] If the bitter class antagonisms that tore prewar France are recalled, and the fact of expanding economic expectations is considered, one must feel concern for the future of the French nation on the basis of these economic data alone. To them must be added the fact that class tensions in France (and, as will be seen, in Italy as well) are greatly intensified, and their resolution rendered doubly difficult, by historical factors—which, moreover, make these antagonisms peculiarly susceptible to a Marxist "interpretation" and to communist exploitation. Reinhold Niebuhr puts it succinctly:

> If the dynamics of an industrial society are superimposed on the class distinctions of a feudal order, the psychological facts correspond much more closely to the Marxist picture of class antagonisms than they do in a purer bourgeois community, such as our own. . . . Significantly, the only Western European nations in which Communism is now a living creed, Italy and France, are those in which the historical dynamism of modern industrialism has never shattered the traditional feudal ethos. In France, where feudalism was ostensibly broken by the classic bourgeois revolution, the bourgeoisie adopted the restrictive and undynamic social attitudes of the older feudalism and created a society in which the middle classes make no great efforts to increase productivity and fight desperately to prevent the working classes from gaining a larger share of productive wealth.[27]

---

[26] See, e.g., Ministry of Finance, *op. cit.*, p. 186.
[27] *The Irony of American History* (New York: Chas. Scribner's Sons, 1952), pp. 103, 111.

In the context of such acute class divisions and of the political conflicts to which they give rise, it is politically impossible to ease tensions
by the British method of redistributing income through taxation. It is
widely acknowledged in France that wage and salary earners bear a
quite disproportionately heavy share of the French tax burden, while
the more prosperous peasants and numerous small businessmen pay
only a small part of what, in justice, they should. But the latter groups
use their political strength to block the fiscal reforms which would dis-
tribute income and the tax burden more equitably. Nor, as long as economic growth is so slow, is it possible to solve the problem by the American method of increasing the real income of all groups simultaneously.

In addition to this acute problem of income distribution and class
conflict, France, like Britain, has been carrying economic and military
commitments—the NATO rearmament effort, the Indochina war, the
maintenance of French rule in North Africa, and investment in the
colonies—too large for its slow-growing resources. These burdens, like
Britain's similar burdens, have been borne in the interest of the whole
Western Community. They reflect also the desire of some Frenchmen
to continue to play a political and military role in the world which is
unfortunately beyond their country's economic capabilities, given the
growing size of the requirements of that role and the inadequate growth
of the French economy. And, as in Britain's case, the attempt to meet
these requirements has aggravated the growth problem by reducing the
resources available for domestic investment.

The danger of this situation is that France may react to the economic
burdens of its international position in a negative and unrealistic manner, by giving up unilaterally a large part of these commitments and re-
tiring into a nationalist-neutralist foreign policy which will make European unification impossible and will undermine the Atlantic Alliance.
It is desirable—in fact necessary—that the burden of these requirements
on the French economy be substantially reduced, as is now widely recognized. But the problem is to carry out their reduction in close cooperation with the United States and other Western countries, in a manner
which does not endanger the vital interests of the West and which
leaves the French, not in a neutralist "little France" mood, but of a
mind to resume their leadership for European unification. The reduction of military and colonial burdens will not be sufficient by itself to
solve France's economic problems. The only visible hope for a re-
vitalization of the French economy—and of French democracy—lies in

the formation of a European union within an Atlantic framework. To achieve that goal in present circumstances demands of the United States a kind of creative and far-sighted statesmanship which we have not exhibited since the inception of the Marshall Plan and the North Atlantic Treaty.

West Germany

Because its recovery lagged two or three years behind that of the rest of industrial Europe, the West German economy is only now emerging from a recovery phase. For, German economic recovery began in earnest only in 1948—after the belated but highly effective currency reform—and for some time thereafter it was hampered by interzonal boundaries, the absence of effective central government, and uncertainties about Western policy. Though production has recovered very rapidly since 1948, the West German economy has not yet fully taken up its slack. The labor force has been greatly expanded over the prewar level—much more than in the rest of industrial Europe—by refugees from the East. As far as labor and plant capacity are concerned, there is still room for rapid expansion before full utilization is achieved.[28] Similarly, on the side of demand, war-caused arrears of industrial investment, construction and consumption have not yet been made up. Thus the rate of growth of the West German economy is still more strongly influenced by "recovery" factors than by long-term limitations.

For this reason, the rate of growth of German output in the last few years gives much less indication of longer-run problems and possibilities than in the cases of Britain and France. The following prognosis for West Germany must therefore be more tentative than that given for Britain and France, where the factors determining longer-term growth

---

[28] Industrial production in West Germany rose from an index (1938 = 100) of 52 in 1948 to 120 in 1952, 131 in 1953, and an estimated 142 in 1954, which was still below the 1954 British index of approximately 160 on a 1938 base. However, the comparison is not exact since there was full employment in Germany but not in Britain in the base year. The existence of some remaining slack in West German industry is suggested by several facts: (1) output per manhour in West German industry has only recently passed its 1938 level, as compared with some 30 percent above 1938 in British industry; (2) there is still registered unemployment equivalent to 5 percent of the wage- and salary-earning labor force in West Germany and the labor force is still being increased by the inflow of Eastern refugees; and (3) productive capacity in the consumer goods industries is still considerably underutilized, a fact which is reflected in the level of output per manhour in industry.

trends have been more clearly revealed. Let us consider first the internal factors, particularly the supply of capital and the quality of industrial enterprise and organization, and then turn to the question of export markets. As we shall see, internal factors seem to be generally favorable to the maintenance of an adequate rate of growth. It is export markets which will probably be the major factor limiting the rate of West German economic growth after recovery is completed.

In comparison with Britain and France, the internal determinants of West Germany's longer-run rate of growth of output and productivity are distinctly more favorable. Labor mobility seems to be fairly high, thanks in part to the large postwar inflow of refugees from the East. The supply of savings—both private savings and business savings—is substantially higher relative to national income, and consumption and government services are relatively lower, than in the United Kingdom and France. It appears that the level, and the degree of political effectiveness, of consumption claims are lower than in other West European countries, as indicated by the acquiescence of German labor in a reduced ratio of wages and salaries to national income as compared with prewar. Consumption has been restricted by a tax system which is more regressive than that of prewar Germany or of most other Western countries today.[29] Social services and other transfer payments occupy a substantially smaller part of the German than of the French and British national budgets. Moreover, German savings have not had to be diverted for political reasons to relatively unproductive or slow-yielding foreign investments, as in the cases of Britain and France.

These differences, as well as a proportionately lower level of military expenditures (occupation costs), make it possible for the West German economy to achieve a substantially higher rate of domestic investment relative to output than can Britain and France.[30] This advantage of

---

[29] See *Economic Survey of Europe Since the War, op. cit.,* p. 74, and Department of State, Office of Intelligence Research, *Postwar Monetary and Fiscal Policies in Western Germany* (OIR Report No. 5171, May 1951), p. 38.

[30] Compare the following breakdowns of gross domestic expenditure in West Germany and the United Kingdom in 1952:

	West Germany	United Kingdom
Personal consumption	56%	68%
Government consumption	18	19
Investment in fixed assets	21	13
Increase in inventories	5	—
	100%	100%

the German economy from a growth standpoint will probably persist, though doubtless in lesser degree, for the next decade barring disruptive political changes, which are always possible. It reflects a greater political tolerance for income inequality, a relative political weakness of organized labor, and a greater propensity to save on the part of other classes— factors which are not likely to change drastically very soon.

German industry is usually credited with a vigor of enterprise and a capacity for technological innovation and adaptation second only to that of American industry. Perhaps this overstates the case. What foreigners often think of as the characteristic aggressiveness and vigor of German industrial management is confined to those capital goods sectors which are dominated by large firms: coal, steel, chemicals, heavy engineering, optical instruments and automotive vehicles being the principal examples. The great bulk of the German consumer goods industries and distributive trades is in the hands of small or very small concerns which are no more energetic nor technically progressive, and no more competitive, than their British counterparts.

It is useful to speculate about the reasons why the German "heavy" and export industries contrast so sharply in this respect with the rest of German production and distribution. Purely economic causes play a part. Relative to the United States and Britain, Germany is still a poor country with a rather unequal income distribution. The thin domestic market for consumers goods offers restricted opportunity for the kind of enterprise in merchandising and in consumer product innovation which is so characteristic of the American economy. More important were the late timing and the historical context of German industrialization. Late industrialization forced the German export effort into the development of new capital goods. It made attractive the adoption of

---

Likewise, the composition of domestic investment in fixed assets in 1952 seems to have been somewhat more "productive" in West Germany than in the United Kingdom.

	West Germany	*United Kingdom*
Fixed investment in:		
Equipment	58%	52%
Housing	22	24
Other building	20	24
	100%	100%

Sources: West Germany: Office of the U.S. High Commissioner to Germany, *Handbook of Economic Statistics* (Bonn, 1954).
United Kingdom: Central Statistical Office, *National Income and Expenditure 1946–1952* (London, August, 1953), pp. 2, 62.

special organization forms (the large combine and the cartel) able to use concentrated economic power to find a place in highly competitive export markets. These forms of organization have also proved conducive to high qualities of enterprise and technical creativity on the part of management.

The cartel form of market organization is not, of course, confined to the German capital goods industries. It exists quite generally throughout German industry. But in the capital goods sector, unlike the consumers goods industries, the principal function of cartels has been the joint exploitation of export markets, and not merely the regulation of prices, production and competition in the domestic market. In this export function, cartels have proved to be a successful institutional form. This is not the place to attempt a general assessment of their economic effects, but one tentative hypothesis may be suggested. In the consumers goods industries, the existence of cartels linking numerous small firms has probably led to maintenance of considerable excess capacity and has contributed to the generally unprogressive business policy characteristic of these industries, just as the similar forms of market organization have had similar effects even more generally in British and French industry. But in the German export and capital goods industries, which are characteristically dominated by large firms, the cartels have not apparently had a negative effect on enterprise and innovation, though they have, of course, prevented domestic price competition and have doubtless supported large monopolistic profits and considerable excess capacity. On the contrary, they have apparently contributed to the technical progressiveness and to the competitive ability of these industries in export markets. The absence of domestic price competition in these industries seems to have been irrelevant to, or perhaps even a positive factor in, their growth.

Moreover, because these capital goods and export industries were also the most important for Germany's growing military strength, they enjoyed a special prestige in the buoyant nationalistic atmosphere of pre-1914 Germany. They were then, and still are, able to attract and hold vigorous personalities in competition with the traditionally more prestigeful German professions of soldier, civil servant and *Akademiker*. For they too, unlike the distributive trades and consumer industries, offer opportunities to exercise power in large undertakings and to share in the prestige associated with national aggrandizement.

Business achievement and wealth have not in themselves been objects of notable respect [in Germany], except where they have been attained on a colossal scale, so great that their direct connection with the national interest, in which the Army, the bureaucracy and the learned professions were supposed to be working, was clear and obvious. This has put a high value on massive business achievements, but very little on those of a minor kind. Moreover, it has put a high value on achievement in those fields which make a direct contribution to Germany's economic strength and development—coal, steel, chemicals, industrial engineering—and relatively little value on achievement in consumers goods' industries. Germany has always been possessed of a number of aggressive and individualistic businessmen and industrial leaders who could never find an honorable place in German society commensurate with their ambitions except in dynamic leadership of large production organizations devoted especially to exploiting the all-important export markets.[31]

Thus it happens that the best German entrepreneurial and managerial talent is concentrated in the capital goods industries which account for the great bulk of Germany's exports. This suggests that Germany's chances in the prospective struggle for export markets are good relative to those of the rest of industrial Europe, at least in markets (like the Western Hemisphere) where competition among the European countries is on an equal basis. It has, however, another and less favorable implication. It means that the rate of Germany's future economic growth is doubly dependent on expanding export markets—not only because German industry as a whole is fairly heavily and increasingly dependent on exports, but also because the export industries are those on which growth particularly depends.[32] For, technical advance and the growth of productivity in other German industries and in the distributive trades is likely to be quite slow.

What, then, are West Germany's industrial export prospects? Again,

---

[31] W. N. Parker, "Entrepreneurial Attitudes and Response in the German Economy," July 1953 (unpublished memorandum).

[32] See International Monetary Fund, *International Financial News* (June 25, 1954), p. 399, and Office of the U.S. High Commissioner to Germany, *op. cit.* The increased postwar dependence of major German capital goods industries on exports as compared with 1936, noted in the IMF publication, is due to a considerable extent to the postwar division of Germany into two parts and to the fact that rearmament was well underway in 1936. It reflects also the fact that the German economy has outgrown its own markets and resources (in the sense explained in the preceding chapter) and that its growth now tends to increase the dependence of its industry on foreign trade.

the question is difficult to answer because the data for the last few years reflect the rapid recovery of German exports from the very low levels of 1948–49. There are, however, indications that the purchasing power of the export markets to which Germany has access is not sufficient to support for long anything like the rate of increase of West German exports of the last few years.[33] Moreover, West German industry has no protected colonial or Sterling Area markets. The relatively favorable export position it enjoyed in Southeastern Europe before the war has been wiped out. It has been severed from its large markets in East Germany. In short, despite the competitive qualities of German export industries, their longer-run prospects are not encouraging, though in the shorter-run they will probably continue to recover prewar markets and to expand their share of world exports. But when this recovery is complete, German exports will feel the effects of the inadequate expansion of world markets for manufactures and of American competition discussed in the preceding chapter.

West Germany's economic growth problem, then, is likely to be a lack of sufficient opportunity to expand exports. How serious a problem it may be cannot yet be foreseen. It could be serious enough to mean that the West German economy would have considerable difficulty maintaining full employment for a growing labor force—i.e., maintaining a level of investment sufficient to utilize fully the high rate of savings associated with the German pattern of income distribution and relatively high propensity to save. When domestic investment and consumption arrears have been made up, a serious retardation of the growth of exports could lead to that result. It could lead also to a revival of Schachtian trade policies.

The significance for the United States of West Germany's potential export problem is not, however, to be found primarily in possible effects on employment or on consumption. It does not appear that economic expectations in Germany are now such that difficulties of this kind would be likely to have political repercussions as serious as would be the case in Britain, France—or even the United States itself—in similar

---

[33] The volume of West German exports increased 11 percent from 1951 to 1952, 12 percent from 1952 to 1953, and an estimated 12 percent from 1953 to 1954. Office of the U.S. High Commissioner for Germany, *op. cit.* But a substantial part of this increase has been financed by credit extended to other Western European countries through the European Payments Union and by means of bilateral credits to other countries.

circumstances. The political problem is rather that the frustration of German exports would tend to lead important business and other groups in West Germany to support a neutralist, or even an anti-Western, foreign policy in the illusory hope of buying with political concessions greater market opportunities in Soviet Europe. Spokesmen for this policy are already to be heard in West Germany, and there has been among German business groups a traditional view that their economic opportunities lie to the East and Southeast—an attitude which seems to have survived to a surprising degree despite the advance of the Iron Curtain.

These economic factors alone would hardly be sufficient to bring about so crucial a shift of German foreign policy. Unfortunately, however, there is danger that they will re-enforce political and psychological pressures working in the same direction. Such pressures are already present in the desire of many West Germans to put German re-unification ahead of all other foreign policy objectives. These pressures are being greatly—perhaps critically—increased as the patient and constructive efforts of the postwar German Government to work with the West are frustrated by French refusal to continue the process of European unification and by Britain's understandable fear of German competition. The coincidence of these three factors—frustration of exports, frustration of Chancellor Adenauer's policy of unifying Germany irrevocably with the West, and the desire for re-unification with the lost provinces—could, in time, bring about a change in German foreign policy that would mean the defeat of the United States' most important postwar European objectives. Soviet policy with respect to Germany and France has increasingly based its strategy on the opportunity which this possibility opens.

For the same reason, the aim of American strategy must be to prevent this possibility from becoming a reality. As far as economic factors are concerned—and without exaggerating their importance—it is perhaps fair to say that no American foreign economic policy which fails to hold the promise of making room for German export expansion is doing its part to assure the continued Western orientation of West Germany. As the preceding chapter has shown, this will be a hard condition to satisfy. It can nevertheless be met if sufficient progress is made in European economic unification and German participation in overseas development.

Italy

The growth of the Italian economy over the last half century has been slow. It might have been supposed that, starting from a much lower level, Italian economic progress in the 20th century would have been more rapid than in countries where industrialization began much earlier. But this has not been true. The Italian national income has grown too slowly to narrow the gap between Italian living standards and those of the other industrial countries. For example, since 1900, real income per capita in Italy has grown no more rapidly than in Britain and France and much more slowly than in the United States.[34] Today, per capita income in Italy is about one-sixth of that in the United States, one-third of that in Britain, one-half of that in France, and two-thirds of that in West Germany. Outside the three northwestern provinces, where most of Italian industry is concentrated, and the capital city, Italy remains an economically underdeveloped and overpopulated country.

The slowness of Italian economic growth can be explained in large part by two circumstances. One is the late start of Italian industrialization: for historical reasons—particularly, the lateness of Italian political unification—Italian industrialization was not fairly begun until the first decade of the present century. The other is Italy's poor endowment of natural resources.

Because of the poverty of natural resources in relation to population, Italy's industrial growth was from the beginning heavily dependent on foreign trade. Lacking adequate domestic supplies of fuel and materials, Italian industry could grow only by expanding exports to pay for the necessary increased imports of raw materials. Similarly, the expanding food requirements of a growing urban population could not be met without a continuing increase of food imports, for good arable land in Italy was, and remains, too scarce to supply these needs domestically.[35]

---

[34] In the fifty-year period 1901–1951, the real national income of Italy approximately doubled while population grew 43 percent. See Bruno Foa, "The Italian Economy: Growth Factors and Bottlenecks," paper delivered at Social Science Research Council Conference on Economic Growth, April 9–10, 1954, p. 3 (mimeographed). This means that real national income and real income per capita grew respectively 1.4 percent and 0.9 percent per year on a cumulative basis during this period. Comparable figures for Britain, France and the United States are given earlier in this chapter.

[35] The amount of agricultural land per agricultural worker in Italy is 25 percent less than in Germany, half as small as in the Netherlands, nine times smaller than in Great Britain and almost fifteen times smaller than in the United States.

But, because of the late start of Italian industrialization, the necessary expansion of foreign trade was inhibited by the increasingly unfavorable international economic environment—an environment far less favorable than that which the older industrial countries enjoyed earlier at a comparable stage of their development. It is true that Britain's economic growth in the 20th century—and to a lesser extent that of the other older European industrial countries—have also suffered from dependence on the increasingly unfavorable external environment. There is, however, an important difference. The British economy encountered serious external obstacles to growth only after it had already attained a high level of per capita income. Italy's growth was stunted from the beginning. A late start and a poverty of natural resources have meant that Italy has never had the opportunity to maintain an adequate rate of growth for more than a few years at a time.

It remains true today and for the foreseeable future that the critical obstacles to Italy's economic growth are external. Internal factors are, on the whole, favorable except for population pressure and a low level of general education. At least, internal factors would allow a rate of growth considerably higher than external limitations now permit. For example, industrial entrepreneurship in Italy is relatively vigorous, and much of Italian industry has been characterized by high qualities of enterprise. There has been a readiness to adopt and to adapt foreign technology, and notable initiative has been shown in seeking foreign trade outlets. Italian industrial science and engineering have been quite creative, and the traditional excellence of Italian design still flourishes. True, restrictive forms of market organization exist in Italian industry; indeed, they are widespread. But they do not seem to be nearly so important a limitation on industrial expansion and technological advance as they are in France and Britain.

As far as the rate of domestic capital formation is concerned, the critical limitations seem likewise to be external rather than internal. The volume of domestic capital formation in Italy is not limited primarily by the supply of domestic savings, as it is in Britain. Savings as a percent of national income are relatively high and military expenditures absorb a smaller share of Italian than of British and French resources. The rate of domestic investment in Italy tends to be immediately limited less by the availability of domestic resources than by the strain on the Italian balance of payments which results from a high rate of domestic investment. For, in a country which is so poor in natural resources relative to population, any increase in investment expenditure induces a large increase in imports of food and industrial materials.[36] Unless exports are expanding rapidly, or foreign capital is available in large volume, there is balance-of-payments strain that must be countered by policies —e.g., restriction of credit and of imports—which limit the rate of investment to a level insufficient to allow full utilization of domestic savings and of existing industrial facilities. Thus, in the postwar period, the anticipated effect of expanding investment on the balance of payments, as well as fear of inflation, have caused the Italian financial authorities to keep a tight rein on credit and public investment—probably tighter than was necessary—at considerable cost to the growth of Italian production and employment.

Some responsibility for the low rate of growth of the Italian economy may be charged to the misallocation of Italian resources by public authorities. In the interwar period, for example, uneconomic industries were fostered for military or prestige reasons. The Italian mechanical industry still contains many plants which can now be used only with large government subsidies—monuments to the waste of Italy's economic resources under fascism. Less obvious, but in sum more important, have been the adverse effects of population pressure and chronic unemployment. These conditions are in large part responsible for the strong political pressure to use public investment not in the most productive ways but primarily as a means of spreading employment as widely as possible—often on mere "make work" projects.

Yet these internal factors have not, in the aggregate, been a major brake on Italy's economic development. The critical obstacle to Italian economic growth has been, and remains, its direct dependence on the rate at which Italy's foreign trade can be expanded.[37] The history of

---

[36] For example, it is roughly estimated that 100 billion lire of additional public expenditure in Italy gives rise to an increase of 33 billion lire in imports. See *Economic Survey of Europe in 1953, op. cit.*, p. 140.

[37] For example, a recent study by the Rome Mission of the Mutual Security Agency concludes that, to expand the Italian GNP by one-third, would require a 40 percent increase in the volume of imports—and therefore presumably a 40 percent increase in the volume of exports, and/or an increasing rate of foreign investment in Italy, in order to pay for them. The major reason why imports would have to increase more than GNP is that "the domestic production of almost all agricultural products . . . is likely to be held down by capacity limits. In other words, total requirements are all likely to expand more than domestic production can accomplish. This is true in spite of the fact that total requirements of these products are likely to increase less than for industrial products in general. Thus agriculture may justifiably be called the principal bottleneck of the Italian economy." Mutual Security Agency, Rome Mission, *The Structure of the*

Italian economic development makes clear that Italy's rate of economic growth has been reasonably adequate only during the relatively brief periods when foreign exchange resources were sufficient to pay for a steadily expanding volume of imports. These have been periods when rapid expansion of exports was possible, as in 1900–1913 and for a few years in the 1920's, or when foreign capital was available in large volume, as during the Marshall Plan.

The growth of the Italian economy has not only been slow; it has been inadequate—i.e., insufficient to keep up with the expansion of economic requirements and claims. The clearest evidence of inadequacy is the fact that economic growth has been manifestly insufficient to relieve Italian population pressure. Here, too, some part of the trouble can be blamed on Italy's late start in industrialization. In the older industrial countries, serious population pressure was avoided, or soon overcome, because industrialization coincided with the acceleration of population growth that occurred generally in Europe during the 19th century. In Italy, however, population pressure had already become serious before industrialization began. The subsequent rate of economic growth has been insufficient to prevent it from getting progressively worse— particularly after World War I, when outlets for large-scale emigration were closed. Thus, during the interwar period, the number of Italians of working age (15–64) was increasing by 200,000 to 250,000 each year, while new employment opportunities were increasing, on the average, by only 50,000 each year.[38] A similar discrepancy persists today.

The results of the long-standing disparity between the growth of population and of jobs are today visible on all sides in Italy. The Italian ratio of employment to total population is well below that of other European industrial countries, while the Italian ratio of agricultural employment to total employment is higher. There has been urban unemployment in Italy of a chronic, "structural" character for the last twenty years; since the war it has remained in the neighborhood of 1 to 1.5 million persons and shows no sign of disappearing. There is widespread underemployment, particularly in agriculture but also in industry, distribution and government services. In all, a quarter of the Italian labor force is either unemployed or works less than the normal

---

Italian Economy if the OEEC Expansion Goal is Attained (Rome, 1953), p. 15 (mimeographed).

[38] See Economic Cooperation Administration, *Italy, Country Study* (February 1949), p. 8.

40 hour week, not counting the large unmeasurable underemployment in agriculture.[39]

It is sometimes said that Italy's population problem is mainly the result of an abnormally high rate of population growth, but this is a one-sided view of the matter. The Italian population has not been growing unusually fast. In recent years, it has grown no faster than the population of the United States or the Netherlands and considerably slower than those of many underdeveloped countries. Granted that Italy's economic health would be better today if, over the past generation, the birth rate had been lower and emigration larger, it nonetheless remains true that the real trouble is the inadequate growth of the Italian economy. Unless emigration increases and foreign trading opportunities expand, population growth at even the present rate remains a serious problem.

Apart from a chronic failure to create sufficient employment opportunities, the Italian economy has also failed persistently in other respects to meet economic aspirations and claims in a tolerable degree. For example, the low average standard of living in Italy, coupled with an unequal distribution of income, means that the least privileged Italian groups—the unemployed, many members of the lower middle class, and much of the southern agricultural population—suffer serious economic privation. The resentments among these groups—and their apparently increasing tendency to express their resentments in "protest" votes for communist or neo-fascist candidates—are a serious threat to Italian democracy. The problem is not simply that income distribution in Italy is unequal; statistically, it is probably not much more so than in the United States. But when the average level is so low, the contrast between the opulence of a few Italians and the wretched existence of very much larger groups leads inevitably, given 20th-century values, to deep resentments. These feelings are embittered by class stratification along traditional lines.

The prevailing dissatisfaction and sense of frustration among Italian industrial workers are less easy to explain in economic terms. As a class, they have not done badly relative to other groups and to their prewar standards; their real income per capita and their share of the national income are both above 1938. Yet they remain, as they were before the war, a disaffected group—a class which feels itself excluded

---

[39] This estimate was made by a special Italian parliamentary committee on unemployment and the population problem, headed by Mr. Roberto Tremelloni, in a report issued at Rome in 1952.

from the privileges of Italian society and is fundamentally hostile to the *status quo*. A part of the explanation is to be found in their deep sense of economic insecurity due to the presence of chronic unemployment and lack of alternative job opportunities. Also, it is probable that the economic claims of organized labor in Italy tend to be pushed up by the knowledge that Italian real wages are lower than in neighboring West European countries. Still, these considerations alone do not suffice to explain the persistent disaffection of Italian industrial workers, nor why they vote almost solidly for communist or fellow-traveling socialist candidates. A generation of Marxist indoctrination may account in part for their attitude and outlook. Equally important (as in France) are the effects on labor attitudes of Italian class hostilities and anti-clericalism of more ancient origin.

It seems reasonable to conclude that Italy's economic health in the 20th century has been bad and has apparently been tending to get worse, and that a large part of the trouble—though certainly not all of it—is Italy's slow rate of economic growth. As one observer concludes, "The fact is that the pressures—open or repressed—which developed within the Italian social structure over the last 50 years outran by far the mitigating impact of Italian economic growth. Economic growth was inadequate to meet the aspirations and social demands of the masses." [40] Unless there is an acceleration of Italy's economic growth, it would be unwise to be optimistic about the prospects for Italy's economic health—or about the future of Italian democracy. Persistently poor economic health will contribute to the continuing growth of communist and radical neo-fascist power, which could lead in time to the break-down of political order and of constitutional government in Italy. Considering the energy and resources which Americans have devoted over the last decade to restoring the Italian economy and aiding the re-birth of Italian democracy, such an outcome would be a bitter defeat for the United States, not only in a psychological and moral sense, but also politically. It would probably mean the neutralization of Italy and the defeat of the European unification movement.

It would be wrong to assert that economic factors alone are necessarily critical for the future evolution of Italian politics, or that an acceleration of Italian economic growth would assure a united, democratic and Western-oriented Italy. As we have seen, the disaffection of

---

[40] B. Foa, *op. cit.,* p. 21.

large portions of the populations of Italy and France is not simply the product of economic frustration. It has also deep ideological and social roots which cannot be excised by economic improvement alone. For these people to overcome their sense of alienation from their national societies and from the values of Western civilization requires profound changes in spiritual outlook and class attitudes on the part of all major social groups in their countries.

Nevertheless, economic factors are undoubtedly of great importance and, in Italy, they are relatively accessible to American policy—a good deal more so than in France. Because the Italian economy is relatively small, and because its growth is not limited primarily by internal institutional obstacles, its rate of growth can be influenced significantly from the outside. The rate of domestic capital formation in Italy is, as we have seen, closely related to the availability of foreign exchange. It could, therefore, be maintained at a higher level if Italy could count on a large and expanding inflow of American capital, most of which would presumably have to be public capital, since attractive opportunities for private American investment in Italy are quite limited. Likewise, an expanded rate of American military "offshore procurement" in Italy would permit a higher rate of domestic investment. For similar reasons, Italy's participation in a European political and economic union would probably make possible a substantially higher rate of Italian economic growth and would provide an outlet for increased Italian emigration.

A whole-hearted effort to increase total emigration from Italy to a multiple of the present rate (150,000 a year) [41] would have important economic and political effects—particularly if there were a large increase in the American immigration quota for Italy.[42] A large increase in the Italian quota would be a convincing symbol of American concern for Italy's welfare. Because of the importance (perhaps exagger-

---

[41] This figure includes only net emigration. It does not include all the movements of Italian migratory workers to and from other European countries. Since the Italian birth rate has been declining markedly in recent years, accelerated emigration could have a substantial effect on unemployment and living standards in Italy over a period of a decade or so.

[42] The annual United States immigration quota from Italy is a mere 5,000, and it cannot be fully utilized because of the restrictions of the McCarran Act. The Refugee Relief Act of 1953 temporarily allots a quota of 60,000 to Italy, but the crippling restrictions written into this Act and the slowness with which it has been put into effect make it clear that this allotment cannot be used rapidly enough to have a significant positive economic or political effect.

ated) which Italians give to emigration as a remedy for their economic problems, enlarging the quota would also advance American political objectives in Italy.

Taken altogether, the political effect in Italy of such developments as an increased inflow of American capital, European unification and expanded emigration, as well as of their economic consequences, might be very considerable over a period of years. There is, in short, much that the United States and the other West European countries could do to arrest political deterioration in Italy, provided there is sufficient understanding and will to act in time.

Japan

The similarity of Japan's and Western Europe's economic problems does not lie in any inability of the Japanese economy to satisfy claims for consumption and economic security in tolerable degree. For historical and sociological reasons, popular economic claims are not nearly as insistent or as politically effective in Japan as they are in the West. The goal of a constantly improving material living standard, if it exists at all, has a subordinate place in the Japanese value-system. The stratified traditional pattern of Japanese society makes for a relatively passive attitude on the part of the mass of the people to the results meted out to them by the economy. If, during the next few years, per capita consumption in Japan fails to rise, or even falls a little, the effect on morale would probably be much less serious than a similar development in the West.[43] Hence, it is probably valid to conclude that during the next decade it would be politically tolerable to apply the major part of the proceeds of Japanese economic growth to purposes other than consumption, with increases in per capita consumption the residual claimant. The opposite is more nearly true of Western Europe.

Nor is the similarity between Japan and industrial Europe to be found in internal obstacles to economic growth. The rate of savings in Japan is still very high, as it has been for many years. There is no evidence of a decline of entrepreneurial vigor, of a crystallization of economic institutions, or of the resistance to innovation so conspicuous in France and Britain. There is a new interest in quality which may in

---

[43] Per capita real income in Japan in 1952 was about at its prewar (1934–36) level, despite a 24 percent increase in population. The recovery from wartime and postwar privation must appear remarkable to the average Japanese consumer.

time overcome the prewar reputation of Japanese products for sacrificing quality to price. Labor mobility is high. The Japanese economy is habituated to a rapid rate of growth, which was not interrupted, as in Europe, by World War I and its long aftermath nor even, except quite briefly, by the depression of the 1930's. Consequently, the Japanese, despite their deep conservatism in many social and cultural matters, are used to considering economic growth and change as normal. In contrast to Europe, there seem to be no strong groups whose interest coincides with a strict maintenance of the economic *status quo*.

The similarity between Japan and Western Europe lies in the great importance of external obstacles to economic growth. The crux of Japan's economic problem, now as in the interwar years, is that its energetic, self-confident and ambitious business class lacks sufficient outlet for its talents and energies at home. Japanese industry has long since outgrown its meager domestic resource-base and must find expanding overseas sources of food, fuel and industrial materials which can be purchased with expanding exports of manufactures. In the interwar period, the Japanese industrialists threw in their lot with the militarists in an effort to solve this problem through imperialism. Today the same problem faces them again in much aggravated form. The Japanese economy has now been shorn of its protected colonial markets, investment outlets and food and raw materials sources, and its trade with the Chinese mainland has been reduced to a trickle.

Japanese exports have been inhibited not only by the external difficulties—reviewed in the preceding chapter—which Japan shares with other industrial exporting countries but also by problems peculiar to Japan. For example, the loss of Manchuria, Korea and Formosa and the interruption of trade with China have closed some of Japan's most important prewar export outlets, as the following figures of the changed area distribution of Japanese exports show:

	1934–1936	1952
Korea & Formosa	24%	8%
China	18	negligible
Other Asia	19	36
North America	17	21
Other	22	35
Total	100%	100%

Other special obstacles to Japanese exports are the war-caused suspicions of, and antipathies against, the Japanese in a number of non-communist

Asian nations and, most important, the anti-Japanese discrimination by the Sterling Area countries—discrimination which is not related to balance-of-payments considerations. Relatively few countries have as yet revived their prewar treaties of commerce and navigation with Japan, and only the United States has concluded a new treaty. Without such treaties, an extension of Japanese commercial activities is difficult. The seriousness of Japan's problem of finding foreign markets is shown by the fact that its exports are still scarcely a third of their 1934–36 volume and its share of world exports of manufactures is far below the prewar ratio. No other industrial exporting country has fared nearly so badly.

Because Japan has had such difficulty expanding its commercial exports, it has remained far more dependent on American financing—in the form of American military expenditures and economic aid—than the countries of Western Europe. Japan's future ability to increase industrial output and to maintain or increase its consumption levels will likewise depend on the willingness of the United States to continue dollar financing of some kind. For, Japan's export difficulties are likely to persist.

In sum, though the Japanese economy has the internal elements of reasonably good economic health, its problem of finding export markets and of paying for necessary imports is considerably worse than that of industrial Europe. The danger in this situation is not that it will lead in the near future to frustration of consumption claims and to disaffection and political trouble among the Japanese people. Rather, the danger is that prolonged frustration of Japanese exports—and thus of the energies and ambitions of the Japanese business class—could contribute to a rift between Japan and the West and a reorientation of Japanese foreign policy toward neutralism. The history of the 1930's should be a warning to the West, and especially to the United States, that failure to make sufficient economic opportunity for the expansion of Japan's exports and for Japanese economic growth can be disastrous for the security of the West and the peace of the world. The logical way to open this opportunity would be to make possible greater Japanese participation in the development of Southern Asia.

The brief analysis of external and internal obstacles to the economic growth of industrial Europe and Japan contained in this and the preceding chapter may be concluded by stressing the several ways in which these obstacles converge and re-enforce each other.

First, the slow growth of agricultural production and exports outside North America, together with the power of American competition, make for slow growing export markets for Western Europe and Japan. Their export markets are also insecure. This insecurity further inhibits the growth of their exports by making export industries relatively unattractive to new investment and by inhibiting the changes in industrial structure and technology necessary to meet American competition and to respond to changes in foreign demand. The inability to count on expanding and relatively secure export markets is a major limitation on economic growth for these national economies which are so heavily dependent on foreign trade.

Second, the weakness of incentives to industrial expansion due to external causes is re-enforced by—and in turn re-enforces—internal restrictionism, private and public.

Third, all of these factors lead to balance-of-payments weakness which further impairs the growth capacity of industrial Europe and Japan.

Fourth, the slow growth of per capita output resulting from this complex of factors tends to be self-re-enforcing in another way. Slow growth makes it difficult to maintain an adequate rate of savings and capital formation in the face of rising consumption claims and defense requirements.

From an American standpoint, the urgency of the economic problems of Western Europe and Japan arises from the possible repercussions on their domestic politics and foreign policies of continued economic weakness and frustration. If these countries are unable to attain more adequate rates of economic growth, they will be exposed to a strong temptation to give up the effort to play a positive role in the free world, and they may try instead to withdraw, politically and morally, from the struggle between communism and the West. Even more serious, continued failure to achieve satisfactory rates of growth will sooner or later confront some of them with the grave dangers of greatly intensified communist subversion, open civil strife, or the need to resort to authoritarian political means to force a reconciliation of economic claims and requirements and to maintain order. These possibilities contain the gravest dangers for the future security and peace of the United States.

Yet it is apparent that the deep-seated and mutually re-enforcing obstacles to growth discussed in these two chapters are not likely to be easily overcome. They will not be overcome by policies concerned with this or that specific problem in isolation from the others. The need is for basic measures which can come to grips with the major external and internal obstacles simultaneously and on a broad front. The need is for remedies which attack not symptoms but roots—the present "nationalized" constitution of the international economy and certain institutional difficulties within the West European economies themselves. The nature of such remedies and the extent to which they may be feasible will be considered in Part II.

4

The Underdeveloped Countries

Background

One of the three basic challenges of our times, the problem of relations between the industrial West and the underdeveloped countries in Asia, Latin America and Africa,[1] has in recent years been approaching a

---

[1] The numerous countries discussed in this chapter may be grouped into four categories:

(a) *Southern Asia*—This group of countries—consisting of South Korea, Formosa, the Philippines, Indonesia, Indochina, Thailand, Malaya, Burma, India, Ceylon and Pakistan— has many characteristics in common. All are part of, or have been influenced by, the complex civilizations evolved over past millennia in India and China. Most have only recently acquired political independence or are still in the process of doing so. Their cultural and religious outlook is comparable and they share common problems of economic development, social re-integration and political evolution.

(b) *The Moslem states*—This group consists of Iran, Iraq, Arabia, Jordan, Lebanon, Syria, Egypt, Libya, Tunis, Algeria and Morocco. The common cultural, religious and historical characteristics of the Moslem countries are well known. Although geographically and culturally part of this group of countries, Turkey has been intentionally excluded since very little of what is said in the following pages about the Moslem states applies to it. Though Turkey had certain initial advantages—e.g., a relatively large area, diversified natural resources, unbroken political independence, etc.—its economic and political development in recent decades has been truly impressive compared with that of the other Moslem countries. The term "Moslem states" is used for convenience, in full awareness of the fact that some of these countries are not entirely Moslem and that two states whose main religion is Islam—Pakistan and Indonesia—are omitted from this grouping.

(c) *Latin America*—These countries, stretching from the Rio Grande River to Cape Horn, are all descendents of a Spanish-Portuguese culture grafted upon an indigenous

critical phase. Though we have sensed its increasing urgency, the West has not yet fully understood why this problem is of fundamental importance, nor the possibilities and limitations which define the task of building better relationships between the West and the underdeveloped countries.

This problem is of vital importance to the West not simply for the reason stressed in the two preceding chapters: that restoration of the economic health of many Western countries and re-creation of a reasonably efficient international economy require a more rapidly growing and calculable supply of primary products from the underdeveloped areas. Important as this objective may be, it is not what today gives such critical urgency to the problem of relationships between the West and the underdeveloped countries. The issue that does so is a much more fundamental one. These countries are now passing through a profound social, political, economic and ideological transformation—a process more difficult and painful than any that they have experienced before, and one which, over the longer term, can have crucial consequences for good or for evil not only for the inhabitants of these areas but for all mankind. If in the course of this transformation free and humane forms of society are evolved by the people of the underdeveloped countries, human freedom and progress everywhere can be preserved or ultimately restored. But the danger is that these countries will instead succumb to the major difficulties now threatening them, that continued economic stagnation, political deterioration and social decay will make possible their conquest or subversion by communist imperialism. In such circumstances, the future of free and humane society everywhere would be seriously compromised.

Today, the efforts of the underdeveloped countries to work out for themselves new and more satisfying social, political and economic institutions of their own choosing are being frustrated by three kinds of difficulties. The first is the unceasing effort of Soviet and Red Chinese communism to annex these countries into the spreading totalitarian

---

Amerindian population. Except in Argentina and Uruguay, considerably more than half the populations of these countries are of pure, or mixed, Indian descent. The Latin American countries are still predominantly primary producers and face similar economic, social and political problems.

(d) *Africa*—The final category covers the dependent territories of the West European countries in Africa south of the Sahara. In large part, the remarks about Africa are also applicable to the remaining possessions of the European powers in Oceania and Latin America.

empires. The second consists of the many internal difficulties—political, economic and social—which block the advancement of the underdeveloped countries. The third is the unsatisfactory nature of their present economic and political relations with the West. Progress in meeting the communist danger and in overcoming the other two obstacles to the free evolution of these countries depends not only on their own efforts but also on the help which the West can provide.

Western policies and Western actions are likely to be adequate to meet this challenge only if the West understands the nature of the problems confronting the underdeveloped countries and has the strength and the forebearance necessary for building mutually satisfactory relationships with them. Unfortunately, in the postwar period, our thinking about the underdeveloped countries has tended to opposite—and equally mistaken —extremes.

On the one hand have been those who recognize the urgency of the challenge of the underdeveloped countries but who have allowed their eagerness to do something about this problem to blind them to the possibilities and limitations actually involved. Their unrealistic optimism commonly takes the form of insisting that if only the West were to provide development capital and technical assistance on a sufficiently large scale, the difficulties now blocking the progress of the underdeveloped countries could all be overcome. We shall attempt to show in this and the next chapter that there are two fallacies involved in this view. The first is the assumption that the problems of the underdeveloped areas are predominantly, if not exclusively, economic in nature and can be solved by economic means—indeed, by technological innovation and a higher rate of capital formation alone. The second is the notion that in any given time period the amount of foreign capital which the underdeveloped countries would be able to absorb effectively is virtually unlimited and that willingness on the part of Western countries, particularly the United States, to invest astronomical amounts of public and private capital each year could be easily generated.[2]

---

[2] Typical examples of unrealistic expectations with respect both to indigenous capital formation and to foreign investment may be found in a compilation of the official development plans of underdeveloped countries published by the United Nations Food and Agriculture Organization in 1949, and in the report to the Secretary-General of the United Nations prepared by a group of experts in 1951. See *Report on International Investment and Financing Facilities*, 5th Session FAO Conference (Washington: Food and Agriculture Organization of the United Nations, November 1949); and *Measures for the Economic Development of Under-Developed Countries*, Report by a Group of Ex-

On the other hand, there are those who are so impressed by the magnitude of the problems of the underdeveloped countries and the difficulty of coping with them that they despair of accomplishing anything worthwhile with the means likely to be available. In consequence, the pessimists tend seriously to underestimate the urgency of practicable Western policies and actions capable of making significant contributions to the advancement of the underdeveloped countries and the improvement of relations between them and the West. Difficult as it may be to influence the profound social changes now occurring in these countries, it is nevertheless possible to help their people consciously to determine the direction of their own development and to accelerate the pace at which it occurs.

The Study Group's view of this controversy will satisfy neither party. We believe it equally fallacious to insist that the process of political, social and economic development can be easily or quickly accomplished as to conclude that little or nothing worth its cost can be done to foster the advancement of these countries or to mitigate the difficulties and dangers now confronting them. Broadly speaking, the error both of the optimists and of the pessimists arises from their common failure to understand the nature of the changes now occurring in the underdeveloped countries and the extent to which the direction and pace of change can actually be influenced by conscious choices and actions. Accordingly, our purpose in this chapter is to describe briefly and impressionistically the nature of the contemporary transformation of these countries—to indicate the deep historical roots of their traditional values and institutions, the kinds of changes now occurring in them, and the complex relations among the political, economic and ideological dimensions of these changes. In the next chapter, we shall narrow our focus to the implications of this transformation for the economic growth of the underdeveloped countries.

Our aim in both chapters is to reveal the actual possibilities and limitations of a practicable Western program of action for fostering the development of these countries—a set of measures which will be outlined in Part II. But, lest the discussion of obstacles unintentionally convey an unduly restrictive impression of what could and should be done by the West to help the underdeveloped countries, we may briefly anticipate our

---

perts appointed by the Secretary-General of the United Nations (New York: United Nations, Department of Economic Affairs, May 1951). An excellent critique of existing capital requirements estimates for the underdeveloped countries will be found in S. Herbert Frankel, *The Economic Impact on Under-Developed Societies* (Oxford: Basil Blackwell, 1953).

conclusion here: it is far better that some resources be wasted in an effort to accomplish too much in too short a time than that the as-yet-uncommitted countries of Asia, Africa and Latin America fail to progress, or be allowed to fall under the communist yoke, because Western help has been too little and too late.

The Social and Economic Transformation of the Underdeveloped Areas

In his recent book, *The World and the West,* Arnold Toynbee recalls to our attention a fact long known but too rarely taken into account in Western policy-making with respect to the underdeveloped countries. He points out that the contemporary problems of Asia and Africa are mainly the result of their "catalytic" encounter with the West over the past several centuries. Although it began many generations ago, this encounter has reached its crescendo only in the post-World War II period. In order to understand the present results of this encounter and to influence its future outcome, it is necessary to know something of the traditional attitudes and institutions of these countries and of the ways in which the impact of the West has been transforming them.

Western policy-makers have also been prone to overlook the fact that in Southern Asia and the Moslem region there has been an age-old history of organized social and cultural life which in complexity and sophistication was, for long periods, superior to anything known in Europe. Despite the extent of Western influence over the past 150 years, many of the traditional institutions and attitudes of these older societies still survive. A major source of error in dealing with the underdeveloped areas is the assumption too often implicit in Western policies that, because the people of these countries may dress like Westerners and use Western concepts to express themselves, their motivations and the meanings they attach to such terms are identical with our own. In fact, the underlying differences are often much more important than the superficial similarities.

To the historian and sociologist, there are profound differences among the traditional societies of Southern Asia, Africa and Latin America [3]

---

[3] For the purposes of this study, it is convenient to consider the economically under-developed countries of Latin America along with the other underdeveloped areas. But, the reason is not simply that the Latin American countries (except Argentina and Uruguay) are themselves underdeveloped and hence can be more meaningfully discussed

which are of such character as to make generalizations intended to apply to all of them exceedingly risky. But to attempt to give even a broad description of these differences here would take us far beyond the scope of this study. Regardless of their social and cultural type or pattern of economic and political organization, all of these traditional societies have had—historically—certain traits in common, particularly when contrasted with contemporary Western society. In varying degree, these common traits have survived into the modern world and constitute some of the major differences between these societies on the one hand and that of the West on the other. For our purposes here, it will be sufficient to describe only those characteristics important for understanding the contemporary attitudes and institutions in the underdeveloped areas which bear significantly on their social and economic prospects.

In virtually all of the countries comprising the underdeveloped areas, large numbers of people still have what may be called "non-market" or "pre-industrial" motivations and attitudes. These are important survivals of the value-systems of the ancient societies of these regions.

In the West the great bulk of the population is habituated to a world-wide money economy; to production for sale rather than use; to wages, interest and profits as the major forms of income; and to large-scale, mechanized methods of production in agriculture and industry. The aim of economic activity in the West is the maximization of money income—in one or another of its forms—by individuals through the investment of capital or of labor on one's own account or for, and under the direction of, others. The motivations and attitudes associated with activities of this kind are, however, conventionally conceived in the West to be universal and immutable, pervading all countries and all ages.

In the older societies of the Orient, Africa, and pre-Columbian America, the basic economic unit was not the isolated responsible in-

in this and the next chapter than in those devoted to industrial Europe and Japan. Though the politically and socially dominant groups in Latin America are certainly part of Western society, they are more representative of the older, pre-industrial, aristocratic tradition—as are Spain and Portugal today—than of the modern, industrial, liberal democratic strand of Western culture. Moreover, the great bulk of the population of Latin America is wholly or partly descended from non-European ancestry, biologically and culturally. Even in Argentina and Uruguay, which have the highest proportion of pure European inhabitants, Western culture has been significantly modified by indigenous influences, just as in Central America and Mexico—which have the highest proportion of Indian inhabitants—the native American cultures have been drastically modified, though not by any means superseded, by Western influences.

dividual, but an organic social unit—the "extended family" in China, Japan and much of Latin America, the village community in India and most of Southeast Asia, the tribe or the guild in the Moslem countries and the more advanced portions of Africa. Local and regional self-sufficiency was pronounced, and production was largely for use rather than for sale. For the great bulk of the population, money incomes were scanty. Those groups who managed to obtain money incomes derived them mainly from "quasi-feudal" [4] rights in land, from simple money-lending, from commerce, and from state activities (such as tax collecting, war, maintenance of the ruler's court, etc.) and not from industry, commercial agriculture or modern types of finance and investment. While in Southern Asia and the Moslem countries urban handicraft production and inter-urban commerce were always extensive, these activities took place, so to speak, in the interstices of predominantly agrarian societies—within and among them—but were rarely regarded by the great bulk of the population as characteristic economic activities or accorded very high social status. Nor did the Oriental cities ever become, as in Europe from the 12th century on, one of the principal active agents of social and economic transformation, helping to erode the high degree of self-sufficiency in the countryside and to weaken the feudal forms of authority through the spread of the market and the growth of urban wealth and power.

In all of these societies, the predominant aim of economic activity was not maximization of the individual's monetary income but the preservation of the complex of non-economic satisfactions and inter-personal relationships expressed by the basic social unit—whether it was the patriarchal family, the village community, the tribe, or the craftsmen's guild. Though these communities were generally at or near minimum subsistence levels, the calculability and security provided by immemorial, essentially changeless, social units of this type were prized above the possible improvements in living standards, social mobility or cultural opportunities which might have come from movement to urban centers and from commercial or industrial occupations. True, individuals and small groups always left, or were driven out of, these

---

[4] We are, of course, aware that medieval European terms such as "feudal" and "manorial" cannot accurately be applied to the forms of authority and income division formerly existing in the Orient and pre-Columbian America. Nevertheless, as the historians have not yet agreed upon more accurate terms, we shall characterize these relationships as "quasi-feudal."

units from time to time, and famine, war or enslavement often swept away whole regions of them. But, for the great mass of the population, religion, ethics, art and custom combined to buttress—and were in turn centered in—the ageless patterns of mutual help and cooperation associated with the primary social units.

Political organization was only a more or less elaborate superstructure resting upon these primary units but leaving them internally unchanged. Dynasties rose and fell, new invaders replaced old aristocrats and bureaucrats, but the functions and responsibilities of the primary units *vis-à-vis* the ruling groups remained the same. Essentially, the primary units provided what—for want of a better word—historians have called a "surplus" over and above their own minimum subsistence needs, whose size relative to the total production varied directly with the ability of the ruling groups to exact it. The surplus was remitted—sometimes in money, more often in kind—by the producers as taxation, as quasi-feudal dues, as interest on debts to merchants and moneylenders, or as payment (generally at unfavorable terms of trade) for needed commodities unobtainable locally (e.g., metals, salt, fibers). Labor services might also be required for such things as roads, fortifications, irrigation and other public works. Toward the primary social units, the functions and responsibilities of the ruling groups were equally simple—the preservation of external defense and internal order, and the supervision of religion, justice and, where such existed, large-scale irrigation. Other activities of the ruling groups and of the commercial classes had little or no relevance to the primary units.

Regardless of the degree of urbanization and of the extent of commercial intercourse, all of these societies were predominantly agrarian —that is, agriculture (in one or another of its forms) was the main type of economic activity and land was regarded by virtually all classes as the only secure, and the most socially desirable, form of wealth. Power over the land and its products was the basis of political authority and social prestige. Incomes derived from land made possible the conspicuous consumption which was a characteristic of the ruling groups of many of these societies. Access to land in amounts sufficient to provide at least a minimum subsistence after taxes, rents and other imposts had been met was the major economic aim of the peasantry, the great bulk of the population in all of these countries.

The transformation of the old agrarian societies of Asia, Africa and Latin America under the impact of the West has been the historical equivalent of the transformation which occurred earlier or concurrently in the West itself, including North America. However, though the historical significance of the process may be everywhere the same, the specific means by which the forms of social and economic organization characteristic of agrarian societies have been dissolved or uprooted and new methods, relationships and motivations introduced have generally been achieved in different ways, by different groups, with differing degrees of conscious compulsion and of passive acquiescence.

In Britain, it was accomplished by private landowners and manufacturers with the at least passive support of a conservatively oriented government, and this was the pattern in much of Western Europe. In the United States, private businessmen were to an even greater degree the agents of affirmative reorganization and transformation, but the social impact of the process was very considerably mitigated by the availability of free land and the tradition, and physical means, of mobility. In both Britain and Western Europe, the process was probably harsher than it otherwise would have been, and the power of the middle class was increased, owing to the very rapid population growth that took place simultaneously with industrialization. But, in the Latin countries of Europe, the process was never completed and the emerging industrial society was rendered both less efficient and less equitable by peculiar characteristics of the middle class, noted in Chapter 3, especially by a lesser sense of social obligation, weak ethical compulsion to public honesty, and greater attachment to feudal values than in the Anglo-Saxon and Scandinavian countries. In Russia, the uprooting and transformation was conducted with a maximum of brutality, both in its early capitalist phase before 1918 and in its more rapid communist phase since that time.

Another important difference must be stressed between the Western transformation and that now reaching its crescendo in the underdeveloped areas. In the former, the major forces responsible for profound social and economic changes were largely indigenous. The native English, continental and American middle classes and governments were the most active agents of transformation in their own countries. In the underdeveloped areas, the most conspicuous instruments and forces of change came from abroad and were not part of the societies on which they operated. Most of the countries of Asia, Africa and Latin America have known other conquerors or have submitted to outside pressures in the past. But few of these previous episodes changed in any significant and lasting respect the internal patterns and relationships of these societies. In the 19th century, the extension of direct colonial rule and of indirect spheres of influence, and the economic penetration of nominally independent areas, had quite different effects. The fact that, to the great bulk of the population, the dissolution or serious impairment of their traditional way of life appeared to be the work of foreigners, helps to account for contemporary bitterness and resentment in the underdeveloped countries.

There can be little doubt that the Western impact on the traditional societies of Asia, African and Latin America would never have produced such far-reaching or rapid effects had it not occurred under the protection afforded by direct colonial rule or by such indirect methods of control as spheres of influence and commercial hegemonies. These new relationships of dominance and subordination made possible the necessary degree of internal political order and economic calculability, effective transportation and communications, and governmental policies and subsidies which fostered the penetration of native economies by Western business enterprise. During the course of the 19th century, region after region was brought within the expanding world economy by these means. Colonialism and imperialist influence also ensured that, once included within the scope of world economic relationships, these regions would not subsequently disrupt the system by divergent economic developments or inconsistent policies and practices.

Once the stage of peripheral commercial contact ended early in the 19th century, the most important forms of Western economic intercourse with these societies were commercial agriculture [5] and extractive industries. Production of primary commodities for export was made possible by the assured and growing market for them which developed in Europe, and to a lesser extent in North America, during the 19th century.

The growth of commercial agriculture was in part the result of deliberate Western initiative and in part the result of unintended pres-

---

[5] Commercial agriculture took many forms. Tea in India, rubber in Malaya and Indonesia, tropical vegetable oils in parts of Africa, tended more and more to be produced on plantations established, owned and managed by Europeans. Other crops, like jute and cocoa were more often raised on small plots owned or rented by natives, and then were sold to European merchants who shipped them to Western markets. In contrast, it is interesting to note that rice, which became a major commercial crop during the 19th century, was left almost completely in the hands of natives, or of the Chinese, because it was produced for Asian consumption and hence was a more difficult and less profitable commodity for European businessmen to handle.

sures.[6] Everywhere in the new colonial areas, the establishment of European standards of governmental service and efficiency, and the resulting need to increase the amount and forms of revenue, were major factors in forcing or inducing natives to raise cash crops or to work for wages in mines and on plantations. There is evidence that in many localities in Africa south of the Sahara the head tax was introduced in part at least to ease the problem of recruiting native labor for the mines, for lumbering and plantation work, and later for industrial activities. By the end of the 19th century, the disappearance of older forms of land tenure and the growth of the rural population drove large numbers of peasants to seek work on the new commercial farms and plantations for at least part of the year, particularly in Latin America.

During the same period, Western manufactures were also introduced into these regions and led, in the course of the 19th century, to the progressive decline of the old native handicraft industries, both urban and rural. In part this resulted from deliberate colonial policies which favored imported Western goods; in part from the fact that, with the growth of commercial agriculture, money was more available and consumers could exercise their preferences; and in part to the severing of the patterns of cooperation which previously made rural handicrafts an integral part of many of the traditional primary social groups.

Finally, toward the end of the 19th century, industrial production began to be established in Southern Asia, Latin America and even

---

[6] The classical example of the latter occurred in India where, after the consolidation of British political rule at the beginning of the 19th century, the East India Company introduced the Western concept of individual private property in land. The primary purpose of this step was to assure an ample cash revenue for the new administration by fixing the responsibility for tax payments on individuals, in accordance with English practice. Two systems were used in different parts of India. Under the first, the *zamindari* system, the former Moghul tax collectors and local nobility, with traditional quasi-feudal rights to portions of the crops produced by the village communities, were made individual owners of the land in the modern sense of the term. These new proprietors then rented the land to the former peasant cultivators as individuals. In the other system, called the *ryotwari*, the lands cultivated by the village communities were divided among the member peasant families, who thereby became individual property owners. In either case, the effect was the same. In order to meet the tax assessments directly, or indirectly through the payment of money rent to the *zamindars*, the cultivators had to produce more and more of their crops for sale, rather than for their own use or for exchange with handicraft workers within the village community. Thus, the institution of individual private property began immediately to weaken the patterns of mutual help and cooperation which had formerly existed within the community. Yet these results, far-reaching as they proved to be, were quite incidental to the intended purposes of the British rulers. See Vera Anstey, *The Economic Development of India* (London: Longmans, Green and Co., 1949), pp. 97-103.

parts of Africa. At first, factories were set up to process, or to semi-process, the raw materials obtained from mines, forests and farms. Soon, however, these were followed by consumers' goods industries established by Europeans and, somewhat later, by natives. Mention must also be made of the railway construction which began in India and Latin America after the mid-century and in Africa and other parts of Asia toward the end of the century.

The growth of commercial agriculture, of extractive and manufacturing industries, of transportation and communications systems, and colonial policies which fostered these developments, all combined to change profoundly, but by no means completely, the traditional social units, internal economic relations, and motivations and attitudes of the native peoples. The change was, of course, most pronounced in the cities, which now acquired far more important positions within their societies as they gradually became the centers of Western-type administration, finance, commerce and industry.

Throughout Southern Asia, however, the process of change is still going on, especially in the countryside. Individual private property, particularly in land; the need to obtain money incomes; the progressive reduction over the past hundred years in the size of individual peasant holdings owing to the nearly universal custom of equal inheritance by all male children, and in some countries even by female children as well; the rapid increase in population; the larger capital requirements of commercial agriculture; and the occasional natural disasters of poor harvests, floods and epidemics—all resulted in a steady increase in peasant indebtedness and to foreclosures and evictions on a growing scale. These countries had always known the village usurer, who had been a hated, though indispensable, member of the village communities. But, in the new circumstances, resort had to be made to his services on a far larger scale. In addition to being moneylender, he also often became local storekeeper, produce merchant and, sometimes, landlord as well. In some countries, he was not a native; Hindus were especially important in this role in Burma and parts of East and South Africa, and the Chinese throughout the rest of Southeast Asia and Indonesia.

This process, superimposed on the usual rural underemployment characteristic of low productivity agrarian societies, gradually produced a large redundancy of labor in the countryside in many Asian countries. While people were generally reluctant to leave familiar village, family or tribal surroundings, they were occasionally driven to do so by famine or, more often, by the chance of obtaining temporary employment elsewhere until rural conditions improved. It was in this manner, and to a lesser extent through the natural increase of the regular urban inhabitants, that a labor supply became available to the plantations, mines, railways and factories which Western capital was developing.[7]

There were, of course, many other aspects to the penetration of these older Oriental societies by Western economic attitudes and forms of enterprise, some obtaining generally throughout these regions and others important only in certain places. It is obviously impossible here to discuss them in any detail or even to catalogue them fully. Suffice it to say, by the mid-20th century, the legal and economic bases of the old primary social units had almost completely disappeared in regions which had the closest or longest contacts with Western society. But today, functioning village communities in their original form can still be found in fairly large numbers in the less accessible parts of India, Burma, Viet Nam and Malaya, and are probably still the dominant type of economic and social organization in Thailand, Laos, Cambodia and parts of Indonesia.

In the Moslem states, similar changes have occurred. There, too, in the course of the late 19th and early 20th centuries, various types of traditional Islamic tenures and rights to arable and pasture land were assimilated to Western notions of individual private property, usually to the benefit of tribal sheiks and new native politicians. To some extent during the last decades of Turkish rule, and more particularly under the colonial and mandate powers during the interwar period, Western influence brought about considerable elaboration in governmental functions, necessitating larger revenues and increased money taxes and rents.

---

[7] Yet then, and to a considerable extent even now, the prospective plantation hand or industrial worker did not seek out an employer as an individual on his own initiative. Everywhere, there grew up systems of labor recruitment, and even of factory management and discipline, which rested to some extent upon the relations of authority and subordination which had existed in the old primary social units. Heads of villages in India and Southwest Asia, heads of families in China and Japan, tribal sheiks in the Arab countries, and tribal chieftains in Africa were used as agents to recruit the members of their own, and later of other, primary units and in many cases to control these workers once they were employed. Wages for the individual laborers were often paid in the first instance to these agents who customarily retained a large share as their commission (sometimes as much as 80 percent). This, like rural moneylending and the trade in native foodstuffs, was one of the most important sources of native capital accumulation for future native businessmen and industrialists. See Wilbert E. Moore, *Industrialization and Labor* (Ithaca, New York: Cornell University Press, 1951), Chapter 3.

Commercial agriculture, mining and industrial production did not, however, become as extensive in the Moslem states as in Southern Asia or even parts of Africa, except of course for the petroleum industry. Nevertheless, population, rural unemployment and indebtedness grew noticeably. The ancient and well-developed urban centers which these countries already possessed grew in size and importance in consequence of these changes. At the same time, the demand for Western manufactures was also increasing with a corresponding decline in the native handicraft industries on which the urban centers had formerly concentrated.

Measured in terms of numbers of people currently engaged in agriculture, most of Latin America, too, is still largely agrarian in character. There are, of course, comparatively few vestiges of pre-Columbian land tenures and village or tribal social units. Those which survive are hidden in inaccessible jungles or mountain regions and contain numerically and politically unimportant fractions of the population.

The Spanish and Portuguese colonists introduced the system of large landed estates at an early stage in the conquest of the native Indian societies. Most of these holdings were worked as plantations using slave labor at the beginning, and later various types of semi-servile peasant tenures. More recently, such unfree tenures have been abolished and forms of rent or of share cropping introduced instead. In some countries (e.g., Mexico) much of the land has been given outright to the peasant cultivators. Yet even where commercial agriculture is extensively practiced, as for example in Guatemala, the peasants generally spend only a relatively small part of the year on the plantations and, during the remainder, return to their villages and to the cultivation of their small subsistence plots which they still regard as their major economic activity.

It is clear, therefore, that throughout much of Latin America peasant cultivators have to some extent become habituated to a money economy, whether they work for wages on plantations or on smaller plots owned by themselves or rented in various ways from the owners. But the available evidence also indicates that the older "pre-market" values and attitudes still persist. The objective of a great many Indian and Mestizo Latin Americans is similar to that of their counterparts in Southern Asia and Africa. They hope some day to acquire enough land so that they and their families can once again live on their own, independent of the international economy. Considerable evidence is available of the extraordinary tenacity of "pre-market" motivations among Latin American workers and farmers and the difficulties which these create for rapid economic development.[8]

Except for the Union of South Africa with its large European population, the other parts of Africa south of the Sahara have lagged considerably behind Asia and Latin America. But even in tropical Africa, growing numbers of natives have left their tribal units to work temporarily or permanently on plantations and in mines. The traditional tribal economies, except in jungle and mountain fastnesses, no longer retain to the same degree their older primitive self-sufficiency.

Contemporary Attitudes and Expectations

In these different ways and varying degrees, the people of the underdeveloped areas have become acquainted with Western economic attitudes and practices. In the course of the 20th century, more and more of them have been raising crops for sale, paying money rents and taxes, working for wages, and learning to save and invest. But even where the older legal rights and economic functions of the traditional primary social units have completely disappeared, the units themselves in their other aspects—domiciliary, religious, cultural, social—may still survive more or less intact and help to keep alive something of the older pattern of relationships and attitudes. The fact that the older units still persist as living social organisms in these limited respects re-enforces the natural conservation of traditional attitudes characteristic of illiterate agrarian societies.

In consequence, over wide and growing areas of Southern Asia, the Moslem states, Latin America and Africa, the great majority of the people suffer today from conflicting values and ambivalent attitudes. On the one hand, they are becoming habituated to Western economic motivations and goals; on the other, the memory of older, inconsistent, attitudes and expectations is still kept very much alive. In some respects, the older is stronger than the new. The familiar psychological security, cultural continuity, companionship, and sense of belonging—in short, the non-economic values—which characterized the older primary units are preferred in many cases to the potential material benefits of a Westernized way of life. Large numbers of natives still conceive their em-

---

[8] Moore, *op. cit., passim.*

ployment in mines, plantations and factories to be temporary and hope for a time when they can return to their original occupations and communities.

The new educated native middle classes have, however, been more strongly affected by their encounter with the West. Almost from the beginning of colonial rule in the 19th century, opportunities for natives to obtain Western-type education, both at home and in Europe and the United States, have been increasing. Thus, there came into being by the interwar period sizeable groups of native intellectuals, professional people and businessmen who were more or less familiar with Western ideas about the self-determination of peoples, nationalism, democracy, trade unionism, socialism and communism. The influence of these Western ideas cannot be overstressed. For the groups which became acquainted with them, though numerically small, were nevertheless the politically active and economically most progressive portions of the population. And, in large part, the importation of these Western ideas into Southern Asia and the Moslem region has been responsible for bringing colonial rule to an end throughout much of this area, and may soon terminate it in the rest.

It is important to remember that what gave revolutionary impetus in the underdeveloped countries to imported Western values and ideas was not that these concepts were necessarily revolutionary in themselves. Rather, it was the fact that these ideas helped to awaken, to make concrete, and to channel into practical political activities the growing resentment of the native populations not only against foreign rule but against the inadequacies and injustices of their own societies as well. This crystallization of grievances, real and fancied, under the banner of Western concepts of democracy, self-determination and nationalism has, of course, been aided and abetted by the Communists for their own ends. Moreover, because many of these Western ideas were essentially foreign to the intellectual traditions and social forms of Asian and even Latin American societies, they have tended to be interpreted in ways which often seem strange and exaggerated to their Western originators. Within their native Western culture, these concepts have usually been expressed and applied in forms which modify their intrinsic absoluteness and mutually reconcile them into a more or less consistent and rational body of doctrine. But there has been a tendency for people in many underdeveloped countries to adopt these ideas without such mutual checks and balances—to espouse democracy without liberalism, equality without equity, absolute national sovereignty without qualifying concepts of domestic order and personal freedom or mitigating concepts of international law and obligation. The uncompromising authority with which such ideals are individually invested helps to explain the passionate, irrational and perverse character of so much of Asian, Moslem, African and Latin American nationalism today.[9]

The widespread use of Western concepts by the people of the underdeveloped areas to express their own resentments and aspirations has also had the effect of blinding many in the West to the nature of the changes desired by the main social groups in these countries. For, the meanings actually attached to Western concepts by these social groups may be significantly different from those which would be readily apparent to a Westerner. In recent years, for example, it has become customary to use the phrase "the revolution of rising expectations" as a summary description both of the motivation for economic development in Asia, Africa and Latin America and of the reasons why it is so urgent for the West to interest itself in this process. There can be no question, as we have seen, that a revolution has been occurring in the underdeveloped areas or that, in general, their economic expectations have been changing. But to grasp the significance of these events, we must ask: which revolution? whose expectations? in what ways have they changed?

It is understandable that Americans should equate the economic expectations of other peoples with their own and should assume that the American standard of living and political system provide universal models to which all "sensible" nations will aspire once they become acquainted with them. To some extent, this is a valid assumption, as we have seen in the case of Western Europe. But its validity for the countries of Southern Asia, the Moslem region, and even of Latin America is neither as universal nor as exact as for Western Europe. The bulk of the population in the underdeveloped areas has very different economic, cultural and ideological backgrounds from that of Europeans and Americans. To assume, nonetheless, that the millhands of Calcutta, the peasants of Egypt and the Indians of Guatemala can never become politically more reliable and economically more cooperative members of

---

[9] Nationalism in the underdeveloped countries is an endemic phenomenon which characterizes many diverse groups with widely varied political viewpoints. It is most vehement and unreasonable at the extreme right and left. Many people of moderate views are nationalistic less by conviction than by the need to avoid vulnerability to attack on this point by radical and reactionary groups.

the free world community until they have been provided with family cars and television sets is clearly too absurd to be taken seriously. Yet this assumption is implicit in much of the thinking of those Westerners who maintain that, unless the living standards of the underdeveloped countries can be quickly raised and transformed to something approximating the American or the West European standards, these societies will surely be conquered or subverted by the communists. It is neither possible to raise the living standards of these countries to anything like the Western level in the foreseeable future nor, if it were, would this necessarily solve the problems of the underdeveloped areas. The capacity for self-control, for rational and morally valid choices, and for responsible actions—without which the existence of free and humane institutions is in the long run impossible—is not as easily exported as tractors or DDT. Nor are these capabilities necessarily increased by a higher standard of living.

In consequence, it is essential to know something about the actual aspirations of the main social groups in these countries, particularly those which tend to be expressed under the guise of superficially similar Western concepts. Accordingly, we shall attempt in the remainder of this chapter to sketch in broad outline the current aspirations of the major functional groups in the underdeveloped countries.

The Modern Middle Classes. It cannot be denied that, at the present time, there are small—but highly articulate and influential—groups in the underdeveloped areas whose aspirations and ways of thinking approximate those of their social counterparts in the West not merely in a superficial sense but more profoundly as well. In the main, these groups comprise what might be called "the middle classes"—numerically still very small but disproportionately important within these societies owing to their literacy, their economic strength and their political power.[10] It is among these people that Western ideas have most directly and fully penetrated and, from them, have radiated to other parts of the population. In general, these middle-class groups can be said to aspire to Western standards of satisfaction not only for themselves but

---

[10] The term "middle class" is used here somewhat unconventionally to include businessmen, politicians, civil servants, professional men, technicians, students, artists and intellectuals generally. However, this grouping has greater merit than mere convenience as it recognizes the common community of background, communication and aspiration which its superficially heterogeneous components possess and is, in consequence, more realistic than the Marxist equation of the middle class with the "bourgeoisie."

—more significant—for the rest of their countrymen as well. These are the groups with which Westerners most frequently come in contact and whose views are commonly accepted in the West as representative of their entire countries. Moreover, these people are the dynamic elements in their own societies, and their decisions, energy and enterprise—in some cases for better and in others for worse—will in large measure determine the success or failure of the underdeveloped countries in the coming decades.

By and large, these middle-class groups are the product of the last hundred years—in a sense, the partly unintentional product of Western penetration and colonial rule. Left to themselves, it is highly unlikely that the older societies of Asia, Africa and Latin America would have generated essentially modern groups of this type. But, the dissolution of the older forms of economic and social organization and the introduction of Western forms provided the opportunities and the incentives for a modern native middle class to emerge.

Yet, in few underdeveloped countries have either the transformation of older attitudes and institutions or the provision of new opportunities and incentives been on a scale sufficiently large to make possible the easy or rapid attainment of Western-type objectives by these middle-class groups. Most fundamental have been the inhibiting effects of traditional concepts of what constitute desirable and appropriate social status, forms of income, and education and training. An obvious example is the Hindu caste system with its rigid limitations on occupations, education, and social and political privileges. But even where a formal caste system like that of India is lacking, these societies are still far more status conscious than are those of the West. Throughout Southern Asia, the Moslem region and Africa, "quasi-feudal" prejudices against manual labor and against direct participation in commercial and industrial activities are still fairly widespread. In much of Latin America, similar attitudes result from the persistence of aristocratic standards derived—via the Spanish-Portuguese colonial inheritance—from the values of an older Europe which had not yet experienced an Age of Enlightenment, a French Revolution or an industrial transformation.

The consequences of the persistence of traditional "pre-industrial" standards may be seen most clearly in the inability of the educational systems of most underdeveloped countries to provide the training and the skills necessary for economic and political progress. In all of these societies, formal education remained the prerogative of the wealthier upper classes for a much longer time than in the West. Moreover, such formal education and training as these societies provided in the past was almost exclusively directed toward professional careers in the law, religion, war, medicine, and the liberal arts. Today in most under-developed countries, preferences for these "liberal" professions are still predominant and continue to be bolstered by the persistence of religious and social prejudices inherited from older cultural backgrounds or from former colonial rulers. In India and in areas influenced by Spanish or Is-lamic culture, the number of students who seek and obtain legal training is still generally far in excess of the capacity of their poverty stricken countries to generate enough legal business to provide them with the types of income and status they expect. An almost inexhaustible need for doctors exists throughout the underdeveloped societies, but the great mass of the population is too poor to pay for medical services, and only those doctors who can acquire a wealthy clientele or who are employed by the government can hope to earn incomes which accord with their notions of appropriate recognition. In the Moslem states and in the coun-tries of Southeast Asia under Buddhist influence, thousands of young men are annually trained for religious careers in the many centuries-old universities and monasteries. Yet a great many of them can look for-ward only to the precarious income of the begging bowl, though few can feel the true religious calling which makes poverty a way to virtue and not to resentment.

The colonial administrations did little to correct the deficiencies of these traditional educational systems and, indeed, in some instances tried to preserve them. Western-type facilities for general liberal arts edu-cation and for the liberal professions were increasingly provided by colonial authorities at both secondary and university levels. At the be-ginning, these arrangements reflected the kind of educational systems still predominant in the West during the late 19th and early 20th cen-turies. Fortunate native students, in modest but growing numbers, managed to go to such Western institutions of higher learning particu-larly after the turn of the century. But even after the West itself began increasingly to develop its own facilities for training in engineering and technology, government administration and business management, applied sciences and skilled trades, institutions for teaching these sub-jects were neither established in the colonies nor were those in Western Europe or the United States generally available to students from the underdeveloped countries owing to their cost, and to their scholastic and other requirements.[11]

In these circumstances, it is not surprising that natives were generally not employed for the middle- or higher-grade positions in government, business and the professions during the period of colonial rule or domination. European-owned enterprises were favored by the colonial administrations and legal and other obstacles placed in the way of native enterprise. Even today in many of the newly independent countries of Southern Asia and the Moslem region, as well as in Latin America, the number of local people who have managed to obtain technological, administrative, managerial, or skilled industrial and agricultural training and experience is woefully inadequate compared with the need for such specialists and technicians.

There are other ways in which the persistence of older values and institutions and the deficiencies of Western rule have inhibited the progress of the new middle-class groups. In a developing country, there is always an obvious and pressing need for socially useful abilities of all kinds and, in theory, opportunities are unlimited. But at the same time, there is usually a lack of capital, of organization, of practical "know-how," of the ancillary agencies, equipment and services without which people with professional, technological, administrative and managerial skills cannot actually be put to work, or cannot be put to work with psychologically satisfying efficiency. In their present state of development, many of these countries are incapable of using fully, or in the most constructive manner, all of the human skills they already possess.

Other factors also militate against the most effective use of potentially available human resources. The occupational limitations of the Hindu castes have already been mentioned. But even where traditional institutions and customs do not restrict freedom of choice and social mobility, the aspiring native businessman frequently encounters obstacles to his self-advancement which were less important, or were absent, at a similar stage of development in the West. In the underdeveloped countries, capital to finance business expansion is scarce and interest rates are very high; existing concerns, particularly the larger ones, already dominate many branches of industry and commerce; and native

---

[11] In Southern Asia and the Moslem regions, the continued traditionalist orientation of education has been in part a perverse response to Western rule or influence—an attempt by native nationalists to preserve or re-assert the ancient learning of their societies in the face of the culture of the despised Westerners.

governments and legal systems are more susceptible to the influence of established firms and businessmen than to the newcomers (or, if the governments are left-wing, they are hostile to all forms of private business enterprise). In the absence of rapid economic growth or of the opening of new areas to settlement, these limitations—combined with the normal risks of enterprise—make the progress, and even the security, of the small or new native businessman particularly uncertain.

Everywhere in the underdeveloped areas, the new middle-class groups bear to a greater or lesser degree the marks of these antiquated prejudices, inadequate opportunities and embittering experiences. Resentment is still deep and bitter over former, and in some cases still current, colonial practices humiliating to native dignity and self-respect—the social and economic discrimination against natives, the inadequate opportunities for native education and enterprise, and the real and imagined shortcomings of colonial development policy, etc. Moreover, the indigenous causes of inadequate progress tend to be overlooked and all difficulties are attributed to the evils of Western rule or influence.

Many of the members of these new middle-class groups have nevertheless succeeded in overcoming both the handicaps and the temptations of this background. Their expectations for themselves and their countrymen, while frequently excessive, are nonetheless directed into constructive channels. Not only do they desire their own economic advancement, but they recognize that it is dependent upon improving the efficiency and increasing the incomes of other portions of the population as well. Hence, they are the leading proponents of technological innovations in industry and agriculture, of adequate transportation and communications systems, of investment in power development, of improved education and public health.

It is understandable that these groups, eager to achieve such objectives, should generally tend to be passionate advocates of rapid and grandiose schemes of industrialization. Industrial development is desired not only for their own enrichment or to raise the living standards of their fellow countrymen, but also because these middle-class groups believe that industrial self-sufficiency is the only way to enhance the international status of their countries and to ensure them an equitable share of the benefits of world trade. The latter objectives of industrialization are in part at least an understandable, if self-defeating, response to previous colonial policies and prewar economic relationships with the West. Some—even considerable—industrialization is beyond doubt necessary, desirable and inevitable over the long term in many underdeveloped countries. But neither the need for, nor the advantages of, industrialization are as great as is commonly believed in these countries, as will be seen in the next chapter.

In addition to the constructive and forward-looking members of these middle-class groups, there are many others who have reacted differently to past experiences and present difficulties and frustrations. These are the people whose resentment has festered, who have fallen victims to passionate, irrational nationalisms, or who have provided leaders and professional cadres for local communist movements. This group of frustrated intellectuals and embittered would-be businessmen—though numerically small—is beyond doubt the most dangerous element in the underdeveloped countries today because it provides the leadership and the organizational skill without which mass discontent, however widespread, could not develop into a sustained revolutionary force. The frustrated writers working for pittances as newspaper hacks, the professionally successful but wretchedly paid professors, the lawyers without clients, the doctors without patients who can pay for their services, the disappointed office-seekers—these are the really "explosive" materials in the underdeveloped societies.

If the destructive activities of these disaffected middle-class groups are to be successfully countered, it is important to understand something of the motivation which impels them. The sincerity of their views need not be doubted, but most of these people are to a greater or lesser extent the unconscious victims of the incapacity of their societies to afford them opportunities for putting their potential abilities to constructive or profitable uses. Owing to the persistence of antiquated values and institutions and to the educational and economic deficiencies noted above, many potentially constructive members of the middle class— Brahmins, Buddhist monks and Mohammedan mullahs, students and intellectuals, lawyers and doctors, unsuccessful businessmen and farmers—find little scope for their talents and inadequate opportunities for realizing their expectations in the underdeveloped countries today. Lacking access to schools in which technical training or skilled trades could be acquired, and prevented by archaic social prejudices from engaging in factory or farm work, they become professional politicians, or swell the governmental bureaucracy and the armed forces to burdensome proportions. Failing these occupations, they may finally sink into the urban masses of petty shopkeepers and casual purveyors of services which make up so large a part of the populations of the major Asian, Near Eastern and South American cities.

Middle-class groups are the "Promethean" elements in the underdeveloped societies today—the only conscious, active and capable agents of social change. A part of the middle class in most of these countries has been trying with slowly increasing effectiveness to build more satisfying and humane institutions for themselves and their compatriots. Another part believes that it, too, is working toward the same goal but, through ignorance, resentment or opportunism, has chosen to do so by irrational or totalitarian methods which in effect make the attainment of humane objectives impossible. The communists have long recognized the crucial role of the middle classes and have been making major efforts to reach and to influence them. In recent years, Iran, Guatemala, Indonesia and other underdeveloped countries have witnessed in various ways the conversion of many disaffected members of the middle classes into conscious or unwitting communist supporters. Indeed, almost without exception, the ablest and most determined native communists in the underdeveloped countries are recruits from such middle-class groups.

In contrast, the West has done far too little to reap the benefits of its own advantages over the communists. If it would make the necessary effort in the spirit of its own ideals, the West might be able to convey a sense of the moral and pragmatic superiority of its values and institutions over those of Soviet or Red Chinese communism. Quite apart from the prestige of Western material and scientific achievements, the West has the as yet unrealized advantage that its institutions express—however imperfectly—those universal ideals of human freedom, individual worth, and economic and social justice which the middle classes of the underdeveloped countries may yet come to value as much as, if not more than, material progress.

Moreover, the things which the West, and particularly the United States, would have to do to help create this sense of moral community between it and the middle classes in the underdeveloped countries are easier, less costly, and would yield greater and earlier benefits than any other type of aid which the West could supply. Help for indigenous efforts to build larger and better-balanced educational systems and adequate professional and vocational training facilities should have a high priority in our public and private assistance programs in the underdeveloped areas. Greatly expanded opportunities for students and technicians from these countries to attend Western educational and technical institutions could also be provided at relatively small cost. A major objective of this training must be to develop local leaders capable of exercising political power. Simultaneously, the West must help in the expansion of permanent political and economic opportunities for increasing numbers of graduates from such native and Western institutions, for the necessarily slow process of economic growth will not automatically provide these employment opportunities in sufficient time or on an adequate scale. To this end, Western business and non-profit organizations operating in the underdeveloped areas will have to make much greater efforts to employ the maximum number of local people at all levels and for all types of work. Public assistance programs should be conducted in such fashion as to employ directly—and indirectly to create additional economic opportunities for—native doctors, technicians, teachers and intellectuals generally. Finally, efforts on a vastly larger scale must be undertaken to make Western learning and Western ideology cheaply and readily available to the people of the underdeveloped countries.

Over the coming decade, the scale on which these, and other similar, measures are carried out by the West—and the sincerity, patience and skill with which the West undertakes them—will be major factors influencing the choices of the middle classes in the underdeveloped areas. In turn, the decisions and actions of these groups will in large measure determine the kind of future which their countries will have.

The Peasantry. The largest group in the population of all of the underdeveloped countries today is still the peasantry—the people who live in the countryside and are dependent on agricultural activities, both commercial and subsistence.

It is among the peasantry that older types of social organization and older attitudes have persisted in largest measure into the present day. The available evidence on peasant attitudes and expectations seems to support the view that the major source of discontent and unrest among the peasants is not so much their failure quickly to achieve a Westernized standard of living, but the disparities between the remembered satisfactions of their ancestral way of life and the lack of these satisfactions today; i.e., the inability to realize the older values of independence, security and a sense of belonging amid the rapid economic and social changes in rural conditions. Native political leaders and middle-class intellectuals may insist that the peasants do—or should—desire rapidly rising material living standards but, by and large, the peasantry does not seem to have such aspirations. Its grievances lie in another direction.

We have seen that—largely in consequence of the encounter with the West over the past hundred years—growing numbers of peasants have been drawn within the range of world economic forces whose operations have been unfamiliar and mysterious and against whose effects they have been unable successfully to adjust, psychologically or economically. Rural underemployment and unemployment have grown; the burden of rents, debts and taxes has increased enormously; individual peasant land holdings have decreased in size, often below the needs of mere subsistence. And, too little is being done in the way of irrigation, introduction of improved agricultural techniques, opening of new arable lands, and agrarian reform to mitigate sufficiently the pressures produced by these developments.

It would, of course, be a great mistake to infer that the condition of the peasants in the older societies was even remotely idyllic. At best, they lived close to bare subsistence levels and, as pointed out earlier, such compensations as they knew—or generally aspired to—were largely non-material in character, e.g., economic independence of outside forces and conditions, status and personal relationships which fostered a sense of security and belonging, individual fulfillment through participation in the internal balance and self-sufficiency of the primary social units, etc. In fact, in Southern Asia, the Moslem states and Latin America, the peasantry has always suffered from oppressive debts and rents, quasi-feudal exactions, and land hunger. In particularly bad periods, widespread rural unrest generally appeared. Historically, this took three forms: flights from the farming areas to escape rural burdens or starvation; endemic banditry; and open peasant rebellions. Every agrarian society, East and West, from antiquity to modern times has known these phenomena. And virtually all peasant discontent has had two main objectives, first formulated to our knowledge in ancient Greece—redistribution of land and abolition of debts (γῆς ἀναδασμός, χρεῶν ἀποκοπή).

Though today the specific causes of rural unrest are different from those of past periods, peasant discontent still expresses itself in much the same forms owing to the sociological character of all peasant societies. If left to themselves, the aims of the peasantry now would be largely similar to those of peasant movements in the past. These aims are not the revolutionary overthrow and reconstitution of the basic institutions of society, but easing of the burden of debts, rents and taxes and satisfaction of the hunger for land. While the realization of these goals might (though it need not necessarily) involve confiscation of the property of others, it would not mean abolition of the institution of private property or the overthrow of basic economic relationships and forms in the society.

There are, however, two new elements which now change the intensity and significance of peasant discontent in major respects—nationalism and communism.

Self-contained primary social units have a natural tendency toward xenophobia, and the distinction between "brotherhood"—the members of the organic social unit—and "otherhood"—outsiders or strangers—is ancient and important, though the membership of each category has varied from period to period. But, in many of the underdeveloped countries today, particularly in the Moslem states and parts of Latin America, groups which naturally resist the reforms required by the peasantry—landlords, moneylenders, tribal sheiks, etc.—and disaffected members of the middle class have exploited this tendency to xenophobia for their own ends. The peasants are encouraged to believe that colonial rulers or Westerners generally are the cause of rural distress and that all would be well if the foreigners could only be thrown out and kept out. There are, of course, other elements in contemporary nationalism in the underdeveloped countries, but this aspect is of central importance.

Far more dangerous for the future of these countries and for the West is the part which communism plays in the agrarian movements today. In themselves, peasant revolts have generally had an inchoate and sporadic character, flaring into sudden violence and as quickly disintegrating when their immediate and limited objectives were achieved, or when organized, determined resistance was encountered. Generally speaking, the peasants have lacked the attitudes, education and experience which would enable them to produce from their own ranks the leadership, the organizational skill and the sense of discipline required for sustained revolutionary activity. Historically, these qualities have often been supplied to agrarian revolts by groups outside of the peasantry, particularly by the middle class. Peasant movements which for one reason or another do not obtain—or will not accept—sustained leadership and direction by other, more experienced, social groups are not likely to last for very long or cause much permanent danger, however violent and destructive they may be in their initial phases.

Modern China provides an excellent example. The "old China hands" in the State Department were correct in one respect. Having seen China with their own eyes, they recognized the basic agrarian character of peasant discontent. But knowing little history, they made the fatal error of assuming that the peasants would be able to control the communists and that the communists themselves were primarily interested in agrarian reforms. In fact, the reverse was true. The postwar Chinese Revolution followed the normal pattern of peasant rebellions when they are led by other social groups. Widespread agrarian discontent was converted into a revolutionary overthrow of society through the leadership and direction of the communists, by whom—in characteristic fashion—the peasants were mobilized, organized and controlled. Once the alternative Kuomintang leadership had, by its own shortcomings, sacrificed its influence over the peasantry, there was little chance that the outcome would be otherwise—unless, of course, the United States had directly and forcibly intervened on a major scale, as in Greece.

These considerations suggest that, as far as the peasantry is concerned, the expectations which must be satisfied to quiet rural unrest are neither of a kind nor of a size which put them beyond reach of well-conceived, long-term efforts. What the peasants want today is what they have always wanted—and what modern technology now makes it so much easier for them to obtain. By and large, they want a scaling down of their debts, rents and other payments to more manageable proportions. They want easy access to adequate, non-usurious sources of agricultural credit. They want opportunities to learn more about Western technological advances in agriculture which can be adapted to the particular needs and capabilities of their soil, climate, crops and level of comprehension. Above all, they want access to land in amounts which will enable them to maintain themselves and their families above mere subsistence levels but not unrealistically above them. This means establishing cooperative and other types of agricultural credit institutions, and bringing additional land under cultivation—by irrigation, reclamation or clearing of virgin forest. It also means land redistribution—but not necessarily in all of the places where, largely under communist inspiration, it is now being demanded.[12]

---

[12] Guatemala was a good case in point. With thousands of acres of arable soil awaiting development in the jungle provinces, the commercial plantations—whose success depends on the economies of large-scale operations, and on whose foreign exchange earnings the entire economy is dependent—were being divided into subsistence plots before the fall of

If by measures of this kind—which are well within the range of economic practicability, though politically most difficult—peasant unrest can be drastically reduced, the peasantry may become a major factor for stability in these societies. Despite the long history of peasant revolts, the stability of agrarian societies under tolerable economic and social conditions is well known, particularly in those societies still permeated with pre-industrial attitudes and containing numerous survivals of older social organisms. Nor is it likely that standards of material consumption approximating those of the West will come to characterize the expectations of most peasant groups within the foreseeable future. The processes of social change in the underdeveloped areas have much further to travel before the aspirations of the average Indian villager will begin to approach in scale and diversity those of a French peasant, much less of a British or American farmer.[13]

If the agrarian problems of the underdeveloped countries are tackled vigorously and intelligently over the next decade, there is no reason why enough progress should not be made to help turn the tide against communism in those regions. This possibility is the greater because remedies for peasant discontent can be found, consistent with Western values and interests, which meet peasant hopes for land and economic independence. In its revolutionary phase, communism promises fulfillment of these hopes. But the history of modern Russia and China, and their satellites, shows that, in the process of consolidating communist rule, peasant hopes are frustrated by the inevitable collectivization of agriculture.

The Industrial and Urban Workers. The industrial working class—in the Western sense of the term—is still much smaller than the actual industrial labor force in the underdeveloped countries. Argentina, Brazil and Mexico are probably the leading exceptions to this generalization.

In most of the other countries, a sizeable portion of the labor force employed in industry and mining conceives itself to be temporary and longs for an opportunity to return to former communities and occupations.

---

the communist-dominated Arbenz Government. See Theodore Geiger, *Communism versus Progress in Guatemala* (Washington, D.C.: National Planning Association, 1953).

[13] Indeed, if real peasant incomes do rise substantially in the underdeveloped areas, there is likely to be an increase in the hoarding of precious metals rather than a much greater demand for consumers' goods. Hoarding is an ancient and characteristic form of saving in peasant societies, European no less than Oriental, as we well know from the case of France.

Part of the labor force does return, or tries to return, constantly, and labor turnover and absenteeism are very high (with consequent bad effects on labor productivity). One result has been that trade unionism has not grown very rapidly in most of the underdeveloped countries not only owing to legal and other obstacles but also because of the continuing preferences of workers for older, more familiar, types of social organization and economic activity.

Where a true industrial working class has developed—feeling itself to be permanent and with characteristically modern attitudes toward work and consumption—the problem is more or less similar to that in the West. Constructive wage and social welfare policies are obviously needed to mitigate industrial unrest. In many underdeveloped countries, particularly in Latin America, the standards in labor relations set for themselves by native business firms are generally worse than those which foreign enterprises would dare even to contemplate in present circumstances. At the same time, however, some of the recent labor and social welfare legislation in underdeveloped countries under leftist or socialist governments is so extravagant that it discourages business enterprise and causes unnecessary labor resentment when resources inevitably prove inadequate for meeting the benefits workers have been led to expect. Such a result only plays into the hands of the communists who, indeed, seek to disrupt economically and politically weak countries by using "popular" or "united front" tactics to promote the adoption of such premature or excessive reforms.

Other considerations, in addition to wage and social security policies, must also be kept in mind in dealing with the problems of that part of the industrial labor force which is not yet assimilated to characteristic industrial attitudes and expectations. Such groups of uprooted peasants will continue to be numerous, and will in all probability grow in numbers over the coming decades. Rural unemployment is already at a dangerous level in many countries, and increases in agricultural productivity are bound to make even more agricultural labor redundant. If the condition of the peasantry is to be improved, these people must be absorbed into industry to the extent that additional land cannot be brought into use to accommodate them. This is one of the major reasons why some industrialization is both necessary and desirable in many underdeveloped countries.

In some ways, the uprooted peasant or primitive tribesman working in mine or factory suffers more than any other group in the population from the consequences of the encounter with the West. The gulf between one pattern of cooperation and discipline and the other is too broad to be crossed in one generation. These people are among the most confused, aimless and unpredictable elements in the underdeveloped societies. Often herded in Oriental slums or wretched mining camps, they can be easily induced to swell a nationalist riot or join a communist guerilla band. But, by paying them decent wages and providing them with adequate opportunities to learn skilled and semi-skilled trades, the difficulties of transition may be eased and constructive attitudes developed.

It would be a mistake if the process of industrialization in the underdeveloped areas were to follow too closely the pattern of the West and to create new Pittsburghs and Manchesters. Rather, the aim should be to decentralize as much industry as is economically practicable to the countryside. If new industries are built in appropriate rural localities, the newly recruited workers can maintain their ties with village agriculture and continue to live in familiar and psychologically more satisfying surroundings. This may be a partial answer to the problems of rootlessness and aimlessness which now plague the vast slums of Oriental and Latin American cities. Since, however, a rural slum is as easily created, and may be fully as noisome, as an urban one—witness 19th-century England—such decentralization of industry requires careful planning and considerable foresight.

In addition to a true industrial working class and the industrial workers newly recruited from the countryside, many of the large cities—particularly in Southern Asia and the Moslem region—contain other, relatively numerous, low income and status groups. Some are small shopkeepers, handicraftsmen and service workers—in most instances survivals of older, formerly organic, urban groups. Others are minor civil servants and public functionaries, especially numerous relative both to need and to population in many of the underdeveloped countries. The majority are a heterogeneous group of domestic servants, unskilled and casual manual laborers of all kinds, beggars, thieves and petty criminals, etc.—partially or wholly unemployed, crowded into miserable slums, or literally living in the streets.

These unfortunate groups are the chief—though by no means the sole—recruiting ground in urban localities for the rank and file of violent nationalist or communist movements. Except for recent arrivals from the countryside, these groups tend to look to the future and not to the past, having to a large extent lost the attitudes and expectations which characterized their formerly functional status in the older societies. Knowledge and envy of the Western standard of living is very much greater among these rootless urban groups than among the peasantry, for they are accustomed to life in the cities where they constantly encounter the most conspicuous and tantalizing manifestations of Western material comforts, and are exposed to movies, the radio, tourists and other purveyors of Western notions of material enjoyment. Thus, these urban groups consist of people who are conscious of, and feel most bitterly, the disparity between their own condition and that which they imagine exists in more fortunate Western countries. Besides the middle-class groups, these are the only other people in the underdeveloped countries to whom the term "revolution of rising expectations" applies in much the same sense as in the West. In consequence of the frustration of their expectations, they fall prey to ideologies which magnify the sense of their own misery and promise them a miraculous translation to lives of ease and plenty. Both irrational nationalism and communism provide these rootless urban groups with convenient scapegoats against whom they can manifest their resentments, and with visions of an utopian age whose coming awaits only the expulsion of Westerners and Western influence.

These functionless urban fringe groups are important in the underdeveloped countries today because, when organized by nationalist or communist leaders into riots, demonstrations and voting brigades, they constitute the only normally recognized *vox populi,* however unrepresentative in numbers and attitudes they may be of the whole population. Although the peasants are far more numerous in these countries than the urban inhabitants, they are generally illiterate, unfamiliar with democratic electoral machinery, and—except when their discontent manifests itself in agrarian revolts—tend to follow the political leadership of economically powerful landowners and sheiks, or to abstain from political activity altogether. In the absence of normal and sustained peasant political activity, the urban mobs at the centers of national and local governments can easily make their influence felt both at the ballot box and in the streets.

The salvation of these functionless urban groups lies ultimately in finding ways and means by which they can be re-integrated into the emerging new societies of the underdeveloped areas in essentially constructive roles. As long as they continue to find a precarious existence in obsolete or marginal activities without real relevance to the economic needs or future of their societies, they will lack the psychological satisfactions of useful integral labor and the ability in time to improve their material conditions of life. Since most of them never participated in, or have long since lost touch with, rural occupations and organic social groups, their settlement as farmers or agricultural workers in the already over-populated countryside would be difficult and uneconomic. Thus, industrialization and the growth of modern-type service industries seem to provide the only solutions to the needs of these low-income urban groups for more productive employment and increased earning power.

The Older Ruling Groups. In many underdeveloped countries, there are survivals of older ruling groups which once played organic parts in their societies but which in some cases now hamper progress by their inertia or by actively seeking to perpetuate archaic prerogatives regardless of the consequences. These groups include large landowners and rural moneylenders, sheiks and tribal chieftains, and the politicians, mullahs and propagandists identified with their interests. They still wield considerable economic and political power in many underdeveloped countries today. Indeed, in the Moslem states and some Latin American countries, they are still the politically dominant groups.[14]

On the whole, these people tend to be satisfied with the present state of affairs in those countries where they continue to enjoy power and authority and, if they aspire to any change at all, they look backward to the days when their rule was unchallenged. Although, for political reasons, they may give lip service to the goal of economic advancement, they tend to oppose changes which would be likely to weaken the economic and ideological bases of their power. Hence, they may supply leadership and funds to extreme nationalist movements in an effort to divert attention from their own shortcomings and to fasten the blame on the West.

---

[14] One of Karl Marx's most striking mistakes was his prediction that the more a country developed economically the more its population would be polarized into two opposite and antagonistic social classes—the capitalists and the proletarians. Ironically, it is precisely in those countries which are most backward that social classes are rigid and are polarized at the extremes of poverty and wealth, while in all of the economically advanced nations the social structure is more complex and fluid, and lower groups tend to rise both in status and in living standards. The modern "welfare state" is hardly the outcome that Marx prophesied for highly industrialized societies.

Though survivals of the older ruling groups may play such dangerously reactionary roles in some of the underdeveloped countries today, the solution to this problem is not the summary prescription of the Queen of Hearts in *Alice in Wonderland:* "Off with their heads!" For, these groups may still be essential to the maintenance of a minimum of internal order in their societies, without which civil war or communist conquest would quickly follow. A simple prescription which proposes to eliminate these people before other social groups—particularly the middle class—have become capable of carrying on their essential function would prove more dangerous than the evil it seeks to eradicate. Thus, there is no quick or easy safeguard against the dangers of a reactionary nationalism which may often deliberately collaborate with the communists against the constructive elements in its own country, or which unwittingly helps to prepare the way for communism by a stubborn resistance to necessary economic and social progress. So long as such groups are essential to the maintenance of internal order, their rule must be tolerated and, if necessary, actively supported. There is no magic formula for transforming overnight a quasi-feudal society into a modern democratic one. Nor, for an underdeveloped country seriously threatened by communist aggression or subversion, would it necessarily be wise to abandon a strong, though reactionary, ruler for a pseudo-democratic regime—called into existence by our fiat—which would be too immature and weak to resist internal disintegration or external invasion. We complain—and quite correctly—that Syngman Rhee is an autocrat, but by whom would he be replaced?

We must also recognize that many of the older ruling groups—like the sheiks of some of the oil-rich Arab states, or the Moslem parties in Pakistan and Indonesia—have proved friendly toward the development of their countries and have seen clearly that their future independence lies in alliance with the West. People of this kind may be preparing the way for the ultimate development of effectively functioning free institutions in their countries and need the help which the West can give them.

In the longer run, it is only through the development of a larger, more mature, and constructively oriented middle class that it will be possible to dispense with the older ruling groups or transform them into forward-looking leaders. But, it must be remembered that neither an Ataturk nor a Magsaysay were created by Western fiat. Nor, for example, have modern Turkey or Mexico achieved their remarkable progress without prolonged efforts of their own to overcome internal difficulties and external dangers. There are, nonetheless, things which the West can do to help foster the growth of constructive middle-class leaders and groups in these societies. Among other things—some of which have already been mentioned in earlier sections of this chapter— achievement of this objective requires closer working relationships between Westerners, on the one hand, and the older ruling groups and emerging middle classes in the underdeveloped countries, on the other hand. If the West can adequately train—and send to the underdeveloped countries in sufficient numbers—devoted and skillful medical missionaries, industrial technicians, agricultural and other specialists, and political and military advisors of the highest caliber, we and the noncommunist countries of Asia, Africa and Latin America can together turn back the tide of Soviet and Red Chinese imperialism and make possible the eventual emergence of free and humane societies in these regions.

Refer to background on page 138

5

The Underdeveloped
Countries

Problems and Prospects of Economic Growth

The economic health of the non-communist underdeveloped countries depends, as does that of the industrial nations, on the character of the requirements and claims on their economies and on the efficiency with which their economies fulfill such demands. It is also affected by the nature of their relations with the international economy and the extent to which the latter increases or diminishes the efficiency of their internal economic institutions. In the preceding chapter, we sketched in broad outline the character of economic expectations and claims in the underdeveloped countries and the general ways in which they have —and have not—been changing during the current profound transformations of these societies. In this chapter, we shall examine the more immediate and specific problems of—and the shorter-term prospects for —accelerating the economic growth of these countries, a requirement which must be met if consumption claims are to be fulfilled, free political institutions fostered, and the capacity for self-defense developed. This analysis will also reveal some of the more important ways in which improved relationships between the underdeveloped countries and the international economy would result in mutual benefits for each.

Economic development—accelerating the rate of economic growth— is at bottom a social phenomenon, the resultant of a complex interaction among institutions, attitudes and motivations. Conventional economic analysis abstracts from this social process certain objectively perceived relationships—e.g., between consumption and saving, investment and productivity, domestic production and foreign trade, etc.—in which changes of various kinds correspond to changes in the rate and direction of economic growth. This is legitimate scientific method so long as the social determinants of these relationships are recognized. In economic analysis applied to Western countries, it is not always necessary to recognize explicitly the social context of economic activity, for institutions, attitudes and motivations are so familiar that they may be assumed as given and, in effect, discounted. But, though this procedure may be valid in the analysis of short-period or static economic phenomena in Western economies, it usually has serious deficiencies —noted in earlier chapters—when used as a method of diagnosing or prescribing for the problems of dynamic processes like economic growth or economic transformation.

The conventional method of analyzing economic phenomena in abstraction from their social context is particularly liable to error when it is applied to the economic growth processes of non-Western societies like those of the underdeveloped countries in Asia, Africa and Latin America. Technically speaking, it may be valid to define an underdeveloped country as one with relatively low productivity, low rate of saving and investment and low per capita national income. But, because their institutions, attitudes and motivations are different from those in the West, the social determinants in these countries of their rates of saving and investment are also bound to operate in different fashions and to produce different results. Hence it would be a grave mistake to infer from this technically valid definition that the only thing needed for developing an underdeveloped country is to increase its rate of net capital formation for a sufficiently long period of time.

Indeed, if the experience of the last decade in trying to accelerate the economic growth of underdeveloped countries has taught us anything, it is that only limited results can be accomplished by purely economic means alone. Social, political and ideological changes must also occur which can induce and sustain a higher rate of indigenous capital formation, larger imports of foreign capital, and greater receptivity to technological innovation. It is only after this stock of "social capital" reaches a certain size that economic development as such can become a self-sustaining—much less a self-accelerating—process. Nor is it clear that any underdeveloped country has as yet reached the stage of this decisive "breakthrough," although Turkey and possibly some of the Latin American countries like Mexico, Brazil, Venezuela, and Colombia may soon be approaching it. Meantime, economic progress is itself a precondition for certain of the social, political and ideological changes on which subsequent economic advancement in turn depends. Thus, economic development is both cause and consequence of social and political development, an aspect or dimension of the general process by which societies are transformed.

In the sections which follow, we shall indicate something of the reciprocal relationships among the social, political, economic, and ideological dimensions of the current profound transformations of the underdeveloped countries. Inevitably, an analysis of this kind must focus attention upon the obstacles to more rapid economic progress which have to be mitigated or removed rather than upon the favorable factors which may already be working to hasten or ease the process of development. Hence, it must be recognized at the outset that the underdeveloped countries today have three advantages which the West did not have—or did not enjoy in anything like the same degree—during the corresponding stage of its own development. The first is the consciousness by these countries themselves of their own need and desire for development, and their consequent eagerness to make this goal an explicit objective of public and private policies and programs. The second is the fact that their economic progress does not depend solely upon their own creativity —their own capacity for innovation in a Schumpeterian sense—but mainly upon their ability to adapt the techniques and tools which they require from the existing, advanced, and still rapidly evolving technology of the West. The third favorable factor is the need and the willingness of the West consciously and actively to assist their economic advancement in various appropriate ways. The importance of these three advantages should not be underestimated. But it is also true that, by themselves, these favorable factors are not sufficient to ensure that development will occur fast enough or in desirable directions. Hence, it is essential that the obstacles to progress be better understood both in the underdeveloped countries and in the West if measures adequate for overcoming them are to be devised and executed in time to be effective.

The Social, Political and Ideological Concomitants of Development

Detailed analysis of the social, political and ideological aspects of development lies outside the scope of this study. A broad sketch was given in the preceding chapter of the ways in which changing social attitudes and values condition the expectations of the main groups in the underdeveloped societies. Here we may briefly suggest certain initial social and political prerequisites for an expanding economic system.

Important among the attitudes and values necessary for initiating and sustaining rapid economic growth are a general willingness on the part of the major social groups to pursue or accept economic and social roles conducive to growth; a government strong enough and respected enough to preserve internal order and a reasonable calculability of political and economic conditions over time; and a minimum degree of external security and of calculable international economic relationships. In turn, these rest upon the persistence of a widely shared community of values and goals both within the country and to a lesser—but nevertheless significant—extent between it and its major trading partners and any powerful neighbors who might otherwise threaten its security. In the absence of such social, political and moral preconditions, an economy may still continue to function, but it is not likely to be one which grows very fast, allocates its resources effectively among competing needs and claims if these are seriously incompatible, or can afford increasing material satisfactions for its members, assuming that these are believed to be desirable.

To what extent do such social, political and ideological preconditions of accelerated economic growth prevail in the underdeveloped areas today? In Southern Asia, the Moslem countries and Africa, the shared community values of thousands of years are threatened or deeply compromised even where they are not in process of rapid decay and transformation. This is true not only in the sense that traditional attitudes and goals are losing their hold over the most active social groups, but more particularly in that many of the institutions and relationships through which basic values were formerly expressed have passed away or have become seriously disorganized. At the same time, attitudes toward production and entrepreneurship—and toward consumption, saving and investment—are not yet of a type conducive to rapid economic growth and, where such exist, are characteristic of too few people within these societies. In regions where independence has been recently won, new national governments are on the whole weak and inexperienced, and in some countries a state of insurrection or civil war is more or less continuous. In older nations, like those of Latin America and the Moslem area, most governments have never acquired the stability and the respect necessary for reasonable security and calculability in the political and legal conditions influencing economic activity. Many of the underdeveloped countries are threatened either from outside by Soviet or Red Chinese aggression or by internal communist subversion, or are seriously weakened by extreme and irresponsible nationalist movements. And, with the "nationalization" of the world economy so characteristic of the mid-20th century, and the success of obscurantist communist and nationalist propaganda, there is no longer between them and their major trading partners that minimum degree of felt community on which mutually beneficial international economic relations depend.[1]

As far as these social and political prerequisites are concerned, most underdeveloped countries are much less favorably situated today than were Western Europe and North America at similar stages in their history. In the West—despite religious, civil and dynastic wars—basic community values were never abandoned, but modified and enriched by the humanistic Renaissance, Protestant Reformation and Catholic Counter-Reformation, they eventually found expression in new forms of individual freedom and vigorous enterprise, orderly and efficient government, and uniform and calculable legal and other conditions of progressive economic activity. No external threat or serious internal subversive movement against its basic economic and social institutions threatened this system during its developing years. Even the pressures of growing populations could be periodically relieved through emigration to new or underpopulated lands. In the underdeveloped areas today, there has as yet been no religious renovation or cultural renaissance capable of redefining traditional values and hastening their expression in new, more satisfying, political and social forms. Everywhere, the dead

---

[1] See Chapter 1, pp. 38–39 for the meanings attached to the phrase "nationalization of the world economy." The underdeveloped countries have contributed importantly to this nationalization not simply by the achievement of national independence but more especially by the parochialism of their economic policies and practices—the economic concomitant of their extreme nationalism and xenophobia. In turn, the relative inefficiency of the nationalized world economy helps to strengthen their economic nationalism.

weight of the past lives on into the present, made increasingly shapeless by the impact of alien ideas and activities.

Japan is an excellent illustration of the importance of moral community, positive attitudes toward economic activity, strong government, and socially responsible class roles for the process of rapid economic growth. The vigor of Japanese economic development over the past ninety years is in no small measure owed to the firm establishment of these political, social and moral prerequisites during the two and a half centuries of the Tokugawa Shogunate.[2] When Japan opened itself to the outside world, it already possessed a long and vital tradition of national purpose, strong central government, self-confident and secularly oriented ruling groups, and industrious and docile working classes. All Japan needed for rapid economic growth was the decision to undertake it, for the necessary foreign capital and technology were also readily available in the still-integrated world economy of the late 19th century.

The case of Japan illustrates another aspect of the relations between political, social, and moral factors and economic growth. Throughout the period of its rapid economic development, Japanese institutions were authoritarian and the state played a much more important role in this development than it did in any Western country, not even excepting Imperial Germany.[3] Thus, it is important to recognize that the political

---

[2] It might prove rewarding to study the extent to which traditional Japanese epistemological and ethical ideas help to account for the differences between Japanese development and that of China, India and even the Islamic countries over the past century. Though derived from Chinese and Indian models, formal Japanese philosophy, as well as popular ideology, had quite different content and significance, particularly in their insistence on what might paradoxically be called "intuitive empiricism" and in their search for individual self-realization in secular attainments rather than in escape through mysticism from the "wheel of life." While characteristic of many strands of traditional Japanese thinking, these ideas were perhaps most fully expressed in Zen Buddhism and influenced directly—and indirectly through Shinto—the attitudes of the samurai groups who played the major role in the 19th-century transformation of Japan. It would be interesting to discover whether this distinctive Japanese intuitive empiricism and secularism could be considered, at least in some of their practical consequences, as equivalents of the many forms of rationalistic secular individualism in the West from the 12th century on. See, for example, the various sections on Zen Buddhism in Charles A. Moore, ed., *Philosophy—East and West* (Princeton: Princeton University Press, 1944) and Charles A. Moore, ed., *Essays in East-West Philosophy* (Honolulu: University of Hawaii Press, 1951).

[3] Basic industries in Japan were planned and initiated by the state and were financed with government funds, part of which were obtained by borrowing abroad. Subsequently, many investments were sold at very advantageous prices to private interests (the *Zaibatsu*) while others continued to be owned and operated by the state. See George B. Sansom, *The Western World and Japan: A Study in the Interaction of European and Asiatic Cultures* (New York: Alfred A. Knopf, 1951), pp. 500–501, 503.

and social conditions of economic growth are not dependent upon one particular set of institutions and moral ideals. In the West, the process of choice and change since the late Middle Ages has resulted in values which stress, and institutions which express, the worth of the individual, the desirability of innovation and enterprise, and the freedom of thought and inquiry. Though threatened today both from within and from without, these basic values still animate our existing political and economic institutions and our efforts to find more satisfying and humane forms of living and working together. But we have also seen over the past generation rapid economic development occurring not only in Japan but in the Soviet Union as well. In the latter country, too, the political, social and ideological prerequisites of growth have obviously existed. But there, the prerequisites of rapid economic expansion have been attained through the utter subordination of the individual to the monolithic state and the extinction of freedom of thought and inquiry in a quasi-religious orthodoxy. Thus, in the West by free consent, and in the Soviet Union largely by compulsion, two different conceptions of the ends and means of social life have each established or imposed a sufficient degree of uniformity of purpose, accepted and socially useful class functions, and stable and effective government, for the economic development of their societies to be substantial and rapid.

The liberal Western way of development is economically more difficult and morally more demanding than the totalitarian or authoritarian way. But its material and spiritual rewards are correspondingly greater. Today, the underdeveloped countries are still free to determine which method they will follow. How are they likely to choose? The growing familiarity of certain groups in these countries with Western ideals and with their current institutional expressions certainly argues the possibility that these countries may eventually succeed in adapting—not in adopting—the institutions and attitudes of freedom to their own cultural potentialities and needs. But it is equally —if not more—likely that the totalitarian way will prevail, particularly if Western interest in the future of these countries continues to be inadequate. For, the historical relationships of domination and subordination in these societies and their traditional attitudes toward the individual are closer to the Soviet pattern of political and moral order than to our own. Moreover, in Southern Asia and the Moslem region, people tend to regard the Soviet Union as an underdeveloped country like their own which has, nonetheless, succeeded in raising itself by its own bootstraps despite Western hostility. Communist propaganda constantly reiterates that only through imitation of Soviet methods can the underdeveloped countries achieve a rapid rate of economic growth in the face of real or imagined Western indifference.

Unless, with adequate Western help, these countries can make more rapid progress in evolving free and humane institutions of their own, it is probable that continued social disintegration, political weakness and economic stagnation will sooner or later produce indigenous totalitarian "solutions" even if the West is strong and resolute enough to prevent outright Soviet or Red Chinese conquest. Already in Iran, Guatemala and elsewhere, nationalistic totalitarian or crypto-communist regimes have nearly succeeded in consolidating their rule, and in other countries (e.g., Indonesia) they may soon be strong enough to reach more openly for power. Such regimes are not just modern versions of the traditional Latin American type of dictatorship but are frankly monolithic, "dynamic" and social revolutionary in the fascist or communist sense. The need to help the underdeveloped countries evolve stronger political and economic institutions congenial with those of the West makes it important that we demonstrate convincingly to their people the ethical and pragmatic superiority of free and humane forms of socially responsible, decentralized, private decision-making and action.

Population Pressure

Next to the establishment of political and social conditions conducive to rapid economic growth, the problem of population pressure is perhaps the most difficult of those facing many underdeveloped countries today.

The consequences of this trend can be seen in the table on page 181 which compares the rate of increase of population with the rates of increase of agricultural and industrial production in selected countries. All of the countries, except Japan, in which food production has grown more slowly than population, are in the underdeveloped category. Moreover, in several of the countries where the population grew less rapidly than food production, levels of domestic food consumption have increased, leaving proportionately less for export.[4]

Prior to the encounter with the West, population in the underdeveloped areas grew slowly, if at all. Religious, social and economic

---

[4] Note that in Australia and Argentina, major exporters of staple foods, population has been increasing much more rapidly than food production.

COMPARISONS OF INCREASES IN POPULATION WITH CHANGES IN FOOD, TOTAL AGRICULTURAL, AND INDUSTRIAL PRODUCTION IN SELECTED COUNTRIES

	Population	Agriculture [a]		Industrial Production [b]
	% increase 1937 to 1951	% increase in food production prewar to 1951	% increase in total agricultural production prewar to 1951	% increase 1937 to 1951
Africa and Near East				
Egypt	29	+23	+12	n.a.
Turkey	24	+35	+40	+79
Far East				
Ceylon	36	+27	+36	n.a.
India	19	−1	−2	+29
Indonesia: Java and Madura	14	−5	−8	n.a.
Philippines	31	+10	+4	n.a.
Latin America				
Argentina	30	+4	+2	+84
Brazil	38	+24	+21	+142
Chile	24	+34	+32	+95
Colombia	33	+71	+71	+422 [c]
Mexico	41	+46	+58	+67
Peru	28	+50	+40	n.a.
Oceania				
Australia	23	+1	+3	n.a.
New Zealand	23	+7	+10	+83
The West				
France	2	+7	+8	+21
Italy	10	+15	+15	+41
Netherlands	20	+22	+24	+45
United Kingdom	7	+24	+23	+29
United States	20	+32	+30	+95

[a] Base = 1934–1938 average in most cases. [b] Includes mining, manufacturing, electricity and manufactured gas. Many of these indices probably also cover an indeterminate portion of construction and services. Except for the Western countries, they are based on estimates rather than on statistically reliable data and probably considerably overstate the growth of industrial production. [c] Percentage increase from 1939 to 1948.

factors generally combined to cause high birth rates, while "Malthusian" influences were relatively unimpeded in keeping the death rate high as well. During the last hundred years, however, birth rates have remained high, but death rates have declined. To a considerable extent, the fall in the death rate is a consequence of the encounter with the West. The growth of commercial agriculture in foodstuffs, more effective anti-famine measures made possible by better transportation and more efficient administration, epidemic control and public health programs, relative internal peace, and many other factors stemming more or less directly from Western influences have in large part been responsible for the fall in the death rate.

The current rates of population increase in many of the underdeveloped areas constitute one of the major problems of these countries. Perhaps it would be more significant to say that population pressures raise all of the other problems of development to a higher level of intensity. They make it more difficult, if not impossible, to mitigate social discontent by increases in per capita consumption. They turn customary rural underemployment into mass unemployment. They force food deficit countries to use scarce foreign exchange for consumption imports rather than for capital goods. They multiply welfare and health problems beyond the capacity of the limited resources available for these purposes in the underdeveloped countries. In a multitude of other ways, inordinate rates of population growth intensify economic, social and political difficulties.

Today, in the countries with excessive rates of population growth, there is more awareness of the problem than there are either willingness or effective measures to deal with it. Some countries are impeded by religious principles or social customs. Others merely hope that somehow a sufficient rise in living standards can be achieved which might provide incentives for a lower birth rate, as was supposed to have happened in Europe. A few countries, like India, are beginning to recognize the need for a sound, positive population control policy.

It is unlikely that, in the absence of positive population policies, the process of economic development will be rapid enough, or substantial enough, to arrest population growth in the foreseeable future, particularly since death rates—still high by Western standards—will continue to decline as health standards improve. In the last two years, world production of food has been increasing faster than world growth of population. But this less dismal global outlook provides small consolation to the many individual food-deficit countries whose low productivity has made it impossible for them either to grow or to import enough food to maintain—much less improve—their consumption in the face of increasing populations. At best, the population problem of these countries may be mitigated in time by improved productivity and by positive population control policies. If it cannot, the political and economic repercussions may become critical long before that general calamity, predicted by the neo-Malthusians, when excessive expansion of world population as a whole will reduce mankind to a diet of seaweed and algae.

Balance of Agriculture and Industry

Though the underdeveloped countries of Asia, Africa and Latin America are today still predominantly primary producers, the economically progressive middle-class groups in most of them either desire or have actually embarked upon industrialization programs. As we have seen in the preceding chapter, the emphasis on industrialization arises in part from the valid needs of these societies to provide productive employment for redundant labor and to raise living standards. In part, however, it is the result of an understandable, but nonetheless debatable, conclusion that only in this way can the economic independence of these countries be ensured and their international trading positions made more favorable.

Despite the valid reasons for industrialization, the primary need of most underdeveloped countries is substantial increases in the diversification, production and productivity of the agricultural sectors of their economies. In those countries where inordinate population growth is a major problem, increased food production is essential unless living standards are to fall or scarce foreign exchange is to be used for food imports. Improvement in the quality and quantity of the diet is probably the first requirement in those areas where per capita consumption must be raised to allay social discontent, both urban and rural. Moreover, the sacrifice of potential, economically feasible, agricultural development to ambitious industrialization projects can be self-defeating, as the recent experience of Argentina, Australia and some of the East European Soviet satellites indicates.

Nevertheless, in countries with population problems, and particularly in those which lack substantial areas of unused arable land, improvements in agriculture will sooner or later generate the need—and the possibility—for some industrialization. The effects of increased agricultural productivity on the requirements for agricultural labor are, however, not likely to be as rapid as, for example, in the United States and Canada in recent decades. In most underdeveloped countries, large-scale mechanization of agriculture is not only beyond the financial resources of the governments and social groups concerned, but it is not yet—and may never be—appropriate to the cultural comprehension, size and types of land holdings, or crops and soils of these regions. Other kinds of improvements in agricultural methods—better hand tools and animal-drawn implements; crop diversification and rotation; soil fertilization, preparation, and preservation; irrigation and water conservation; insect, weed, and pest control; improved food storage, transportation, marketing, and processing—are on the whole cheaper and, at least over the short-term, are more likely to be better suited to peasant needs and capabilities. They will, therefore, yield more rapid and substantial productivity increases than ambitious mechanization schemes.

But even these agricultural innovations cannot be easily or quickly accomplished. Techniques, tools, and biological and chemical products originally developed for temperate zone physical and economic conditions are generally not suited for adoption in the tropics without extensive testing and adaptation. Cultural differences, illiteracy, and social and religious customs also limit the applicability of many types of Western techniques and equipment. Thus, the achievement of a substantial and sustained increase in the rate of growth of agricultural productivity—per acre and per man—is a slow and difficult process, as postwar experience with technical assistance programs proves.[5]

While in the interests of these countries themselves, agricultural reform and development must have priority, some regions have already reached a stage of labor redundancy and underemployment where industrialization also becomes urgent. There is, however, considerable

---

[5] The physical limitations of agriculture in tropical and semitropical regions must also be kept in mind. Except in the river valleys and deltas, tropical soils are generally neither as fertile nor as durable under cultivation as those of the temperate zones owing to the more rapid oxidation of minerals and the leaching and erosion which result from the combination of high mean annual temperatures and greater, more concentrated, rainfall. Land reclaimed from tropical jungle or rain forest is particularly fragile and, if it is to be continuously and intensively cultivated, requires careful management to preserve its fertility. Much of it may be suitable only for extensive, and not for intensive, methods of cultivation. See Pierre Gourou, *The Tropical World* (London: Longmans, Green and Co., 1953).

disagreement over the extent of industrialization and the specific industries which should be fostered.

The industrial countries are inclined to claim that the industrialization of underdeveloped areas should be undertaken only to the extent that it contributes to maximizing the output of the international economy as a whole, and that this consideration requires the use of resources in underdeveloped countries in accordance with the traditional doctrine of comparative costs. In fact, considerable industrialization in underdeveloped countries could be justified even by this restrictive standard. Under the control of metropolitan industrial countries, primary production in many colonial and semidependent areas was formerly pushed beyond the limits that the comparative advantage principle would itself have dictated. But it is also true that, unless greatly qualified, this conventional economic standard is not very helpful in the conditions of the mid-20th century.

In the first place, the doctrine of comparative costs neglects the adverse effects of the unstable character of raw material prices on the stability of incomes in the primary-producing countries. A policy of expanding agricultural output for export involves increasing the vulnerability of the underdeveloped countries to this instability and, more generally, to all the adverse effects on economic growth of the incalculability of contemporary international economic conditions.

In the second place, without considerable qualification, the simple comparative costs criterion is not equitable. For example, if the doctrine of comparative costs is applied on the basis of *existing* comparative costs, it uses *existing* relative levels of productivity and real income in industrial and agricultural countries as its starting point. In effect, it treats existing levels as normative—as factors to which policy should conform and which it would not be "economical" deliberately to alter. But the existing distribution of income in the non-Soviet world, and the related pattern of comparative costs, are historical facts, not norms. They exist, in part, simply because Western Europe and the United States were the first areas to industrialize.[6] To apply the doctrine of compara-

---

[6] Industrial productivity and costs are to an important extent determined by the size which particular industries and national outputs have reached, owing to the dependence of so-called "external economies" on the size of individual industries and the size of the total national output. Perhaps the best formulation of this point was made by Allyn Young in the article entitled "Increasing Returns and Economic Progress," *Economic Journal* (December, 1928). These "external economies" in the process of industrialization are ignored in a static comparison of the costs of producing newly introduced manufactures in under-

tive costs without qualification to the question of industrialization of agricultural countries amounts to an attempt to deny to the agricultural countries the right to alter, by conscious policy, a pattern of distribution of world income and of opportunities for economic growth given by history—a pattern which today has neither an ethical nor a political sanction.[7]

If, however, the comparative cost doctrine is modified to take into account these two major contemporary qualifications, it would become a more relevant and useful criterion, though not by any means a controlling one. In general, it would provide a fairly broad justification for industrialization in underdeveloped countries. But even on this liberalized criterion, it is clear that the industrialization programs of a number of underdeveloped countries go beyond the dictates of social need or economic efficiency.

In the light of their very limited capital resources (and in theory their virtually unlimited needs), the underdeveloped countries should try to make the most economical and efficient use of what they have. Since the objective is to increase productive employment opportunities and improve living standards as rapidly as possible, the industries to be encouraged should logically be those with relatively modest capital requirements, which do not need a high proportion of technically skilled labor, and which produce goods directly suitable for consumption. Food processing, textiles and clothing, building materials, house furnishings, farm implements, and allied "soft" and consumers' goods industries

developed areas with the costs of producing the same products in established industrial economies. "External economies" in industry are, in general, a function of the total volume and degree of diversification of industrial output in the industrializing country. At a certain stage in industrialization—witness Japan—the "external economies," if indeed they can be so called, crisscross the whole industrial structure and may produce a new manufacturing economy competitive in many lines with established industrial areas.

[7] Of course, classical 19th-century economic thought was never guilty of so gross a methodological error. It was recognized quite early that the possibility of realizing increasing returns in industry, once a certain level of industrialization was reached, created a case for tariff protection of "infant industries." That is, it was recognized that the process of industrialization would itself change the pattern of comparative costs and would justify protection for a while. But, from a contemporary standpoint, this doctrine, too, is incomplete in holding that, at some unspecified point, "artificial" promotion of industrialization should end and thereafter economic growth should be governed by reference to comparative costs alone. Today, such a conclusion overlooks the fact that the problem of distributing opportunities for economic growth among countries is a continuing one which cannot, in mid-20th century conditions, be left solely to the "automatic" allocation of an impaired international market.

best meet these requirements. In contrast, the "hard" and producers' goods industries—metals processing and finishing, machinery, machine tools and vehicles, chemicals and drugs, electrical and electronic goods, etc.—do not. Their capital and technical requirements are very high, indigenous demand for their products is likely to be limited for many years to come, and their competitive position—both in domestic and in foreign markets—quite disadvantageous compared with similar products made in advanced industrial countries.

This guiding principle is easily stated but very difficult to apply. The widespread demand in these countries for the development of heavy industry arises in part from the belief that it would ensure economic independence of, and fair treatment by, the industrial nations of the West. Steel mills, chemical plants, machine tool factories and the like tend to be evaluated in such political terms by the underdeveloped countries and not in the light of the most economical use of their own scarce capital and trained manpower resources. Not only are proposals of this type unrealistic, but they are generally promoted with such passion as to reduce local interest in, or actually to block, more modest and more practicable projects for which foreign assistance, private or public, might be obtained.

Thus, the attainment of a desirable order of development priorities —of proper balance between agriculture and industry and among different branches of industry—is by no means easy in the underdeveloped countries today. Factors are operative which work both for and against a desirable pattern. In the absence of general agreement on the priorities and direction of development, the process is likely to be slower and more wasteful than it might otherwise be. To the extent to which free market forces are permitted to operate, natural selection could eventually weed out and discourage uneconomic efforts. But, the influence of the market place is now—and is likely to remain—very much less important in the underdeveloped areas than in the West at a similar stage of its evolution.

Incentives, Investment and Consumption

The rate and pattern of economic development will be affected as much by the incentives for, and the limitations on, the economical use of resources as by the availability of resources. These limitations are of special importance in the underdeveloped countries where the motive of maximizing money incomes does not yet operate as universally or as freely as in the West.

The growth of agriculture is overwhelmingly dependent upon peasant attitudes and activities. Yet it is by no means certain that, even if sufficient capital were obtainable, investment in agriculture would occur on a corresponding scale or would result in increased supplies available for consumption by other portions of the population, or for export. As we have seen, social, cultural and religious factors limit and distort the most effective use of investment resources. In some countries, the initial increments in the food production of individual peasant families are likely to be consumed by these groups themselves. Even in the case of nonfood crops, or of food crops customarily raised for sale, production increases may occur only to the point where the additional money income is sufficient to provide a slightly more ample and secure —but still traditional—standard of living. Once this level is reached, additional time for noneconomic activities may be valued more than the qualitative and quantitative changes in consumption which further production increases might bring. Such passive peasant attitudes toward a large and sustained rate of increase of agricultural productivity are widely prevalent among the two thirds of the Latin American population of Indian or mixed descent, in Africa, in the Moslem countries, and in those areas of Southern Asia least influenced by Western activities and motivations.

Among the middle classes, there are analogous—though different —attitudes which work against a division of income between consumption and investment more conducive to economic growth and to the most productive types of investment. In Latin America and the Moslem countries, the middle classes are still heavily influenced by older aristocratic or quasi-feudal standards and a considerable portion of middle-class income is used for conspicuous consumption. In these regions, too, investment in the purchase of land and non-productive real estate is still popular for reasons of social prestige and security. But, unlike many of their counterparts in England before the 20th century, few of these landed *bourgeois* become "improving landlords." Even today, the standard of efficiency on native-owned plantations and estates is generally lower than on those owned or managed by Westerners.

Finally, for much the same reasons, many of these middle-class groups become *rentiers* at an earlier stage of their capital accumulation than has been customary in the West. They prefer to invest their savings in mortgages and other forms of high-interest-bearing obligations and, more recently, in foreign (Western) securities rather than in new productive enterprises involving risk-taking and active management at home.[8] This tendency, always strong in Latin America and the Moslem countries, has been re-enforced in the postwar years by internal disorder, inflation, and the threat of communist aggression and subversion.[9]

Among the industrial workers, we have also noted evidences of the persistence of pre-industrial motivations which in part account for the lower productivity and high absenteeism and labor turnover in the underdeveloped areas. While the demand for higher wages is now universal in these countries, it may be motivated as much by a desire to accumulate sufficient funds for enabling the worker to return to some traditional occupation or residence as it is by the expectation of permanent employment in industry and an improved material living standard along Western lines. These attitudes may, however, change as the satisfactions of urban life—and the returns from, and security of, industrial occupations—increase compared with those of agriculture or other traditional forms of work.

These relatively weak incentives for productive investment and for substantial and sustained increases in productivity and production are also affected by the low level of income and the existing patterns of income distribution. Most of the populations of these countries live too near minimum subsistence levels to afford even a moderate rate of

---

[8] With respect to business ability and motivation, the following quotation from an unpublished memorandum by Everett E. Hagen of the Center for International Studies, Massachusetts Institute of Technology, illustrates the effects of the persistence of pre-entrepreneurial attitudes in the underdeveloped countries: ". . . administrative-managerial ability is not lacking [in the underdeveloped countries]. The histories of underdeveloped countries with which I happen to be familiar record many instances of effective prosecution of magnificently conceived large scale enterprises, mainly warlike or with religious significance. . . . Lack of training in industry and in administration is superficially the explanation of the lack of managerial-administrative ability in productive projects. I suggest that the explanation is seriously incomplete. An important reason why entrepreneurial ability to develop industry and agriculture is lacking is that interest in such entrepreneurship is lacking. It does not have high honorific value in the culture. The people and the leaders want the fruits of entrepreneurship, but few of them are interested in being the entrepreneurs."

[9] There is reason to believe that at least some underdeveloped countries may never pass through a period of vigorous competitive enterprise, individual or corporate. This is particularly likely in Latin America where business attitudes and methods resemble those in the more stagnant economies of Western Europe.

saving. Moreover, such income as is potentially available for capital formation tends to accumulate in the hands of groups often uninterested in productive investment. This is particularly true in the countryside, where the landlord, the moneylender, the local shopkeeper and produce merchant—frequently the same person—manage to obtain a shamelessly disproportionate share of the returns from agriculture. Without widespread agrarian reforms, which cover agricultural credit and marketing as well as land tenures and rents, the peasantry will generally be unable to afford even those investments which its limited incentives might induce it to make.

To a lesser extent, there is also a nonprogressive pattern of income distribution in the other sectors of the economy. Though business taxes are generally low, interest rates are high and banking and credit facilities are proportionately more expensive than in the West. This tends to restrict new indigenous investment to a self-financed basis. At the same time, the willingness to use income for investment conflicts with socially acceptable consumption standards.

Thus, the poverty of these economies, their nonprogressive patterns of income distribution, and the persistence of traditionalist attitudes toward investment and consumption all combine to limit the process of indigenous private capital formation and to make it less efficient and productive than it might otherwise be. Also, they restrict the effectiveness of measures which might be taken by the industrialized nations to stimulate additional primary production in the underdeveloped countries through higher prices and more stable demand for primary exports. In consequence of these factors, the elasticity of supply is significantly less in the underdeveloped countries than in the advanced industrial economies of the West.

Economic Policy in the Underdeveloped Countries

Native private initiative and resources in the underdeveloped areas are likely to fall short by a very considerable margin of achieving the rate and pattern of economic growth desired by these countries themselves and necessary for an effectively functioning world economic system. In the circumstances, a heavy responsibility rests upon the governments of the underdeveloped countries to play an active role in the process of internal development and to establish and maintain conditions under which foreign capital and foreign cooperation—private, governmental and international—can provide maximum help.

In assessing the ability of the governments of the underdeveloped countries to discharge these tasks, the primary considerations are the newness and inexperience of many of them, their susceptibility to nationalistic pressures, their shortage of trained policy-making and administrative personnel, and the limitations on the specific governmental instruments and techniques which can be effectively employed at the current stage of political, social and economic development in these countries. The first three are obvious, or have already been discussed, and need no elaboration here. But the last requires fuller explanation.

In many, if not most, underdeveloped countries today, the largest source of indigenous investment capital is the governmental budget. This will undoubtedly continue to be the case until changes in attitudes and income distribution and the process of growth itself have induced much greater and more spontaneous private capital formation. But the domestic resources which governments can mobilize for publicly financed investment, and the techniques available to them for this purpose, are also limited by the poverty of their economies and by existing economic and social structures.

Westerners do not generally realize that, in most of these countries, the principal source of government revenue is still taxation of imports and exports and, to a lesser extent, excise and sales taxes. Taxes on business incomes and private capital gains are generally very low— except in the case of foreign-owned businesses—not only as a matter of deliberate development policy but also because tax morality and social customs do not permit the collection of substantial revenues from these sources. Personal income taxes are either nonexistent or nominal, for the great bulk of the population is too poor to pay them and the difficulties of collection are virtually insurmountable. Instead, capitation and land taxes of a type traditional in these societies have in many instances been kept in force, but their yield is low and their value chiefly symbolic in maintaining the right of the government to levy direct taxes on the entire population.

In the circumstances, government revenue is particularly dependent upon the state of foreign trade and fluctuates with the rise and fall of exports and imports. Expenditures, however, have a tendency to rise steadily, owing to the need to foster development and increase social welfare, to support a growing bureaucracy, and to restore and maintain internal order and national security. These expenditures are not easily curtailed as revenue fluctuates, particularly in the case of national security and development projects, which run for several years and must have assured financing if waste and inefficiency are to be minimized.

Owing both to the limited revenue available and to its uncertainty, considerable reliance must be placed upon borrowing, and the capital items in the budget may be financed wholly or partly from this source. In most underdeveloped countries, however, the private market for government obligations is very small and, in the absence of foreign credits, inflationary forms of financing are common (e.g., central bank advances).

Thus, the fiscal situations of the underdeveloped countries contain inherent tendencies to generate inflationary pressures. Persistent mild inflation is not necessarily an evil in underdeveloped economies where a rapid rate of growth must be stimulated in the face of relatively weak economic incentives and a nonprogressive social structure.[10] But strong inflationary pressures, which nullify these benefits, are constantly being generated in the underdeveloped countries by overly ambitious development and social welfare programs, irresponsible nationalist passions, and internal disorder, or in response to inflationary movements originating in other parts of the world. Owing to the limited economic control techniques available to these governments and to the limited effectiveness of such anti-inflationary measures in underdeveloped economies, major inflationary pressures soon get out of hand, aggravating already inequitable patterns of income distribution, stirring up additional social unrest, and diverting scarce resources to uneconomic uses. While the use of foreign aid funds to finance large consumers' goods imports may effectively dampen inflationary pressure, the effects may only be temporary and are usually achieved at the expense of permanently useful capital goods imports.

---

[10] Earl J. Hamilton has recently documented and analyzed the important role played by mild inflationary pressures in the economic development of Western Europe from the 16th to the 19th centuries. He notes particularly how a persistent tendency to inflation hastened the redistribution of wealth from traditionalist to more progressive social classes and increased the accumulation of productive capital owing to the lag of wage rates and raw material prices behind the prices of finished goods. See "Prices and Progress," *Journal of Economic History* (Vol. XII, No. 4, Fall, 1952).

The problems of mobilizing through the governmental budget, and using efficiently, the resources needed for development purposes, while holding inherent inflationary tendencies in reasonable check, are made more difficult by the nonprogressive character of existing social and economic relationships. But they are also compounded by political and ideological factors which heavily influence the economic policies of these countries. Politically powerful interest groups may slow down the necessary modernization and expansion of the tax system. At the same time, demands for the protection of new domestic industries from foreign competition not only result in rising costs for the government and consumers but also restrict the tariff revenue which might be obtained through larger imports. The weakness of many of these governments and their susceptibility to popular pressures make it difficult for them to hold in check the growth of social welfare expenditures and the unnecessary expansion of the bureaucracy, particularly in the lower ranks.

Finally, and perhaps most importantly, prevailing nationalist passions produce uneconomic uses of available resources and in various ways diminish the resources which might be obtained from abroad. The obstacles to rapid and efficient economic growth resulting from exaggerated and irresponsible nationalism are too familiar to require extended discussion here. Suffice it to say, they have had the effect, as *The Economist* once put it, of "cutting off the native nose to spite the Western face." Nationalism accounts for much of the antipathy to private foreign capital investment. It tends to discourage economic assistance from other governments and international organizations by making impossible demands for, and setting unreasonable conditions on, foreign investors, public and private. It seriously reduces the willingness and the ability of the underdeveloped countries to participate in arrangements for international economic cooperation in their own interest and that of the world economic system as a whole.

In their external economic policies, the underdeveloped countries tend to be among the most active practitioners of economic nationalism not only because of xenophobia but also because of the vulnerability of their economies to unpredictable and drastic changes in international economic conditions. The instability of world prices and demand for primary products may cause major changes in their balances of payments and internal employment levels. As already noted, government revenue is inordinately dependent upon taxes on imports and exports. In the interest of the international economy as a whole, it is important that the underdeveloped countries become better integrated into world economic relationships and more responsive to the long-term need for balance between primary-producing and industrial countries. But the underdeveloped countries are unlikely to modify their economic nationalism unless and until more effective mechanisms are in existence for protecting them against excessive short-term fluctuations in world demand for their products.

Internal Measures for Accelerating Economic Development

At bottom, the obstacles to the economic growth of the underdeveloped countries are results of the profound social transformations through which they are now passing. The constructive liquidation of moribund institutions and the creative resolution of the dilemmas of existing class attitudes and relationships would do incomparably more to accelerate economic growth, and ensure its continuance, than any other changes that could be conceived. In turn, considerable economic progress is necessary before these societies will be flexible enough, and have sufficient resources, for such essential social and political reconstruction.

It is this reciprocal dependence of economic, political and social development which provides both the opportunity and the means for the West to assist significantly in the process of growth and creation in the underdeveloped countries. But before this possibility can be realized, it is necessary to be rid of the notion—fashionable both in the West and in the underdeveloped countries—that Western efforts could directly, substantially and rapidly improve the living standards of the people of those regions. Even the largest conceivable contribution by the inhabitants of the West would be insignificant compared to the vast quantities of goods and services which would be required directly to raise the living standards of the underdeveloped countries to a per capita level remotely comparable to that of Western Europe, much less of North America. Something may be done along these lines in particular localities or even in certain entire countries where political considerations or other factors warrant such extraordinary efforts. But it is inconceivable that any substantial results could be achieved by the direct method which would affect more than a small proportion of that half of the world's population now living in the underdeveloped areas.

There is no substitute for self-help—for the slow, painful, and difficult process by which the people of these countries learn to produce more and more goods with less and less expenditure of effort and resources. It is only by increasing their own productivity—their ability substantially to expand their production of goods to consume directly and to exchange with the rest of the world for other goods that they need or desire—that these countries are eventually going to enjoy significantly higher living standards. In this fundamental sense, the solutions to the problems of the underdeveloped countries lie in their own hands and depend on their own efforts.

Yet when the many kinds of actions which the underdeveloped countries will have to take in their own behalf are summarized and grouped into appropriate categories, some of the specific ways in which Western help could be of decisive importance become apparent. The most essential economic and social changes in the underdeveloped countries are along the following lines:

1. Agrarian reform, where relevant, affecting not only land tenure and rent and share relationships, but agricultural credit, marketing and purchasing arrangements.

2. Stimulation of maximum possible increases in agricultural productivity and production.

3. Encouragement of a more progressive (i.e., conducive to growth) pattern of income distribution and use through tax reforms (which would encourage savings and productive investment and discourage conspicuous consumption and nonproductive investment), wage policies, fiscal and monetary policies, etc.

4. Development of light industries and consumers' goods industries where countries have natural advantages, potentially important domestic demand (e.g., for food-processing industries), excessive rates of population growth, or inadequately employed urban populations.

5. Development of primary production for export in order to obtain capital funds and goods from abroad for further economic growth.

6. Stimulation of opportunities for productive employment of middle-class groups whose expectations have hitherto been frustrated. This might be done through low interest loans to small, new, and expanding businesses; more rapid expansion of health and educational facilities so

as to provide more and better job opportunities for doctors and teachers; etc.

7. Reform and expansion of educational systems so as to reduce the relative stress on the liberal arts and professions and to provide more and better facilities for training in applied science, technology, business management, public administration, skilled trades, etc.

8. Expansion and improvement of public health facilities including positive programs for population control, where necessary.

These internal reforms will not be easily or rapidly accomplished. If they are to be carried out, the governments and socially responsible groups in the underdeveloped countries must address themselves seriously to the task. This means not only continuity of purpose, energy and continual application. It means also that short-term interests will often have to be subordinated to more substantial long-term benefits for the national community as a whole. Above all, it means that problems must not be obscured, and attention diverted, by irresponsible nationalist passions, utopian expectations, or simple panaceas.

The burden of carrying out these objectives can be made much lighter —and in some cases can alone be made possible—by adequate and appropriate kinds of assistance by Western nations, particularly the United States. The introduction of a new administrative, managerial or technological skill, the firm establishment of a new industry or energy source, the eradication of malaria or some other endemic disease, and many other types of specific improvements, may in particular situations provide the decisive increment of change, the last additional element which, though small in itself, may complete the preconditions necessary for some major new advance over a broad front. It is to specific effects of these kinds that the West can make major contributions. The cost of such assistance programs is well within the limits of political possibility and economic feasibility. Indeed, the chief difficulty to be overcome is our failure to understand the need for such Western efforts and the methods by which they can be successfully carried out. Specific discussion of such methods will be reserved for the appropriate sections of Part II.

If the foregoing review of the obstacles to economic growth is valid, some underdeveloped countries cannot be expected to make much more rapid progress during the coming decade than they have during the preceding one. Their own indigenous capital formation will probably be considerably less than that envisaged in their optimistic plans. Social and political reforms will continue to be frustrated by archaic prejudices and short-sighted interests. Irresponsible nationalists or native communist groups may prevent such countries from making effective use of Western protection, encouragement and assistance.

In present circumstances, these conclusions have particular applicability to many of the countries in Southern Asia and the Moslem region. There, the formation of the minimum stock of "social capital" required for self-generating and accelerated economic growth has been inhibited by the failure to undertake necessary internal reforms or by inordinate rates of population growth, or by both. In addition, many of these countries are hampered by special difficulties of a political or ideological nature—e.g., Indian-Pakistani relations, Arab-Israeli relations, and their attendant refugee problems, etc.—and by the imminence of the communist threat (as in Indochina, Malaya, Burma, Indonesia and Iran) which divert attention and resources from the arduous task of social, political and economic development.

Elsewhere, however, the outlook is considerably brighter. Though the process by which attitudes, institutions, and relationships are transformed is necessarily slow, once it gets underway its effects begin to be cumulative at a certain point and make further progress considerably easier and more rapid. Turkey and some of the Latin American countries may soon demonstrate the reality of this possibility. In its own way, Turkey has been developing reasonably strong and stable central government and social classes increasingly willing and able to raise their productivity and incomes. Agrarian reforms are being accomplished and aggressive native entrepreneurial groups are beginning to emerge. However, in Turkey and Latin America, the state has had to play a much larger role in this process than it did in the Western nations. Barring adverse political developments, it seems reasonably assured that some, at least, of these countries will soon accumulate the minimum necessary stock of "social capital" and will enjoy an accelerating rate of economic growth.

The current stage of social and economic transformation in the underdeveloped societies appears to be the crucial one. First, from the point of view of the underdeveloped countries themselves, the coming decades will determine the character of the political and economic systems now emerging in those regions. The present phase represents the period of fusion between what is left of traditional values and institutions and the newer ones generated by prolonged contact with the West.

There is little possibility of, and even less desire for, re-creating the ancient patterns of moral, political and economic order in the under-developed countries. At the same time, it is highly improbable that they can become fully Westernized, even if they wanted to—which apparently they do not. They are, therefore, much more likely to become new societies which—the West must hope—may eventually achieve a new organic blending of ancient and Western features combined with the novel characteristics required for successful adaptation to their present situations.

The second reason why the current phase may be considered crucial is because it will witness the success or failure of efforts to integrate the developing countries of Southern Asia, Africa, and Latin America into a more effectively functioning international polity and economy. As we have seen, the underdeveloped areas are of major importance to Western Europe and Japan as sources of foodstuffs and raw materials and as markets for industrial products. Conversely, the industrialized nations must for many decades continue to be a major source of capital and the main source of the technology required by the underdeveloped countries for increasing their national wealth and per capita incomes. Satisfactory economic relationships between these two groups of countries are essential to each. The events of the current period will decide whether new patterns of reciprocity can be achieved to replace 19th-century dominance and subordination.

The results of these two processes will affect deeply the worldwide conflict between the Western democracies and the totalitarian Soviet and Red Chinese empires. The as-yet-uncommitted underdeveloped countries represent a potentially vast increment of manpower and other resources, for they already contain almost half the world's population and the greatest reservoir of untapped natural materials remaining on the planet. It is possible to exaggerate the consequences for the West of the conquest of large portions of these regions by communist imperialism. But it would be foolish for the West to underestimate the determination of the Soviets and Red Chinese to accomplish this conquest or the magnitude of the efforts they are now making to do so. In this competition, the West can achieve a decisive advantage only when it can summon the will and the wisdom to demonstrate in convincing fashion the natural superiority of free societies over totalitarian ones.

PART II

Prescription

6

What Kind of World
Economic Order?

In the present generation, the foreign policy of the United States has been undergoing a major transformation. Before 1914, the United States was distant from the main centers of world power, secure behind its ocean barriers and the protection of the British navy, and absorbed in its own economic and political development. Americans had little need or inclination for an active foreign policy, except on the infrequent occasions when the security of national boundaries was believed to be threatened. The great powers of Europe rarely considered American interests or actions as relevant—much less important—in the major issues of 19th-century world politics. Isolationism and protectionism were the dominant features of the American conception of the proper relations between the United States and the rest of the world. There were exceptions, of course. There was, for example, a tendency to intervene sporadically, and often naively, in world affairs on moral grounds. Again, before the end of the 19th century, the American concept of national interest was extended to include active concern with developments in the Caribbean and Pacific areas. But, at bottom, American attitudes were complacently isolationist and were only occasionally disturbed by such impulses to participate in world affairs.

Traditional American isolationism and protectionism rested on assumptions about the position of the United States in the world economy and polity which were, however, ceasing to be true even before World War I. By 1910, the American economy was already a large net exporter of manufactures and its earlier dependence on imported manufactures had been greatly reduced. With few exceptions, American industry was no longer struggling to establish itself in the face of older and more powerful European competitors; as we have noted in Chapters 2 and 3, American manufactures were already making large inroads into British export markets. After 1900, a high rate of capital formation in the United States no longer depended upon investment from abroad. At the turn of the century, American national income was approximately equal to that of the United Kingdom and Imperial Germany combined. The population of the United States was by then substantially larger than that of any of the great powers, except Russia. Thus, even before World War I, the United States had become a great power in terms of size and wealth, though its political influence and military strength were as yet only potential. Both were realized in the course of that war, from which the United States emerged as the leading democratic nation of the world.

But the American conception of foreign policy was not as yet consistent with the actual role played by the United States in World War I and in the immediate postwar settlements. President Wilson's efforts to make the American people understand their new position and exercise continuing leadership in world affairs were unavailing in the face of the deep-seated, traditional reluctance to engage in an active foreign policy on a worldwide scale. The United States was slow to grasp and accept the obligations entailed by its new power, and by the growing inability of England, even with the help of France, to carry on its traditional role of leadership. Instead, Americans continued to assume that England was responsible for maintaining world order and that any failure of Britain to do so resulted wholly from mistaken British policies and not from any decline in British political and economic strength. Throughout the interwar period, the United States refused to commit itself to cooperate with other countries in the preservation of world order by any means more binding than good conduct pledges like the Kellogg Peace Pact.

In the course of World War II, this lag in American understanding and acceptance of responsibility was rapidly overcome. The decade of the 1940's saw the United States assume international obligations—military, political, economic and moral—which would have been inconceivable as recently as 1939. Our leadership during the war itself was largely a reaction to the obvious threat to American security and to the fact that we were able to devote many more resources to the collective effort than were the other allied countries. But the continued willingness of the American people to bear the responsibilities of world leadership after the war has been a real intellectual and moral achievement—the more so because the years from 1945 to 1950 saw the frustration of the optimistic wartime hopes for the postwar world. During that five-year period, we took over from Britain responsibility for the defense of the eastern Mediterranean and, by implication, of the whole Middle East. We initiated the North Atlantic (NATO), South Pacific (ANZUS), and other (Japan, Formosa, Korea, etc.) defensive pacts and thereby guaranteed the security of those regions. We revitalized the system of Pan-American alliances and organizational arrangements. We commenced economic and rearmament aid programs on a major scale affecting all non-Soviet countries, allied and neutral, willing to participate on reasonable terms. As the culmination of this period, we did not fail to resist communist aggression against our Korean allies by the direct use of our own armed forces when other means proved inadequate. These were unmistakably the actions of a nation which at long last recognized that, among the countries with which it shared common values or consistent interests, it alone possessed the resources and the flexibility required for effective leadership. It is true that, since 1950, neo-isolationism has been growing in the United States. But it is unlikely that nostalgia for a comfortable isolationist past will again become so strong as to compel us to abdicate our recently assumed responsibilities of world leadership.

Effective leadership depends not only on continued willingness to assume it and on resources adequate to discharge it. It depends equally upon understanding the nature of the difficulties to be faced and the means appropriate for dealing with them. In Part I, the Study Group has sketched the broad outlines of the major economic problems faced by the non-Soviet countries. The analysis reveals that these economic problems—like the major political problems of the free world—are not simply the products of marginal maladjustments within and among the member states of an international order whose fundamental constitution is still adequate and unimpaired. Rather, many present international economic and political problems spring from the basic structure and functioning of the nation-state system itself. American postwar foreign economic policy has been slow to grasp this fact and to accept its implications. Though the development of an adequate American policy is no longer prevented by failure to recognize the changed position of the United States in the world, it is still inhibited by our slowness to adopt a foreign economic policy which is fully relevant to the problems of world economic and political order in our times. Just as the failure of the United States to recognize the implications of its new international position was a key factor in the increasing insecurity of the interwar period, so American slowness to appreciate the fundamental character of the difficulties now confronting the non-Soviet countries helps to explain why our leadership has not been more successful in the postwar period.

Some of the worst defeats of Western policy in recent years have resulted from this failure to appreciate the fundamental character not only of international problems but also of national ones in certain countries. Thus, one of the reasons for the loss of Indochina and the defeat of the European Defense Community was our erroneous assumption that France was still a world power, capable of leadership, decision and action at home in Europe and abroad in the French Union. In France, Italy and probably other European countries, the inadequacies of the nation-state form are now so great as gravely to handicap not only the national economy but the national political institutions as well. This adverse effect is aggravated in France by the peculiar difficulties inherent in the French type of parliamentarianism. In these countries, a strictly national solution for the basic problems of economic health, political effectiveness and social cohesion and morale no longer seems possible.[1]

This chapter will examine American foreign economic policy since World War II to discover how far it has accepted—in theory and in practice—the implications of the problems analyzed in Part I. We shall then attempt to describe goals or general directions for foreign economic policy which would be as relevant to contemporary problems as is possible within present political and moral limitations. In effect, the following contrasts the kind of world order at which American postwar policies have been aiming with another kind of world order, more relevant to mid-20th century conditions, which the United States should help to create.

---

[1] See below pp. 274–275.

Postwar American Foreign Economic Policy in Theory and Practice

The history of postwar American foreign economic policy properly begins in the mid-1930's with the adoption of Secretary of State Cordell Hull's reciprocal trade agreements program. It was not until the United States had suffered through the most severe years of the great depression that the interest of a competitively powerful economy in opening up international markets on a reciprocal basis was able to assert itself successfully against traditional isolationism and protectionism.[2]

Though the change of direction marked by the Reciprocal Trade Agreements Act was motivated primarily by belated recognition of American economic strength, and by an immediate national interest in greater freedom of international trade,[3] American foreign economic policy soon acquired a more positive and "internationalist" tone. Recognition of American economic strength gave rise to a feeling of American responsibility to contribute actively toward the better functioning of the international economy in the long-term interest not only of the United States but of all friendly countries. When World War II further emphasized the preponderance of American economic power, this sense of responsibility was strongly reinforced and, under that influence, American foreign economic policy moved into a new phase—which we shall call the "Bretton Woods period." This may be roughly defined as the five years between 1942, when serious "postwar planning" began in the Executive Departments in Washington, and 1947, when the proposal of the Marshall Plan marked the start of another phase.

---

[2] For example, as late as 1930, the Smoot-Hawley Tariff raised import duties to the highest point in American history.

[3] The competitive strength of the American economy and its relatively low dependence on foreign trade also help to explain why American economic policy in the 1930's did not follow that of the other trading countries very far down the path of the "new economic nationalism." There were, of course, important exceptions to this generalization. Unilateral devaluation of the dollar in 1933, American behavior at the London Economic Conference of the same year, and the trade policies incident to domestic agricultural programs during the 1930's can fairly be described as typical examples of the new economic nationalism. They were, in a sense, the international consequences of the priority which the early "New Deal" gave to domestic economic recovery and reform. However, after 1935, such nationalistic practices were usually regarded as exceptions—necessitated by domestic political considerations—to the official doctrine of economic liberalism which was being formulated under Cordell Hull's leadership.

In the Bretton Woods period, the United States used its great war-time and postwar influence in a wholehearted effort to turn back the tides of economic nationalism which had run so strongly in the inter-war years. This effort was guided by an explicit set of ideas about the kind of world economic order toward which American policy was working. The intention was to re-create an integrated and—as far as possible—automatic world economy, largely free of interference by national governments, on the model of the 19th-century system, as it was conventionally understood.

Three authoritative documents sum up the guiding principles of the Bretton Woods period: the Articles of Agreement of the International Monetary Fund (1944); the Charter for an International Trade Organization (1947) proposed by the State Department but abandoned because of Congressional opposition; and the General Agreement on Tariffs and Trade (1947) which contains, in addition to its tariff provisions, most of the substance of the ITO Charter except for the provisions setting up the ITO itself. Though these international agreements are long and complex, their essence can be simply stated. It is that if national governments would pledge themselves to refrain from controlling their foreign commerce and would agree to maintain domestic monetary policies consistent with reasonable balance in their external accounts, an integrated, self-adjusting and privately trading system of competitive national economies would again prevail over the world—or at least over the non-communist part of it. To this end, these agreements collectively established a code of "good economic behavior" for national governments whose two essential prescriptions were: no interference with international trade or international commercial payments, except for non-discriminatory tariffs; and no exchange controls on ordinary international commercial transactions—i.e., full interconvertibility of national currencies for current transactions—except under specified exceptional and temporary conditions.[4]

---

[4] It was recognized during the Bretton Woods period that re-creation of an integrated world economic order would have to be postponed until the economic damage of World War II had been overcome by the efforts of affected countries helped by American assistance. But the means of reconstruction were not themselves of central concern during this period —of so little concern, indeed, that the scope of the task of reconstruction and the magnitude of the dollar aid required were not realistically appraised until 1947. (For one of the first official critiques of this earlier unrealistic approach to the reconstruction and recovery problem see House of Representatives' Select Committee on Foreign Aid, 80th Congress, 2nd Session, *Final Report on Foreign Aid*, pp. 21–29, 39–41, 57–74.) Throughout the Bretton Woods period, attention was focussed instead on the return of normality expected to follow the "transition period" during which war-damaged countries were to be allowed, in recog-

Behind these prescriptions lay the assumption—largely implicit—that the international economy of the 20th century was still (as its 19th-century predecessor was supposed to have been) an essentially autonomous and automatic system, whose proper functioning had been upset, but not basically impaired, by two world wars and the intervening great depression. The economic nationalism of the interwar years was for the most part thought to be a temporary and perverse response of national governments to these severe, but nonetheless transitory, disturbances. While political and ideological causes were also recognized for the nationalistic policies pursued by certain countries (e.g., Nazi Germany and Soviet Russia), it was generally believed that if war and depression were avoided and if all governments would pledge themselves to eschew quantitative trade restrictions and tariff discrimination, private international markets would be able to work again, as they had worked before 1914, for the best interests of all countries.

Nevertheless, there was an important difference between the prescriptions of the Bretton Woods period of American foreign economic policy and the conventional explanation of how the 19th-century system functioned. According to the classical explanation of the working of the international gold standard, the maintenance of national balance-of-payments equilibrium was essentially automatic. It resulted from the effects of international gold and short-term capital movements, via the banking systems and money markets, on national price and wage levels and (in more modern terms) on levels of aggregate demand. But this mechanism had actually depended on the freedom of national banking systems and money markets from active governmental control or influence. Largely in deference to the universal fear of postwar unemployment, the IMF Articles of Agreement attempted to substitute for this automatic mechanism a code of conscious economic behavior which recognized that national economic authorities would actively try to influence domestic monetary conditions, but which bound them (except

---

nition of their reduced export potentials and extraordinary import needs, to control imports by quantitative restrictions. Thereafter, all quantitative restrictions were to be ended and current account convertibility was to be assured by all member countries. According to the IMF Articles of Agreement, this period of grace was supposed to come to an end on July 1, 1952, after which import quotas were to be abolished and current account convertibility restored. An indication of how temporary and superficial the problems of the transition period were thought to be during the Bretton Woods phase may be seen in the abortive and nearly disastrous attempt to accelerate the restoration of the free international market by making sterling convertible on July 1, 1947, as required by the Anglo-American Financial Agreement of 1945.

in specified temporary emergencies) to respond readily to a disequilibrium in the balance of payments by appropriate corrective financial and monetary measures; i.e., to conduct their domestic financial and monetary policies so as to maintain balance-of-payments equilibrium without resort to import quotas or to currency discrimination of any kind.

Thus, it was expected that national economic authorities could and would adhere to a code which would require them, in the event of conflict, to give priority to freedom of international trade and payments over other considerations, including the level of domestic employment and the interests of powerful domestic claimant groups. That this expectation was seriously intended was itself symptomatic of the extent to which policymakers during the Bretton Woods period failed to appreciate the significance of the political and economic changes which had occurred since the 19th century. In 20th-century conditions, the likelihood that national authorities would be willing or able to give priority to freedom of trade and payments varies inversely with the seriousness of domestic unemployment or inflation, with the intensity of the desire for rapid economic growth, and with the degree of national dependence upon foreign trade. It is precisely when the pursuit of domestic economic objectives gives rise to balance-of-payments difficulties—or threatens to be seriously impeded by such difficulties—that national economic authorities are least able to cope with balance-of-payments problems by nonrestrictive means.[5]

In sum, the Bretton Woods prescriptions were based on the premise that an international economy freed of most governmental controls would be the most efficient from a cosmopolitan standpoint, and would also be accepted by each national economy as best serving its own national interest. It was assumed—though seldom explicitly—that the national and the cosmopolitan standpoints were consistent; that the many individual national economic interests were fundamentally harmonious, at least in the longer run; that national governments were politically capable of making their foreign economic policies on these assumptions; and that the national governments of the non-communist world—or most of them

---

[5] Economists were, of course, aware of the inconsistency between the theoretical priority accorded to freedom of trade and payments and the actual priority enjoyed in practice by such national economic objectives as full employment, rapid economic growth, stabilized shares of foreign or home markets, and the like. Though the implications of this inconsistency were widely understood and taken into account in domestic economic analysis and policy-making, there has been a peculiar blindness about their applicability to international economic problems which no doubt springs from the failure to appreciate the profound differences between the 19th- and 20th-century world economic systems.

—could and would trust each other to adhere to the Bretton Woods prescriptions as embodied in intergovernmental agreements, despite large differences in historical backgrounds, contemporary aims, and political and economic capabilities.[6]

The Bretton Woods doctrine was liberal economic internationalism. It was liberal in the classical sense because it believed, correctly, in the vitality and efficiency of private competitive economies. It was internationalist both in a moral and in a political sense. Morally, it rightly recognized limitations upon the means by which national interests could be pursued —limitations which acknowledged the concern of Americans for the welfare of the human community as a whole. It was internationalist in a political sense because it assumed, erroneously, that a world consisting of a multitude of sovereign national states could automatically enjoy a high degree of international economic integration. Thus, its prescriptions were based on the mistaken "universalist" premise that all countries could participate in this kind of liberal international economy on an equal footing —that is, with equal rights and obligations, though not necessarily with equal influence—despite gross differences in economic health, cultural backgrounds, and degrees of political and economic effectiveness.

It is instructive to observe the parallels between this internationalist and universalist conception of the objectives of American foreign economic policy and the concept of world political order which was the aim of American foreign policy generally during the same period. The political aim, too, represented a decisive break with traditional isolationism and an acceptance, both on moral and on national interest grounds, of a special responsibility to establish a peaceful world political order. The goal was to create a universal system of sovereign nation-states living in harmony with each other. In pursuit of this objective, political foreign policy during World War II had two central principles: to restore the countries liberated from enemy occupation to full national sovereignty;

---

[6] These premises were not, of course, unanimously and consciously held by those who tried with such dedication to establish a world economic order based upon them. Certainly, there was much difference of opinion during the Bretton Woods period and many reservations were expressed about the possibility of success (cf. for example, John William's testimony on the Bretton Woods legislation and early reservations expressed by Jacob Viner). Nor does the Study Group wish to minimize the significant concessions to realism in the IMF Articles of Agreement, such as the "transition period," the "scarce currency clause," the provisions for exchange rate adjustments and for IMF advances to members. Yet, taken as a whole, the structure of policy which emerged in the 1942–47 period—particularly its insistence on non-discrimination and on universally inclusive participation—is difficult to understand except in the light of such implied premises.

and to establish an all-inclusive world organization to maintain peace by cooperation among the great powers and not by a power balance between actually or potentially antagonistic coalitions. It is not easy to-day to recall the almost utopian quality of much official American think-ing in the wartime years when the United Nations Charter was under discussion. Something of it is suggested by the following passage in a speech by Secretary of State Cordell Hull in 1944:

> As the provisions of the four-nation [Moscow] declaration are carried into effect [that is: when "a general international organization, based on the principle of the sovereign equality of all peace-loving states" has been established] there will no longer be need for spheres of influence, for alliances, for balance of power, or any other of the special arrangements through which, in the unhappy past, the nations strove to safeguard their security or to promote their interests.[7]

The implicit premise of this idealistic political internationalism was the belief that there were no fundamental or irreconcilable conflicts of inter-ests or aims among national states, and particularly among the great powers—that all states (except fascist states) were essentially "peace-loving." This is, of course, the political analogue of the assumption that national economic interests are fundamentally in harmony, and it springs from the same philosophical roots in 19th-century liberalism and posi-tivism. However, not all official American thinking about political for-eign policy in the Bretton Woods period had as idealistic a tone as the quotation from Cordell Hull. A provision for regional security arrange-ments (Article 51) was written into the United Nations Charter at American and British insistence to take account of our Pan-American policies and of Britain's Commonwealth relations. But even those who held to what was thought to be a more "realistic" concern with immediate national interest, and whose model of a desirable and attainable world order was the 19th-century balance-of-power system, assumed tacitly that conflicts of national interest in the 20th century were, on the whole, not much more serious than they had been in the past. In short, American political foreign policy—like economic foreign policy—unquestioningly accepted the nation-state system as unimpaired and immutable, and pre-scribed a universal code of good political behavior (the United Nations

---

[7] Cordell Hull, "Bases of the Foreign Policy of the United States," *Bulletin* (Washington: Department of State) March 25, 1944, p. 276.

Charter), or a return to the 19th-century balance-of-power system, as the alternative bases for a peaceful international political order.[8]

The year 1947 ushered in a new phase of American foreign policy, political and economic. On the political side, the change was abrupt and clear. As soon as the fact of implacable Soviet expansionism was accepted, it was obvious that the earlier conceptions of political order were irrelevant to the postwar world. To block Soviet imperialism, the Western community of nations now understood that it had to organize itself permanently into a politico-military coalition. The military inability of the continental European nation-states, and even of Britain, to provide for their own security on a national basis was now clear for all to see. To most Americans as well, it appeared that, unless the freedom of Western Europe were preserved, the chances for the security of the United States itself would be slim indeed. This new conception of a regional Western defensive coalition, with some degree of permanent organization, was embodied first in the Vandenburg Resolution and then in the American proposal for an Atlantic defense treaty. Its first concrete expression in action was the American guarantee of the independence of Greece and Turkey and the aid program instituted to make that guarantee effective.

Moreover, the Mutual Defense Assistance Program (1948) and the other defense activities under the aegis of the North Atlantic Treaty involved a new concept of American responsibility. Hitherto, it had been assumed that our special responsibility for maintaining world order was discharged with the establishment of the United Nations, in which the United States would be only *primus inter pares,* acting as impartial arbiter of possible disagreements among the other members and keeping a benevolent but detached interest in the operation of the world organization. This conception of the respective roles of the United Nations and the United States was now superseded by American acceptance of the continuing responsibility to lead positively and to participate actively in

---

[8] The concept of the United Nations Charter as a universal code of good political behavior was not explicitly formulated but was inherent in the official American attitude toward the organization. In practice, particularly from 1945 to 1947, an even more unrealistic notion about the United Nations was fashionable not only among the public generally but to some extent within the United States Government as well. This was the expectation that the United Nations would soon prove to be an embryonic form of world government which would become more fully developed in the foreseeable future. The frustration of this illusory hope has been one reason for the more recent tendency unduly to deprecate the United Nations and to deny the organization its rightful value as a symbol of the ideal goal of universal human community and as a useful forum of world opinion.

the planning and execution of a regional Western defense program, of which the United States would bear the major part of the economic and military costs. This change was as important and as radical in its way as the earlier shift from isolationism to internationalism, for it marked abandonment in practice of unrealistic assumptions with respect to the efficacy of the United Nations, the practicability of a universalist approach to world political problems, and the possibility that the United States would be able to play the role of an infrequent arbiter rather than an active and partisan leader in international affairs.

These political and military developments are mentioned only to recall the general context in which a parallel and equally radical shift in foreign economic activities was also taking place. The shift in the economic field, however, has been more gradual and much less self-conscious than that in political and defense policy. The change has been reflected more in American actions than in new conceptions of goals. The new kinds of economic activities undertaken since 1947 are still generally regarded as temporary expedients necessitated by what, from the standpoint of official Bretton Woods theory, could be little more than transitory perversities of national economic policies. Even in the 1950's, the consciously formulated goals and the preferred means of foreign economic policy continue to be heavily colored by the precepts of the orthodox Bretton Woods doctrine. This lag of understanding behind action has probably been responsible for the most serious deficiencies of our foreign economic policies in recent years. Because our understanding of what we have been doing has been inadequate, actions wholly appropriate and desirable in themselves have too often failed of their purposes because they have been incomplete, uncoordinated, and pursued with insufficient vigor or for too short a time.

In practice, six major advances have occurred since 1947 which have made American foreign economic activities significantly more relevant to the actual problems and possibilities of the postwar world than they were during the Bretton Woods period.

First, the years since 1947 have witnessed the increasing acceptance in practice—though not yet in theory—of the fact that achievement of the objectives of the United States demanded not only a continuing active foreign economic policy but the use of a wide variety of means—financial and technological as well as diplomatic and organizational. Large-scale economic and military aid, military "offshore procurement," technical assistance, stockpiling of strategic materials, "counterpart funds" and other devices were added to the tool kit of foreign economic policy, or assigned a more prominent place in it. These means were, however, regarded as temporary—and generally disparaged—supplements to the main prescriptions and strategy of the Bretton Woods doctrine. But the inability to realize the goals of Bretton Woods policy except marginally, combined with the growth in the size and variety of the new programs and the establishment of new government agencies to administer some of them, inevitably shifted the center of gravity and the orientation of American foreign economic policy away from attempts to apply universal trade and monetary prescriptions to the more active and empirical work of providing material and technological assistance. By the end of 1948, the relationship between the two approaches to foreign economic problems was reversed, with the new programs and techniques occupying the center of the stage and internationalist trade and monetary policies and universal intergovernmental agencies playing a peripheral or waiting part.[9] Yet, the original expectations of the Bretton Woods period have not been abandoned. It is still officially hoped that somehow the need for "exceptional" measures of these kinds will end in the near future. Partly for this reason, and partly as a concession to remaining isolationism, short termination dates continue to be written into aid legislation, and "temporary" and "emergency" tags are generally attached to the new devices.

Second, this change in the content of American economic activities has helped to break down the former separation between foreign economic and political policies. Earlier, the two were kept in separate compart-

---

[9] This unintended reversal of roles has had important consequences, both good and bad, for American foreign economic policy since 1948. On the good side, the administration of foreign aid programs—military, economic and technological—has, by its very nature, directed the attention of analysts and policy-makers toward the more fundamental causes of the deficiencies which aid is supposed to alleviate. The new agencies administering aid—American, foreign and international (e.g., OEEC, EPU, NATO)—have perforce been concerned with problems of economic growth; of resource availability and allocation, both internal and external; of comparative competitive positions; of incentives for saving and investment; and of intergovernmental coordination of national economic policies. Since an aid program is essentially an activity, those concerned with aid here and abroad have been predisposed not merely to analyze these problems but also to try to do something about them. Thus, aid funds have provided the incentive, the means and the leverage for a more active attack on the problems of the contemporary international economy. The progress made since 1947 both toward a better understanding of world economic problems and in coping more adequately with them has been owed in no small measure to the unintended predominance of the foreign aid programs in American foreign economic policy. At the same time, the indefinite continuation of foreign aid has tended, at least in part, to be self-defeating.

ments—each with its separate objectives, means, and personnel—true to the rigid separation of the political and economic realms in neoclassical liberalism. Beginning with the Truman Doctrine and the Marshall Plan proposals of 1947, foreign economic policies commenced to be seen, and to be used explicitly and continuously, as means to particular political and defense objectives—especially after 1950, when rearmament of the Western Community became a major American goal. Conversely, political and diplomatic means have more and more been used to influence the economic policies of other governments as, for example, during the European Recovery Program. In short, after 1947, American foreign economic policy was increasingly recognized as an integral part or dimension of general foreign policy.

Third, an important change occurred—again, much more in practice than in theory—in the attitude of American policy toward discrimination against dollar imports by nondollar countries. As the dollar shortage persisted from year to year despite large, continuing foreign assistance and military expenditures, as the end of the IMF's "transition period" and of the European Recovery Program (July 1, 1952) came and went, the Bretton Woods ideal of universal currency convertibility and worldwide non-discriminatory trade still appeared remote. Active American participation in originating and establishing the European Payments Union (EPU) and the OEEC's trade liberalization program in 1949 meant that the United States would in effect, though not in name, countenance—indeed, encourage—the formation and indefinite continuation of a large nondollar trade and payments area practicing discrimination against dollar goods and services. Likewise, the earlier American antipathy to the Sterling Area, due to the latter's discrimination against the dollar, gradually subsided. Official theory, however, still regards these and other similar concessions to 20th-century conditions as purely temporary and hopes that the need for them will soon pass. From the perspective of this study, the unofficial countenancing of discrimination may be differently interpreted. It is a recognition—reluctant, and as yet only partly conscious—that the dynamic, competitively powerful and structurally balanced American economy cannot be fitted into the contemporary international economy in a manner consistent with the broader objectives of American foreign policy unless the other industrial economies are shielded in some orderly and flexible fashion against the consequences of their own economic disadvantages *vis-à-vis* the United States for as long as these disadvantages persist.

Fourth, American policy has tended to move away from the universalist insistence of the Bretton Woods period. Experience is finally teaching us that all nations are not equally capable of assuming the rights and obligations of full membership in a freely trading international economy; that all regions do not have similar, or even important, parts to play in the creation of world political and economic order; and that the relations which are possible and desirable among the countries of the free world depend in large part upon the degree of homogeneity in their historical backgrounds, current economic and political institutions, and aspirations for the future. In consequence, the United States has recognized (e.g., in the European Recovery Program) that its interests in, and relations with, Western Europe are essentially different from those which it has, or could have, with the independent underdeveloped countries. This distinction expresses, as the next two sections of this chapter will make clear, the strength of the sense of community and of common destiny in the face of internal and external challenges among the nations sharing the traditions and values of Western civilization; and the relative weakness, or absence, of such a sense among the other non-communist nations —who stem from different and diverse historical traditions—and between them and the West.

Fifth, the growing awareness of the differing capacities of nations to participate in the international economy, and of the disproportionate strength of the United States, has been accompanied by recognition— again, largely in practice—that the international economy of the mid-20th century is not able to maintain its equilibrium and allocate acceptably the gains from trade in the automatic and impersonal fashion believed to have operated in the 19th century. As noted above, it was already recognized in the Bretton Woods period that an integrated and automatically self-adjusting international economy could not be restored unless national governments adhered to an explicit and detailed code of good economic behavior, the monetary portions of which were embodied in the IMF's Articles of Agreement.[10] In practice, the consultative machinery of the IMF has been largely superseded by the more active and efficient arrangements for deliberate economic cooperation and pol-

---

[10] Indeed, the creation of an organization like the IMF was itself a confession that such good conduct pledges were insufficient. One of the major purposes in establishing the IMF was to provide an institution in which member governments could consult with one another on international financial problems expected to arise despite general adherence to the Bretton Woods rules.

icy coordination among national governments provided by smaller, more homogeneous, regional organizations like the OEEC, the EPU, and the Sterling Area committees and conferences. Though an automatically operating international economy is still the goal of official policy —properly so to the extent that it can be attained in the conditions of the mid-20th century—such international equilibrium and freedom of trade as has been achieved in the postwar period has in large part depended upon the conscious coordination of national economic policies among the major trading nations of the free world.

Sixth, American policy since 1947 has included one major objective— the political and economic unification of Western Europe—which is clearly premised on the conclusion that, for this group of countries, even the continuous coordination of national policies through intergovernmental organizations like the OEEC and the EPU is insufficient, and that a formal merging or joint exercise of their national sovereignties is necessary if they are to achieve economic and political health and to play their proper part in Western defense. American sponsorship of European union has thus involved a quite basic qualification of the internationalist assumption that the nation-state system is adequate and immutable.

From this summary of the major developments in American foreign economic activities since 1947, it is apparent that practice has been more relevant than theory to the needs and possibilities of the mid-20th century. Here, as so often in human affairs, the wisdom of practical experience has proved greater than that of theoretical doctrine. The novelty of the newer policies should not, however, be exaggerated. They have been motivated by the same national and moral imperatives which underlay the earlier political and economic internationalism; they have grown out of the same American interest in, and concern for, the political stability, the economic health, and the military security of noncommunist countries which motivated the earlier support of the United Nations, the Bretton Woods institutions, and the ITO. Nor have the changes in foreign economic activities after 1947 involved a basic disagreement with the conventional view that the ills of the international economy are traceable in large part to economic nationalism or, more generally, to the undesirable and anarchic interventions of national states in the international economy. But changes in foreign economic activities since 1947 imply an explanation quite different from that of liberal internationalism of the origins, nature and probable duration of economic nationalism and of the other causes of poor economic health in the free world—an implicit diagnosis of contemporary problems which Part I of this study has endeavored to make explicit and clear. The measures of foreign economic policy adopted since 1947 have been increasingly inconsistent with the universalism and economism of Bretton Woods doctrine, and with political and economic internationalism's obliviousness to the precarious condition of the nation-state system, particularly in Western Europe.

What is now imperatively needed is that the theory and ideology of foreign economic policy should catch up with practice and fulfill their proper function of providing guidance for future actions. A major advance in thinking is required today even to maintain the progress made since 1947 in improving the international economy of the free world. The concern of American foreign economic policy for the successful functioning of the international economy is rendered less and less effective by the failure not alone of thought but also of action to keep pace with changes in political and economic conditions and needs. Nor is this backwardness of policy being overcome by new, more adequate, approaches to the problems of world economic order. Instead, popular disillusionment at the lack of greater progress toward the desirable goals of foreign economic policy has helped to provide an opportunity for the resurgence of protectionist and neo-isolationist attitudes which threaten seriously to impair the quality of American leadership in the free world. In these circumstances, a new creative advance in our thinking about the problems of world economic order is among the most urgent tasks facing the American people today.

Specific suggestions as to how the advances of recent years might be consolidated and their implications developed and realized more adequately will be made in the following chapters of Part II. But the real significance of the short- and medium-term measures to be considered can only be grasped in the context of longer-run goals. Without the sense of direction provided by a broad view of the kind of world order which—in the conditions of the second half of the 20th century—it is necessary, possible and desirable to create, immediate policy measures are likely to be mere haphazard improvisations that cancel each other or that cannot in isolation produce results worth the effort and expense they entail.

It is in this respect that the lag of understanding behind action produces its most serious consequences. It means either that there are no longer-term goals at all to guide policy-making and execution or that the consciously accepted goals are obsolete and hence irrelevant to present problems. Before turning to a consideration of immediate measures, therefore, we shall attempt in the remainder of this chapter to sketch in broad outline the longer-range objectives of American policy which follow from the analysis of world economic problems presented in Part I. Explanation of these long-term considerations will also serve as a unifying rationale for the specific policies and measures prescribed in Part II.

The Western Community

Implicit in the practice of American foreign policy in the postwar period has been an emerging concept whose validity is derived from the most basic facts of contemporary life. This concept is that American interest in, and concern for, the nations of the West are different both in kind and in degree from American interest in the other countries of the free world.

There are good reasons for this special relationship, some obvious and others not. The most obviously important reason is that Western Europe possesses the only complex of human skills and productive capacity comparable in size and efficiency to those of the United States and the Soviet bloc. The conquest of those resources by Soviet imperialism would be a fatal blow to the free world. Indeed, the belief that Western Europe must not fall under the control of any power hostile to the United States (i.e., seeking the revolutionary overthrow of the democratic world order) has been the cardinal principle of American foreign policy since 1917, though it has not always been so recognized and acknowledged. That principle has been to American policy in the 20th century what the Monroe Doctrine was in the 19th century. It expresses the most direct and obvious national interest of the United States in the preservation of freedom in Western Europe.[11]

But, American interest in Western Europe is not simply the passive one of preventing its conquest by any hostile or revolutionary power. It

---

[11] American concern and responsibility for the preservation of freedom in Western Europe are the logical successors to Britain's similar concern and responsibility prior to World War I, particularly with respect to the smaller European states. The decline of British power and the rise of the United States has shifted responsibility from British to American hands. At the same time, technological changes have drastically reduced the military significance of distance, making the Atlantic Ocean not much more of a defensive barrier for the United States than the English Channel was for Britain in the 19th century.

has a positive aim—to mobilize Western Europe's human and material resources for an active part in the task of advancing the security and progress of the free world. Large as may be the capacity of the United States for this task, it is not large enough for Americans to be able to dispense with the help of allies and friends. Nowhere else in the free world except in the West could the United States find allies capable of contributing substantially to this effort and willing to do so. Thus, the direct interest of the United States inevitably leads it to seek its major allies in Western Europe.

These reasons for American concern with the other countries of the West are, however, only the surface aspects of more fundamental historical and moral relationships. If North America, Western Europe and the English-speaking countries of the Commonwealth possess human skills and productive resources adequate to lead and defend not merely themselves but the whole free world, and if loss of a significant part of these resources would prove fatal to the rest, it is because this group of countries created and developed the ideas, the institutions and the techniques which today constitute political, economic and military strength. If the individual countries of the West are able and willing to cooperate effectively with one another to promote human freedom and progress, it is because they are all members of a single historical and moral community. Their basic value systems and institutions are the same. They share a common history, a common civilization, and common problems and dangers. Important as the cultural differences and conflicts of interest among the Western countries may be, they are nevertheless smaller and less significant than are those between the West as a whole and any other country or group of countries. The fact that the West is a moral community—that it has a deep sense of its own unity and uniqueness— is the underlying reason why the United States has a fundamental interest in the well-being of the other Western countries, why it must seek its principal allies among them, and why the Western countries are able and willing to work more closely and effectively with one another than they ordinarily can with non-Western nations.

Though the West has always had the sense of being a unique historical and moral community, it has not since the Renaissance thought of itself as a single political or economic community. To feel themselves a political community, people must have a strong sense of the need for a common political authority arising from common external dangers or internal disorders (or, as today, from a combination of the two) which are urgent and beyond the capacity of the separate political units to withstand. From 1815 to 1914, the West faced no external dangers or critical internal disorders. The rest of the world was dominated by the West, politically and economically. Within the West, the international anarchy always latent in separate national sovereignties and national loyalties was providentially held in check, as we have seen in Chapter 1, by the moral values embodied in economic liberalism, constitutional government and international law; by certain features of the 19th-century social structure and economic institutions; and by the *Pax Britannica*. In the 20th century, the passing of this complex equilibrium has unleashed within the West (as elsewhere) the anarchic forces of extreme political and economic nationalism—forces which are in part the products of changes in traditional Western values and which are, in consequence, much too powerful to be held in check by nostalgic remnants of 19th-century attitudes in the absence of deliberate authority transcending national boundaries. Today, the rise of communism, the expansion of Soviet power, and the political independence of Asia have created external challenges of a military, economic and moral character which an internally weakened and disordered West cannot meet successfully on a separate and uncoordinated national basis.

In these circumstances, it is not surprising that the nations of the West are beginning again to think of themselves as a political community—and even as an economic unit—and to act on that premise. To mention only the major examples, this emerging concept has been embodied in, or symbolized by, the Marshall Plan, the North Atlantic Treaty Organization, the Organization for European Economic Cooperation, the European Payments Union, the Commonwealth, the European union movement, and the Atlantic Community idea. Implicit in this concept and in these actual or proposed institutions are a need and a hope—a sense on the part of the Western nations of the urgent requirements of their predicament and a desire to move toward a long-run goal. Essentially, that goal is the increasing political unity and economic integration of the West.

The specific form in which this goal might ultimately be realized cannot yet be foreseen. What is needed now is not a detailed blueprint but a sense of direction and the willingness at each stage to take the immediately indicated steps leading in that direction. The Study Group believes that the start represented by the organizations and proposals mentioned above is in the right direction and that the next steps required develop logically from those already taken and from better understanding of the structural problems of world order which American policy must be designed to mitigate. Chapters 7 and 8 discuss such next steps for Western economic policy which could lead in the direction of closer and more effective economic organization of the Western Community.

Whether these steps—or others having the same general purpose—will be taken depends heavily upon the quality of American leadership in the coming years. By virtue of its economic size, independence and rapid rate of growth, the United States has far greater freedom of action than other Western nations, whose economic health and military strength have been impaired by the West's internal disorders and external challenges. Probably alone among the Western nations, the United States still possesses a sufficient combination of material strength and moral vigor to take the lead in trying to move the West toward the long-run goal of political and economic unification.

This American responsibility has two aspects. On the one hand, it is an urgent continuing duty to invent—and to encourage Western adoption of—a strategy leading toward the general objective of growing Western unification. The United States will have to use its full power and influence to achieve that end, and must be ready to bear a share of the economic costs of that strategy proportionate to its economic size and health. On the other hand, the responsibility also involves the duty of self-restraint—the obligation to respect the political and economic rights and opportunities of other Western nations in accordance with the best Western conceptions of political and economic justice. At the moment, Americans do not seem to be greatly tempted to misuse their political and military power. Indeed, we still feel great reluctance to exercise our leadership and we still toy with isolationism from time to time. But we are, nonetheless, in danger of misusing our economic power unconsciously—in the name either of doctrinaire economic internationalism, or of a narrow protectionism—in ways which could deprive our industrial partners in the West of adequate opportunities for economic growth.

It will not be easy to convince the non-Western countries of the free world that they, too, have an important stake in the more effective organization of the Western Community. Yet, for the foreseeable future, the security of the independent underdeveloped countries against communist imperialism depends essentially upon the military strength of the West. Likewise, the extent to which—and the ease with which—these countries can obtain the foreign capital, technology and export markets needed for their own economic development depend upon improving the economic health of the Western nations. Unless the West can make substantial progress in overcoming its own internal disorders, neither the military security nor the economic advancement of the independent un-derdeveloped countries can be assured.

Thus, the more effective organization of the Western Community is in the interest of the United States, of the other Western nations, and of the whole free world. This principle is basic to American policy in the mid-20th century. It provides a long-range objective in accordance with which the shorter-run problems of policy can be decided and measures for their solution made consistent with one another. A clear understand-ing of the necessity of Western unification, and a willingness to move toward it by any effective and morally valid means, are two of the main conditions of success for American foreign policy. They are in no sense easy to satisfy. The parochial forces of nationalism at home and abroad will not yield readily even to the most urgent and logically compelling need for more effective organization of the West. The very concept of a Western political and economic Community is still struggling to be born against the inertia of the traditional belief in the immutability of the nation-state system and the conventional faith in the efficacy of the universalist prescriptions of political and economic internationalism. Only if our ways of thinking can be made more relevant to the real problems of world economic order in the mid-20th century are we likely to make much progress in overcoming these difficulties.

The West and the Underdeveloped Countries

Though there is a fundamental difference between the aims of Ameri-can policy within the Western Community and its aims in the rest of the non-Soviet world, the essential political and moral imperatives of American policy do not differ in the two cases. The right of self-defense, the duty to support self-determination, and the obligation to widen and deepen human community—these three imperatives apply equally to the external as well as the internal relations of the West. But in the West's relations with the independent underdeveloped countries, the operational meaning of these imperatives—the long-run goals and the strategy which they imply—is different primarily because of the great differences in past history, present circumstances, and future aspirations which distin-guish the West from the other countries of the non-communist world.

Within the West, these imperatives seem to demand the creation of a real Western political community and a more or less closely integrated Western economy. This goal is the rational answer to those common problems of the Western countries which arise from the growing inconsistencies between the nation-state system and the requirements of military security, economic health and political stability. It is a rational goal because the West is already an historical and moral community. If the Western nations are to survive and progress, they will have to come within a generation to believe—and to act on the belief—that their characteristic values and ideals can no longer be realized without a basic reform of the political and economic constitution of the West. It is morally valid for the United States to shape its foreign policy in relation to this long-run objective because its voluntary achievement in some form is possible, and it would permit a far better realization and harmonization of Western security, freedom and welfare than is likely to be attained by many countries within the existing nation-state system in the prospective conditions of the second half of the 20th century.

When, however, relations between the West and the independent underdeveloped countries are considered in the light of the same three imperatives, the results for Western policy are quite different. The societies of Asia and Africa—and, in the sense defined in Chapter 4, even Latin America [12]—do not form part of the same civilization, the same historical and moral community, as the West. Hence, it would be neither realistic nor morally valid to set as the goal of Western policy in the foreseeable future the creation of a unified political community and an integrated economic system embracing the whole non-communist world. This goal would not be realistic because it is not responsive to the contemporary economic and political aspirations and problems of the independent underdeveloped countries. It could not now be achieved by morally valid means—that is, by the voluntary consent and active cooperation of the independent underdeveloped countries—though it could perhaps be achieved imperialistically. Granted that the reaction of the underdeveloped areas to what they consider "economic colonialism" has often been carried to irrational extremes, it would be equally irrational for the West to believe that it is in the interest of Asia, or even Latin America, to restore anything resembling their 19th-century political and economic relations with the industrial countries, or that they are at all likely to be

---

[12] See p. 142, footnote 3 for the reasons why in this study the Latin American countries are included in the underdeveloped areas and are not treated as part of the West.

willing to do so. These considerations mean that the goal of unification of the whole free world (or, for that matter, of the entire planet) is not likely to be a realistic one even for as long a period as a generation ahead, because it could not be achieved by voluntary and constitutional methods but only by some new form of Western domination over other civilizations. Thus, the creation of a unified political community and an integrated economic system by morally valid means presupposes an antecedent historical and moral community, which does not now exist between the West and the underdeveloped countries, nor—except perhaps in Latin America—is likely to be created within the lifetime of living persons.

What, then, should be the general direction of American and Western policy with respect to the independent underdeveloped countries? The United States cannot validly claim to speak for these other civilizations in setting goals and strategy for foreign policy, as it can within limits for the Western Community of which it is the natural leader. The United States does have, however, the right and the duty to try to define and to protect vital Western security and economic interests which are threatened by the designs of communist imperialism and the profound transformations now occurring in non-communist Asia, Latin America and Africa. We must try to influence the course of that transformation—not to dominate it or to force it into a Western mold, but to render its outcome at least compatible with Western values and vital interests both in the near future and the long run. The West should be clear on this point. The moral duty to respect the freedom and self-determination of these other societies is real and is genuinely felt in the West, as the voluntary Western freeing of colonies has shown. But, it does not require the West to surrender its own security and its truly vital economic interests in the name of a self-determination which insists upon expressing itself exclusively in a *national* form. Nor does this duty require the West to be indifferent to the longer-run possibility that, even if Soviet aggression or subversion can be prevented, the transformations now occurring in the underdeveloped countries may well eventuate—as did similar transformations in Japan and Russia—in ideologies and policies antithetical to Western interests and values and ultimately backed by real economic and military power.

Unavoidably, then, Western governments—and especially the United States—must be as concerned in their relations with the underdeveloped countries to protect the vital security of the West as they are to express the values of Western humanitarianism and to advance the long-range Western interest in strengthening the bonds of moral community between itself and the free societies of Asia, Africa and Latin America. In the context of the cold war, this concern for Western security means primarily the prevention of successful communist subversion or aggression. In a few underdeveloped countries—those subject to direct Soviet or Red Chinese pressure or where domestic communists have been acquiring significant economic and political power—these Western aims have to be pursued by a variety of appropriate means. Military and political actions may in certain circumstances be of more immediate importance than economic measures in the tasks of external defense, winning a civil war, or ensuring that a local government is freed of communist control or influence. Because they are critical, situations of this kind will continue to absorb much of the attention and energy of the West and especially of the United States. They will raise exceedingly difficult moral and political problems. It will not always be possible for the West to avoid interventions which are too reminiscent of colonialism to win the approval of Western and native liberals even when such actions are the only alternative to communist conquest. Neither will it always be possible for the United States to be on the side of *national* forms of self-determination against other means of terminating colonialism, as we have been rather too easily and self-righteously on occasions in the past.[13]

Outside of such critical countries and situations, Western strategy in the underdeveloped countries must perforce rely more heavily on economic means (as, for example, in India and the Moslem states). In these less critical areas, the West has two main objectives, as indicated by the analysis in Chapters 4 and 5. One general aim must be to provide the means for widening the economic and social opportunities of the native intellectual and middle-class groups who might otherwise supply leadership and cadres to subversive movements. Lack of organic social functions and adequate opportunities makes these groups highly susceptible

---

[13] In a speech on October 3, 1953, Henry A. Byroade, at the time Assistant Secretary of State for Near Eastern, South Asian and African Affairs, observed, "It is a hard, inescapable fact that premature independence can be dangerous, retrogressive and destructive. Unless we are willing to recognize that there is such a thing as premature independence, we cannot think intelligently or constructively about the status of dependent peoples." The entire speech is one of the most thoughtful, and thought provoking, made by any high official of the State Department since World War II. In this connection, it is well to recall the rather stringent standards which a people had to meet before that apostle of liberty, John Stuart Mill, was willing to consider them eligible for self-government. See John Stuart Mill, *Representative Government,* Chapters 1, 4 and 18.

to communism or irresponsible nationalism. The second main objective must be to hasten the process of social and economic development—and, incidentally, to deprive the communists and extreme nationalists of their "mass following"—by promoting social and economic reforms, like those discussed in Chapters 4 and 5, which are the necessary prerequisites for progress and are also capable of significantly mitigating agrarian and urban unrest.

This strategy is not difficult to describe in general terms, but there are narrow limits within which the West can in fact expect to carry it out. There is a tendency in the underdeveloped countries to assume that the successful achievement of political, social and economic development depends mainly upon the willingness of Western countries to provide freely and unconditionally the capital and technology required. This thought is often echoed in the West, usually coupled with the belief that sufficient Western pressure for necessary internal reforms in the underdeveloped countries is all that is needed to achieve these reforms. We have indicated in Part I our reasons for believing such views to be gross over-simplifications. The major sources of agrarian and urban unrest and of inadequate economic opportunities for middle-class groups are internal to these countries and can be influenced only marginally from outside. There will undoubtedly be many situations—such, perhaps, as the Indian Five Year Plan—where the local will and organization are at least partially mobilized and a margin of external economic resources and technical assistance could be of decisive importance. But, more typically, basic internal problems are not likely to be resolved, or even very substantially mitigated, by the economic means which the West could bring to bear in a manner acceptable today in most underdeveloped countries. Our ability to do so will be very limited unless and until native middle-class groups have been created within these societies which actively seek internal reform and are strong enough to accomplish it with the increment of resources that the West can provide. Essentially, the task of American and Western strategy in the underdeveloped countries is to find acceptable and efficient ways, political and economic, for breaking through this dilemma: on the one hand, in the absence of a constructive middle class, Western efforts in the underdeveloped countries will be relatively ineffective; but, on the other hand, such middle-class groups are not likely to be created without much more effective Western help.

Another major interest of the West in its relations with the underdeveloped countries is its concern for expanding the sources of primary products and increasing the markets for industrial exports. From the standpoint of Western Europe, this is predominantly an economic interest. From the standpoint of the United States, it is primarily a function of our political and military concern for the economic health and military strength of Western Europe and Japan. Direct American economic interest in the underdeveloped countries is important but more limited, owing to the continental character of the American economy. For their part, the underdeveloped countries also have an important economic interest in adequate trade and financial relations with the capital-exporting nations of the industrial West. Logically, there would not be much difficulty in harmonizing these economic interests in ways which would yield important benefits to all parties concerned. But, in practice, the longer-term mutual advantages of improved economic relationships between the West and the underdeveloped countries tend to be obscured by more immediately pressing problems, by irrational nationalism, and by memories of former colonial injustice or nostalgia for departed imperial rule. At present, most Western countries—other than the United States and Canada—are so preoccupied with difficult problems of their own that they can spare neither the attention nor the resources required for a substantial change in the character of their relations with the underdeveloped countries. At the same time, the main conscious purpose for which many underdeveloped countries now seek to obtain capital and technology from the West is to achieve what they call "national economic independence" rather than to mitigate their internal economic difficulties or to help improve the effectiveness of the international economy. With respect to primary products, the independent underdeveloped countries are more often interested in stable export markets at favorable terms of trade than in substantially expanding their production and exports. Thus, in practice, inconsistencies arise between the professed economic aims of the underdeveloped countries and those of the West.

It is, nonetheless, true that these apparently conflicting interests contain the elements of a mutually advantageous relationship—the exchange of capital and technology from the industrial nations for an assured and adequate supply of primary products from the underdeveloped countries. A proper Western strategy would deploy the major instruments and measures available to the industrial countries—e.g., public and private capital exports, technical assistance, stockpiling, etc.—in ways which maximize their effectiveness in helping the independent underdeveloped countries to adopt policies that are in their own longer-term interest and are conducive to expansion of primary production for export to Western Europe, Japan and North America. This does not mean, of course, that the industrial countries should behave as if their own economic interests were the only issues involved in their relations with the underdeveloped countries. In many situations, the broader interests of the West in preventing political and economic decay and communist subversion will require economic policies toward the underdeveloped countries which are of a more immediate and emergency character and hence do not contribute directly to the kind of permanent relationship here envisaged. Moreover, above and beyond economic and political interests, the West is morally bound to respect the right of the underdeveloped peoples to find their own destiny.

There is need for the industrial countries to recognize more clearly and to accept in practice the implications for Western policy and strategy of the present limitations and longer-term possibilities here suggested. The failure to do so in the past has resulted in a dissipation of Western bargaining power—particularly American—in a large number of piecemeal and uncoordinated efforts in the fields of international investment, technical assistance, stockpiling, and other developmental activities. Nor has the lack of coordination and of unifying strategy in economic development policy been harmful to Western interests alone. It has also meant a much less effective use of available capital and technical assistance from the standpoint of the underdeveloped countries themselves than might otherwise have been possible.

Finally, we must not be reluctant to admit that there is much more to American and Western concern with the underdeveloped countries than the pursuit of Western security and economic health, tempered as they may be by regard for the right of self-determination of the peoples of Asia, Africa, and Latin America. The concern of Westerners, and especially of Americans, with the deep transformations now occurring in the underdeveloped countries also has another dimension which cannot truly be explained simply in terms of Western self-interest, although it is often so rationalized. For, the West has a genuinely humanitarian interest in the economic, social and political progress of non-Western peoples which transcends national and cultural divisions and finds expression in many types of humanitarian activities, public and private, which Westerners carry on or finance in the underdeveloped countries.[14] This hu-

---

[14] Jacob Viner has written:

"There is also, I am convinced, a genuine humanitarian interest on the part of the

manitarian motivation finds both symbolic and concrete expression—though not unmixed with other motives—in public assistance programs like Point IV; in the willingness of the United States to channel a part of its economic aid through international organizations, like the IBRD, over which the United States Government has relinquished direct control; and in emergency relief measures like the wheat loans to India and Pakistan. More clearly—and less mixed with considerations of national or Western self-interest—this humanitarian concern finds expression in private religious, educational and welfare activities in the underdeveloped countries too numerous and diverse to mention here.

Closely allied to this humanitarian impulse is the Western concern that the social and political development of the underdeveloped countries should be consistent with Western values of individual freedom and social responsibility and with the Western ideal of justice. In this concern, Western pride and self-interest are no doubt present, but there is also a genuine conviction that the underdeveloped countries must "also enjoy the benefits and the virtues, as we see them, of political democracy, of social security, and of freedom from degradation of human dignity and from over-arduous, overlong or servile toil" [15] if these benefits are to continue to be enjoyed in the West.

All of these motivations spring from deep moral and religious roots in the Western tradition and they are right and proper elements in Western policy toward the underdeveloped countries. A concern for other peoples' material welfare and for progress in individual freedom and dignity expresses the ultimate Western social ideal of a universal human community, living in peace and justice, transcending geographical, racial

---

American people in the welfare of the masses of people elsewhere who are living in a state which seems to us, and increasingly to them, one of distressful misery. The floor of Congress is not ordinarily the platform from which the more generous impulses of the American nation receive their most outspoken and vigorous expression. The Administration, which lives closer to Congress and has to respond to its views more fully than do those whose operations are confined to the academic lecture hall or the pulpit, has to be guarded in revealing any feelings of generosity to other peoples, lest Congress charge it with giving away the substance of the American people to gratify a soft-minded humanitarianism. It is not easy, therefore, to prove to foreign skeptics that a genuine sympathy on the part of large sections of the American people for the economic plight of low-income peoples is influencing American policy. I believe it nevertheless to be a fact—one which a properly conducted public opinion poll would verify and which we could verify for ourselves if we were to examine our own motives." Jacob Viner, "America's Aims and the Progress of Underdeveloped Countries" from *The Progress of Underdeveloped Areas,* Bert F. Hoselitz, ed. (Chicago: University of Chicago, 1952), p. 176.

[15] *Ibid.*

and cultural divisions. But the profession and expression of this ideal must be neither sentimental nor naively rationalistic. Humanitarianism alone is not a sufficient basis for policy toward the underdeveloped countries. An outcome of the transformations now occurring in these societies compatible with Western freedom and progress cannot be obtained simply by financially generous and morally correct behavior on the part of the West. We have seen too much of collective irrationality and human evil in this tragic century to believe—as our grandfathers could have believed —that these revolutionary changes would inevitably be guided by a "Law of Progress" into the path of liberalism, constitutionalism and international harmony. We must not be misled by our positivistic notions of social perfectibility—nor mislead the underdeveloped countries—into expecting that anything we could do would actually, in the words of a former President of the United States, "wipe poverty, ignorance and human misery off the face of the earth" or, in Nehru's words, make "the causes of misery and conflict disappear." Nor will it be possible to transfer wholesale to Asian, African and probably even Latin American soils the principles and institutions of constitutionalism and freedom under law which contain the quintessence of the Western political tradition. Indeed, we are having trouble maintaining them within the West.

Yet the West must equally avoid the opposite error of a cynicism which is ashamed or contemptuous of humanitarian impulses and denies the possibility of human progress, or which leads too easily in a crisis to the abandonment of moral restraints in dealing with non-Western peoples. The ultimate hope of creating uncoerced community between the West and other societies lies essentially in this possibility: that the genuinely humanitarian ideals of Western society can find sufficient expression in our relations with other peoples to evoke an answering sympathy, and that the Western values of freedom and constitutionalism may be ultimately adapted to alien cultures to an extent which makes possible political and economic unity among different civilizations despite great cultural diversities. The growth of mutual sympathy and respect, together with the slow, historical process of convergence of values and institutions through prolonged contact, may ultimately—though by no means inevitably— bridge the spiritual and political gulf which now separates the West from the independent underdeveloped countries. This is not, to be sure, even a long-term goal of policy as we have been using that term in this study. It is an ideal, but an ideal which should, for the sake of the West's moral and material well-being, be allowed its relevance to Western policy. For, if it is not, the West will fail to meet creatively the challenge of the underdeveloped countries, with disastrous consequences not alone for itself but for them as well.

The Criteria of a Successful American Foreign Economic Policy

The chapters which follow will outline more immediate policy measures which the Study Group believes the United States should now take, or should encourage other countries to take, to move the free world toward these longer-range goals for the West and for the underdeveloped countries. But before turning to such specific measures, it is important to be clear about what they could be expected to accomplish. The actions to be discussed in succeeding chapters are not proposed as "solutions," fully capable of overcoming the economic difficulties of the free world. Obstacles to economic growth in the industrial and underdeveloped countries are too deeply rooted in existing institutions and attitudes to be affected more than marginally during the next few years by such American actions as would be politically feasible and morally valid. What, then, can American foreign economic policy accomplish within the next few years, given the political and moral limitations within which it must operate? What, in effect, are the criteria of a successful foreign economic policy?

Foreign economic policy is a part of general foreign policy and the criteria of its success are, therefore, political and psychological as well as material. The growth or decline of communism, neutralism and isolationism within the Western Community, the improvement or deterioration of national morale in the Western countries—criteria of this kind are as relevant as increases in productivity, living standards and hard currency reserves. The significance for American policy of such economic changes in other countries depends, in the last analysis, principally on their presumed effects on political, psychological and military factors. Thus, two ways in which American foreign economic policy can influence politics and attitudes in foreign countries should be distinguished: through its effects on economic conditions (consumption, employment, etc.); and through its symbolic and psychological impact.

In the shorter run, American foreign economic policy cannot have very large effects on politics and attitudes abroad through its immediate impact on economic conditions for the obvious reason that the economic effects of American actions cannot usually be very large—though this is not always true. Occasionally, American policy can bring about large economic changes in other countries in a short time. For example, in the first two or three years of the Marshall Plan, American aid was the critical factor which made possible a very substantial increase in Western Europe's production and living standards, which in turn had large and beneficial psychological and political results. But such situations are unusual. Typically, the United States is not able deliberately to exert this much leverage on economic conditions in other countries. In the shorter run, therefore, foreign economic policy achieves results mainly through peoples' reactions to the policy itself. Even in the case of the Marshall Plan, a large—perhaps the major—part of the beneficial psychological consequences during the first year at least was not the result of actual economic change. The conspicuous upsurge of West European morale in 1948 and early 1949 came too soon to have been primarily the result of economic improvement. Rather, it came from the sense of American support and the promise of economic improvement and independence symbolized by the Marshall Plan itself.

This is one major reason why the Study Group has stressed the importance of the longer-run aims of American foreign economic policy—that is, the conception of the kind of world order that our policy seeks to create. The capacity of American policy to bring about favorable changes in political attitudes and morale abroad depends in considerable part on how other people understand and react to its longer-run goals. The people of other countries either may reject American goals, or may passively acquiesce in them, or may be so inspired by them that they will themselves be willing to undertake the complementary actions necessary to achieve such objectives. Moreover, the orientation of American policy toward a more rational and relevant conception of the kind of world order which is necessary, possible and desirable in the second half of the 20th century, is not only a psychological requirement. It is also needed if policy is to be internally consistent and effective in bringing about the desired results. Both considerations emphasize the ideological and strategic function of longer-run goals.

The importance of clarity about longer-range objectives has not been adequately appreciated by those concerned with the making and execution of American foreign economic policy. In part, this has been the result of the tendency of conventional thought to keep economics and economic policy in a water-tight compartment, separate from the rest of society and policy. It is owed also to an overly pragmatic approach to foreign policy-making on the part of many government officials and legislators, who often act on the assumption that the only test of policy is short-run success and that any attempt to sketch long-run goals—or even to project policy objectives which are not immediately attainable—is impractical and useless. There is, of course, an important place for pragmatism and for an experimental attitude in foreign policy-making. A pragmatic attitude about the appropriateness of particular means to achieve desirable goals is a necessary antidote to doctrinaire attachments to policies even after their premises have ceased to be relevant and their failure has been demonstrated. As we have seen, the major advances in American foreign economic activities since 1947 have been more the result of *ad hoc* experimentation than of a new conception of goals. Likewise, a pragmatic attitude is a defense against the naive or fanatical enthusiasms of an overly rationalistic perfectionism which insists upon immediate radical solutions of all problems and is scornful of political or moral limitations and of half-way measures. But when the pragmatic attitude is carried to the point of denying the relevance of longer-run objectives, it is likely to degenerate into a crude and amoral opportunism, masquerading as political realism, whose only test of the success of a policy is whether it is immediately "salable" to all articulate interests.

The chief weakness of an excessively pragmatic approach to foreign policy is that it is self-defeating. It cannot maintain morale in the face of inevitable difficulties, setbacks and disappointments because it provides no sense of direction, no conviction of that meaningfulness of effort and sacrifice which is required to sustain courage when the going is tough. This is why a clear conception of longer-run aims capable of providing a sense of direction, and the articulation of a strategy for moving in the direction indicated by these goals, are essential parts of successful policy making. Without the perspective of long-range goals and the guiding principles of a relevant strategy, there are no reference points by which the multitude of specific policies and actions can be made consistent with one another and with their intended purposes. Without long-range goals and effective strategy, foreign policy-makers are likely to lack the conviction and the courage to resist the forces of particular interests, partisan passions and national prejudices which beset them on every side. Much of the recent decline of morale and failure of nerve in the West can be charged to an excessive preoccupation since 1950 with short-run military objectives and with the day-to-day tactics of the cold war. The sense of a positive direction and constructive meaning in Western policy, once symbolized by the Marshall Plan and Point IV, has been largely dissipated. Unless Western policy-makers can explain their immediate objectives in terms of the kind of world they are trying to build over the longer-term, and in symbols capable of evoking enthusiasm from the peoples of the West, the necessary participation, effort and sacrifice will not be forthcoming. As Lord Acton wrote:

> The pursuit of a remote and ideal object, which captivates the imagination by its splendor and the reason by its simplicity, evokes an energy which would not be inspired by a rational, possible end, limited by many antagonistic claims, and confined to what is reasonable, practicable and just.

It is not too serious an exaggeration to conclude that the success of the measures discussed in the following chapters should not be judged primarily by whether, if adopted, they turn out to be notably successful in producing short-run improvements in economic conditions abroad. If they fail to achieve adequate economic results in a reasonable time, they can be replaced by better measures born of growing experience and understanding. In the longer perspective, however, their success will rather be judged by their ability to convey to the peoples of the West a sense of movement in the right direction, which depends, before anything else, on the longer-range goals which these measures are understood to serve.

Within limits, the will of a society to survive, its ability to respond creatively to successive challenges and to modify its day-to-day actions in the light of experience—in short, its courage and morale—depend more directly on the firmness of its conviction that it is moving in the right direction than upon the early or complete success of its efforts. The Marshall Plan was, at best, a very partial success in terms of its short-run objectives—to restore Western Europe's economic health and political stability and to make it independent of "extraordinary outside assistance." Yet, mainly because of the attractiveness of its symbolic meaning, it succeeded for a time in giving to the peoples of Western Europe and the United States a new sense of direction and purpose in their common political and economic life. Perhaps the West will be able to find again its sense of direction and to improve its morale when its people become convinced that they are really engaged once more in building a better Western political and economic Community.

7

The Economic Organization of the Western Community

Trade, Payments and Economic Integration

What is now being done and what more might be done to overcome the obstacles to the economic growth of Western Europe and Japan? The answer to this question is concerned primarily with external obstacles—not because the internal obstacles to growth are less important, but because they are less accessible than the external problems to remedial action by the United States. Also, some improvement in the external economic environment of the West European economies is probably a necessary—though by no means a sufficient—condition for overcoming internal obstacles to growth, such as restrictionism and the inadequate vigor of industrial enterprise.

The external economic problems of the other industrial countries are owed in considerable measure to the fact that these countries are no longer parts of a world trading system within which the movement of goods, money and persons is relatively unrestricted and the conditions of doing business are reasonably secure and calculable.[1] To put it positively, the other industrial economies need to be parts of a wider-than-national economic unit, or units, within which freedom of international trade and capital movements, free convertibility of currencies, and the *continued assurance* or *calculability* of that freedom are much greater than in the

---

[1] See Chapters 1 and 2.

contemporary international economy and more nearly approach the degree of economic freedom and calculability within a national economy. We say "more nearly approach" because economic relations among independent national states cannot normally be as free or as secure as within a state—even in the 19th century they were not.[2]

Today, a major improvement in this respect is, clearly, a necessary condition of any sustained advance in the rate of economic growth of Western Europe and Japan. As explained in Chapter 2, these industrial economies can enjoy adequate rates of growth only if they can achieve a rapid and sustained increase of industrial exports and primary imports at satisfactory terms of trade. According to international trade theory, this is made possible by participation in a universal trading system essentially similar to the world trading system of the last century. But since, for reasons already explained, that universal solution is not a historic possibility in our times, it is necessary to think in terms of regional groupings of countries, among whose members it may be possible to create greater freedom and calculability than on a wider, or universal, basis.

To be effective in mitigating Western Europe's and Japan's external problems, such regional groupings would have to satisfy certain criteria of size and resource availability. Specifically:

(1) The regional grouping would have to be large enough in terms of total population and income to constitute an "internal" market of a size sufficient to provide large new possibilities of gains in productivity through increases in the degree of subdivision and specialization of industrial operations.

---

[2] "The area given by politics, within which there is a uniform law, police, money and weights and measures, is an area within which economic relationships are far easier to establish than they are across the boundaries of such areas. Modern thought [i.e., economic liberalism] has tended to ignore this factor and to hold not only that free trade should be, but that it practically can be, the condition of economic relations between state areas. This mode of thought turned its back on the recognized economic significance of the area of government expressed in the term 'commonwealth' in the 17th century. In order to understand the meaning of the nation-state system for such an area as Europe, it is indispensable to recover the concept of the area within a state as a commonwealth." George S. Pettee, *Union for Europe* (Chicago, Illinois: Human Events Associates, 1947), p. 8. One reason why this difference has been ignored by economic liberalism may be the fact that, as explained in Chapter 1, the degree of difference was not great enough to be a major consideration in economic decisions during the latter half of the 19th century.

(2) The countries forming the grouping would have to be sufficiently diverse in their endowments of the factors of production, yet sufficiently similar in initial economic structure, to provide important new opportunities for gains in productivity through increased geographical specialization of agriculture and industry.

(3) At the same time, the countries forming the grouping would have to be sufficiently complementary in economic structure, and have a sufficiently favorable ratio of population to natural resources, that the dependence of the grouping on the rest of the world for food and industrial materials and for industrial export markets would be, or could become, fairly low. That is, such a grouping should be able to increase its internal agricultural and mineral output rapidly enough, and at sufficiently low real costs, for its future economic expansion to be reasonably "balanced" and not excessively dependent on the incalculable vicissitudes of its external economic environment. In short, the industrial countries of Western Europe and Japan need to be part of wider-than-national economic units considerably larger and more balanced than any of their existing individual national economies.[3]

---

[3] For a clear formulation of the economic criteria of desirable economic groupings, see Jacob Viner, *The Customs Union Issue* (New York: Carnegie Endowment for International Peace, 1950), pp. 41–54. Viner's analysis deals principally with customs unions and his criteria refer to a situation in which tariffs are the only barriers to international trade. He therefore abstracts from the effects of the other, and considerably more important, obstacles to trade, including the incalculability of present-day international economic relations. The differences between the economic criteria explained above (particularly the Study Group's emphasis on the desirability of a relatively balanced economic structure) and those adduced in Viner's lucid analysis of customs unions arise primarily from this difference in starting point. If the whole range of present-day obstacles to international economic relations is taken into account, the economic case for integrated wider-than-national trading areas becomes even stronger than Viner's analysis suggests—even from a cosmopolitan point of view, and *a fortiori* from the standpoint of American foreign policy—as far as the other industrial countries of the free world are concerned. Apart from this question, Viner's analysis may also understate the extent to which a large customs union or other economic grouping can make possible "increasing returns" in industry by providing an enlarged internal market. This is perhaps because Viner is thinking only of the effect of a larger internal market in making possible economies of scale for individual plants and firms and omitting from consideration its effect in making possible "external economies" through the increasing subdivision and specialization of industrial production processes seen as an interrelated whole. "The mechanism of increasing returns is not to be discerned adequately by observing the effects of variations in the size of an individual firm or of a particular industry, for the progressive division and specialization of industries is an essential part of the process by which increasing returns are realized. What is required is that industrial operations be seen as an interrelated whole." Allyn Young, "Increasing Returns and Economic Progress," *Economic Journal* (December, 1928).

To satisfy such economic criteria in tolerable degree, the economic unit need not include the whole non-communist world but, ideally at least, it would have to consist of a rather large group of countries. A grouping comprising two or three small industrial countries, such as the projected Benelux economic union (Belgium, the Netherlands and Luxembourg), offers its members relatively small economic advantages even in the present international environment, although the political and psychological benefits of Benelux and its value as a symbol of movement toward a supranational European union have undoubtedly been great.[4]

Let us, therefore, assume for the purposes of discussion that ways could be found to include Western Europe and Japan in a grouping, or groupings, which satisfy these economic criteria. A more difficult question then arises. How can a group of countries assure a high degree of freedom and calculability in their mutual trade, payments and other economic relations? By what institutional means can countries today constitute themselves a regional trading area within which international economic relations are significantly freer and safer than among independent national economies? This is the crucial question for American foreign economic policy insofar as it is concerned with the external economic problems of Western Europe and Japan. The answer to this question given by liberal economic internationalism—that nations have only to agree to renounce economic nationalism in order to restore freedom and calculability to their mutual economic relations—is not now adequate, nor is it ever again likely to be so. It is impossible simply to exorcise by international agreement the deeper causes of economic nationalism and the social values and national interests which it serves. Rather, an attempt must be made to find alternative means—consistent with greater freedom and calculability of international economic relations—by which national communities can achieve the purposes they now seek to realize through economic nationalism.

---

[4] Benelux and the abortive proposals for Franco-Italian and Scandinavian economic unions have also contributed significantly to Western understanding of the economic and political problems of regional economic integration. For example, the experience of the Belgian and Dutch governments in trying to create an economic union between their countries has led them from the earlier hope that union could be accomplished largely by intergovernmental agreements to remove trade and payments barriers to the realization that, in contemporary conditions, close international integration presupposes a measure of supranational control over national economic policies. See below, p. 246.

International Economic Integration in the Mid-20th Century

Freedom and calculability of economic relations among a group of countries depend on many things. They depend most fundamentally on whether military security, political stability and a legal order favorable to the conduct of international business prevail throughout the trading area. Apart from this basic requirement, they depend on a common ordering of economic activities and conditions throughout the trading area. In some circumstances, that common ordering may occur "automatically," by the action of private markets. When national states customarily allowed a high degree of freedom of private trade and investment and when private economic power was restricted in scope, economic conditions could be ordered by market forces in a reasonably calculable way throughout the trading world, as in the 19th century. Today, in contrast, organized interest groups and national communities are reluctant to submit their economic fortunes to the impersonal and automatic regulation of international markets and of an international monetary system. This reluctance is expressed in a variety of public and private economic controls and interventions, which restrict the freedom of international economic relations and introduce major elements of uncertainty and risk into the international economy. Explicit governmental trade and payments barriers (quotas, tariffs, exchange controls, etc.) are only one form which this intervention takes. National governments and private organizations also intervene in national economies at many other points.

In consequence, freedom and security of international economic relations will not normally occur automatically in present circumstances. They have to be consciously created by coordinated action of national governments to prevent public and private restrictions from destroying the freedom and calculability of international markets. Yet coordinated action of this kind is most difficult to accomplish. National economic policies are too often made by organized interests seeking short-run economic advantages through economic nationalism, and with little concern for the long-run economic and political benefits which a more efficient international economy would bring. This is the essence of the problem of international economic integration in the contemporary world.

To test this general reasoning, the question of currency convertibility may be considered. Continuous and assured interconvertibility of their currencies is essential to the freedom and security of international economic relations among the members of any grouping of countries. However, continuous convertibility of currencies within a wider-than-national trading area can only exist if there is some institutional arrangement which orders monetary conditions throughout the region so as to keep payments imbalances among its members within tolerable bounds. The arrangement must be, by convention or by law, secure from undue interference by national governments or private interests. In the 19th century, the institution which filled this role was the sterling-gold standard mechanism. Its workings were accepted throughout the trading world as impersonal economic forces to which private traders and public authorities alike were accustomed to conform. In this century, however, the workings of an impersonal mechanism of that kind cannot be made consistently acceptable in most countries to major economic interests or even to national governments themselves. Governments may allow it to work for a time, as in the late 1920's, or where circumstances are unusually favorable, as within the dollar area today. But, in contemporary conditions, the functioning of a largely automatic international monetary system is normally precarious—and hence incalculable—either because the political tolerance of most national communities to deflationary or inflationary pressures from abroad is too low or because their desire to follow independent national economic policies despite external difficulties is too strong. Rather than submit to unwanted external pressures or obstacles, most national governments today resort as a matter of course to unilateral restriction of their foreign trade and payments. Thus, continuous convertibility of national currencies over a wide area cannot be assured by a return to the gold standard or by any similar—i.e., largely automatic—mechanism. In most cases, continuous convertibility can be assured only to the extent that means can be found to harmonize national economic conditions by deliberate coordination of national monetary and financial policies.[5]

---

[5] The emphasis in contemporary discussions of international economic problems on inflationary or deflationary national monetary policies as a cause of trade restrictions sometimes gives the impression that ill-conceived monetary policies are the only obstacle to a high degree of international economic integration. That is hardly true; the harmonization of national *monetary* conditions is not the only requirement for effective integration of national economies with each other. Though national inflations and deflations have been conspicuous causes of the restriction and insecurity of international economic relations since 1930, they have not been the only cause. Today, national economies are subject to many economic interventions and controls, public and private, which discriminate against foreigners; which support a structure of wages, prices and exchange rates impossible to maintain without restriction of imports; and which greatly increase the risks of doing interna-

International economic integration today is a very different matter from what it was in the last century. As Professor Viner has put it:

> There has occurred, since 1914, and especially since the 1930's, a new development which makes the removal of trade barriers between countries with important actual or potential economic relations a much more formidable matter than it was in the 19th century. This is the growth of governmental intervention in industry, and especially of planned economies, socialist or otherwise. In the 19th century, the free market predominated, prices were flexible and unregulated, exchange rates were relatively stable without need of exchange control, and costs were not made rigid by wage-regulation, social security programs, cartelization, or extensive collective bargaining. . . . Now, however, tariffs and other barriers to trade—quotas, import licenses, exchange controls, state import monopolies, etc.—protect not merely the allocation of employed resources but the whole artificial national price and wage structures, the volume of employment, the social security programs, the exchange rate pegs, the monetary and fiscal policies, and so forth. . . . Two neighboring countries contemplating complete customs union today must therefore contemplate also the necessity of harmonizing their general patterns of economic controls, which would involve a much more complete degree of economic unification than would a representative 19th-century customs union.[6]

There is another sense, too, in which the integration of national economies—particularly advanced industrial economies—is a very different and much more difficult problem than it was in the 19th century. Over the last forty or fifty years, there have been profound changes in the character of industrial markets, the nature of industrial organization, and the structure of industrial production which have tended to increase the dependence of international economic integration on the security and calculability of the conditions of doing business across national frontiers. For example, many industrial products are today sold under monopolistic conditions created by product differentiation, large-scale sales promotion, special servicing facilities, and the like. The purpose of

---

tional business as compared with business at home. The prevalence of this public and private interventionism and protectionism is such that, even if a group of countries could manage to keep their monetary conditions in harmony, the degree of economic integration possible among them would not be very high—unless their economic policies were also closely coordinated for the purposes of inducing mutual adaptation of their economies and reducing national protectionism and restrictionism in all their other forms.

[6] Viner, *op. cit.*, p. 136.

such arrangements is, of course, to attach a large group of purchasers as securely as possible to a particular producer's products. The profitability of these arrangements, which represent a very large investment in resources, funds and executive energy—and of the mass production which they make possible—depends on a high degree of assurance that this nexus between producer and customers will not be broken. In consequence, to establish selling arrangements of this kind across national frontiers is today ordinarily too risky for most manufacturers. For industries which depend on large-scale sales promotion, the risks of international business are a formidable obstacle to increased international trade and an important cause of the nationalization of industrial markets. It is, for example, an important obstacle to European manufacturers of consumer goods who may desire to increase their share of American mass markets.

Again, the changed structure of industrial production today demands a degree of calculability in commercial relations between industrial firms substantially greater, on the average, than was true fifty years ago. Industrial growth involves, characteristically, an increasing subdivision and specialization of production operations, both within firms and industries and among them. A growing proportion of industrial output has accordingly come to consist of specialized capital equipment and intermediate products—semi-manufactures, components, sub-assemblies, etc. To reap fully the gains in productivity which this increasing "roundaboutness" of production permits, each specialized production operation must work at capacity and as continuously as possible. It is this need for continuity of industrial operations that creates a requirement for a high degree of calculability—i.e., a minimum of unintended interruption—in the linkage between them. Thus, for example, industrial firms will hesitate to become dependent on a foreign supplier of some specialized machine, part or component, and will be reluctant to rely heavily on foreign outlets for specialized intermediate products.[7] In sum, these two familiar

---

[7] For example, a cotton textile mill in Lancashire takes far less risk in depending on foreign supplies of a relatively unspecialized commodity—cotton—than would a British producer of tractors in depending on a German or Japanese supplier for a specialized component—e.g., a specially designed ignition system. For, the textile mill can ordinarily be sure of finding the kind of cotton it needs in any of a dozen foreign markets, while the producer of tractors may lose several months of production if his foreign supply is interrupted, for example, by changes in government regulations in his own or the supplying country. Broadly speaking, the textile example is typical of 19th-century industry and the tractor example of the newer 20th-century industries.

changes in the structure of modern industry—its growing dependence on large-scale "selling" to consumers and its increasingly complex, specialized and "roundabout" methods of production—both require greater calculability in economic relations and, therefore, make for the nationalization of industrial production and markets.[8]

The conclusion reached above that international economic integration depends on the deliberate coordination of national economic policies and controls is not, of course, equally true everywhere. Within the dollar area, and particularly between the United States and Canada, it seems to be possible to maintain continuous convertibility of currencies and a rather high degree of economic integration "automatically"—i.e., without deliberate coordination of national policies. The reasons for this are illuminating.

The case of the United States is the easier to explain. Chapter 1 has sketched the main reasons why the American balance of payments has been consistently strong. For these and other reasons, it is possible for the United States Government to follow the internal monetary and financial policy dictated by domestic considerations without need to resort to payments restrictions. Nor do other domestic policies have to be adjusted to the state of the balance of payments. Then, too, the low dependence of the American economy on foreign trade, together with its high rate of growth and its flexibility, make it proportionately far better able to adjust spontaneously to external market conditions than, for example, the British economy. Indeed, the size and competitive power of the American economy are such that it tends to create its own external market conditions; as noted in Part I, American economic conditions and capa-

---

[8] One further aspect of this phenomenon should be noted. The increased requirement for calculability has given rise to the combination of related industrial and selling operations within single firms (e.g., vertical and horizontal integration) and to the elaboration of new forms of long-term contractual or agency relationships between independent firms. Thus, industry today is far more "organized" and "organic," and far less "atomistic," than fifty years ago. It follows, then, that international economic integration, to be effective, has to involve not merely a growth of trade in the usual sense but also a good deal of organic growing together of industrial firms across national boundaries. When the matter is put in that way, it becomes apparent why the incalculability of international conditions is now so imposing an obstacle to the international integration of industrial economies. It also becomes apparent why differences in the outlook and spirit of industrial management among countries, and in their forms of industrial organization, are today obstacles to international economic integration in a way which they were not a generation ago. The uniquely high degree of integration between American and Canadian industry illustrates the combined effects of relatively high calculability and of a similarity of management outlook and industrial organization.

bilities are active rather than dependent forces in the international economy.

In contrast, the Canadian economy is heavily dependent on foreign trade—almost as much so as the British—and is a relatively small economy. It is, therefore, subject to the necessity of adjusting to external changes and to the risks of heavy external dependence in the present international environment. But, its rate of economic growth is very high—in fact, the highest in the free world. As in the United States, the structure of the Canadian economy is relatively flexible, its entrepreneurs vigorous and progressive, and the competitive ability of many of its exports strong. The Canadian Government has been politically able and willing to allow the exchange rate of the Canadian dollar to move in response to market forces. Thus, the Canadian economy is able to respond adequately to external market changes, to avoid chronic inflation, and to maintain its competitive position in foreign markets. Moreover, the traditional sense of community between Canada and the United States—their historical friendship and mutual trust—as well as their relatively liberal domestic economic policies and their geographical proximity, make for a degree of freedom and security of trade and private investment between them that is almost unique between sovereign nations in the present-day world. Despite these factors, however, the continued strength of the Canadian dollar is considerably less assured than that of the American. At bottom, it depends on American commercial policy and on a high level of demand in the United States—factors which are not as calculable as they might be. And trade between the two countries is even now restricted to a significant extent by tariffs, quotas and other protectionist devices which are susceptible to rapid increases at times of economic stress.[9]

Despite this and other exceptions, it remains true for much of the noncommunist world—and certainly for Western Europe—that a high degree

---

[9] Generally speaking, the other countries of the dollar area (Northern Latin America and the Philippines) are members by virtue of the structure of their exports and their proximity to the United States. For the most part, their exports consist of a few minerals and tropical agricultural products which are not competitive with American output and which, unlike European manufactures and some Asiatic raw materials, enjoy a rapidly expanding market in the United States, largely free of import restrictions. Several of these dollar countries also offer attractive and reasonably secure outlets for American investment —in part for traditional reasons, as in the Philippines; in part because they are, like Canada, well within the United States' inner security zone. Nevertheless, the convertibility of other dollar-area currencies is, in most cases, considerably more precarious than that of the Canadian dollar, particularly where domestic economic policies have been inflationary, as in Mexico and the Philippines.

of international economic integration presupposes formal institutional means of coordinating national economic policies. Among countries belonging to an historical community, sharing a similar outlook, and having a sense of mutual trust, considerable coordination of this kind can be accomplished merely by continuous informal negotiation and agreement, or by formal adherence to multilateral treaties and active participation in international organizations. The Sterling Area and the Organization for European Economic Cooperation (OEEC) are such intergovernmental arrangements and they are able in different degrees to increase considerably the freedom and security of international economic relations among their members.

But the effect on national policies of intergovernmental arrangements which leave national economic sovereignty substantially intact is necessarily limited. Such arrangements can, as we shall see, mitigate considerably the disorder of the present international economy, but they cannot create the conditions of a high degree of continuous international economic integration. Except in unusual circumstances (e.g., during a major war or economic crisis), voluntary agreements, whose performance is solely the responsibility of the individual sovereign parties to them, cannot be made strong enough to restrain national governments from taking unilateral action when powerful domestic interests press for it—especially since the citizens of any country cannot normally count on the ability of other governments to abide by these agreements. To put it another way, the drastic lowering or removal of trade and payments barriers among, say, a group of European countries would give rise to conflicts of interest among economic groups in the different countries and thus to conflicts of interest among national governments. If these conflicts of interest were severe, it would be impossible to resolve them by compromise and agreement because each government would have the easier and safer alternative of resorting to unilateral action—e.g., of reimposing import restrictions. Indeed, domestic political pressures may allow governments no other alternative, for the concern of domestic economic interest groups is usually with their immediate problems or, at best, with short-run national interests. Only rarely do such groups act on the basis of concern for the longer-run interests of the nation, much less of any wider-than-national community to which their country may belong.[10]

---

[10] "The arguments for freer trade on the ground of abundance are cosmopolitan rather than national. They are concerned with long-run tendencies in an open world economy,

This line of reasoning leads back to the conclusion arrived at in Chapter 1. By reason of changes in the nature of economic life and in the relations of governments to economic affairs, international economic integration is no longer consistent with the unfettered exercise of national sovereignty. Where governments are concerned with employment, wages and prices, and with transferring incomes from some groups to others, and where the pressures of private groups are so effective, old-fashioned free trade no longer obtains even *within* nations and it is plainly out of the question to revive it by agreement *among* nations. Today, therefore, a high degree of freedom and security of international economic relations presupposes enough supranational authority to prevent unilateral national action, to decide how conflicts of national economic interest are to be reconciled, and to enforce its decisions. Where a high degree of economic integration among a group of national economies is desired, and where the nature of these economies is such that freedom of trade and payments among them would give rise to acute conflicts of interest, genuinely supranational organs of a governmental or quasi-governmental character are required—organs which are capable of making and executing decisions about economic policy by some method other than unanimous consent and voluntary execution by the national governments concerned. In contemporary conditions, the fully adequate alternative to economic nationalism is not economic internationalism but economic supranationalism.

This conclusion will be unwelcome to those who have hoped that much less radical means would be sufficient to restore an integrated international economy, at least in the West. It is obviously difficult for a group of national governments voluntarily to surrender any significant degree of control over economic matters which affect group and national interests —even if the surrender is to a supranational body which their citizens control jointly through democratic institutions. Such a body will never be created solely or even primarily for economic reasons; a lesson taught

rather than with short-run considerations in a closed national economy. But economic and political decisions are seldom taken on such long-term grounds. Ordinarily, they are governed by immediate expectations of local gains. The general good has little appeal to a businessman whose investment is threatened by competition, or to a worker who clings to his present employment because he must find food for his family next week. The gains from international specialization are regarded dimly by those whose interests must be sacrificed if such specialization is to develop." J. B. Condliffe, *The Commerce of Nations* (New York: W. W. Norton & Co., 1950), p. 818. This quotation perhaps oversimplifies the issue by assuming, in the tradition of economic liberalism, that the cosmopolitan interest and long-run national interests are somehow "naturally" in harmony.

by the history of existing federations is that economic motives alone have never been sufficient to bring about voluntarily the political union of sovereign states. The voluntary creation of true supranational authority presupposes an organic, historical sense of community among the nations concerned. It requires a wide and deep consensus on many matters—including many crucial questions of economic policy—among the component national communities. It depends upon a strong desire on their part to become, in some degree at least, a single political community.

These considerations imply that a solution of the external economic problems of the other industrial countries is beyond the present limits of political feasibility—although the possibility may exist of creating a European grouping of a supranational character. They do not mean, however, that nothing worthwhile can be accomplished to improve the external environment of the West European economies until it may become politically possible to create some kind of political union embracing all or most of the Western Community. In the following sections of this chapter, we shall examine two existing regional groupings of European and other predominantly Western countries, which involve no explicit central authority, yet which have already improved materially their members' external economic environment, and are capable of further improving it if certain changes are made in their methods of operation.

We may now return to the concrete policy issue posed at the beginning of this chapter: What wider-than-national trading areas exist, or might be created, to mitigate the economic problems of Western Europe and Japan? The West European countries are already part, or are now trying to create, three major economic groupings whose purpose is to increase the freedom and security of international economic relations among their participants. The oldest of these—and the most successful—is the system of economic arrangements linking together the members of the British Commonwealth and some other countries. The second is the grouping defined by membership in the Organization for European Economic Cooperation and by participation in the European Payments Union. The third is the proposed European political and economic union. In the remainder of this chapter, we shall examine critically each of these groupings, actual and proposed, and consider ways in which its effectiveness might be increased.

Economic Organization of the Commonwealth

Though the Commonwealth is primarily a political and symbolic institution, it is also the political framework of the most effective existing wider-than-national trading area. The mechanisms and the geographical scope of that area are difficult to explain simply, since they are more products of historical evolution than of a deliberate plan.

The major economic institutions of the Commonwealth are the Sterling Area financial arrangements, the imperial preferential tariff agreements, and a number of intergovernmental committees, such as the Commonwealth Finance Ministers, the Commonwealth Liaison Committee, the Sterling Area Statistical Committee and the administrative machinery of the Colombo Plan.[11] Participation in these institutions is not strictly confined to Commonwealth countries and the membership of the different institutions is not always the same. Canada, for example, is a "dollar country" and not a member of the Sterling Area. Several non-Commonwealth countries, such as Ireland, Burma and Iraq, are members of the Sterling Area. Nor are the signatories of the imperial preferential tariff agreements identical with the members of the Sterling Area. Several Asian countries which are not Commonwealth members participate in the Colombo Plan, and so on. Thus, there are several overlapping groupings, organized for different economic purposes, with the United Kingdom and colonies and a majority of the Dominions as the common nucleus.[12]

Nevertheless, is seems best to consider these groupings as a unit, not only because of their common membership and their connection with the Commonwealth, but also because they have a common origin and a common

---

[11] In addition to these formal institutions, there are a number of other important intergovernmental economic arrangements within the Commonwealth—for example, the bulk-purchase contracts which cover a portion of the United Kingdom's imports from the Dominions. The influence of the Sterling Area arrangements extends somewhat beyond their formal membership, because of the Sterling Transferable Account System and the use of sterling in the monetary reserves of a number of non-Sterling Area countries.

[12] Good brief descriptions of the major Commonwealth-Sterling Area economic institutions and their evolution may be found in Economic Cooperation Administration, *The Sterling Area, an American Analysis* (London and Washington, 1951), Ch. 1; A. R. Conan, *The Sterling Area* (London: Macmillan & Co., 1952); D. H. Robertson, *Britain in the World Economy* (London: Allen & Unwin, 1954), Ch. 2; and League of Nations, *International Currency Experience* (Montreal, 1944), Ch. 3.

aim. The existence of all these groupings is explained in large part by the fact that their members were once, in varying degrees, parts of an integrated imperial polity and economy. The complementary structure of their economies, their long-established commercial and banking ties, and their special sense of community—all products of their former imperial bonds—explain in large part why these concentric groupings came to be and why they continue to hold together. Such historical factors made it natural for the member countries to respond to the disintegration of the 19th-century world economy and to growing American competition by evolving a currency and trading area of their own, within which the conditions of international trade, payments and investment are more free and calculable than outside, and which gives some protection from outside competition to trade between Britain and the Dominions.

Among the institutions of this currency and trading area, the Sterling Area financial arrangements have been the most conspicuous and important in the postwar period. To understand their function—and their value and limitations in mitigating the external problems of the British economy—a brief sketch of their history is necessary.

The Sterling Area was not formally constituted until the outbreak of World War II but it was a logical outgrowth of the developments of the interwar period which led to the emergence of a Sterling Bloc. Before 1914, the pound sterling, tied to gold, was the universal currency of international trade; the British banking system, together with the Bank of England, acted as the central monetary institution of the whole trading world. With the emergence of national central banking in the interwar period, the control of national monetary policies and the financing of external trade were increasingly assumed by national authorities. This process was accelerated after 1931 when sterling ceased to be convertible into gold and national financial authorities everywhere sought to play an increasingly active role in combating deflation. The disintegration of the pre-1914 monetary system was not, however, as complete among the Dominions (except Canada), the British colonies and a few other countries with particularly close commercial and banking ties with the United Kingdom. This group of countries came to be known as the "Sterling Bloc." They followed sterling in abandoning the gold standard and continued to keep their currencies pegged to sterling. They also continued, as in the past, to allow the British banking system to function as their common central bank in clearing and financing their trade and payments with each other and with non-sterling countries, although the former grip of the British banking system on their internal monetary systems was greatly weakened.[13]

When war came in 1939, Britain's most urgent financial problems were to conserve dollars for imports of war supplies from North America and to augment its own financial resources by borrowing as extensively as possible from the Dominions. The Sterling Bloc's financial arrangements were quickly adapted to these purposes. A ring of exchange controls was put around the sterling countries and the dollar holdings and earnings of the members were treated as a pool to be used only for military and other essential imports. Because the other members customarily settled their foreign accounts in sterling, the United Kingdom was able to borrow freely from them simply by allowing its current sterling obligations to them to grow. Thus, there emerged the now familiar financial arrangements of the Sterling Area: the "dollar pool," the system of coordinated restriction of dollar payments, and the large sterling indebtedness of the United Kingdom to certain other Sterling Area members—the so-called "sterling balances."

It has been possible in the postwar period to maintain within the Sterling Area a substantially greater freedom of international trade and payments than elsewhere in the free world, and even substantial freedom of private capital movements.[14] The freedom of trade and payments within the Sterling Area is not, however, complete and it is substantially less than before 1914. But effective currency convertibility has existed within the area since World War II, although, in several instances, quantitative restrictions have been imposed temporarily by certain Dominions on imports from the United Kingdom, primarily for balance-of-payments reasons.[15] Likewise, the Dominions maintain stiff—albeit preferential—tariff protection against British manufactures as well as other, more subtle, forms of protectionism. Nonetheless, the Sterling Area members still enjoy in their mutual economic relations a considerably greater

---

[13] That is, the Sterling Bloc countries were distinguished from the rest of the trading world in that (a) they adopted sterling as the "standard" of their national currencies and (b) they continued to conduct their foreign payments in terms of sterling, to hold their external reserves in sterling, to sell foreign exchange earnings to British banks for sterling balances held in London, and to obtain foreign exchange by drawing on their sterling balances.

[14] Except, of course, within the dollar area, where, as we have seen, currency convertibility has been fairly consistently maintained in the postwar period.

[15] For example, by South Africa in 1949 and Australia in 1951.

freedom from restrictions, and from the threat of restrictions, than is true outside.

What makes this possible? The answer to this question reveals both the advantages and the shortcomings of the Sterling Area system from the standpoint of Britain's economic health. The dollar pool and the system of coordinated restriction of dollar payments have made it possible to maintain a high degree of convertibility within the Sterling Area despite its postwar dollar shortage. Without this coordination of commercial policy *vis-à-vis* nonmember countries, trade and payments among the Sterling Area members would have been forced by the dollar shortage into the same kind of restrictive bilateralism which characterized postwar trade and payments among other nondollar countries until the formation of the European Payments Union in 1950, and which still prevails outside the Sterling and EPU Areas. Nonetheless, from a British point of view, the coordination of commercial policy has been insufficient. Some Dominions have made claims on the dollar pool which seem excessive in the light of the Sterling Area's total dollar earnings. The only two Dominions which have been regular net earners of dollars (South Africa and Ceylon) have been unwilling to participate in the dollar pool.[16] In effect, the Sterling Area system has worked because Britain has been willing to finance the dollar deficits of some of the Dominions out of the net dollar earnings of the colonies and American dollar aid. Without that aid, the Sterling Area would probably have broken up.[17]

The fact that a high degree of currency convertibility has been maintained within the Sterling Area shows that methods have been found to preserve the liquidity of international payments within the Area despite the absence of any formal machinery for the coordination of the monetary and financial policies of the members. In the first section of this chapter, it was argued that such coordination is normally a prerequisite to maintenance of international convertibility in the mid-20th century. What is it about the Sterling Area which makes a high degree of convertibility possible within the Area without such formal coordination? There seem to be three principal reasons. The first is that the absence of formal coordinating machinery is in part compensated by the continuing prestige of the British Government and of the Bank of England in the Common-

---

[16] See A. R. Conan, *op. cit.*, p. 154.

[17] A fuller explanation of the relation between the dollar shortage, discrimination, American aid and the maintenance of multilateral trade and convertibility of currencies among a grouping of nondollar countries is given in the next section of this chapter.

wealth, and by the economic bargaining power which the British Government possesses *vis-à-vis* some of the Dominions. A second reason is the sense of community that exists in varying degree among Commonwealth countries, coupled with the habit of many Commonwealth governments to look to London for guidance on international economic questions, particularly financial ones. These traditional attitudes tend to restrain—though not always to prevent—the adoption by some of the Commonwealth countries of those arbitrarily nationalistic economic policies which are standard practice among most other nations. There is within the Commonwealth a greater tolerance for the effects of Sterling Area freedom of trade and payments on domestic economic conditions, and a greater feeling of responsibility to adjust national economic policies to the interests of other members, than is true elsewhere.

A third reason why the Sterling Area is able to work without formal coordination of the members' policies is the willingness of the United Kingdom to bear a disproportionate share of the burden of assuring the liquidity of international exchanges within the Area. By allowing large releases from the sterling balances and free private capital exports to the sterling Commonwealth countries, the United Kingdom has enabled some of the Dominions to avoid or to postpone the choice between internal monetary restriction and restriction of imports. Thus, Britain's willingness to meet a disproportionate share of the sterling—as well as of the dollar—costs of maintaining freedom of exchange within the Area has been a necessary condition of that freedom. Moreover, the freedom of trade within the Sterling Area is also somewhat one-sided to Britain's disadvantage. The degree of effective protection which the British economy has against competition from the Commonwealth is substantially less than Commonwealth protection against British competition. The willingness of the British to accept Dominion protectionism without retaliation is easily explainable in terms of the history and structure of the British and Dominion economies. Nevertheless, it contrasts sharply with the commercial policies of other industrial countries and with Britain's own commercial policy toward countries outside the Commonwealth. It provides a strong economic inducement to the independent sterling Commonwealth countries to accept the limited degree of external discipline involved in the Sterling Area arrangements, despite the absence of formal intergovernmental coordinating machinery.

The fact that the United Kingdom endures these costs willingly is explained in part by the support which the Sterling Area arrangements give to the political cohesion of the Commonwealth. It is evidence also of the economic benefits Britain derives from the Sterling Area. Among these benefits is considerable protection for British industrial exports in Commonwealth markets against American, European and Japanese competition. In the postwar period, this protection has been owed mainly to the barrier of quantitative restrictions between the sterling and dollar countries, whose immediate purpose has been financial rather than protectionist. But if and when it may be possible to lower this barrier and even to eliminate it from time to time (i.e., to make sterling convertible with the dollar on current account), the other means of protection which surround the Commonwealth will become more conspicuous and important. These include not only greater calculability of economic relations within the Commonwealth but also the imperial preferential tariff and the many other, less formal, preferences which British and Dominion exports enjoy within the Commonwealth by virtue of governmental policies and traditional commercial and financial ties. Some of these less formal preferences have been strengthened in recent times by the growth of economic interventionism—for example, the bulk-purchase contracts between Britain and some of the Dominions. The traditional private commercial and financial ties, however, have lost much of their former power to direct the Dominions' trade toward the United Kingdom.

American policy has been generally hostile to the imperial tariff system —though we have had to accept it—as to other forms of regional tariff preference. Yet the imperial tariff and other less formal preferences are favorable to British economic growth, though at some cost to the expansion of American exports and those of the other industrial countries. Without them, the pressure of American and European competition would affect the rate of growth of British exports to the Dominions more seriously than it has—perhaps as seriously as in Latin America. The traditional American attitude toward these preferences seems to give our rather small economic interest in the promotion of our own exports priority over our much greater political interest in British economic health, in the solidarity of the Commonwealth, and in close Anglo-American relations. But, the United States cannot afford, politically or morally, to act as though it were unaware that the competitive power of its exports is a factor tending to restrict the opportunities for economic growth of its most important ally. As John Williams has said: "The danger for Britain and for Western Europe is that, unless by some form of organization a basis can be laid for expansion of exports and relief from the necessity to meet every crisis with import cuts, the direct trade between the United States and the non-European world will be strengthened and Europe will be forced into a backwater. . . . The solution seems to lie in the development of larger trading units able to cope on more nearly equal terms with the United States." [18] An approach along these lines is more consistent with real American interests, as well as more equitable, than our customary doctrinaire disapproval of trade preferences—at least those of other countries, for we cling to some of our own.

This is not to say that the United States should be unconcerned about the degree and form of the Commonwealth preferences. The application of these preferences against the continental countries of Western Europe and against Japan is undesirable from an American standpoint, since these countries also need wider export markets and the United States has a strong political interest in their economic health. The extension of the Commonwealth tariff preferences to include—at least to some significant degree—the whole EPU area (as proposed in the "Strasbourg Plan" [19]) and even Japan would be desirable. The United States has also a direct economic interest in ensuring that the degree of protection involved in these preferences is not excessive, just as we have an interest in the convertibility of sterling as circumstances permit. Organizational means through which these concerns could be more effectively expressed are suggested below.

The Sterling Area financial arrangements, then, and the accompanying Commonwealth preferences, together make an important contribution to British economic growth and health. But, unfortunately, that desirable result is now being obtained at too high a cost in current resources to the British economy. This cost results precisely from the relative freedom of trade and payments within the Commonwealth without sufficient coordination of the members' economic policies.

Lack of coordination of monetary policies has meant too great an export of capital, in the form of releases of sterling balances, for an economy as short of capital as Britain's, though it has benefited the rest of the Commonwealth. Lack of coordination of investment policies has meant a direction of investment and economic development in the overseas Commonwealth which is clearly contrary to Britain's longer-run opportunities for export expansion. Lack of sufficient coordination of dollar im-

---

[18] *Trade Not Aid: A Program for World Stability* (Cambridge, Mass.: Harvard University Press, 1953), p. 27.

[19] See Council of Europe, *The Strasbourg Plan* (Strasbourg, 1953).

port policy among Sterling Area countries has resulted in some overseas Commonwealth countries enjoying a dollar import surplus at the
expense of the central reserve and of American aid appropriations whose
intended purpose was quite different. At the same time, lack of an adequate voice in financial policy on the part of some Commonwealth members has permitted British financial policy, public and private, to inhibit
more rapid development of the colonies—and even of the Dominions—
by its conservatism and by many forms of subtle and official discrimination against private foreign investment, particularly American. Finally, the freedom of private capital movements within the Sterling Area
has resulted—in the absence of greater consistency among national economic policies—in large flows of "hot money" out of the United Kingdom which have little or no justification from the standpoint of the economical use of resources in the Sterling Area as a whole. In sum, present
arrangements for consultation among the finance ministers, central banks
and economic officials of the sterling Commonwealth countries have
proved to be too discontinuous and informal to provide a sufficient coordination of economic policies among the members for the system to
work without excessive cost to the British economy. In recent years,
there has been an increasing recognition of this fact in Britain and the
Commonwealth as well as in the United States.

The remedy for the current financial burden of the Sterling Area on
the British economy and dollar reserves—as well as for the inadequacies of current British and Commonwealth policies—is not to break
up the Sterling Area. That prescription has had its supporters among
those who have not understood that the relative freedom of trade and
the calculability of economic conditions within the Sterling Area have
depended—and are likely to continue to depend—on the existence of
the dollar pool and the common system of control of dollar payments.
The value of this freedom and calculability to British and Commonwealth economic growth clearly outweighs the current cost to the United
Kingdom imposed by the Sterling Area arrangements in their present
form. The remedy is so to reorganize the Sterling Area, and to improve
and harmonize the policies of its members, that its great value can be
preserved and increased, while its current cost to Britain can be reduced.

The kind of organizational arrangement which would be ideally desirable from the standpoint of Britain's economic growth and health is
clear. It should make possible complete or nearly complete freedom of
trade and payments among Britain and those overseas Dominions whose

natural resources and present economic and institutional structures would permit rapid expansion of low-cost agricultural production: Canada, Australia, New Zealand and South Africa. It should subject the economic policies of the Commonwealth members to close coordination. The high degree of economic integration of Britain with the Dominions which such an arrangement would make possible would provide a much improved opportunity for Britain to expand its industrial exports and for these Dominions to increase their agricultural output for export to Britain and their industrial raw material production for export to the United States.

But, as we have seen, integration of this degree of closeness would depend on the creation of a supranational political and economic authority—some kind of Commonwealth union or federation. This thought has only to be stated to demonstrate its present political impossibility. For the Dominions, close economic integration with Britain would mean a slowing down of their prized industrialization (probably quite radically) under the impact of unrestricted competition from British industry. It would presumably be politically unacceptable to them to restore so close and dependent an economic and political relationship with the United Kingdom in which—however equal juridically the members might be—Britain would be the dominant factor and memories of former colonial status could be so easily revived. Projects for federation of the English-speaking Commonwealth have been put forward unsuccessfully in the past and there is now no important sentiment for a Commonwealth federation, even in the United Kingdom. The time may come when the pressure of external danger, or other events not now foreseeable, may make that project politically feasible —though a wider union of the whole English-speaking world, or of the whole Western Community, would be more in keeping with the basic economic, military and political needs of the West. For the foreseeable future at any rate, full economic integration of the Commonwealth—or of any substantial part of it—under a supranational political authority is not politically feasible.

Nevertheless, considerable improvement in the economic organization of the Commonwealth is possible on a cooperative basis, without central authority. In addition to a real sense of community and traditional political ties, there are strong common economic interests among the Commonwealth countries which provide the basis for a more effective economic organization of the Commonwealth. All have a common interest in a high degree of freedom of trade and payments within the area and, therefore, a common interest in maintaining a system of coordinated limitation of dollar payments in periods of dollar scarcity. The Dominions have an interest in the stability of British demand for their agricultural exports and in the continued availability of British capital. There is also the desire of the Dominions to participate more effectively in the making of policy concerning the economic relations of the Sterling Area with the United States and the European continent—for example, on such matters as the exchange rate of sterling and relations with the EPU and the OEEC. These economic interests of the Dominions are probably strong enough to make them accept a degree of voluntary coordination of economic policies considerably greater than now exists, if Britain, too, will accept and propose it. The British Government, for its part, will need to overcome its reluctance to share economic policy-making with the Dominions and to use its economic bargaining power to accomplish improvements in the economic organization of the Commonwealth.

Specifically, the present loose consultative arrangements among the Commonwealth governments with respect to trade and payments questions could be strengthened and formalized by the creation of a permanent Commonwealth economic organization modeled, perhaps, on the OEEC. The principal functions of this body might be:

(1) To provide a mechanism by which the mutual obligations of the Sterling Area members of the Commonwealth with respect to their domestic monetary policies, restrictions on dollar payments, drawings on the central dollar reserve, and maintenance of general balance-of-payments equilibrium, can be defined more precisely; and by which performance of these obligations can be subjected to a degree of formal and continuous comment and review by all the members.

(2) To provide a mechanism by which the economic policies of Commonwealth countries toward the United States and continental Europe can be more effectively coordinated. The occasional meetings of the Commonwealth Finance Ministers and the creation of the Commonwealth Liaison and Statistical Committees have been steps in this direction, and in the direction suggested in the preceding paragraph, but not very long ones.

If a Commonwealth economic organization having these functions were created, the United States should be associated with it in some manner. We have a commercial interest in the trade and payments policies which such an organization adopts. We have a political interest in preventing undue discrimination against European and Japanese exports in Commonwealth markets. Furthermore, the effective functioning of the Sterling Area financial arrangements is likely to depend in the future, as it has in the past, on American financial support and on American acquiescence in its discriminatory and preferential features. Without more participation in Commonwealth decision-making on trade and payments questions, the United States should not be willing to continue this support and acquiescence. American participation could take various forms. One possibility would be informal American association with the proposed Commonwealth organization—at least an associate or "observer" membership, for example, such as we have had in the OEEC. Possibly, formal American membership would be desirable. The organizational proposals made in the following section and in Chapter 8 would also increase American participation in Commonwealth economic decisions.

Apart from trade and payments questions, there is need for a more effective coordination of investment and economic development policies and programs among Commonwealth members. Specifically, a mechanism is needed by which the investment and development plans of Commonwealth countries could be reviewed with respect to their consequences for the Sterling Area as a whole—e.g., their consequences for the Sterling Area's external balance of payments, for primary production in the overseas Dominions and colonies, and for British exports. This review ought to take place in connection with the provision of development capital from Britain and other countries.

Unlike the Sterling Area's trade and payments problems, however, these development questions cannot be adequately handled within a Commonwealth or Sterling Area framework, for several reasons. The major potential source of capital for development of the Dominions and the British colonies is not Britain but the United States. Without greater and more formalized American participation than at present, it would not be possible to undertake development programs in the overseas Dominions and colonies large enough to be effective. Moreover, it would be politically unwise and practically inconvenient to exclude the non-Commonwealth countries of Southern Asia—Indonesia, Burma, Thailand, free Indochina and the Philippines—from any regional economic development organization which would include India, Pakistan and Ceylon.

The present membership [20] of the Colombo Plan—which includes the United States and most of these non-Commonwealth Asian countries—reflects these considerations, particularly the importance of having Japan, a potential capital-exporting nation, in any regional arrangement for Southern-Asian development.

What seems to be needed, then, is some kind of Southern-Asian development organization—in effect, an enlarged and strengthened Colombo Plan. Its membership would consist, on the one hand, of industrial capital-exporting countries and, on the other hand, of primary-producing or underdeveloped capital-importing countries. In addition to the present membership of the Colombo Plan, continental European countries should be included in the role of capital-exporting members, particularly West Germany and France. Britain and the other capital-exporting members might agree to channel a substantial part of their public investments in the Southern-Asian countries through the organization.

An organization of this kind would be in the interest of the primary-producing and underdeveloped members because it would assure them a larger and more calculable flow of foreign capital. It would be desirable from Britain's standpoint because it would accelerate Commonwealth development and provide a better mechanism than now exists for ensuring that the use made of capital by the overseas Dominions would be beneficial to Britain as well as to the Dominions.[21] It would give Japan and continental Europe greater access to investment opportuni-

---

[20] The Colombo Plan now includes Australia, Burma, Canada, Ceylon, India, Indochina, Indonesia, Japan, Malaya, Nepal, New Zealand, Pakistan, the Philippines, Thailand, the United Kingdom and the United States.

[21] With respect to private capital exports from Britain within the Sterling Area, it may be that they should be subject to control in order to eliminate "hot money" movements which do not contribute importantly to the future economic growth of Britain. There is no *a priori* reason to suppose that, in the present nationalized economy of the free world, private international capital movements will always (or even normally) be economically desirable, either from the standpoint of balance-of-payments equilibrium or of the economical use of resources, unless there is a high degree of coordination of economic policies among the countries concerned. There are important exceptions, of course—for example, American private investment in Canada and some parts of Latin America, and overseas investments by the oil companies. In contrast, much investment of Latin American capital in the United States is of extremely doubtful desirability. Other than American private capital exports, the bulk of private international capital movements in the contemporary world have been essentially flight capital, usually illegal, and nearly always perverse from a balance-of-payments standpoint. See Arthur I. Bloomfield, *Speculation and Flight Movements of Capital in Postwar International Finance* (Princeton, N.J.: Princeton University Press, 1954).

ties and markets in the Commonwealth. For all these reasons, and because of the critical position of Southern Asia in the cold war, it would be in the political interest of the United States.[22]

The proposals here made, though relatively modest, could add to the effectiveness of the Commonwealth-Sterling Area economic arrangements in mitigating the external obstacles to Britain's economic growth. In the main, the organizational changes envisaged continue a trend toward closer cooperation observable in Commonwealth arrangements since 1939. Today, there is a growing recognition, particularly in the United Kingdom, of the need to accelerate this trend. Otherwise, the centrifugal economic forces at work in the Commonwealth—products of economic nationalism and of the continuous pressure of American competition—may again become dominant as they were in the interwar years. "The time has passed when the Sterling Area can long survive on the present informal and almost organization-less basis." [23]

Wider Trade and Payments Arrangements

The second of the existing regional economic units considered here links Britain and the Sterling Area with 15 countries of continental Europe and their overseas colonies in a trading and currency system which includes almost half of world commerce.[24] This wide grouping is defined by the membership of the Organization of European Economic Cooperation (OEEC) and the European Payments Union (EPU). The outer Sterling Area countries also participate (though not as members) by virtue of British membership in the OEEC and the inclusion of sterling in the EPU system. Though the United States does not participate in the trade and financial arrangements of this grouping, American initiative and financial support have been responsible in no small degree for their creation and success, and American and Canadian representatives take part in the meetings of these organizations. For reasons to be examined, the freedom and security of international relations within this whole trading area is less than within the Sterling Area, but substantially greater than exists among other non dollar countries.

---

[22] See also Chapter 9, p. 344.

[23] J. Williams, *op. cit.,* p. 27.

[24] This proportion is based on import values for 1951. It includes trade within the Sterling Area, trade among the continental European OEEC members and their colonies (including trade between metropolitan countries and their own colonial territories), and trade between the Sterling Area and the continental EPU members and colonies.

The OEEC-EPU trading system arose as a reaction to the quantitative restrictions and bilateralism which characterized trade among the West European countries in the early postwar years. When the war ended, production in continental Europe was a fraction of the prewar level, and intra-European trade was at a standstill. As European production recovered, intra-European trade also revived, though much more slowly and in the form of bilateral barter. At first, bilateralism was owed to physical shortages and the consequent pressure on each government to make sure that its trickle of exports was exchanged only for the most essential foreign goods. But as European production and exports increased, the purpose of quantitative restrictions and of bilateralism became primarily financial—arising less from shortages of particular goods than from the general shortage of foreign exchange, particularly gold and dollars, which nearly all the West European countries shared. In this situation, it appeared to each government that it was in its interest to conduct trade and payments under bilateral quota agreements in order to maximize its ability to extract gold, dollars or credit from its neighbors, and to defend itself against such exactions on their part. No European government could afford, in these circumstances, to treat foreign currencies as freely interchangeable—or to forego bilateral negotiation of import quotas—for fear that it would be forced to pay to other European countries the dollars it needed more urgently for purchases in the Western Hemisphere, or to export goods on credit, which it could not afford to do.[25]

The gross economic inefficiency of bilateral barter among this group of highly interdependent economies was apparent from the beginning. But not much could be done about it until the European countries' foreign exchange shortage had been eased by further recovery of exports and by the assurance of an adequate dollar supply through the Marshall Plan. As these developments occurred, the European governments began to search for ways of breaking down the system of restrictive bilateral quotas within which their mutual trade was confined. Even so, without a suitable locus for multilateral negotiation and without strong leadership, it is unlikely that much progress would have been made. Fortunately, both were available in the OEEC. During three years of negotiation, trial and

---

[25] With the revival of production, the desire to assure protected export markets also came to play an increasing, though still subordinate, role in the motivation of European bilateralism. In the interwar period, such protectionism, rather than financial considerations, had been the principal cause of bilateralism.

error, and with the continuous participation of the United States, the countries of Western Europe evolved a series of trade and payments arrangements culminating in the European Payments Union and in the OEEC's intra-European trade liberalization program. In combination, these two unprecedented international developments have made the West European currencies (including sterling) freely interchangeable on current account for non-residents, have freed a large part of intra-group trade from quotas, and have caused remaining quotas to be applied in a less discriminatory manner with respect to the members of the grouping. Together, these accomplishments have meant a considerable improvement in the freedom and security of current trade and payments within this large trading area.[26]

This is not the place for a detailed account of the EPU,[27] but it is necessary to explain in general terms how the EPU permits so large a group of countries to maintain the interchangeability of their currencies (on current account) and a considerable freedom of trade from quantitative restrictions. Quantitative restriction of trade and bilateralism among the European countries since the war have been principally caused by their shortage of means of payment with which to settle their international accounts with each other. This shortage has had two aspects. On the one hand, it reflects recurrent balance-of-payments strain among the European countries themselves—strain due in the main to divergences of domestic economic and financial policies. On the other hand, it reflects the European countries' persistent shortage of the only generally-acceptable means of international payment—gold and American dollars. The EPU meets this double problem by several devices, which may be briefly outlined.

The EPU enlarges the supply of means of payment for inter-member settlements by an agreement among the members to settle their debts with each other only partly in gold or dollars, and the remaining part in credit. That is, each member agrees in advance to finance a part of the others' trading debts by extending credit to them. Next, the EPU provides central clearing machinery for offsetting the members' bilateral payments surpluses and deficits with each other on a multilateral basis,

[26] An excellent account and interpretation of this evolution may be found in William Diebold, Jr., *Trade and Payments in Western Europe* (New York: Harper and Brothers, 1952), Chs. 2–5.

[27] Good brief descriptions of the EPU may be found in Diebold, *op. cit.*, Ch. 5, and in Commission on Foreign Economic Policy, *Staff Papers, op. cit.*, pp. 491 *et seq.*

thus greatly reducing the total volume of intra-European settlements and dollar payments. The EPU's Managing Board and the OEEC provide a means through which member governments can bring diplomatic pressure to bear on each other to alter domestic policies which lead to unmanageably large payments deficits and surpluses. The pressure exerted in this way cannot be very great, and it would have little effect if the member governments did not feel themselves parts of a European community with some mutual responsibility to adjust domestic economic policies in order to maintain trade liberalization. Nevertheless, over the past five years, the EPU's Managing Board and the OEEC have been able to exert a significant influence on members' domestic policies, though not enough to free intra-European trade entirely from quotas nor to prevent reimposition of quotas in a number of cases. In addition, the shortage of dollars available for intra-European settlements has been eased by a large continuing flow of dollars from the United States Government (in the form of aid and military expenditures) and by means of quotas restricting the demand of Western Europe and the Sterling Area for dollar goods. OEEC members are not committed to relax quantitative restrictions on dollar imports along with restrictions on trade with each other. So long as Europe and the Sterling Area are short of dollars, some discrimination against dollar goods is a necessary condition of the relative freedom and security of trade and payments within the Sterling Area and the whole OEEC-EPU grouping.

Successful as it has been in comparison with what preceded it, the OEEC-EPU trading area does not enjoy as much freedom or calculability of economic relations among its members as does the Sterling Area. Some quantitative restrictions are still maintained among its members and the degree of trade liberalization achieved is much more precarious than within the Sterling Area. Private capital movements within the OEEC-EPU grouping are still generally restricted, while in the Sterling Area they are largely free. The greater success of the Sterling Area is not owed merely to differences in the institutional arrangements of the two groupings. Rather, the institutional differences reflect more basic disparities: the greater sense of community and mutual responsibility within the Commonwealth than within Western Europe, and the fact that, in the Sterling Area, one country—Britain—exercises strong leadership and assumes the burden of assuring the internal liquidity of the entire system, at considerable cost to its own economy. In the wider grouping, no member country has been able or willing to play that role.

In sum, the OEEC-EPU grouping works for two basic reasons. First, its members have at least a minimum sense of community and a sufficient degree of common interest in greater freedom and security in their trade and payments with each other. Second, the United States has supplied the minimum necessary leadership and dollar support, and has been willing to accept persistent discrimination against American exports.

While the Sterling Area is now generally accepted as a continuing feature of the free world's economic organization, the future of the OEEC-EPU trading system has been in doubt. For several years, official and professional opinion on this question in Europe and the United States has been sharply divided. Official American doctrine still considers this successful venture in regional trade and payments liberalization to be a temporary expedient which should give way as soon as possible to the universal scheme envisaged at Bretton Woods. That is, this regional arrangement should now be replaced by a system which would be more "automatic" and less dependent than the EPU on deliberate coordination of national policies; which would use gold or dollars as the means of international settlement; which would involve no greater degree of trade liberalization among non dollar countries than between them and the dollar area—i.e., no discrimination; and whose membership would include most, if not all, non-communist countries, rather than being confined to West European countries, their overseas territories and the Sterling Area. In the view of many others, however—and in the Study Group's own opinion—the OEEC-EPU system has demonstrated its relevance to the facts and the needs of the postwar period, and some variant and improvement of it should continue for the foreseeable future.

The Study Group's preference for the approach toward convertibility [28]

---

[28] Except where the context indicates otherwise, the term "convertibility" is used in this discussion to mean a situation in which both resident and nonresident holders of a national currency are entitled to convert it freely into any other currency for any use other than the international transfer of capital. This right to convert implies the absence of quantitative restrictions on imports and exchange controls on non-capital transactions. Thus "convertibility" and "trade liberalization" are two sides of the same coin. The phrase "nondollar convertibility" means a situation in which the right to convert for noncapital purposes is confined to conversion among nondollar currencies. The existence of nondollar convertibility, therefore, implies a degree of discrimination against dollar goods and services as compared with nondollar goods and services. Conversely, the phrase "dollar convertibility" is used to describe a situation in which there is no such limitation or discrimination as far as noncapital transactions are concerned. The phrase "nonresident con-

and trade liberalization exemplified by the OEEC and its subsidiary, the EPU, follows from our conception of the prerequisites of international economic integration and from the analysis of the dollar shortage presented in Part I. A major reason why the OEEC has been able to maintain a relatively high degree of convertibility among its members is that it has exerted some influence to harmonize their economic policies. It would be a pity to give up this activity on the mistaken assumption that the "automatic disciplines" of gold or dollar settlements would accomplish the same result. For most countries today, convertibility cannot be merely automatic; it has to be organized. As we saw in Chapter 1, the 19th-century sterling-gold standard system was itself not wholly automatic but depended on the coordination exercised by the Bank of England and the London money market.

There is another sense, too, in which Western Europe's and the Sterling Area's approach toward convertibility requires international organization and cannot be merely automatic nor the result of uncoordinated decisions by national governments. In Chapter 2, it was argued that the countries of Western Europe and the Sterling Area will tend to be short of dollars, intermittently at least, for the foreseeable future.[29] That is, they will find it necessary or desirable from time to time to restrict their current dollar payments—i.e., to make their currencies inconvertible in some degree with the dollar—in the interest of their economic growth and health. If this is true, there will be a continuing or a recurrent danger that, without the OEEC-EPU mechanism or its equivalent, trade among the West European countries and the Sterling Area will be forced back into narrow bilateral channels. Without a mechanism of this kind, settlements among OEEC members would revert to a 100 percent gold or dollar basis, so that a general shortage of dollars would also involve a scarcity of means of settlement among them. This scarcity would tend to cause a breakdown of their mutual trade liberalization and a reversion to bilateralism in their trade and payments. In consequence, whenever the countries of Western Europe and

---

vertibility" refers to a situation in which nonresidents of the country concerned are free to use their holdings of its currency freely for noncapital purposes, but residents are not. It is important to keep these distinctions in mind—particularly that between "convertibility" and "nonresident convertibility." In the last year, much of the public discussion of convertibility has really referred only to the "nonresident" type but has omitted the qualifying adjective. The difference between, for example, full sterling convertibility and mere nonresident sterling convertibility would be very great indeed.

[29] See above, p. 94.

the Sterling Area as a group are significantly shorter of dollars than of each other's currencies (on current account), the maintenance of a high degree of trade and payments liberalization among them will depend on arrangements which have the same general functions as the EPU and the OEEC trade liberalization program—i.e., arrangements which (a) keep European currencies fully interchangeable on current account but only partially convertible into dollars, and (b) maintain a higher degree of trade liberalization among the member countries than between them and the dollar area. The arrangements need not be identical with those now existing; a number of other possible forms could be suggested. But they must be able to accomplish these two purposes quickly and efficiently in periods of dollar scarcity.

There may well be times in the future when the dollar supply of the European countries will be so adequate that 100 percent gold or dollar settlements among them, and an end to discrimination against the dollar on balance-of-payments grounds, would be feasible without danger of restricting intra-European trade. Provision for this possibility should be made by suitable modifications of the EPU and of the trade liberalization program, such as those suggested below. Yet as long as the threat of recurrent dollar shortage persists, arrangements which can accomplish the two purposes mentioned in the preceding paragraph should be kept in existence, if only on a "stand-by" basis. International financial arrangements of this kind would not be easy to re-establish if allowed to lapse, and their existence provides considerable assurance that trade liberalization within the European-Sterling Area grouping will not be permitted to break down. Without them, any significant deterioration of Europe's or the Sterling Area's dollar position could start a vicious circle of restrictionism and bilateralism whose damage would be considerable and which would not be easy to break again.

It is sometimes said that, if only Western Europe's and the Sterling Area's gold and dollar reserves were large enough, there would be no need for arrangements like the EPU to assure a substantial degree of freedom and security of trade and payments on a nondiscriminatory basis throughout the Western Community. This might be true if there were no persistent tendency to dollar shortage. Given that tendency, however, this argument misconceives the function of foreign exchange reserves. Their purpose is only to finance temporary and self-reversing international payments deficits. No level of reserves is sufficient to finance persistent deficits.[30] Even if the reserves of Western Europe and the Sterling Area were greatly augmented by dollar loans or grants, or by some kind of dollar stabilization fund or "line of credit," these countries would still have to take concerted action, involving discrimination against dollar goods, to avoid a breakdown of liberalization of trade and payments among them in prolonged periods of dollar scarcity. This is the weakness of proposals made from time to time to re-establish the permanent dollar convertibility of other major currencies by means of large stabilization funds or loans.[31] Given a recurrent shortage of dollars, the only way to assure continued dollar convertibility of European currencies consistent with Western Europe's economic health would be for the United States Government to undertake to supply dollars to European countries in whatever amount might be needed to keep international payments liquid at all times. Such an arrangement would be neither practical nor desirable. It would hardly be to the interest of the United States to make so one-sided, unqualified, and potentially expensive a financial commitment.

The Study Group favors measures to augment or supplement the hard currency reserves of Western Europe and the Sterling Area, but such measures are not a substitute for financial and trade arrangements like those of the OEEC-EPU grouping. Rather, the purpose of creating larger European dollar reserves (or their equivalent) would be to make the liberalization of trade and payments within this grouping less subject to breakdown and hence more calculable. Larger dollar reserves would also allow the European countries to take greater risks in liberalizing their trade with the dollar area.

---

[30] "Monetary reserves by their very nature can only be a *temporary* means of financing imbalances in international payments. No level of reserves is adequate to finance *continuing* deficits. Reserves can provide only a breathing space until the country concerned takes measures to eliminate the deficit in its balance of payments or until its trading partners, through their own actions, increase their purchases from it. The concept of adequacy [of monetary reserves], therefore, can have meaning only within a framework where there are occasional temporary fluctuations of a self-reversing character in the balance of payments of a country which is in a fundamentally 'strong' or balanced payments position." Commission on Foreign Economic Policy, *Staff Papers, op. cit.*, p. 476.

[31] For example, the proposal made in 1952 by *The Economist* to set up an Atlantic Payments Union. The proposed Atlantic Payments Union would use dollars as the currency of settlement. It would include the United States on the same basis as other countries and the United States would extend to other members a very large dollar line of credit in the form of a "drawing right." See "Living with the Dollar," *The Economist* (London, November 22, 1952), p. 594.

For the countries of Western Europe and the Sterling Area, then, convertibility and trade liberalization cannot be merely automatic or the fortunate product of independent national actions. They have to be internationally organized. Organization is required to harmonize national economic policies, to assure adherence to trade liberalization rules, and to prevent a breakdown into bilateralism in the face of dollar shortage.

The OEEC and the EPU are not, however, the only possible organizational means of carrying out these tasks. An alternative which has been suggested is to abolish these agencies and to adapt the International Monetary Fund (IMF) and the General Agreement on Tariffs and Trade (GATT) to serve the same purposes. Thus, the GATT Agreement could be amended and the GATT machinery modified to incorporate into them the equivalent of the OEEC trade liberalization program for those GATT members willing to accept such obligations. In periods of dollar scarcity, the IMF could authorize nondollar members subscribing to a trade liberalization program to discriminate jointly against the dollar, in accordance with the "scarce currency clause" of its Articles of Agreement. At such times, the IMF could also provide the equivalent of clearing and partial dollar settlements among these nondollar members. But there are major practical difficulties in the way of this alternative. Most serious is the basic difference in philosophy and attitude between the IMF and the OEEC-EPU. The IMF is still imbued with the doctrine of Bretton Woods, awaiting a permanent end of the dollar shortage and expecting an early return of an essentially automatic international trading and monetary system. Hence, the IMF has been—and apparently remains—unalterably opposed to being used in the manner suggested above. Until the coming of that time when it would be able to operate in strict accordance with the precepts and expectations of the Bretton Woods doctrine, the IMF has preferred to watch, to wait and to warn.

For these reasons, it seems best to continue on the basis of the OEEC-EPU arrangements. There are, however, a number of respects in which these arrangements could be improved. Among them, the following may be suggested:

(1) There is need for coordinated action among the West European countries and the United States to reduce the degree of discrimination against the dollar, and to increase the degree of dollar convertibility of European currencies, in periods when the current supply of, and demand

for, dollars are approaching balance. These things might be done in a variety of ways which cannot be considered adequately here. Suffice it to say that two kinds of arrangements among the member countries are needed.

First, a flexible code of trade liberalization with the dollar area, which would reduce or eliminate discrimination against dollar imports in periods of relatively plentiful dollar supply, but which would permit countries to reimpose discriminatory import restrictions and exchange controls when required by a renewed scarcity of dollars.

Second, some means of "hardening" settlements among the member countries—i.e., of reducing or eliminating the content of credit in such settlements—in periods of ample dollar supply. This could be accomplished in several ways. One way would be to change the gold-credit settlement ratios within the present EPU framework. Another way would be to allow member countries able to do so to make their currencies convertible with the dollar for nonresidents—thus taking these countries' settlements with other members out of the EPU, at least temporarily. Other member countries, unable or unwilling to make their currencies convertible with the dollar for nonresidents, would continue to have access to credits from the EPU. These, or similar, financial arrangements should be so established as to be readily reversible in order to make possible a return to multilateral clearing and partial gold or dollar settlements among the members in the event of renewed dollar scarcity.[32]

(2) It would be desirable to supplement the dollar reserves of Western Europe and the Sterling Area for the reasons suggested above. Probably the best means of doing so is to provide a source of substantial, but relatively short-term, dollar credits on which the OEEC countries could draw with the agreement of the United States Government. Dollar credits of this kind should be "administrative" rather than "automatic." That is, they should be extended only at the discretion of the United States Government, and perhaps on the recommendation of an Atlantic Trade and Payments Committee [see (4) below], so that the decision to grant or withhold credits could be used to influence national economic policies. Possible sources of such dollar credits include—in addition to the IMF

---

[32] For a fuller discussion of these questions, see K. Knorr and G. Patterson, *A Critique of the Randall Commission Report, op. cit.,* pp. 50–54; Commission on Foreign Economic Policy, *Staff Papers, op. cit.,* pp. 488–9; Raymond F. Mikesell, *The Emerging Pattern of International Payments* (Princeton, N.J.: International Finance Section, Princeton University, 1954); and *The Economist* (London, July 24, 1954), p. 289.

—the United States Federal Reserve System, the United States Treasury's Stabilization Fund, and appropriated aid funds.[33]

(3) The mutual obligation of OEEC members concerning trade liberalization should be put on a different basis. At present, the members have agreed to free 75 percent of their private trade with other members from quantitative restrictions, and a higher percentage is now under consideration. Several countries have gone further than 75 percent, while others have been prevented by balance-of-payments difficulties from fulfilling this obligation. The time may have come to try a different approach. The OEEC members should agree to the complete removal of quantitative restrictions on trade with each other, except in certain carefully defined circumstances. A redefinition of the mutual obligation of the members—the "rules of the club"—in these terms would give the OEEC a firmer legal basis for its efforts to harmonize members' domestic economic policies in order to maintain trade liberalization.

(4) In the last few years, American leadership in the work of the OEEC has greatly diminished. In part, this has been a desirable result of Western Europe's economic recovery. But it has also reflected the loss of a positive sense of direction in American foreign economic policy and, in particular, the lack of a clear American conception of the economic organization of the Western Community. The conception outlined above requires closer and more formalized American participation in the trade and payments activities of the OEEC and the EPU, just as it requires a closer American relationship with the Sterling Area. This is needed not simply to protect the interest of American exporters in keeping EPU currencies as convertible—and discrimination as low—as is consistent with Western Europe's economic health. More important, continuous American participation in, and financial support of, these activities is needed because such American action appears to be essential to their success.

Accordingly, the Study Group believes there should be created—within the framework of the OEEC or its successor organization [34]—an Atlantic Trade and Payments Committee, with the United States and Canada as full members. The Committee would be concerned, in general, with

---

[33] Concerning the use of the IMF and Federal Reserve Bank funds for this purpose, see Commission on Foreign Economic Policy, *Report to the President and the Congress* (Washington, D.C.: January 1954), p. 74.

[34] A proposal that the OEEC be succeeded by an Organization for Atlantic Economic Cooperation, paralleling the North Atlantic Treaty Organization, is made in the following chapter.

policies of its members affecting trade and payments relations between the West European-Sterling Area grouping and the dollar area—more specifically, with the liberalization of dollar imports by the OEEC countries and the Sterling Area, with the degree of dollar convertibility of EPU currencies, and with American and Canadian import and financial policies.

(5) Finally, there is the question of whether membership in the OEEC-EPU grouping should be widened to include other nondollar countries of the free world. The OEEC-EPU arrangements have often been criticized—particularly from the standpoint of Bretton Woods doctrine—because of their regional character. The implication of this criticism is that an alternative and preferable scheme could be set up which would include on the same footing most, if not all, non-communist countries. But the present membership of the OEEC-EPU arrangements is not the result of an arbitrary preference for regional, as against wider, arrangements. It is a response to mid-20th century economic and political facts and needs. The dollar countries cannot be included on the same footing as other OEEC members because of the latter's tendency to dollar shortage. And the possibility and desirability of including other nondollar countries depend on whether those countries feel a need for the facilities which OEEC membership would provide and whether they would be willing and able to abide by the "rules of the club."

On both of these criteria, the independent underdeveloped countries are, generally speaking, in one category while Japan—the only industrialized nondollar country which is not now in the OEEC-EPU grouping—is in another. It does not seem that, on the whole, membership in the grouping is necessary or desirable for the independent underdeveloped countries either from their own standpoint or from that of the West.[35] By and large, these countries would be neither able nor willing to accept the obligations of membership in the grouping, particularly the obligation to eliminate import quotas except in a few limited circumstances. The sense of community between them and the West is not yet great enough to make either side sufficiently responsible in undertakings of the kind required. Nor would it be equitable or politically feasible for the West to try to force the underdeveloped countries to dispense with quantitative restrictions on imports. Such restrictions are required

---

[35] This generalization is not meant to suggest the exclusion of underdeveloped countries which already participate in the EPU either directly or by virtue of membership in the Sterling Area.

in many cases to promote economic growth. To foster their internal development, it is often necessary for these countries to follow economic policies which make their domestic monetary conditions more inflationary on the average than in the industrial West. If they were included in a payments system involving credit margins, their credits would be quickly used up for development purposes.[36] But this is not the purpose of such credits. International public development credits should be extended by agencies especially designed for that purpose and not as the unintended by-product of participation in trade and payments arrangements.

Nor do the underdeveloped countries need to participate in formal international clearing among non dollar currencies—the other function currently performed by the EPU. Their clearing problems are small enough to be manageable by ordinary currency arbitrage, and it is now possible for "third countries," and for the EPU countries themselves, to clear small current surpluses and deficits in the principal EPU currencies in the private foreign exchange markets which have been re-established in the last few years. Underdeveloped countries which conduct their nondollar trade in sterling can now accomplish the same result through the Sterling Transferable Account System.[37]

Japan's situation is quite different from that of the underdeveloped countries. Japan is a major trading nation and has the same need as industrial Europe for participation in a wider-than-national economic grouping. Specifically, Japan needs the credit facilities, the participation in nondollar trade liberalization, and the large-scale clearing privileges which membership in the OEEC-EPU grouping confers. The question remains, however, whether the sense of responsibility and common concern between Europe and Japan is sufficient to make it feasible to include Japan in the grouping. This issue is especially difficult for Britain, which would feel the brunt of Japanese competition in Sterling Area

---

[36] For example, this has been the experience of Turkey in the EPU.

[37] The present status of the Sterling Transferable Account System is reviewed in International Monetary Fund, "Extension of the Sterling Transferable Account System," *International Financial News Survey* (Washington, D.C., March 26, 1954), p. 295. A recent study by a technical working group of the United Nations Economic Commission for Asia and the Far East (ECAFE) concludes that, with the exception of Japan, ECAFE members do not need greater access to the clearing facilities of the EPU than they already have by means of the Sterling Area and the special monetary arrangements which link Indonesia to the Netherlands and free Indochina to France. See *Report of the Working Group of Experts on Payments Problems of the ECAFE Region* (Bangkok, August 31, 1954).

markets if the OEEC trade liberalization rules were applied to Japan. The Japanese, too, might hesitate to give up their freedom of action with respect to import quotas, although Japan would undoubtedly be a large net gainer from membership in the grouping. From an American standpoint, however, it appears that Japanese membership should be supported, in view of Japan's uniquely difficult foreign trade and payments problem and its great political and military importance to the West.

To summarize, the way of organizing trade and payments relations envisaged above is already emerging out of the common efforts of the Western Community to create greater freedom and calculability of international economic relations over a wide area. The basic concept is a large, organized, nondollar trade and payments system within which trade and payments are kept relatively free and calculable by coordination of national policies, including the administration of a flexible degree of discrimination against the dollar. This system would also involve a degree of protection against American competition by means of regional tariff preferences. With the exception of Japan, it seems neither desirable nor feasible to make any special effort or concessions in order to add other countries as full members.

The concern of the United States with the economic growth and health of the other industrial countries makes this organization of trade and payments desirable on grounds of political interest and economic equity, despite its small adverse effect on potential increases in American exports. At the same time, greater and more active participation by the United States Government in the administration of these arrangements is also desirable in order to ensure that the degree of discrimination against the dollar is no more than necessary and to provide the required leadership and financial support.

European Political and Economic Union

The third grouping considered by the Study Group exists as yet only in embryo, but its ultimate aim is some form of European political and economic union. To date, the major efforts in this direction have been made by six industrial countries of continental Western Europe: France, West Germany, Italy, Belgium, the Netherlands and Luxembourg. Known as the "Community of Six," this group has been responsible for the establishment of the European Coal and Steel Community (the Schuman Plan), for the abortive effort to create a European Defense Community (EDC), and for the preparation of a plan for a European Political Community.[38]

The European union movement has been a far more radical venture in wider-than-national organization than the two groupings already discussed. Its ultimate aim is not intergovernmental cooperation but a fundamental reform of the European nation-state system. The European union movement expresses a widespread feeling among continental Europeans that the European nation-state system is in decay because it no longer provides a political constitution adequate to safeguard the values of European civilization and to permit its characteristic ideals to be progressively realized.

> The average continental European feels himself a member of an enfeebled nation, the nearly helpless prize in a world power struggle in which his government plays no effective part. He knows that his economic horizons, his freedom of movement and opportunity are constricted within narrow national boundaries. He believes that the major factors determining his economic well-being, his military security and even his personal survival are beyond the capacity of his government to control or even to influence very much. Unlike the average American or Briton, he feels that his national state is no longer capable of adequately discharging the increasingly heavy responsibilities of political sovereignty. As a consequence, and no matter how much the traditions and culture of his [national] society still mean to him, his belief in and loyalty to his government as a sovereign political entity, his willingness to sacrifice and, if necessary, to die for it have been very severely impaired.[39]

This decline of positive faith in the national state, this weakening of West European political nationalism as a positive ideology and source of social cohesion and morale, have been compounded of political, military and economic judgments. But it has been the more strictly political aims of the European union movement which have been most persuasive to Europeans. The movement's leadership and most active support come from those Europeans who understand that division and weakness make Europe vulnerable to the efforts of the Soviet Union to neutralize or subvert the continental governments. These men, too, have grasped the

---

[38] The only public document defining the proposed institutions of the European Political Community is the Draft Statute of a European Community adopted by the Ad Hoc Assembly at Strasbourg in March 1953. See Ad Hoc Assembly Doc. 15R, Strasbourg, March 10, 1953.

[39] Theodore Geiger and H. van B. Cleveland, *Making Western Europe Defensible* (Washington, D.C.: National Planning Association, 1951), p. 43.

fact that, in a world where the standard of effective size is set by great powers of continental dimensions, their own separate national states can never again play a part in world affairs commensurate with their historical roles or their present aspirations. They see that the relationship between the United States and Europe will remain unsatisfactory and unstable—threatening to degenerate into neutralism and isolationism, or into imperialism—until there is in continental Europe a political entity with sufficient morale and material strength to be a responsible partner, rather than a dependent client, of the United States.

The European union movement has gained one notable victory—the establishment of the European Coal and Steel Community—and has suffered one serious defeat—the French Assembly's rejection of the European Defense Community. But the prospects for ultimate success or failure cannot yet be judged with any assurance. In the following chapter, we shall suggest certain American actions which might improve these prospects. Here, our concern is with economic questions—with the potential economic significance of European union, and with the main economic problems which would be encountered during the progressive unification of the industrialized countries of Western Europe, regardless of whether membership in the grouping were limited to the Community of Six or included other European nations as well.

Though the main impetus of the European union idea has been political, there is also a belief—widespread among continental Europeans—that political union would enable them to cope more successfully with their economic problems. The political and military aims of the European unification movement are premised—though not always consciously—on the assumption that political union would also make possible the economic health and strength which these aims presuppose. Is this assumption sound? How true is it that, if a union embracing at least the Community of Six and possibly other European countries could be established, it would improve the rate of economic growth and the economic health of its members, and what precisely is meant by "union" in this economic context?

These questions require answers on two levels: that of economics and that of political institutions. The economic question is: assuming that institutional means could be found in a European union to make the conditions of economic intercourse much more free and calculable than at present, does such a grouping have the economic characteristics—the size, natural resources and economic structure—which would make possible a substantial improvement in the rate of growth of industrial and agricultural productivity? The political question is: what institutional means would be required to make possible a major improvement in the freedom and calculability of economic relations within a European union?

In the Study Group's opinion, the answer to the first, or economic, question is a qualified "yes." It would take us too far into technical questions to try to justify this conclusion fully here, but the argument may be briefly summarized.[40]

First, even within a union including only the Community of Six and their colonial territories, the geographical distribution of material and human resources, and of managerial and labor skills, is undoubtedly *diverse* enough to make possible a much more efficient geographical specialization of production than now exists in these countries if there were much greater freedom and calculability of economic conditions throughout their area. This is true for industry and perhaps even truer and more important for agriculture.[41]

Second, the Community of Six is *large* enough in terms of income, population, and rate of growth of population to provide a very substantial internal market. Unification would, therefore, open up to European industry opportunities for much greater subdivision and specialization of industrial production processes than it now enjoys. In the

---

[40] It will be observed that this argument is based on the criteria of an adequate economic grouping given on pp. 236–237 above.

[41] Compare the following comment: "The potential advantages to be gained from a closer international integration of agriculture in Western Europe are very considerable:

"First, there is the problem of utilizing more efficiently the soil and manpower of France, Western Europe's biggest agricultural producer. If guaranteed markets were provided in other European countries, France could produce much larger quantities of grain and of animal products than at present and thereby reduce the dependence of other countries on dollar imports.

"The second, much more intricate, problem is that of making better use of the great surpluses of agricultural labor in southern Europe. The aim should be to arrange for larger exports from those countries of particularly labor-intensive crops—such as vegetables and fruits—to other, mainly northern, countries where labor is scarce, or will become scarce if there is further industrial development. Exports of labor-intensive products from southern to northern Europe would raise the productivity of labor not only in southern European agriculture—where the alternative is idleness—but also in importing countries, where more manpower could then be transferred to industry.

"The need for a more adequate international specialization in Western European agriculture can be stated, then, as follows: given the limited scope for transferring surplus rural labor to other countries and the improbability of international capital transfers, the structure of production, and hence the flows of international trade, will have to be adapted to the actual location of agricultural manpower." *Economic Survey of Europe since the War,* op. cit., pp. 234–5.

longer run, unification could make possible the development of an industrial technology characterized to a much larger extent than today by mass production and declining real costs.

Third, the Community—including its colonial territories—is large enough in terms of population and natural resources to be proportionately much less dependent on external markets and sources of supply than are its separate national members today. Their economic growth would, therefore, be notably less inhibited by the incalculability of international economic relations than at the present time.

Finally, an improvement in the rate of growth of productivity and a reduction of external dependence—together with the increase in economic flexibility which would result from these and other consequences of union—would improve the group's competitive position in export markets. This would tend greatly to strengthen a European union's balance of payments with the dollar area, which would contribute to its economic efficiency by making discriminatory restrictions on imports from the dollar area unnecessary.

For all of these closely related reasons, a European union which embraced at least the Community of Six would make possible a higher rate of economic growth for its members. This is only a possibility, however. Its realization would depend not only on finding means to eliminate the most conspicuous barriers to trade among the member countries— quotas, tariffs, discriminatory state trading, discriminatory taxation, and the like. It would depend also on a major loosening of the *private* restrictionism and protectionism which is so characteristic of these economies. And, assuming these things were done, the potential economic benefits of unification would still be opportunities only. Whether they could be realized would depend on the adequacy of enterprise—generally weak in France and inadequate in some sectors of Italian and German industry.

In sum, optimism about the potential economic benefits of a European union must be qualified. Yet there is reason to suppose that the process of unification would mitigate private restrictionism and stimulate enterprise. The removal of governmental trade barriers would by itself weaken private restrictionism and restore some competition to European industrial markets. The loosening of public and private restrictions would help to create general conditions favorable to the growth of expansionist attitudes. The general improvement in European morale which would accompany the process of unification might make it possible for the more vigorous European industrialists to infuse in their conservative or lethargic brethren some of their own belief in economic expansion.

We come, then, to the question of institutional means. It has been shown in general terms that supranational authority is necessary to create a high degree of economic freedom and calculability among a group of European countries. Now, we must try to see more concretely what kind and degree of supranational authority would be required to unify national economies. For the purpose of this discussion, we shall assume that the union would embrace at least the Community of Six and that central institutions would be created which would gradually acquire considerable supranational economic authority. Under the European Coal and Steel Treaty, the Community of Six already has supranational regulatory powers over the coal and steel industries within its members' territories. Until the defeat of the EDC, it had been envisaged that a European Political Community would be established which would gradually assume the supranational economic powers necessary to create an integrated economy—a "common market"—over the whole area of the six nations. At the time of present writing, it seems probable that European unification will follow a longer and more tortuous path than that envisaged by the authors of the Draft Statute of a European Political Community. Nevertheless, this statute may be taken as a convenient starting point of our discussion.[42]

The Statute defines its economic aim as establishment of "a common market among the Member States, based on the free movement of goods, capital and persons." In the following discussion, however, a more limited meaning will be given to this objective. We shall confine attention to the measures necessary to create a common market in goods and services only—that is, freedom of trade among the member states and free interchangeability of their national currencies on current account—while migration of labor and capital movements within the proposed Community remain subject to control at national boundaries.

---

[42] The relevant provisions of the Draft Statute are as follows:

"The Community has the following mission and general aims: . . . to promote, in harmony with the general economy of Member States, the economic expansion, the development of the employment, and the improvement of the standard of living in Member States, by means, in particular, of the progressive establishment of a common market, transitional or other means being taken to ensure that no fundamental and persistent disturbance is thereby caused to the economy of the Member States. . . . (Art. 2)

"The Community . . . shall establish progressively a common market among the Member States, based on the free movement of goods, capital and persons . . ." (Art. 82)

There is no doubt that freedom of migration and capital movements within the proposed Community would, in principle, tend to accelerate the rate of economic growth and contribute to maximizing the economic welfare of the Community.[43] But, complete economic integration, including free capital movements and migration, would require a much broader delegation of national powers to central organs than would be possible in the early stages of economic unification, and would multiply in other ways the political obstacles to union.

The minimum supranational economic powers which appear to be necessary to create a common market in goods and services may be briefly outlined under four headings: (1) money and banking; (2) taxation; (3) direct economic controls; and (4) restrictive practices.

(1) The most obvious requirement of a common market in goods and services is adequate supranational (i.e., central) control over money and credit. Such power is necessary to ensure that imbalances of payments among the member states are kept within the limits of available means of settlement. Without that power, it would not be possible to assure continuous interconvertibility of the currencies of the member states on current account. A European union would, therefore, require a central bank of its own, possessing the usual powers of central banks over the national banking systems of the member states—including central control over the use by member states of nonmember currencies (especially dollars) and over the rates of exchange of the members' currencies.[44]

It does not seem likely, however, that the substitution of a single European currency for the individual national currencies would be necessary, or even desirable, during the initial stages. The creation of a single currency would deprive the central authorities of an essential tool of economic policy: the power to adjust the exchange rates of the national currencies. Without this power, which the abolition of the national currencies would preclude, almost the whole burden of managing imbalances in payments among the member states would fall on the monetary policies of the central organs of the union. Imbalances in

---

[43] There are, however, important exceptions to this principle. See, e.g., J. E. Meade, *Problems of Economic Union* (Chicago: Chicago University Press, 1953), pp. 76–82.

[44] Limitations of space prevent an adequate discussion here of the supranational powers over money and credit necessary to create a common European market in goods and services. An analytical description of the necessary powers may be found in H. van B. Cleveland and H. J. Spiro, "Federal Powers over Currency, Banking, Credit and Foreign Exchange," in C. J. Friedrich and R. R. Bowie, *Studies in Federalism* (Boston: Little, Brown and Company, 1954), pp. 413, 431–438.

interstate payments, no matter how large or persistent, would have to be brought under control by the central authority primarily through deflationary actions in the deficit member country and inflationary actions in the surplus member country. Unless supplemented by exchange-rate adjustments, actions of this type would often have to be too severe or prolonged to be politically acceptable. For that reason, it would very likely prove impossible to keep member currencies convertible unless monetary policy could be supplemented by the supranational power of the union to alter their rates of exchange.

Centralized control of monetary policies would deprive the members of the possibility of pursuing their own domestic stabilization and employment policies. From a national standpoint, this is an unavoidable cost of creating a common market. The question of whether it will prove to be an acceptable cost is a political and psychological, not an economic, problem. The answer depends on whether these countries come in time to value the many benefits of economic and political unification more highly than the ability to pursue separate national employment and stabilization policies.

(2) Assuming, then, that adequate central control of money has been established, the creation of a common market in goods and services requires additional supranational powers adequate to assure continuous freedom of trade in goods and services among the member states. What precisely is meant by "freedom of trade" in this context? Obviously, it would include abolition of governmental trade barriers, such as import quotas, tariffs and export restrictions. But it also means something more. It would mean that the central authorities would have power to ensure that national taxes and direct controls on production, distribution and consumption of goods and services, public and private, would be administered without discrimination against the products of other members. Freedom of trade in this context would mean no governmental trade barriers and no discrimination by national origin. Broad as this delegation of power to the union would be, it would nevertheless leave to the member states sufficient power to affect substantially the distribution of income and other matters of social and economic welfare within their own borders. On political grounds, this would be essential. Member states might be willing to delegate to central authorities the powers strictly necessary to create a common market in goods and services, in the interest of economic growth, political effectiveness and military strength. But there is no evidence that Europeans would be willing

to turn over to supranational authorities the primary governmental responsibility for income distribution and questions of social welfare. The following discussion of taxation and other economic powers is, therefore, based on this conception of the division of economic functions between a European union and its member states.

It would not be necessary that income taxes be uniform throughout the union in order to have a common market, any more than it is necessary that state income taxes in the United States be uniform. General differences in national production costs between two member states resulting from differences in rates of business income taxation could be offset by appropriate adjustment in the interstate rate of exchange. The same is true of any generally applicable national tax, whether levied on production, distribution or consumption.[45]

In contrast, national production, excise or consumption taxes on particular industries, products or classes of products raise a more difficult question. A specific tax of this kind can easily be used as a disguised substitute for a tariff, even if the tax does not openly discriminate in favor of nationals of the taxing country. Presumably, the central organs would need authority to prohibit special taxes wherever they were found to be unreasonably protectionist in their intent or their effect. A similar supranational authority would be needed to prohibit national production subsidies; for they inevitably discriminate against producers in other countries. The High Authority of the European Coal and Steel Community already has both of these powers with respect to national taxes on, and subsidies to, the coal and steel industries.[46]

---

[45] "It is sometimes argued that even in the case of general taxes of this kind . . . the levels of taxation must be brought to an equality in any economic union. Otherwise, it is argued, the costs of production including tax in the taxing country will be raised above those in the rest of the union, and the taxing country's trade will thereby be subject to an artificial obstacle from which the trade of the rest of the union is exempt. But this is to fall into the error of applying absolute instead of comparative costs to international trade. Provided that the exchange rates between the currency of the taxing country and the currencies of the other countries are properly adjusted to take care of differences in such tax levels as well as of differences in other internal costs, there need be no obstacle to balanced commerce of a kind which will both optimize trade and maximize production." J. E. Meade, *op. cit.*, p. 23.

[46] In the United States, state excise and sales taxes on particular products are not held to be invalid under the interstate commerce clause of the Federal Constitution unless they are found to be discriminatory against interstate commerce. Similarly, the High Authority of the European Coal and Steel Community has decided that national taxes on steel need not be uniform within the Community but must be applied by each member government without discrimination.

In the light of these considerations, the reasons for not including freedom of capital movements and labor migration in the initial characteristics of the common market may now be seen. If capital and labor movements were free, the central authorities would need power to reduce differences in income taxes and in social security and welfare charges and benefits among the member states wherever such differences might give rise to seriously uneconomic or politically unacceptable interstate movements of capital or labor. This power would put the central authorities far more deeply into questions of economic welfare and income distribution than would be politically acceptable, at least during the early years of a European union.[47]

(3) What would be the respective roles of the union and the member states in the administration of direct controls on the production, distribution and pricing of products—i.e., allocations, production quotas, rationing, and maximum and minimum price controls? Freedom of interstate trade would prevent controls on production, distribution and prices from being effectively administered at the national level; for such controls can work only within an economy which has been administratively insulated. For example, a national price support scheme for agricultural products would quickly break down unless competition from imports could also be limited by tariffs or quotas. A national allocation or rationing scheme would be unworkable unless exports of the allocated or rationed goods were also controlled. A system of production quotas to limit competition during a recession of demand would break down unless imports of the controlled items were also subject to quotas. In a European union, therefore, powers of this type would have to be exercised at the supranational level, where they could be supported by control of external trade, or not used at all.[48]

---

[47] In addition to this reason for not freeing interstate labor and capital movements, there are others equally compelling. For example, freedom of interstate capital movements would probably give rise to periodic interstate balance-of-payments difficulties due to irrational or politically motivated capital movements. Freedom of labor migration would probably result in continuing labor migration from Italy on a scale which would be politically unacceptable, particularly to organized labor, in the other countries.

[48] In the case of some agricultural commodities, for example, central price supports, buttressed by appropriate union tariffs or quotas on imports from nonmember countries, would be necessary. For most industrial products, however, the best arrangement would probably be a general power to prohibit direct controls by the state governments, with central authority to adopt and enforce direct controls, or to order the harmonization of state controls, under certain limited circumstances, e.g., allocations of basic materials in the event of a persistent shortage. This is the way price, production and distribution controls are dealt with in the European Coal and Steel Community Treaty.

(4) Finally, there is the problem of private restrictive arrangements. In European industry, the most important direct controls on prices, production and distribution are those created by private restrictive agreements, often with the blessing or active support of national governments. Like public control of prices, production and distribution, such private restrictions can work only when supported by national tariffs and quotas or when they are international in scope. Thus the removal of quotas and tariffs would undermine private restrictive arrangements unless they were reconstituted as international agreements covering all competing producers in the common market.[49]

The process of economic unification would provide a unique opportunity to loosen the grip of these arrangements on European industry.[50] If the union had authority to prohibit private restrictive arrangements, and if its central organs were to become imbued with a philosophy of economic expansion and with a willingness to rely on competition and freedom of economic adjustment to a greater degree than has been customary in European industry, much might be done to overcome this major obstacle to European economic growth. A few years ago, this hope would have seemed utopian. Yet that is what the Coal and Steel Community is now trying to do for the European coal and

---

[49] A detailed examination of private restrictive arrangements in European industry would probably show that public support of them through tariffs, quotas, and other, less formal, means has usually been necessary to their success, even in the case of so-called international cartels.

[50] Removal of trade barriers would have a somewhat parallel effect on collective bargaining and the structure of wages within the Community. At present, collective bargaining in continental countries tends to be conducted on a national scale. This results from the fact that European trade unions are usually integrated into centralized national confederations and that employers' organizations are similarly centralized. Collective bargaining, therefore, takes on the character of a political struggle at the national level, in which differences in the situation of individual industries—particularly differences in labor productivity—are given little weight in fixing wage rates. The necessity for state intervention in collective bargaining from time to time in the interests of economic stabilization has re-enforced this centralizing tendency. The result is, as noted in Chapter 3, a pattern of wages which does not adequately reflect differences in productivity among industries, thus adding to other causes of inadequate labor mobility. Frequently, absence of competition among employers means that prices cover costs for even the least efficient producers and industries. Thus, there is little incentive for individual industries or employers to try to put collective bargaining on a firm or industry basis. The removal of interstate trade barriers would tend to loosen the grip of the national confederations on the trade unions and, at the same time, to create a strong incentive for some unions and some employers to bargain on a firm or industry, rather than a national, basis. This would help to produce a wage structure which would better reflect differences in labor productivity among firms and industries and create desirable wage incentives for labor.

steel industries—formerly among the most effectively cartelized of European businesses.[51]

In addition, the formation of a continental European union would give equal rights to all of its citizens in the remaining dependent overseas territories of any member. At an early stage of unification, responsibility for colonial development could be transferred to the new central authorities. This would probably be the best way to ensure that larger developmental resources would be available, that a fresh and more vigorous approach to colonial development would be made, and that the many legal and unofficial forms of discrimination now practiced by colonial administrators against the businessmen and investors of other countries would be abolished, at least with respect to the members of the union.

The foregoing has perhaps been enough to suggest the kind of institutional arrangements which could serve as transitional steps toward the economic unification of the Community of Six or of a larger group of European countries. A few words may now be said concerning the practical problems which would arise in dismantling trade barriers and establishing supranational economic institutions.

To create a common European market, ways would have to be found to make the necessary measures—removal of protective restrictions and assumption of important economic powers by supranational authorities—acceptable to a political majority of the interests most directly concerned and to the national governments. In economies which have been heavily protected for so long, the removal of trade barriers, even if done gradually, would cause considerable competitive injury. The political power of the affected interests would be brought to bear on national governments to arrest the unification process or to prevent it from having its intended effects on prices and economic structures. Important elements in national governments would resist each additional transfer of economic sovereignty—in part simply because of the loss of power involved; in part because it would remove from the national communities means of pursuing their own separate interests.

That is why it would probably be necessary for the member governments, before they attempted to agree on precise institutional arrangements, to make an unequivocal commitment to the general objective of

---

[51] See, for example, Raymond Vernon, "The Schuman Plan," *American Journal of International Law*, April 1953, pp. 196–7.

a common market.[52] If that goal could be formally accepted and clearly symbolized, a political momentum might be built up, based on broad popular support, and capable of gradually overcoming the stubborn resistance of special interests, public and private. Interests which stood to gain immediately from a removal of trade barriers would be encouraged to form alliances across national frontiers and to put pressure on national governments which could help to offset the influence of those who would postpone indefinitely the removal of barriers and the establishment of supranational economic powers.

What disturbance of existing interests and what supranational economic powers would be politically acceptable to the peoples of a European union would depend in part on economic philosophies. European liberals usually regard unification as an opportunity to dismantle not only the controls whose purpose is economic nationalism but also most other kinds of governmental intervention in the economic process. Cartel-minded industrialists would like to achieve unification of their industries by extending and formalizing their national and international forms of restrictive "industrial self-government." European socialists think of economic union in terms of supranational socialism and not as a way of creating greater scope for private business enterprise. So far, these thorny ideological issues have been avoided by the leaders of the unification movement—deliberately and wisely avoided. Until there has been a clear-cut commitment by governments to the general objective of a common market, these divisive ideological and theoretical questions, so dear to many European politicians and intellectuals, should be postponed as far as possible. But when it comes to setting up supranational economic institutions and deciding what their economic powers are to be, the question of the kind of wider-than-national economic system to be created cannot be avoided. For example, the powers outlined above would be adequate only if the economy of the union were to remain largely in private hands, and only if national and central economic authorities preferred to use indirect (i.e., monetary and fiscal) rather than direct means to achieve their aims. Different assumptions on these crucial questions would imply the need for much more extensive supranational economic powers.

To be politically acceptable, the removal of trade barriers and the

---

[52] That is, for example, the purpose of Articles 2 and 82 of the proposed Statute of the European Political Community, cited above.

opening of national markets to union-wide competition would have to be done gradually. Presumably, there would have to be general legislation of some kind establishing the legal framework of the common market and setting a final date, or dates, by which national trade barriers and other discriminations would be eliminated. This general legislation would provide a new basis for future economic calculations throughout the union.

It would, however, be naive to suppose that a common European market could simply be legislated into existence by general prohibitions against trade barriers and discrimination. It would also be necessary for the central authorities to come to grips with the concrete problems of adjusting particular industries to a regime of free trade and union-wide competition. Not all European industries would require this special treatment. Some have economic or technological characteristics which would make their problem of facing union-wide competition relatively easy or, conversely, too difficult to deal with as a unit; others would have little political leverage on their national governments. Such industries might be left to work out their own transitions to a common market, aided only by time to make the necessary adjustments and access to the resources of a European re-adaptation fund.[53] For a number of other industries, however, it would prove economically efficient and politically expedient to provide for the working out by management and labor of a special reorganization and adjustment program, under supervision of a specialized supranational agency. Where, for example, the industry is one with very heavy and highly specialized capital investment, with a highly trained labor force which would have difficulty in finding alternative employment, and with large differences in costs among national sectors, such special attention would be desirable—particularly if the industry or its labor were in a position to exert strong pressure on national governments to block removal of trade barriers.[54]

---

[53] Article 85 of the proposed Statute of the European Political Community envisages the establishment of a European Readaptation Fund.

[54] In such industries, the economic and social cost of a purely competitive adjustment to a regime of free trade, without benefit of a special industry program, would often be too high. It would, therefore, be strongly resisted by appeal to national governments, or by restrictive arrangements, unless a rational adjustment program could be worked out with the participation of interested groups. The purpose of the program would be twofold: (1) during a transition period in which continuing protection would be allowed, to bring the high-cost sectors of the industry into a condition in which they could meet competition without protection—e.g., by modernization, reorganization, reconversion of hopelessly un-

It is in European agriculture rather than in industry that the most difficult transitional problems occur. Both for economic and political reasons, European agriculture could not make its transition to a European market freed of trade barriers or national discrimination primarily through the action of competitive market forces. This is the conclusion reached, with varying shades of emphasis, by a number of official and unofficial studies of the problems of creating a common European market in agricultural products. It is the common starting point for a number of plans for agricultural integration in Europe.[55]

The difficulty lies in the great inflexibility—inelasticity of supply—in European agriculture. No doubt inelasticity of supply in the shorter run is characteristic of agriculture in most countries, but it is especially true of European agriculture owing to several factors—the lack of sufficient alternative employment opportunities in industry; the traditional conservatism of the continental peasant; problems of land tenure and excessive subdivision of holdings; lack of adequate capital and, in some cases, of access to technical knowledge; etc. This inflexibility, coupled with the political power of European farm groups, has made it both undesirable and politically impossible to eliminate price supports, buttressed by protection and often by production control, from European agriculture. An attempt to integrate European agriculture simply by removing interstate barriers and thereby rendering existing price supports ineffective would cause serious hardships to the higher-cost producers and would run into overwhelming political resistance.

Existing proposals for European agricultural integration are in agreement that the establishment of a common European market in agricultural products would have to follow a different path. Since it would not be possible to eliminate price supports for many products, it would be necessary to transfer the responsibility for setting the support prices, and for coordinating the administration of supplementary direct

---

competitive capacity to other uses or its scrapping; and (2) to provide alternative employment for workers who would be displaced by the removal of protection at the end of the transition period. Financial assistance would be provided by the central authorities to make the program possible. This method of handling the adjustment problems of such industries would have the further advantage of giving the central agency an opportunity to influence the industry in question to adopt a technically progressive and expansionist attitude toward the new opportunities provided by the common market, and to assist it financially to do so. On this problem generally, see John C. L. Hulley, "Protect or Compensate?," *World Politics* (April 1953), p. 318.

[55] See, for example, European League for Economic Cooperation, *The Role of Agriculture in the Formation of a Single European Market* (Brussels, June 1952).

controls, to supranational agencies. The central task of such agencies would be to promote the structural adjustments necessary to make possible the gradual removal of national protection, and thereby to establish common prices in European agricultural markets. The agencies would also have the task of bringing the policies of the member states with respect to external trade in agricultural products into harmony.

In sum, two conclusions have been reached concerning a European economic grouping of a supranational character. First, although the support for European union is not motivated primarily by economic considerations, union could make an important contribution to the economic health of Western Europe. Second, supranational arrangements can be envisaged which, if established, could make possible a degree of regional economic integration sufficient to induce major changes of economic structure and outlook within the Community of Six or on a wider basis in Western Europe.

The three regional economic units considered in this chapter differ significantly in their size, their economic institutions, and their ability —actual or potential—to create among their members the freedom and security of economic relations on which a high degree of economic integration depends. The two existing groupings—the Sterling Area and the OEEC-EPU trading system—are sufficient only to mitigate in varying degree the external obstacles to Western Europe's economic growth. Without them, the problem would be much worse than it is; but even with them, it is still a long way from solution. The supranational union of European countries which has been proposed is a far more ambitious project whose possible economic benefits would be correspondingly greater.

Throughout the preceding discussion, the crucial dependence of these groupings on American political and economic support has been indicated. The survival of the Sterling Area, the conception and creation of the EPU, and the progress made toward European union have depended directly on American leadership and American economic support. Beyond this, the fact that the two existing groupings are not in themselves adequate to meet their members' economic difficulties, and that the creation of a supranational European union in the near future is problematical, suggests the need of further American action directed toward closer economic integration between these groupings and the

United States. Some steps in that direction have already been suggested
—e.g., closer association of the United States with the Commonwealth
economic arrangements; measures to supplement Western Europe's dollar reserves and to create an Atlantic Trade and Payments Committee.
These and other, more important, American policies required for the
effective economic organization of the Western Community are discussed in the next chapter.

8

The Economic
Organization of the
Western Community

The American Role

The preceding chapter examined the contribution which the Commonwealth and the OEEC-EPU trading system can make to the economic health of Western Europe. One conclusion was that the external economic problems of Western Europe cannot be solved merely by intensifying economic relations within these regional groupings. To be sure, the economies of Western Europe and the Sterling Area are probably, in combination, large enough and sufficiently varied in their resources to enjoy an adequate rate of growth if they could achieve a sufficiently high degree of international economic integration. But, so high a degree of integration—demanding, as it would, supranational authority over important areas of national economic life—is not yet a realistic possibility, although a supranational union of several West European countries may in time be established. Even if such a union were created in the near future, however, it would be many years before it would become a highly integrated economic unit. For these reasons, industrial Europe needs new opportunities for foreign trade in addition to those which these groupings could provide. Specifically, industrial Europe needs an expanding volume of imports of primary products from non-European sources at satisfactory terms of trade. It needs freer and more secure access to overseas markets, which are also expanding, where it can earn the currencies needed to pay for such imports and where its export industries can be stimulated to more rapid growth.

To state these needs is to state the reason why industrial Europe has to have closer economic integration with North America. For North America is the only place in the free world where Western Europe might be able to find this particular combination of trading opportunities on a large enough scale. In addition, West European industry could profit from the stimulus of easier and more secure access to American technology. It also needs more participation by American enterprise in its management and more American competition in its home markets. Finally, Europe requires American capital and enterprise to help expand its industries and develop primary production in its colonies and in the Dominions. These requirements all point to closer economic integration of the Western Community as a whole.

If that objective could be approached on a truly reciprocal basis, the task would be very much easier than it is. The difficulty is that the European economies need the benefits of intensified economic relations with North America, but they cannot afford, under the conditions likely to occur in the foreseeable future, to extend equivalent economic benefits to the United States in return. They need more economic integration with the United States, but on a favored—partially unilateral—basis; that is, one which would enable them to some extent to shield their domestic economies and their trade with each other from the consequences of unrestricted American competition. To increase Europe's opportunity for economic growth, the United States will have to find effective ways of opening up its domestic market to larger imports from Europe, while continuing to acquiesce in regionally organized restrictions on its own export opportunities for at least a considerable period ahead. Indeed, the United States will have not merely to tolerate such regional arrangements but actively to foster and support them, as the preceding chapter has shown. If, then, Western Europe's economic health is to improve, its economic relations with the United States will have to be organized in this asymmetrical, one-sided manner.

This concept of the economic organization of the Western Community has been implicit in our postwar policy toward Western Europe and the Sterling Area. It has found expression, for example, in the European aid programs and in continued American acceptance of discrimination against the dollar by the Sterling Area and the OEEC countries. If the Study Group's analysis in Part I of Western Europe's economic needs is substantially correct, this concept of economic organization—though not necessarily the particular policies and arrangements which now exemplify it—is a continuing requirement of Western Europe's economic health for some time to come. It is a necessary consequence of the goals of American foreign policy and of the structural characteristics of the international economy. Improvement in Western Europe's economic health requires that means be found to increase progressively the economic integration of the Western Community on a basis which is more advantageous economically to Western Europe than to the United States. The ultimate result should be to make Europe a stronger system, no longer in need of such special support.

Means of that kind are outlined in this chapter. Most of the measures recommended, beginning with liberalization of the American tariff, are familiar and relatively modest, but their adoption in the degree proposed is politically extremely difficult. The difficulty is, precisely, that most of them have a one-sided character when considered from an economic standpoint. In the main, the shorter-run economic benefits they confer go to other countries while the economic costs they entail are domestic American costs. Therefore, so long as these measures are considered in a strictly economic context, their costs to certain American producers will outweigh their benefits to American exporters and consumers generally on the scales of domestic politics, and there would be little prospect that they could be carried out in sufficient degree to achieve their purposes. Action along the lines proposed in this chapter is, in consequence, unlikely unless these or similar measures come to be supported by the American public because of the larger ends they would serve.

The larger objectives served by the measures discussed in this chapter are political and moral rather than economic. If American public opinion has accepted in recent years the economic cost of aid programs and other one-sided economic arrangements with Western Europe, it is because political and moral concerns have outweighed short-term domestic economic interests, though the latter have still operated to set relatively narrow limits within which the former could find expression. Many Americans have recognized that our national interest in Western Europe's economic health offsets by far the economic costs involved in organizing our economic relations with Western Europe in a one-sided fashion—so long, at least, as the European nations are making serious efforts toward their own economic and political union.

Many more have been willing to support a foreign economic policy of this kind less because they have grasped its relation to our national security than because of a feeling of identity with, and concern for, Western Europe as the source of our common Western civilization faced by the same communist threat. Thus, further progress in the economic integration of the West depends on tapping more effectively than in the past these sources of American motivation, which rise from the genuine moral internationalism of many Americans and from the fact that the United States shares with Western Europe a common civilization, common dangers and a common destiny.

The measures outlined below can attract sufficient popular support only if they are seen as the economic aspects of a broader policy whose theme is the progressive unification of the Western Community in political, military and economic terms, to the end that Western civilization may survive and prosper. If, for example, those who support an effective reduction of the American tariff continue trying to "sell" it to the public mainly on the ground that increased trade is good for the American economy, as well as for other trading nations, the attempt will in all probability continue to fail as it has in the past. The strictly economic consequences for Europe of American tariff reduction are not large enough to be dramatized in the way that, for example, Europe's economic need for dollar aid in 1947 could be dramatized. At the same time, the anticipated domestic economic benefits of tariff cuts are much too small and too widely diffused to attract enough political support, while the fear of damage from increased import competition is concentrated and politically effective. Moreover, an economic rationale obscures the principal reason why tariff liberalization is a good policy for the United States, particularly in the shorter run. It is good policy less because of its immediate economic effects here and abroad than because it is one of the steps the United States could now take to create within the Western Community a feeling of political solidarity and a sense of progress toward eventual greater unity. A rationale of that kind would bring out the positive political and psychological importance to the United States of tariff liberalization and of similar economic measures which, in themselves, are prosaic and lacking in popular appeal. But since it offers a general and long-run advantage and entails short-run and specific disadvantages, political wisdom and maturity are required to accept this reasoning.

It will, however, be futile to propose the concept of American economic relations with Western Europe outlined here unless the European countries are considerably more willing than they have recently been to move ahead decisively with their own economic and political unification along the general lines discussed in the preceding chapter. It is reasonable to hope that Americans will continue to value Europe's long-run economic health and the solidarity of the West highly enough to make economic sacrifices for them in the shorter run, if we are convinced that the major European nations are trying seriously to come to grips with the fundamental obstacles to their economic growth and health. But it would be foolish to suppose that this motivation would persist if Western Europe is content to drift along on the present basis, counting on existing regional economic arrangements and continuing American financial support to make unnecessary an attack on basic problems through closer economic integration and political unification.

Japan, too, has need of more secure access to the American market and of the other economic benefits which closer integration with the United States on a partially unilateral basis could bring. Measures to that end are also considered in this chapter. But Japan and the United States lack organic, historical elements of community like those which already unite in some degree the nations of the West. There is not the sense of familiarity, respect and trust between Japanese and Americans that exists among Western peoples, and there are, in consequence, much narrower political and psychological limits to what the United States can do for Japan, notwithstanding the importance of Japan's economic health to the United States. Nevertheless, such measures as would be feasible are urgently necessary, for the dependence of Japan's economic growth and health on American policy is, in present circumstances, greater even than Western Europe's.

The measures discussed in this chapter can be grouped into several sections. The first relates to American tariff policy and kindred questions. The two following deal with the things that need to be done within the American economy to make it better able, economically and politically, to take larger commercial imports—namely, to maintain the growth of aggregate demand and to assist particular industries and communities to adjust to increasing competition from imports. Because the probable extent of tariff liberalization is nonetheless limited, the fourth section considers measures of a more direct and positive kind to bring American buying power and capital to bear on the expansion of European and Japanese industry and dollar earnings—in particular, military "offshore procurement." The final section deals with the problems of improving the organizational arrangements of the Western Community and giving more positive content to the symbols of Western unification.

Reducing the American Tariff

Among the steps which the United States could now take to increase the economic integration of the Western Community and to expand Japan's trading opportunities, the most obvious is a reduction of the American tariff. It seems clear, however, that even a drastic reduction of the tariff would not be sufficient, by itself, to induce a large-scale increase in American imports, particularly in imports of manufactures. The only detailed estimate available suggests that the increase in imports resulting from a complete suspension of the tariff would not exceed a range from $800 million to $1.8 billion annually, at least in the first few years.[1] Why this is true may be seen by considering the changes which, in addition to tariff reduction, would be necessary to bring about a really major increase in American imports of European manufactures.

The principal obstacles to American imports of European products have been considered in previous chapters and arise from causes other than deliberate tariff barriers. They may be summarized as follows:

(1) The area of comparative cost advantage which European manufactured products would enjoy in the American market if the tariff were eliminated is relatively small—particularly with respect to the sectors of the American market where demand is expanding rapidly.

(2) European exporters face great difficulty in establishing the large-scale sales promotion, distribution and servicing facilities which would

---

[1] See Commission on Foreign Economic Policy (Randall Commission), *Staff Papers* (Washington, D.C., February, 1954), p. 380. This estimate is based on the work of Dr. Howard S. Piquet, presented in his book *Aid, Trade and the Tariff* (New York: Thomas Y. Crowell, Co., 1953). His estimate refers to the short-run (3 to 5 year) effects of a suspension of the tariff which is temporary, with no assurance of permanence. It is, therefore, no indication of the possible increase in American imports over a longer period of time if obstacles other than the tariff—particularly, the incalculability of international economic relations—could be mitigated. The estimate is based on 1951 American import data and the figures in the text are accordingly expressed in prices of that year. For an earlier semiofficial estimate, see the so-called "Bell Report," A Report to the President by the Public Advisory Board for Mutual Security, *A Trade and Tariff Policy in the National Interest* (Washington, D.C., February 1953), p. 65.

be necessary to gain and hold a substantial share of the American market for many kinds of manufactured products.

(3) There are persistent supply limitations in European industry—that is, insufficient capital and enterprise are available to expand European productive capacity and to redesign products in order to take advantage of market opportunities in the United States. (This obstacle might be considerably reduced if Western Europe itself can achieve more economic integration.)

Such non-tariff obstacles to imports are critically dependent, directly or indirectly, on the business risks which arise from the incalculability of the conditions governing commercial relations between Western Europe and the United States. Uncertainty about the future course of American tariff policy is one—but only one—cause of this incalculability. All three kinds of non-tariff obstacles to imports would, therefore, be mitigated if European exporters and American importers could count on free and secure commercial relations with each other. If, for example, European manufacturers could count on secure access to the American market, the area of their comparative advantage in it could be expanded, for the size of that area is not wholly determined by unalterable economic factors. If the area is small today, it is at least partly because European firms cannot now count on market opportunities which are secure enough to justify equipping their plants, redesigning their products and expanding their output in order to compete successfully on a price basis in the more rapidly growing sectors of the American market, where tariff barriers are even now of minor importance in most cases. Accordingly, if the risks of doing so were reduced, more European manufacturers would find it profitable to take advantage of lower European wages and to adopt volume production techniques in order to exploit the American market on a volume basis. True, the higher price of capital relative to wages in Europe, as compared with the United States, sets some limits to this possibility. But, in theory at least, the area of Europe's comparative advantage in the American market could be considerably broadened irrespective of tariff liberalization. Indeed, even with present production techniques and costs—i.e., with the present pattern of comparative costs—many European industries have the ability to compete with American products on a price basis and could expand their exports to the United States considerably were it not for the extraordinary risks in doing so.

Similarly, if these risks were reduced, more European manufacturers could afford to establish large-scale sales promotion, distribution and servicing facilities in the United States. American capital, enterprise, management, technical services, and knowledge of the domestic market would become available on favorable terms to European industry to help expand exports to the United States. For example, if secure access to the American market were reasonably assured, many more American manufacturing firms would find it profitable to set up European subsidiaries to produce for the American market. It would become profitable to establish licensing and agency arrangements between European and American firms (such as now exist to a limited extent) to supply European machinery and components for use, assembly or distribution in the United States. In short, the organic growing-together of economic organizations, which is so important an aspect of industrial growth, could occur on a significant scale between industrial Europe and the United States.

Institutional and structural changes of these kinds, then, are prerequisites to a major increase in European exports of manufactures to the United States. Within present political limits, however, there is no way of creating the degree of freedom and security of commercial relations between Europe and the United States which such changes presuppose. Economic freedom and calculability in that degree would require some kind of political and economic union of the Western Community—in effect, a supranational Atlantic union. But a union of that kind, desirable as it might be, is not within the feasible limits of politics for the foreseeable future.[2] It has been useful, nevertheless, to examine this possibility because it puts the narrower question of tariff reduction in proper perspective. It demonstrates that the American tariff is not the principal obstacle to a successful integration of the United States into the international economy, as many advocates of tariff liberalization suppose.

Nonetheless, the tariff is a significant obstacle to imports and one which could be modified in the next few years. Tariff liberalization is, therefore, a desirable and necessary policy. The resulting increase in American imports, though small relative to Western Europe's and Japan's need for export opportunities, would be considerable in comparison to their present exports to the United States, particularly if the tariff itself could be made somewhat more calculable.

---

[2] For further discussion of this question, see below, pp. 320–322.

It is as a political and psychological measure, however, that tariff liberalization is most significant and urgent. Indeed, the political and psychological effects of a lowering of American import barriers are in themselves of sufficient importance to justify a substantial effort in this direction even if the prospective economic benefits were negligible. Such action would be an earnest of our good intentions toward our Western allies and Japan—and even toward the independent underdeveloped countries—who have convinced themselves, rightly or wrongly, that one of the principal tests of American leadership is liberalization of American import policy. It is politically desirable that this action be taken, particularly at a time when the Soviet Union is making a major propaganda effort to convince the rest of the free world that the Communist bloc is a prospectively better trading partner than the American economy. Finally, it could serve to widen the domestic political limits on import liberalization by demonstrating that import barriers could be reduced without causing anything like the fearsome damage that protectionists have predicted.

In present circumstances, a worthwhile and practicable program for reducing American important barriers must strike a balance between two opposing requirements. To be worthwhile, reductions must be substantial enough to have the desired political and psychological results and actually to increase imports; to be practicable, they must not be so drastic as to create insuperable domestic political obstacles. Harmonizing these requirements is not easy; it may not even be possible. The political difficulties may be eased if it is clear from the beginning that import barriers will be reduced only gradually; that, for many commodities, differential degrees of protection will still remain which will reflect to some extent the relative competitive positions of American and foreign products; and that effective readjustment efforts will be vigorously supported for those industries and communities adversely affected by tariff cuts. At the same time, it must also be emphasized that every economy has efficient and inefficient producers; that marginal industries and producers have no inherent right to protection against competition, domestic or foreign; and that a valid case for continued protection of them can be made only if important security interests or humanitarian concerns are involved which cannot be satisfied by more desirable means.

The changes in tariff policy here advocated are a beginning only. They are designed to restart the process of tariff liberalization which

—begun by Secretary of State Hull and furthered by the Reciprocal Trade Agreements Act in 1935—has since 1948 been gradually brought to a standstill by protectionist elements in the Congress.[3] The first requirement is broadened legislative authority for the President to reduce tariff rates. A substantial expansion of imports through changes in the tariff can be achieved only by a further lowering of rates already reduced and by a lowering of rates not yet reduced. The reason is that the reductions hitherto made under the Reciprocal Trade Agreements program have, with minor exceptions, merely eliminated the excess protection embodied in the Tariff Act of 1930 or generated by economic changes over the past twenty-five years. Hence, if imports are to be increased through tariff liberalization, the President will have to be empowered to make further substantial cuts in tariff rates already reduced. In addition, if the President is to be able to use effectively even his existing authority to cut tariff rates, the peril-point amendment will have to be abolished and the escape clause modified to encourage a much less restrictive interpretation than the Tariff Commission now follows. The determination of the specific reductions to be made requires a careful and dispassionate weighing of the national and private interests involved. If the objectivity and flexibility needed for this purpose are to be ensured, the primary responsibility for decision and action should remain where it has been for the past twenty years—with the President,

---

[3] The year 1947 marks the high point of the trade agreements program. Since then, the original Act has been amended so as to curtail greatly the President's power effectively to reduce trade barriers. In 1948—with Republicans in control for the first time in over fifteen years—the Congress enacted the so-called "peril-point" amendment requiring the Tariff Commission to survey all commodities on which the President proposed to negotiate agreements and to specify rates of duty below which, in the Commission's judgment, tariffs could not be lowered without injuring the American industry affected. The President is permitted to reduce tariffs below the points specified but, whenever he does so, he is required to send an official communication to the Congress explaining his reasons for such action. In 1949, the Congress—again Democratic—repealed the 1948 version of the Trade Agreements Act, including the peril-point amendment, and restored the Act almost to its original form for a period of two years. In 1951, when the Act again came up for renewal, Congressional opposition—even with the Democrats in control—was sufficiently powerful to overcome the Administration's proposal for renewal without changes. The Act was renewed for two years (to June 1953) but with several major amendments, one of which restored the peril-point provision. It also included an "escape clause" in the form of a tightened version of the escape clause procedure that had been followed by the Administration, under Executive Order, since 1947. In 1953 and again in 1954, the Congress —again Republican—extended the Act for a single year, with both the peril-point and the escape clause provisions included. Thus, since 1948, the power of the President to reduce tariffs has been whittled down. The peril-point provision, together with the escape clause, provide an effective brake upon the tariff-cutting power of the President.

acting under authorization of the Congress and in accordance with general policies specified by it.

There is both a feasible maximum and a worthwhile minimum to possible changes in the legislation governing tariffs and other import restrictions. These limits are approximately defined by the recommendations of two recent official bodies—the February 1953 Report of the Public Advisory Board for Mutual Security (the Bell Committee), and the January 1954 Report of the Commission on Foreign Economic Policy (the Randall Commission). The Bell Committee's recommendations represent the maximum reductions likely to be politically feasible in the foreseeable future.[4] In contrast, the recommendations of the Randall Commission probably represent the minimum that could be considered economically or politically worthwhile.[5] Increases in imports are unlikely to be quantitatively very significant unless reductions in import barriers are at least of the magnitude advocated by the Bell

---

[4] The Bell Committee recommended: (a) abolition of the escape clause and peril-point amendment, and adoption of the concept of the national interest as the guiding principle of import policy in place of the necessity of avoiding injury to particular domestic industries or groups; (b) the preparation of a new simplified tariff providing for general reductions of duties and eliminating present uncertainties in the classification of goods by consolidating the many hundreds of present tariff rates into seven basic schedules—a Free List; four groupings of commodities bearing duties of 10, 20, 30 and 40 percent *ad valorem;* a Specific List for basic agricultural and mineral raw materials; and an Extraordinary List where commodities might be placed whose importation, for security or other reasons, should be limited by quotas or other restrictions, or by exceptionally high rates; (c) the President should be authorized without limit of time to enter into reciprocal trade agreements and to reduce tariffs, within the limits specified in (b) above, in return for reductions in tariffs or trade restrictions by other countries, or unilaterally; and (d) other recommended reductions including simplification of customs procedures; revision of agricultural import quotas; easing of mandatory shipping restrictions; and liberalization of government procurement policies (i.e., "Buy American" restrictions).

[5] The Randall Commission proposed: (a) the existing escape clause and peril-point amendment should be retained but modified to permit the President to disregard the findings of the Tariff Commission on injury to domestic producers whenever he deems it in the national interest; (b) instead of a thorough revision or general reduction of the tariff, piecemeal studies of commodity definitions and rate schedules should be authorized by the Congress and the President given authority to promulgate desirable modifications and simplifications provided they do not materially alter the total duties collected on any existing group of rates; (c) the Reciprocal Trade Agreements Act should be renewed for three years and the President authorized to reduce existing rates by not more than 5 percent each year in return for reciprocal trade concessions; (d) the President should be authorized to reduce rates, with or without reciprocal concessions, on commodities not now imported or being imported in negligible volume, provided the reductions do not exceed 50 percent of the 1945 rates and are spread over a period of three years; and (e) other recommendations including some simplification of customs procedures, some Presidential flexibility under the "Buy American" Act, repeal of the mandatory shipping restrictions, etc.

Committee. Hence, those who believe that better integration of the American economy into the international economy is one of the necessary conditions for the security and progress of the United States and of other free countries should not cease to work for the adoption of an import policy along the lines of that recommended in the Bell Report. However, until such a policy can be achieved, the United States cannot afford for political reasons to undertake less than the minimal measures recommended by the Randall Commission. While the latter would probably not increase American imports appreciably, they would nevertheless help to maintain a feeling of movement in the right direction. In the absence of perceptible momentum, not only our allies and friends abroad but the American people as well are likely to suffer a serious weakening of confidence in American leadership.

Measures to increase the calculability of the tariff are as desirable from an economic standpoint as the reduction of tariff rates. Uncertainty about the tariff arises on three levels. There is, first, uncertainty about the future course of American tariff policy as a whole—uncertainty which has been growing because of the peril-point amendment and the recent Congressional practice of authorizing only short-term extensions of the Reciprocal Trade Agreements Act. This uncertainty could be substantially reduced if the Congress would repeal the peril-point provision and enact a new, permanent basic tariff law involving a general reduction of rates, as proposed by the Bell Committee. It could be mitigated even if only the existing Reciprocal Trade Agreements Act could be made continuing legislation or were extended for a considerable period—say ten years. Second, there is uncertainty whether particular tariff rates will be raised as a result of decisions under the escape clause of the Trade Agreements Act. Modification of the escape clause, as suggested above, would reduce—but could not wholly eliminate—this source of uncertainty. Third, the standards and procedures for valuing imported merchandise, and the complexities of the Tariff Act of 1930, frequently lead to uncertainty about the duty to be paid and to serious delays in determining it. The proposals either of the Bell Committee or of the Randall Commission—if carried out in their intended spirit—would reduce substantially this third source of incalculability.[6]

There are, however, narrow limits to what can be done by unilateral

---

[6] A discussion of these three sources of uncertainty may be found in the Commission on Foreign Economic Policy, *Staff Papers, op. cit.,* pp. 287–292.

national action to increase the calculability of the American tariff and its administration. In the last analysis, the psychological effectiveness of national action is seriously qualified by the possibility that the Congress or the Executive will later find it expedient to alter American policy. This basic uncertainty cannot be removed by declarations of national policy or by national legislation, for it is inseparable from national sovereignty itself. There is no getting around the fact that the calculability of commercial relations between the United States and other countries depends on a reasonable assurance of the stability of American commercial policy—or, at least, on the assurance that policy will not be subject to changes which deal arbitrarily with foreign trading interests. But assurance of that kind can be created only within a community which exercises in common some of the attributes of sovereignty; as between sovereign national communities, the assurance will necessarily be greatly qualified by the freedom at any time to resort to unilateral national action.

It would be quite unrealistic to propose that elaborate supranational arrangements be set up for the entire free world—or even for the Western Community—to limit national freedom of action with respect to tariffs and other matters of commercial policy, in the interest of greater calculability of commercial relations. It would be worthwhile, however, to consider a short first step in that direction—the establishment by treaty within the Western Community of a permanent arbitration and appeals agency of some kind for questions of commercial policy and related matters. Appeals to this body might be taken both by governments and by interested private parties—American and European—concerning alleged violations by any member government of tariff concessions, investment guarantees, and other formal intergovernmental arrangements for increasing trade and capital flow within the Western Community. At first, this body might be merely an arbitration tribunal. In time, however, its decisions could come to be recognized formally by the participating governments as legally binding interpretations of international agreements, enforceable in national courts on the initiative of interested parties, governmental or private. Over a period of years, an institution of this kind might have a significant effect on the calculability of economic relations within the Western Community, even though enforcement of its decisions would depend, in the last analysis, on the good faith of national governments.

Present legislative authority to reduce tariffs (the Reciprocal Trade

Agreements Act), permits American tariff concessions only in exchange for equivalent tariff concessions by other countries. Tariff reciprocity of this kind may have been appropriate in the 1930's. Today it is no longer so, for several reasons. If its purpose is to expand American exports of manufactures, tariff reciprocity is no longer an effective means of doing so, because most other countries' imports of American manufactures tend to be limited more by their supply of dollars (that is, by import quotas and exchange controls) than by their tariffs. A more fundamental objection to tariff reciprocity is that expanding the level of our exports of manufactures should not be a high priority aim of American foreign economic policy. In many situations, that aim is inconsistent with a more important objective—to help improve the economic health of Western Europe and Japan by enlarging their export opportunities. It is inconsistent with the concept of the economic organization of the Western Community outlined above. What the other industrial countries need—and what our own interests suggest—is a primarily *unilateral* liberalization of the American tariff, in conjunction with progress by the Europeans in regional economic integration.

The difficulty with tariff reciprocity is not with the idea of reciprocity itself. The thought that the lowering of American import barriers should be exchanged for real benefits to the United States is a valid one; indeed, it has obvious diplomatic and psychological advantages. Mutuality in economic relations with other countries is as important for their morale—and for the psychological stability of the relationship—as it is for the United States. But tariff reciprocity wastes on an objective which is either meaningless or, at best, of minor significance the bargaining power which a willingness on our part to make major tariff cuts could give us. The appropriate kind of reciprocity—or mutuality —is to use tariff reductions, along with such other benefits as the United States may be willing to extend to other countries, to help obtain from them the actions which we believe to be essential to our national interest, broadly defined, and to the ends we share with them. A strategy of that kind would also tend to avoid the dissipation of our economic bargaining power which results from using the principal instruments of foreign economic policy—such as tariff cuts, economic aid, governmental foreign investment, military "offshore procurement," and procurement of strategic materials abroad—in a series of piecemeal and uncoordinated negotiations. It would permit our economic bargaining power to be focused more sharply in order to obtain from other countries the actions we deem truly important not simply to ourselves but often to them as well.

How, concretely, tariff reductions and other American policies might be used in this kind of strategy cannot be fully outlined here. Two illustrations may, however, be given. In the preceding chapter, a series of proposals was outlined for action by the West European governments to make the Sterling Area and the OEEC-EPU economic grouping more effective. It would be appropriate to offer these governments major American tariff reductions, together with arrangements to supplement Europe's dollar reserves (see above, p. 269), in exchange for a commitment by the European governments to take some, at least, of those actions. American tariff concessions granted to Western Europe should also be extended to Japan—possibly in connection with steps to bring Japan into the EPU and to extend the OEEC trade liberalization rules to Japan. A bargain of this kind could be presented to the American public and the Congress in terms of its significance for American security and for the unity of the West. It would be a far more important diplomatic achievement and would have greater domestic political appeal than a multilateral reciprocal tariff agreement of the conventional type.

Again, American tariff concessions might be used to obtain other objectives. Tariff cuts might be exchanged for a commitment by countries willing to enter it guaranteeing full "national treatment" to American businessmen and private investors within their territories. A commitment of this kind might also include enactment by the countries receiving the benefit of tariff cuts of special legislation to increase the attractiveness of foreign direct and portfolio investments within their territories.[7] Such an arrangement would be more than a *quid pro quo*, for the other countries would benefit not only from the *quid* (American tariff cuts) but also from the *quo* (increased American private investment).

These examples are not necessarily intended as recommendations for action; they might be neither practical nor desirable in precisely the form described here. They do, however, illustrate how the desire of other countries for lower American tariffs might be better used to further not only American interests but the common ends of the Western Alliance and of the whole free world.

---

[7] Measures of this kind are considered in the following chapter. See below, pp. 333–334.

This way of using American tariff concessions would require abandonment of the unconditional most-favored-nation policy with respect to tariff reductions. In effect, the United States would in time come to have a "multi-column" tariff. The present tariff has two columns of tariff duties: one for countries which have signed the General Agreement on Tariffs and Trade (GATT) and a higher one for non-GATT countries. Under the policy proposed here, additional—and lower—columns would apply to those countries willing to enter into agreements to exchange American tariff concessions for other kinds of benefits to the United States. Thus, there would be created—within the present GATT membership—an inner group enjoying lower American tariff rates in return for other concessions. The group which would enjoy the lowest American tariffs would presumably include, at a minimum, Western Europe, the Commonwealth and Japan. This arrangement would be analogous in certain respects to the British Commonwealth system of imperial preferences. Existing preferential American commercial policies for Cuba and the Philippine Republic are precedents, on a small scale, for what is here proposed: a preferential tariff relationship based essentially on a special political relationship.

Maintaining Adequate Demand in the American Economy

It may be superfluous to say that the prevention of a major American depression is an absolute precondition of an effective American foreign policy. One need only recall that the more or less chronic depression of the American economy in the 1930's contributed to economic stagnation in many Western countries, both through its effects on the world monetary climate and because it helped to stimulate economic nationalism. Apart from economic consequences, our ability or inability to avoid a major depression has become for the rest of the world—as for ourselves—a test not only of our qualification for international leadership but of the efficiency or inefficiency, the justice or injustice of a liberal economic system.

Preventing a serious depression does not, of course, mean preventing any temporary underutilization of capacity or unemployment. In a growing economy, whose vitality depends in part on the decentralized and private character of economic decisions, temporary imbalances inevitably occur from time to time. Various elements of capacity and demand do not always change in the right proportion to each other, and corrections become necessary. The capacity to produce may at times exceed the ability and the willingness to buy consumer goods and capital goods for further expansion. Therefore, continued growth is not possible without periodic adjustments of capacities to demands, and vice versa. Such adjustments lead to temporary curtailments in the purchase and production of specific goods, though they need not affect adversely the levels of employment, income and production as a whole if the curtailments in some areas of economic activity are more than offset by simultaneous expansion in other areas. However, such adjustments may—and often do—occur simultaneously in large sectors of the economy and then spread by a cumulative process through the economy as a whole, leading to a generalized inadequacy of demand. If it continues for long, a cumulative process of this kind leads to a serious depression.

It is widely acknowledged that important structural and institutional changes in the American economy have occurred since the 1930's which increase substantially the "built-in" resistance of the American economy to a generalized cumulative downward spiral of production and demand. These changes are, for the most part, reflections of the rise of powerful claimant groups, of greatly expanded defense requirements, and of new attitudes and economic expectations—changes which are not peculiar to the United States and whose economic and political consequences have concerned us throughout this study. The most obvious and perhaps most important of these changes for the subject here considered is that the government budget has become very much larger, both absolutely and relative to the gross national product. In the event of an economic downturn, tax revenues will drop promptly while government expenditures are likely to decline but little. Thus a large employment-inducing deficit would occur, which would help automatically to inhibit a cumulative development of the original deflationary impulse.

Formerly, the onset of deflation tended to produce a "liquidity crisis" which accelerated the downward spiral. When debtors began to fail in substantial numbers because of difficulties in their particular lines of business, banks were inclined to restrict lending sharply and to liquidate outstanding credits in order to prepare for the possibility that an alarmed public would withdraw its cash deposits. Today, the fact that deposits—up to a certain amount—are insured has very much reduced the pressure on the banks to increase their liquidity in the event of a rise in business failures. Another new source of stability is the change in the situation of workers who lose their jobs because of the curtailment of production in a particular sector of the economy. Formerly, the unemployed had to reduce their purchases at once and very drastically. They thereby became one of the links in the chain reaction which produced depressions. With unemployment benefits now provided through social insurance, this factor is at least somewhat mitigated today.

In the past, one medium through which depressions spread was the reaction of many businessmen who, in consequence of weakening of markets, attempted to liquidate even normal inventories, or curtailed plans for modernization and expansion of their plants and equipment. Again, a change for the better has occurred. The fact that the United States Government is committed to an economic stabilization policy has reduced the fear of many businessmen that a downturn will lead to a prolonged and severe depression. Today, businessmen are less inclined to succumb to "depression psychology." Some may even recognize that a time of general slackness in the labor market, of cheapening credit and falling prices of materials may be especially favorable for the modernization of their plants and equipment. Many businessmen will realize that, even in an economic downturn, consumers may be willing to increase their purchases if attractive goods are offered at attractive prices. The fact that a large number of consumers now have greater liquid reserves than they had in the past makes such an aggressive business policy a more promising possibility than in earlier decades.

At the same time, it cannot safely be assumed that the American economy has become *automatically* depression-proof. For example, with respect to the favorable change in business attitudes, we cannot be sure of its extent, nor is it certain that business confidence would survive even a temporary failure of governmental attempts to reverse a downturn. We are even less sure about the resistive capacity of consumers. If job prospects become uncertain, consumers are likely to postpone purchases of durable goods, particularly purchases on installment. Today, a larger portion of consumer purchases fall into the category of "deferable" demand than twenty-five years ago. This may be one factor making for greater instability now as compared with the past, and it is not known whether this factor would be offset by the increase in the liquid assets of consumers and their responsiveness to better and cheaper products when they appear on the market. In sum, we may conclude that the American economy has gained greatly in stability but is still exposed to the danger of depression. And, any complacency on this score would knock out one of the main stabilizing factors—public confidence that the United States Government is committed and ready to act for the purpose of counteracting an economic downturn.

It is unnecessary to review here the arsenal of weapons actually or potentially available to the United States Government for combating a depression.[8] Properly used, they are adequate to exercise a powerful influence toward economic stability, and there are grounds for confidence that, if needed, they would be used to avoid major depression and mass unemployment. This confidence rests not only on the Federal Government's existing commitment and ability to adopt necessary measures. It rests equally on the expectation that business will be guided increasingly by the long-run prospects for the expansion of market opportunities and by the technological possibilities of our age rather than by the short-run fluctuations of markets. It should be emphasized, however, that these hopes will materialize only if the Federal Government prepares in time for the actions which might be needed. Such economic preparedness is, in effect, one of the conditions which would induce business to orient itself more toward longer-range prospects and away from the hopes and fears of the moment. In the Marxist view, the American private enterprise economy is bound to move through increasingly severe depressions to its own eventual self-destruction. Contrasted with this view is the American conviction that—though adjustments and fluctuations are inevitable in a free, dynamic society—we are in process of conquering the threat of severe depression and mass unemployment. This job is a far more difficult one in a free society with high levels of consumption than in a totalitarian society with low living standards, and it would be dangerous to assume that we have already mastered it. But the simple fact that avoiding mass unemployment has become one of the nation's prime objectives and is generally accepted without controversy provides ground for confidence that the United States will succeed in avoiding another major depression.

There is, however, more to the problem of maintaining demand than avoidance of major depressions. Demand cannot remain at static levels but must grow in order to utilize the growing capacity of the American

---

[8] For a recent discussion of means of preventing depression see *Defense Against Recession,* A Statement on National Policy by the Committee for Economic Development (New York, March 1954).

economy to produce. Over the next few years, the American labor force will be rising by not much less than 1 million workers annually. Each worker's output per manhour will also be rising by something on the order of $2\frac{1}{2}$ percent annually, and probably by more.[9] To the extent that Americans do not want to realize their increasing productivity in shorter hours of work—or cannot afford to do so because of the growing economic requirements of world leadership in the cold war—demand in the American economy must continue to expand in order to make full use of this growing capacity. Indeed, postwar experience suggests that the typical demand problem in the American economy for the next few years may not be preventing a major depression but supporting necessary economic expansion.

Inadequate growth is not, of course, nearly so serious a matter as depression. But quite apart from the human suffering and frustration and the economic waste involved, stagnation would be dangerous for a nation in our historical situation. It would retard growth of our total economic capacity—something we can hardly afford while the economic power of the Soviet bloc is growing so rapidly. Inadequate growth of demand would make it far more difficult for the United States to carry out an effective foreign economic policy. It would increase the political resistance to tariff cuts and other measures—such as expanded military "off-shore procurement"—which involve increased foreign competition for American manufactures. It would tend to increase the trading problem of Western Europe and Japan by improving the competitive strength of American manufactures at home and abroad and by retarding the growth of income generally in the trading world. It would give rise to demands by American exporters for special governmental assistance—e.g., "tied" export credits and other devices designed to improve by governmental action the competitive position of American products abroad.

For these and other reasons, American domestic employment policy should not be confined to economic stabilization or avoidance of severe depression. The objective should be to achieve a reasonably regular expansion of production and demand while avoiding strong inflationary pressure. Minor recessions cannot be avoided; they are probably a necessary accompaniment of rapid growth and technological change in a private enterprise economy, and to prevent them would probably re-

---

[9] See, e.g., Joint Committee on the Economic Report, *Potential Economic Growth of the United States During the Next Decade* (Washington, D.C., 1954), p. 7.

quire deliberate, continuing inflation. The essential thing is that employment policy be growth policy and not merely anti-depression policy. It is not possible to suggest here, even in broad outline, how this could be done.[10] Suffice it to say that our success or failure in maintaining an adequate growth of demand in the American economy is a major condition of progress in the economic integration of the Western Community and of the success of our foreign policy as a whole.

Facilitating Adjustment to Larger Imports

An adequate level of demand in the American economy will of itself facilitate the political task of opening the American market more effectively to the other industrial countries. The political acceptability of lower tariffs would also be increased by more specific measures to facilitate the adjustment of particular enterprises, groups of workers, and communities to increasing imports.

There are, broadly, two methods by which domestic producers could be helped to adjust to the effects of increased competition, whether arising from domestic sources or from imports. The first would be by direct payments to producers, either as continuing subsidies to enable them to remain in business, or as compensation for losses incurred by firms in liquidating their business and by workers in obtaining new employment. The second method would be by "depressed industries and communities programs" which would involve Federal support of local and state initiative in helping particular industries and communities to adjust to increased competition (whether from imports or domestic sources) so severe as to be beyond their capacity for self-adjustment without undesirable economic or social consequences.

Widespread direct Federal subsidies or compensation payments are definitely undesirable for a variety of reasons. Subsidies ostensibly given for the purpose of enabling an industry to continue operations for a transitional period while it adjusts to increased competition tend instead to be used indefinitely to offset the higher production costs of relatively uneconomic methods, thereby forestalling precisely those changes which the subsidy is supposed to facilitate. If the payments are intended to compensate for damage, major practical difficulties will be

---

[10] For some recent suggestions along these lines, see Report of the Steering Committee, *Opportunities for Economic Expansion* (Washington, D.C.: National Planning Association, 1954).

encountered in trying either to relate the loss of profits or assets to any single cause, or to measure the quantitative effects. For these reasons, it would be well to limit the use of direct subsidies to those industries which have to be maintained for national security purposes. Even in this case, however, the use of long-term purchase contracts would often be preferable. Where such contracts could not be used and a continuing direct subsidy is the only remaining means available, Federal subsidies could perhaps be better controlled if they were included in the Defense Department's budget, where they would be in competition with other military requirements.

The main reliance for facilitating adjustments to increased imports should be placed on programs for transforming depressed industries and communities. Generally speaking, such programs should originate at the local or state level and be supplemented by the Federal Government. The importance of local initiative and control should not be underestimated. Unless the people directly affected are willing and able to assume most of the responsibility for making necessary changes, there is little that can be done for them from the outside except indefinite subsidization—which only perpetuates their plight. It is clear, however, that in many cases local and state resources will be insufficient for the task of economic transformation or relocation. Several Federal agencies already have responsibilities and powers which are relevant to the problems involved in readjustment programs. But, local programs are now receiving very little active assistance from the Federal Government. In some cases, this is owed to lack of funds; in others, it results from inadequate interest and ingenuity on the part of the Federal agencies concerned. Even without a broadening of existing Federal functions, much more could be done to assist local programs than is now being undertaken by Federal agencies. In particular, there is need to establish within the Executive Branch an office with responsibility, and with sufficient authority and funds, to ensure that Federal powers are used effectively to encourage and support local and state initiative.

In addition to the provision of adequate unemployment benefits, there are various appropriate ways in which the Federal Government could assist local readjustment programs. Federal aid to local and state readjustment agencies could be provided in the form of grants for the retraining of labor; for meeting workers' costs of moving to new locations where employment is available; for investigating the possibilities of diversifying the industries of individual communities and regions;

and for research to improve technology and managerial skills. Federal loan funds might be made available to state and local development authorities for such purposes as the building of new plants and the modernization of old ones for sale or rental to private companies; the construction of needed transportation, power and other public facilities; etc. Finally, low interest Federal loan funds and accelerated amortization certificates might be given directly to business firms willing to undertake costly readaptations which would have a reasonable chance of making their operations profitable in the changed competitive situation.

The effectiveness of Federal support for such programs will depend directly upon the principles governing the use of Federal funds. Federal benefits available to private persons, state government organizations and local communities should generally be for the purpose of paying part of the cost of readjustment, and not as compensation for injury. Where benefits are granted, they should normally be contingent upon evidence that the readjustment is actually being made. Finally, the Federal Government should normally require the presentation of a plan or program developed on local initiative.

The development of long-term readjustment programs by depressed industries and communities, and adequate Federal assistance in carrying them out, will foster not only the growth and stability of the American economy but the foreign policy of the United States as well. In cases where the difficulties of a depressed industry or community result wholly or in part from changes in import policies, a vigorous readjustment program could provide the increment of energy and resources needed to make an affected domestic industry more efficient or to enable affected businessmen and workers to shift to other activities or locations. General recognition that the private groups and the local, state and Federal agencies concerned are capable of cooperating in the formulation and execution of such programs might help to mitigate the objections of many businessmen, workers and farmers to significant reductions in American import barriers.

American Military "Offshore Procurement" and Economic Aid

In view of the relatively narrow limits of what could be accomplished for Europe's economic growth by changes in American import policy, it is necessary to consider measures of a more direct kind to create the equivalent of dollar markets for European manufactures and to overcome the internal obstacles in Europe to an expansion of output for export. One action of this type by which the United States Government could help significantly to expand European industry and to ease Europe's dollar shortage is in fact already in use on a considerable scale—the "offshore procurement" of supplies and equipment from European industry by American military authorities for the American armed forces stationed in Europe and elsewhere abroad, and for the rearmament of our European allies. The importance of this dollar procurement activity for Western Europe's industry and balance of payments is shown by the fact that, in 1954, American offshore procurement expenditures in OEEC countries were equal to about 15 percent of their commercial exports of manufactures to other areas and to about 60 percent of their total dollar exports.

So far, however, these expenditures have been considered by the United States mainly as military procurements, secondarily as a substitute for direct dollar aid, and not at all as an instrument of long-range foreign economic policy. Indeed, off-shore procurement has been generally regarded as a purely temporary expedient. A change in concept is, therefore, needed. United States Government procurement for military purposes in Europe should be used to stimulate expansion of British and European heavy industry, in much the same way that American domestic military procurement serves that purpose at home in accordance with the industrial mobilization base concept. Since industrial Europe's trading opportunities cannot now be sufficiently expanded through ordinary commercial channels, special government action of this kind is a necessary supplement.[11]

This change in concept would be consistent with the realities of American military relations with Britain and continental Europe. So long as Soviet imperialism is a serious challenge to the West, that relationship should be maintained. It is now, and should continue to be, a partnership to which the United States regularly makes a large contribution out of its own military budget. Why should not a part—a larger part than at present—of that contribution take the form of continuing

---

[11] American military stockpiling purchases of materials produced in European colonies and the Sterling Area also serve the function of increasing Western Europe's dollar receipts and help indirectly to expand overseas markets for European and Japanese manufactures. Proposals concerning stockpiling policy are made in the following chapter.

procurement of military supplies and equipment in Europe? Such procurement need not only be for European rearmament and for the American forces in Europe, but might also be for American forces in other parts of the world. Moreover, why should not that contribution involve some financing of plant expansion in Europe both for producing finished armaments and necessary components and for strengthening the basic European industries which are ultimately the source of industrial war potential as well as of more rapid economic growth? In short, the necessity of large continuing American military outlays for the defense of the Western Community should be used abroad—as it is in the United States—to stimulate the industrial expansion which is one of the essential sources of military strength.

The complex questions of means involved in this shift in the objective and scale of American military expenditures in Europe cannot be discussed here in any detail. Three points should, however, be noted. First, the change in concept and purpose of offshore procurement would need to be made explicit. Second, the program would have to be given the same kind of continuity as the American domestic military and mobilization base program. Otherwise there would be lacking the calculability of future demand on which a vigorous response of European enterprise to the stimulus provided by American procurement and special financing would depend. Third, there would be need for close coordination of military procurement and mobilization base activities in Britain, continental Europe and the United States. Coordination would be necessary to ensure that American procurement and financing activities were used in ways best calculated to serve not only short-run military and balance-of-payments purposes but also the long-term expansion of European industry, while keeping production of the most strategically important weapons safely located.

Important as this change in concept would be for Western Europe, it would be even more important for Japan. As explained in Chapter 3, Japanese industry and Japan's balance of payments are uniquely dependent on American "special procurement." In 1952 and 1953, such American procurement in Japan for various military purposes was more than two-thirds as large as Japan's total commercial exports. The level has declined substantially in the past year, with unfortunate results for Japanese industrial expansion and Japan's balance of payments. For the foreseeable future, the rate of Japanese industrial growth will depend in large measure on the size of American expenditures of this or similar kinds. Japan's opportunity to participate in regional economic integration is very considerably less than Western Europe's. Hence, a long-range American offshore procurement policy in Japan, similar to that sketched above for Western Europe, is—relative to Japanese economic needs and prospects—of even greater importance than in Western Europe. By this means, Japanese industry should be enabled to fill a substantial part of the needs of Asian defense, particularly as SEATO requirements expand.

The continuation of military offshore procurement on a large scale in Western Europe and Japan, together with other dollar outlays incident to the stationing of American troops abroad, should very largely obviate the need for further economic aid of the traditional type to these countries, except in possible future emergencies. This is fortunate because "aid," especially "economic aid," has become a negative political symbol in the United States and in Western Europe.

The negative reaction to economic aid is in part justified and in part the result of confusion about the nature and purposes of such aid.[12] The term "aid" has two distinct meanings which are often confused, not only in ordinary discourse but also in policy-making. In one sense, the term "aid" means any transfer of economic resources by the United States Government to other countries for any purpose other than payment of an obligation, and regardless of whether the transfer takes the form of a loan or a grant, money or commodities, technical services or military equipment. In the second and more restricted sense, such a transfer of resources is "aid" only if it is strictly unilateral and nothing material and specific is received in return—that is, only if it involves no element of mutuality, bargain or *quid pro quo*. In this second sense, a loan would not be "aid," but a grant would be considered "aid" unless it were given in exchange for some specific benefit to the United States, or as part of some mutually beneficial arrangement (e.g., as a contribution to a joint military program). The failure to distinguish between the first and second meanings of aid—between aid in an economic sense and aid in a moral and legal sense—has been a fruitful source of confusion.

Aid in the sense of voluntary charity, without mutuality, cannot by its nature be a continuing feature of the relationships between countries

[12] See, for example, the discussion of aid policy in the Randall Commission's Report, *op. cit.,* Ch. 6, and the analysis of the Commission's confusion on this subject in K. Knorr and G. Patterson, *A Critique of the Randall Commission Report, op. cit.,* pp. 34–41.

which consider themselves in some sense as equals. In such circumstances, the relation between the giver and receiver of charity is almost inevitably corrupted if unduly prolonged. The donor country comes to think of itself as morally superior and to expect recognition in the form of overt demonstrations of gratitude. The recipient country soon resents its dependent status and, in defense of its self-respect, will often tend to act as though it had a right to aid as a matter of economic justice. In turn, the donor will resent this presumption and will generally conclude that it is being "exploited." Unfortunately, we have seen such attitudes developing in the United States and in other countries in the last few years. It is, therefore, sound policy to terminate aid which has this character as rapidly as possible and to confine its future use to emergency situations where it can be politically justified as a temporary measure in the national interest, or morally justified as an act of spontaneous humanity.

But this conclusion does not mean that all economic aid should be brought to an end, except for temporary emergencies. Quite the contrary. Aid of the economic type remains one of the most effective and flexible tools of foreign policy possessed by the United States. Hence, we must not deprive ourselves of its use by confusing it with charity. Where it is possible to obtain important results beneficial to the United States by the transfer of resources to other Western countries, and where such transfers can be made psychologically and morally acceptable to both parties by including an element of mutuality in the relationship, then, clearly, aid is a useful and morally valid tool of policy. The practical meaning of this principle is that the element of specific mutuality should be present in all future aid transactions, except those of an emergency character. This will often mean the use of the loan form rather than the grant form. Nevertheless, there will sometimes be situations where grants can be justified; for example, in order to dispose of surplus agricultural commodities abroad and as contributions to joint military undertakings, such as the NATO military program. What is needed is a flexible approach under which the specific form of aid best suited to the actual purpose at hand can be employed. A doctrinaire approach—which regards loans as intrinsically good and grants as inherently bad even if they involve mutuality—restricts too narrowly the effectiveness of this technique of foreign economic policy.

As progress is made toward the closer economic integration of the West outlined in this and the preceding chapter, it would be advisable to channel as large a part as possible of American military and economic aid through existing and new international institutions, European and Atlantic. This would continue a practice already begun in the cases of the EPU and the European Coal and Steel Community, and would help to provide existing and new regional organizations with the resources needed for successful operations and to strengthen their prestige and bargaining power *vis-à-vis* their member national governments. In time, we may hope, the need for large-scale transfers of American economic resources will diminish with the growth of Europe's unified strength in place of its present divided weakness.

Strengthening the Organization of the Western Community

In this and in the preceding chapter, a number of suggestions have been made which involve cooperation among Western countries on a new range of economic problems. Some of the proposals would also require formal international treaties and agreements which imply the creation of international agencies among Western countries. The existing organizational arrangements of the Western Community—the North Atlantic Treaty Organization (NATO) and the Organization for European Economic Cooperation (OEEC)—are not now adequate to serve these new purposes. The economic activities of the NATO have been confined narrowly to negotiations concerning the economic capabilities of member countries to make military expenditures. The OEEC has been concerned very largely with intra-European questions. It has had no jurisdiction over problems of trade policy involving non-European countries outside the Sterling Area. Although they participate as associate members, Canada and the United States are not full members of the OEEC and there has been no provision for bringing in other non-European countries, such as Australia and Japan, as appropriate. For these reasons, it would be desirable to make certain changes in the existing Atlantic machinery to enable it better to serve these additional economic purposes by providing a place to negotiate about them and an organizational framework to which to attach new economic functions.

One method would be to change the OEEC into an Organization for Atlantic Economic Cooperation. This could be done simply by adding the United States and Canada to the OEEC as full members and changing its name to signify the broadened scope of its interest. Some other non-European countries, such as the southern Dominions, Japan and certain Latin American nations, could be associated with it for activities of particular concern to them. The Atlantic Trade and Payments Committee, proposed in Chapter 7, would be an integral part of such an Organization for Atlantic Economic Cooperation and could also appropriately absorb the functions of the permanent GATT Committee.[13] Many different kinds of negotiations on substantive economic policy and on policy coordination could be conducted within this new Atlantic-wide framework. Such a development would be particularly advantageous to the United States in that it would permit our great economic bargaining power to be used comprehensively and, hence, more effectively. It would avoid much of the present piecemeal handling of closely related international economic problems in a variety of different and unconnected negotiations and agencies. For example, an Organization for Atlantic Economic Cooperation would provide the organizational framework for the kind of comprehensive negotiations on tariffs and other economic policies suggested above. Led by the United States and Britain, an Organization for Atlantic Economic Cooperation would be in fact, if not in name, a kind of economic "high command" for the Western Community and for most of the free world.

These practical considerations are not the only reason for favoring formal American participation in an Organization for Atlantic Economic Cooperation. As a symbol of Western unification, this action would also have considerable political and psychological value. It would point far beyond itself to an emerging Western political and economic Community. At present, that goal is expressed by the idea of an Atlantic Community, the geographical and historical heart of the West. But the Atlantic Community idea is still a weak symbol, with but little power to attract the loyalty of Europeans and Americans, because it has now so little concrete institutional content, and such content as it has is largely military. An Organization for Atlantic Economic Cooperation would add content of a more positive character, symbolizing as it would the permanence of economic cooperation between Europe and the United States.

---

[13] The General Agreement on Tariffs and Trade (GATT) would also require amendment, or at least reinterpretation, to bring its philosophy into line with the conception of the economic organization of the Western Community and the free world sketched in Chapters 7, 8 and 9.

A start, too, could now be made in providing some political, as well as economic, content to the Atlantic Community symbol. Perhaps the most practicable and useful way of doing this would be to carry out recent proposals for an Atlantic Consultative Assembly similar to—and possibly growing out of—the existing Consultative Assembly of the Council of Europe.[14] The proposed Atlantic Assembly would consist of delegations appointed by national legislatures from among their own members. The Assembly would meet at regular intervals to discuss common economic, political and defense problems of the Western Community and, when appropriate, to make recommendations regarding them to the governments of member states.

The importance of providing some positive economic and political content to the symbol of a unified Atlantic or Western Community has not been adequately grasped by American policy-makers. That the meaning of particular policies is not exhausted by their practical results has been a recurring theme of this study. Indeed, the practical results may be of relatively minor significance compared to their symbolic importance. One of the weaknesses of an excessively pragmatic approach to foreign policy is its obliviousness to the energizing value of symbolic representations of longer-range goals. The improved organizational arrangements proposed in this study for the Western Community would have the value not only of their more immediate and tangible results. They would have the greater value of symbolizing in a living form the basic concern of the peoples of the West for closer unity in the face of mounting challenges, internal and external.

These, then, would be appropriate next steps in the political and eco-

---

[14] This suggestion has had considerable support in recent years not only among influential sections of the American public but in the Congress as well. The Study Group's own suggestions for improved organizational arrangements within the Western Community are quite similar to those contained in a "Declaration of Atlantic Unity" by prominent citizens of the United States, Canada, Britain and continental Western Europe. See *New York Times,* October 4, 1954. The Declaration proposed: "(a) Development of NATO as a central agency to coordinate the political, trade and defense policies of the member nations; (b) Elaboration of a comprehensive mutual program for lowering tariffs, freeing currencies and eliminating trade restrictions, so that an adequate economic basis may be established for the Atlantic Community and associated nations; (c) Establishment by the legislatures of each of the member governments of a legislative committee to promote further organization of NATO within that country; (d) Creation of an advisory Atlantic Assembly, representative of the legislatures of the member nations, which would meet periodically to discuss matters of concern; and (e) Establishment by NATO of an Economic Advisory Council."

nomic organization of the Western Community. Can anything concrete be said about the longer-run goal of Western unification toward which they point?

Among those concerned with longer-range objectives, there are numerous advocates of an Atlantic Union—a federal union of the West—as the fully adequate answer to the West's economic and political problems. A federal union of the Atlantic Community would indeed be a formidable economic and political unit. With a population of some 400 million, with the combined industry and industrial growth potential of Britain, Western Europe and North America, and with the great agricultural resources of the latter, such a union of the West would create an economy fully adequate to satisfy the claims and requirements on it, and a polity able to overcome the West's internal disorder and to meet its external dangers. Voluntary Western union along federal lines would likewise be a morally valid solution of the problem of creating central political authority in the Western Community. But it is not likely to be a relevant goal of official American policy for the foreseeable future.

Understood symbolically, the Atlantic Union idea is valuable because it expresses dramatically an important truth—namely, that the weakness and the disunity of the West logically and ideally demand a solution which is both supranational and constitutional. But if taken literally as a goal of policy, it may be, like so many other comprehensive schemes for political change, illusory. Transformations in social attitudes and institutions, however radical, are never merely artifacts of reason imposed on the stuff of history by a creative act of will. (Not even the Philadelphia convention of 1787, from which came the Constitution of the United States, and which is often cited in this connection, was a pure act of rational will.) Human reason and creativity can indeed transcend any given historical context, but they cannot leap clear of it into a realm of pure freedom; they can only use existing interests and social forces gradually to reform existing institutions in the light of new concepts. In revolutionary situations, the limits of possible changes are much broader than usual owing primarily to the abandonment of customary moral restraints. But even then, though the new in history may more quickly transcend and often destroy the old, it is nevertheless continuous with the old, emerging organically from it, not leaping too far ahead of it. However abstractly necessary or desirable, reforms of the existing political and economic organization of the Western Community cannot reach very far ahead of present interests and felt needs, particularly if they are to be achieved by morally valid means. There is, to be sure, far more realism in the Atlantic Union idea than in projects for World Federation. The former at least relates to an existing international community with real historical roots which already senses a need for greater political unity. But the idea of a voluntary federal union of the West—desirable as it might be—seems to be too far removed from present economic and political interests to be other than the attractive symbol of an ideal—a general direction rather than a specific goal.

This conclusion applies particularly to the situation of the United States. There is now far too little mutuality of economic interest in an Atlantic Union as between Britain and continental Europe on the one hand, and the United States on the other. Europe needs America economically far more than America needs Europe. Free and secure access to the American market, a high level of American capital outflow to industrial Europe and its dependent overseas territories, the stimulus to European industry of American technology and of the participation of American enterprise— all these essentials of Europe's economic health could be made fully available by an Atlantic political and economic Union. But such economic benefits as an Atlantic Union might reciprocally provide the United States are not now urgently needed. The American economy is itself a continental economy. It does not need to join with others in a regional grouping—within which trade and payments are relatively free of restrictions—in order to enjoy good economic health. Its economic growth still depends only marginally on expanding foreign trade. The competitive strength of its industrial exports and its ability to finance a continuing export surplus give it the foreign markets and supplies it needs either automatically or by unilateral action of the United States Government.

Indeed, the economic case for Atlantic Union from an American standpoint is actually weaker than the foregoing considerations indicate. What industrial Europe, especially Britain, needs is free and secure—but at the same time largely unilateral—access to the American market, while the more vulnerable sectors of the European economies retain a considerable measure of tariff or other protection against American competition. For, the full impact of American competition within an Atlantic free trade area would, at least in the short run, create widespread unemployment and entrepreneurial demoralization in Europe. Over the longer term, it might rob much of European industry of any opportunity for future growth and whole industries and industrial areas might stagnate or fall into chronic depression. Thus, to make free trade in an Atlantic Union consistent with Europe's economic health would probably require massive migration from Europe to North America. In contrast, unilateral free trade within an Atlantic Union would probably mean some sacrifice of our own rate of growth and certainly some serious readjustment problems —much more serious than would be occasioned merely by liberalization of the American tariff with national sovereignty left intact. Large-scale immigration from Europe would entail even more serious adjustment problems here. Neither of these alternatives would have much appeal to the United States. In short, the gross differences between Europe and America in density of population, vigor of enterprise, competitive power, economic institutions and external dependence make the kind of Atlantic Union which might be acceptable to Western Europe, and adequate to solve its economic problems, quite unattractive to Americans.

Present political considerations lead to a similar conclusion. The discrepancy between the United States and Europe in material power, in the feeling of responsibility for the security of the free world against communist imperialism, and in the sense of having a positive mission in the world, would make voluntary Atlantic Union on federal lines unattractive to the United States, and probably inconsistent with the security of the West for some time to come. The creation of a federal union in which the United States could be outvoted (or nearly so) by the other members would involve an increase of their power, but a sharp diminution of American power and freedom of action. Thus, it would entail the serious risk of paralyzing the political will of the West during a period in which such paralysis could mean the end of Western civilization. Considerable American freedom of action is now essential to the security and progress of the West and of the whole free world. This is not because we Americans are individually or collectively wiser, more farsighted, or more moral than our Western allies. Probably we are not. But material power, responsibility to decide and act, and a sense of positive mission must all be joined together, or the result is paralysis and drift.

Doubts of the desirability and feasibility of Atlantic Union in the foreseeable future need not, however, detract from its value as a symbol of the general direction in which the Western Community ought to move in the coming years. Atlantic Union may not be a relevant goal of policy for the United States Government, but it is nonetheless a legitimate end to be proposed by private citizens, individually and collectively. Perhaps, in time, their efforts and the turn of events may combine to make it a practicable, as well as a desirable, possibility.

Though it is probably illusory to project a blueprint of Atlantic Union as the answer, in any but a symbolic sense, to the West's political and economic problems, it is nevertheless possible to discern a direction of development for Western organization which is both politically feasible and relevant to these problems. That direction of movement is already implicit in the existing pattern of cooperation among the Western governments. Its further development will have to be guided by two principles.

The first is that the United States is the main source of leadership for the unification of the West and American power provides the principal means of unification—i.e., of coordinating national policies. This has clearly been true in the past. When American initiative and ideas have been adequate, there has been progress in the political and economic integration of the West; when they have been inadequate, there has been drift and disintegration. The same is likely to be true in the future. No supranational center of power and leadership for the West can now be—or is likely soon to be—created and the United States is the only Western country with the material and psychological resources to substitute for it. To put it another way, the progressive unification of the Western Community will depend upon the progressive extension of American influence, power and responsibility within and on behalf of the Atlantic Community. Whether the United States will accept this role, and whether Americans can define their aims in terms which will evoke the willing cooperation of other Western nations, are questions to be considered in the final chapter of this study.

A second and contrasting principle is that American leadership will be acceptable to the European nations only if they are able to counterbalance to some extent the disproportionate power of the United States by the creation of regional economic and political groupings which do not include the United States. This principle is implicit in the concept of the economic organization of the Western Community which underlies the Sterling Area, the OEEC-EPU grouping, and the policies recommended in this and the preceding chapters. It is expressed even more clearly in the European union movement. Without the united strength provided by these groupings, the separate European countries would individually confront the disproportionate economic power and political influence of the United States on such unequal terms as to inhibit the growth of mutual trust and cooperation. When disparities of power are too great, they prevent the growth of community among nations, as among individuals and groups within a nation. This principle is one of the essentials of constitutionalism. It is as relevant to relations between the United States and Europe as it is, for example, to relations among business, labor and farmers within our national community. It is for this reason that, despite the setback entailed by the defeat of the European Defense Community proposal, some form of European political and economic union must continue to be a central objective of Western policy for Europeans and Americans alike.

It is noteworthy that these two principles of Western unification are complementary and interdependent. The progressive organization of the West depends on the exercise of American economic and political power. But if that power is to be acceptable to the European nations—if it is to be leadership rather than domination—it must be counterbalanced by strengthening the institutions of European unity and creating—if, and as soon as, possible—a supranational European union. Conversely, European unification depends upon progress in the unification of the Atlantic Community as a whole—that is, upon the willingness of the United States to take measures, such as those already suggested, which involve it ever closer in European affairs. Europeans know that a European union, valuable as it would be, would still not be strong enough to be independent—militarily or economically—of assistance by the United States. Nor could a European union ensure an internal balance of power between France and Germany, or guarantee preservation of constitutional democracy, without continuous close support of the United States. Unification on both levels—the European and the Atlantic—must move together or not at all.

The main lines of American action today—as distinct from conscious doctrine—are consistent in their general trend with the direction of development defined by these principles. The measures we have recommended in this and the preceding chapters carry that same trend forward, as far as foreign economic policy is concerned, another step or two. Yet American policy-making has hitherto given little evidence of conscious recognition of this direction of movement. Obsolete ways of thinking still obscure the needs of the West for the exercise of American organizing power. Policy-makers still too often seem to ignore the implications for policy of the gross disparity between American military and economic power and that of other Western countries. The lack of a conscious sense of direction in its political and economic policies is a luxury that the West can no longer afford. It is time that the West, and especially the United States, became more conscious of where it is going, and found ways to symbolize its purposes more adequately and to pursue them with less intellectual confusion and more moral energy. A proper sense of direction and a clear understanding of its necessity and urgency are the qualities most urgently required to improve the effectiveness of American leadership of the Western world.

9

Economic Development Policy

—

The two preceding chapters have sketched the measures which the other industrial countries and the United States might take, jointly and singly, to improve the economic health of the Western nations and the efficiency and calculability of their mutual economic relationships. We must now consider the steps which might be taken to make the economic relationships between the industrial countries, on the one hand, and the independent underdeveloped nations, on the other, more satisfactory to both parties. The necessary steps are indicated by the phrase "economic development policy," which is a shorthand expression for those foreign economic policies and activities of the United States, and of the other Western nations, which are intended to influence the growth of production and incomes in the underdeveloped countries and to expand their trade with the industrial countries. These are matters in which both the industrial and the underdeveloped countries have major economic interests.

The nature of these economic interests is made clear by the analysis in Part I. From the economic standpoint, Western Europe and Japan are concerned with the underdeveloped areas primarily as expanding sources of supply of primary products and as growing markets for manufactured goods. The independent underdeveloped countries are economically interested in the Western nations and Japan mainly as sources of capital and technology and as stable markets for their exported primary products. As noted in Chapter 6, these economic interests conflict to a considerable extent—particularly over the terms of trade between the two regions, the conditions governing governmental and private investment by the industrial nations in the underdeveloped countries, and the relative emphasis placed by the latter on industrial development as compared with the growth of primary production.

Nevertheless, the economic interests of the two groups of countries also contain the elements of a mutually advantageous economic relationship—i.e., the exchange of Western development capital and technology for an adequate supply of primary products from the underdeveloped countries. But to realize such a relationship requires two types of mutual concessions—those in the field of foreign investment, governmental and private; and those affecting stabilization of international demand for primary products. The aim of American policy is to achieve concessions of these two kinds. In the field of public and private investment, the task is to determine (a) what could and should be done by the United States (and the other industrial countries) to increase and regularize the flow of private and governmental capital and technology to the underdeveloped countries; and (b) what could and should be done to induce the underdeveloped countries to take the complementary steps necessary to encourage private investment, and to make foreign governmental investment and technical assistance more effective. Similarly, in the field of commodity trade, the task is to decide what the United States could and should be doing to help stabilize international demand, and to induce the underdeveloped countries to expand their primary production at an adequate rate.

Accordingly, this chapter is concerned with American policies and activities directed toward these two objectives. The first section deals with measures for stimulating private American investment in the underdeveloped countries; the second section discusses the investment and technical assistance programs undertaken by the United States Government directly and through the medium of international organizations; and the third section explores possible arrangements for international commodity stabilization.

The fact that measures of these kinds are discussed in a chapter devoted to the underdeveloped areas does not imply that private American investment in the other industrial countries and international commodity stabilization are unimportant to Western Europe and Japan. Quite the contrary. These activities would also benefit them directly, as well as indirectly through their effects on the underdeveloped countries. But they are not the sole, or even the most important, means for improving the economic health of the other industrial nations, and they would supplement the institutional and other measures for Western economic integration discussed in the two preceding chapters. In contrast, the types of measures considered below constitute the principal—indeed, the only —feasible economic means available to the United States for influencing the policies and actions of the independent underdeveloped countries.

Private Capital Investment

While the importance of a large flow of private investment funds from the industrial countries to the underdeveloped areas is generally recognized, the reasons for its importance are not always as well understood. As a means for achieving the objectives both of the underdeveloped countries and of the West, private foreign investment is generally superior in two respects (noted below) to the investment of funds through governmental or international agencies. To realize these advantages, however, private investment cannot take the form of short-term speculative ventures from which, it is hoped, profits greater than the original investment could be withdrawn after a few years, and often the capital itself repatriated soon after. Its benefits—as well as its own security—can be achieved only if its purpose is the management of an indefinitely continuing operation, and a significant percentage of its profits are reinvested year after year either in the expansion and improvement of the original enterprise or in new activities within the recipient country.

First, direct private investment of the latter kind is capable of building relationships between the industrial and the underdeveloped countries which are organic and continuous. It usually involves relations between people, not governments; relations which become integral parts of the economic and social fabric of the recipient country. It normally carries with it the technical knowledge which is as sorely needed in the underdeveloped areas as are capital funds. Such continuous, and often cumulative, transfers of capital and technology under private auspices are much more likely to result in durable capital assets and permanently absorbed technological innovations in the underdeveloped countries than are publicly financed investment and intergovernmental technical assistance programs with their necessarily limited scope and short-term character.

Second, direct, long-term, private investment fosters in various ways the growth within the underdeveloped countries of a constructive middle class and habits of private, decentralized decision-making and enterprise. As explained in Chapter 5, both the cultural backgrounds of many of these countries and the nature of the internal difficulties and external threats which they now face are strongly conducive to centralization of initiative, decision-making and control in authoritarian governments. If liberal values compatible with those of the West, and indigenous institutions capable of realizing them, are ever to evolve in Asia, Africa and Latin America, it is necessary for alternative modes of choice and action to be increasingly available within these societies. By precept and example, as well as by actually involving growing numbers of local people in privately directed economic activities, private foreign investment can help to foster democratic patterns of decision and action in the underdeveloped countries.[1]

These "qualitative" advantages of private investment abroad tend to be underestimated, while its supposed "quantitative" effects are generally exaggerated.[2] The argument is often heard, for example, that an expansion of private foreign investment would make possible a proportional decrease in the amount of capital transfers among governments. To the extent that new private investment provided scarce currencies previously unavailable except as loans or grants from foreign governments, the argument would seem to have validity. However, offsetting factors would also operate. Governmental funds invested abroad in recent years, either directly or through international organizations, have been largely limited to the fields of transportation, communications, water control, and power generation. Private foreign investment, which typically occurs in the production and distribution of goods and services, would have only an indirect influence on the expansion of these activities. Indeed, the greater the amount of private investment in production and distribution, the

---

[1] To achieve benefits of these kinds, private capital must act in a socially responsible manner. Most American business firms operating abroad have long since recognized the value of this principle both for the profitability and security of their foreign investments and for the advancement of the recipient countries. For examples see *Case Studies of American Business Performance Abroad* (Washington, D.C.: National Planning Association, 1952 to date).

[2] This tendency is strikingly evident in the Report of the Randall Commission, where the qualitative benefits of private investment are dismissed in a brief sentence and much stress is placed on the dubious argument that increased private foreign investment would be a major factor in overcoming the dollar shortage. See Commission on Foreign Economic Policy, *Report, op. cit.,* pp. 16–17.

greater might be the eventual need for additional transportation, communications, and power facilities, and possibly, therefore, for increased loans and grants from foreign governments or international organizations.[3]

The view is also widely held that an expansion of private foreign investment would help to eliminate the tendency to dollar shortage of the other non-Soviet countries. Here, again, an important qualification must be made. The relatively small current flow of private foreign investment usually involves as much, if not more, capital equipment exports than actual dollar expenditures abroad. Thus, only private capital investment which provided new supplies of scarce currencies would contribute in the short term to mitigation of exchange imbalances. But this short-term effect may not be as large as is generally believed, for private investors seek a maximum of security and are more than likely to look for investment opportunities in countries with currencies already strong. The long-term effect of private investment on payments problems would, however, tend to be significant to the extent that such investment helped —directly or indirectly—to expand production for export at prices that could compete effectively in world markets. Again, this long-run result may not be as large as anticipated because amortization charges, interest, and dividend payments gradually catch up with, and may eventually exceed, the annual volume of new capital exports unless the latter also continues to expand indefinitely.[4]

On balance, then, the influence of private foreign investment on the character and rate of economic and social development abroad appears to be much more important than its clearly demonstrable consequences for payments problems. As a practical matter, the expansion of private foreign investment possible in the foreseeable future would probably be large enough to make an important contribution to economic growth;

---

[3] It is true that successful expansion of private business activities would itself generate capital which, under appropriate inducements, might be attracted to the fields that are now typically provided with capital funds by governments. But this is a long-term result, and does not have the immediate effect of diminishing the need for investment assistance by foreign governments. It follows that, in present circumstances, only in a somewhat tenuous long-term sense is private foreign investment important as a means of diminishing governmental investment.

[4] Indeed, the United States has been for the past quarter of a century a "mature creditor" in the sense that annual earnings from private long-term foreign investments have exceeded the annual net outflow of American private long-term capital. With new petroleum investments now declining and income from existing investments rising, the difference— in present circumstances—is certain to grow substantially in the decade ahead. The follow-

but, it is also likely to be too small to have much of an effect upon international payments problems, one way or the other.

In recent years, private American investment abroad has been mainly for two purposes—the extraction and refining of oil and other minerals, and the establishment of manufacturing or assembling facilities in foreign countries to provide products for markets previously supplied by finished exports from the United States. Since World War II, almost 70 percent of direct private American investment abroad has been in petroleum extracting, refining and distributing facilities.[5] Of the remainder, more than three-quarters has been invested in Canada and Latin Amer-

---

ing figures show the extent to which American income from private long-term investment abroad has exceeded new private foreign investment in the postwar years, and a projection of the present trend for 1962:

	American Private Long-Term Foreign Investments (Net of Repayments) [a]	American Income from Private Long-Term Foreign Investments [a]	Resulting Net Inflow of Funds into United States
	(millions of dollars)		
1945	454	569	115
1946	59	784	725
1947	810	1070	260
1948	748	1260	512
1949	796	1296	500
1950	1168	1624	456
1951	963	1789	826
1952	831	1615	784
1953	517	1649	1132
1962 (Proj.)	1100	3850	2750

[a] Not including reinvested earnings. If reinvested earnings were included, both income and investment figures would be raised by the same amounts. The differences between them would be unaffected.

Source: 1945–53, United States Department of Commerce. 1962 projection, United States Department of State, Intelligence Report No. 5911, *The Long-Term Outlook for the Supply of U.S. Dollars,* March 10, 1953.

[5] The heavy concentration of American private investment in the petroleum field may not be conducive to the optimum use of resources from the standpoint of balanced and more evenly distributed development opportunities. But, it has a major potential significance for the economic future of those countries fortunate enough to possess petroleum resources. With known reserves of nearly 40 billion barrels—and unexplored reserves probably more than double that quantity—the Moslem countries have an immense prospective income which could be devoted to economic and social development. Their capacity to realize the potential benefits of this resource depends directly upon their degree of political development. A major objective of Western policy in the oil-rich underdeveloped countries is to assist their political evolution so that they will be able to realize more of the potential benefits of their natural resources.

ica. Thus, only some 8 percent of total direct private American investment has gone into activities other than petroleum in Western Europe,
Africa, Oceania and non-communist Asia. So-called "portfolio" investments—the purchase by Americans in the major security markets of the
world of newly-issued bonds or stocks of foreign companies or governments—have been practically non-existent in the postwar years.[6]

Though the importance of private foreign investment for economic
growth has come to be more widely recognized in the United States
and abroad, an expansion in its volume and scope is not likely to occur
automatically. The major economic and political obstacles to such expansion include the poor economic health of many national economies,
the incalculability of the international economy, the cold war, and the
profound social transformation of the underdeveloped countries. These
factors lie at the roots of most of the specific deterrents to private investment which postwar discussions of the subject have made familiar.
So long as the underlying difficulties persist, private foreign investment is
likely to be restricted in volume and range of activities, and incentive
measures designed to overcome symptomatic deterrents will have limited,
though useful, effects.

The immediately apparent obstacles to an expansion of private foreign
investment are broadly of two kinds—those arising from competitive uses
of capital and those unduly enhancing risks. The most important competition with which private American investment abroad has had to
contend has been the alternative opportunities for investment at home.[7]

---

[6] Old issues outstanding for many years are still traded, but there has been little or no
new capital export by this means since the early '30s. Yet the revival of portfolio investment would be worthwhile, for it is a possible method whereby large indirect private investors could be tapped, e.g. institutional investors such as insurance companies, the increasingly important investment trusts, etc. Indeed, some of the projects now dependent on
public lending might be financed in this manner. This is also the logical device by which
"multiple country" foreign investment might be stimulated—for example, a flow of private
capital from the United States through the United Kingdom or Japan to the underdeveloped
areas. An obvious advantage of this indirect flow would be the primary endorsement of the
initial borrower.

[7] The only important deterrent effect on private foreign investment of large-scale investment of United States Government funds abroad is that it gives rise to misunderstanding
of what is a reasonable return commensurate with risks. However, the specific purposes for
which governmental investment has taken place have not been seriously competitive with
the development of production and distribution facilities—the typical field for private investment. It is hard to be certain whether the governments of the underdeveloped countries
would have behaved with more or less rectitude if United States Government grants and
loans had been unavailable to them; or whether there might not even have been some improvement in their attitude toward new private investment, as well as in their compliance

The Western world has lived under a sustained period of full or nearly full employment of productive resources for a decade and a half. Returns on domestic investment, while not extravagant, have seemed quite satisfactory to American businessmen when measured against alternative returns available from foreign investment—and the risks, needless to say, have been far smaller. The greatest obstacles to increased private investment abroad have been the high risks—over and above those traditionally considered to be normal business risks—which the private investor, corporate or individual, recognizes as entailed in the commitment of capital funds in most parts of the world today. Where these new 20th-century risks have not been evident, as in Canada, there has been a large and continuing investment of private capital from the United States. But elsewhere in the non-Soviet world, three kinds of deterrents have tended to impress themselves increasingly upon potential private investors—political risks, the risks of war and civil disorder, and the risks arising from the incalculability and restrictiveness of the contemporary international economy.

It is sometimes argued that any measures taken by capital-exporting countries to reduce the deterrent effects of these 20th-century risks would only serve to weaken the incentives of the underdeveloped countries to facilitate an improvement in the "climate" of investment. But, at bottom, the problem is not a matter of a given minimum of encouragement which is provided less by the capital-importing country if the capital-exporting country provides more. It is a matter of finding ways and means whereby both types of countries can take steps to mitigate the deterrents inhibiting international private investment. This is because the measures which capital-exporting countries could adopt to stimulate the outflow of private capital would be of very limited usefulness unless they were matched by a substantial lessening of the hostility in many capital-importing countries to private foreign investment. Granted the profound economic and social transformation through which the underdeveloped countries

---

with existing contracts with old private investors, as a result of the prospect of greater American assistance if they could demonstrate more satisfactory behavior. It must be acknowledged that American grants and loans to the underdeveloped countries have in part been brought about by the unwillingness of private capital either to accept necessarily large risks, incommensurate with any probable returns, or to undertake development work where no returns at all could reasonably be expected. In general, both United States Government agencies and international organizations like the International Bank for Reconstruction and Development have scrupulously attempted to avoid competition with private capital in fields which would be legitimate and attractive for private investors.

are now passing, and their current phase of irresponsible nationalism, it is probably too much to expect that most of them would be able or willing to provide strong positive encouragement for private foreign investors. But, at the least, they will have to reduce significantly their deterrents, particularly those of recent origin—the various forms of legal, fiscal and economic discrimination against foreign business firms, the threat of expropriation and civil disorder, undue restrictions on repatriation of earnings and capital, etc.—if private investment is to be increased to its presently practicable limits.

For this reason, the strategy of economic development policy must be to induce as many as possible of the underdeveloped countries to help mitigate the factors now making the climate for private foreign investment so unfavorable. The things which the underdeveloped countries desire from the United States and from the other industrial countries— governmental investment funds, technical assistance, commodity stabilization arrangements, etc.—can certainly be offered in exchange for measures which would reduce the discrimination against, and the abnormal risks of, private investment in those regions. It will, however, take considerable skill and patience to carry out such a policy in the present state of the underdeveloped countries.

As part of this strategy, there are a number of measures which the capital-exporting nations, particularly the United States, could adopt on their own account to provide greater incentives for private capital exports. The advantages and disadvantages of the steps which the United States might unilaterally undertake are briefly indicated here.

In recent years, there has been considerable discussion—but little use made—of United States Government guarantees covering various kinds of risks in private foreign investment. Risks arising out of currency inconvertibility or of expropriation actions can now be covered in the United States with existing legislation. But little avail has been made of these possibilities by American investors. Some believe that this arises from the fact that war and civil disorder risks are not covered, and that the costs of these guarantees are unavoidably too high. It may be that if additional risks were covered, and if the guarantees were made available to old investments as well as new, the costs could be reduced and the arrangement would be more widely used.[8]

---

[8] It is well to recall, however, that capital is by nature timid, and the existence of the necessity for a guarantee is itself a recognition and constant reminder of the factors which would make a new investor hesitant to commit his funds abroad. A guarantee against un-

Tax measures are probably the most effective devices available to the United States Government for stimulating private foreign investment. Comparative returns on alternative investment opportunities are measured on a net basis after payment of all taxes, and the differentials that arise from tax concessions are especially meaningful when taxes are at high levels.

A number of tax suggestions have been made in recent years, such as abatement of all United States taxes on business income derived from foreign sources; an extension to all business income earned abroad of tax rates that are now applicable to so-called "Western Hemisphere trading corporations"; the granting of deductions from United States taxable income of a certain percentage of the amount invested abroad in any year; deferring the tax levy until such amount is returned to this country; a more generous credit for taxes paid abroad; and the application of the same United States tax to foreign branches as is now applicable to foreign subsidiaries. Other suggested devices would attempt to encourage portfolio investment more directly; for example, the granting of partial or total tax exemption to income received from bonds and stocks of foreign countries and companies. Finally, accelerated amortization of foreign investments has been proposed along the lines of the amortization incentives provided for domestic investments necessary to the national defense.

Tax concessions of these kinds would undoubtedly be at least partially effective, but there are, nonetheless, some perplexing issues of policy involved. On the one hand, the loss of government revenue would probably be more than outweighed by the benefits of increased private foreign investment. But, on the other hand, it is by no means equally clear that these advantages would counterbalance the possible long-term consequences of so serious an impairment of the principle of equal tax treatment of all types of business, domestic and foreign, old and new. Tax concessions which discriminate in favor of foreign investment as compared with domestic investment might set a precedent for the preferential treatment of other—perhaps much less desirable—special purposes.

---

compensated expropriation might even invite seizure, for foreign governments sometimes find it easier to deal with another government than with private firms. Moreover, there is often a disinclination on the part of private investors to become too involved with government, either at home or abroad. Administrative procedures, especially, must be simplified if guarantee provisions are to be extensively used. Despite these doubts, the possibility of achieving a wider use of investment guarantees merits fuller exploration.

In consequence, the Study Group would not favor going beyond the tax concessions recommended by the Commission on Foreign Economic Policy (Randall Commission),[9] with the reservation that these privileges should be available only to long-term investments—i.e., of at least five years' duration—and should not be granted to short-term speculative ventures. In addition, tax concessions should only be allowed by the United States Government on investments in countries which do not increase their own taxation of American investors in anticipation, or as a consequence, of a reduction in the United States tax. Perhaps the best way to guard against this contingency would be to permit tax concessions only on investments in countries which have signed investment treaties with the United States.

Among other measures which the United States Government could take to stimulate increased private foreign investment should be a clarification of the degree to which domestic antitrust laws are applicable abroad. Existing uncertainties regarding the applicability of domestic antitrust laws limit the ability of American companies operating abroad to conform to local laws and competitive practices. Clarification of this problem might significantly influence the willingness of some companies to make foreign investments.

More might be done to make government loan capital available for jointly financed ventures under private management, i.e., in which private equity capital would be invested in some agreed ratio to the government loan capital made available to the enterprise. Such jointly financed enterprises could help to stimulate the export of the technological and managerial experience of private domestic firms, or of their foreign affiliates. The Export-Import Bank, in particular, might explore the possibility of making inexpensive loan capital available on this basis, both to foreign affiliates of United States firms and to foreign firms, without the guarantee of local governments. Some arrangements along these lines have already been authorized, but much more should be done. The merit of this proposal is that it encourages an increased flow of private investment in the short run. But, it may have the limitation

---

[9] The Randall Commission recommended: (a) the so-called "Western Hemisphere Trade Corporation" tax reduction privilege to be applied to all private American investments abroad and the reduction somewhat increased; (b) several discriminatory restrictions on types of investors and forms of investment eligible for tax concessions to be abolished; and (c) larger and more liberal deductions from United States tax liabilities to be granted for taxes paid to foreign governments by private American investors abroad. See Commission on Foreign Economic Policy, *Report, op. cit.*, pp. 18–22.

of being effective only for as long as the government subsidy continues.

There are also measures that the United States might propose with respect to international organizations which could help to stimulate private investment. The International Bank for Reconstruction and Development (IBRD) is making, and will doubtless continue to make, its contribution to mobilizing private capital for investment abroad through the sale of its securities to private investors in various capital-exporting countries, particularly in the United States. Its loans to member countries —for which it is required to obtain the guarantee of the receiving governments—have been for the most part directed toward water developments, power resources and transportation; although in recent years loans have been made for industrial development. The IBRD has been one of the most successful of the postwar international organizations and its activities have been of significant value. Nevertheless, criticisms have been made that its charter is unduly restrictive and should be liberalized to permit it to make loans without government guarantees, and to make equity investments as well. If private investors would buy the IBRD's securities without government guarantees, it would certainly be worthwhile to dispense with the troublesome negotiations which the guarantees entail. The Study Group doubts, however, that the IBRD should extend its activities into the equity field. There is considerable question about the wisdom of combining in the same institution both equity ventures and the kind of investments now made by the IBRD. As a practical matter, the IBRD is still very far from having exhausted the opportunities for worthwhile investments within its existing limitations.

To increase private capital investment in equity ventures abroad, the Study Group believes that a new international institution specifically designed to operate in the venture capital field would be quite useful. The Executive Branch of the United States Government has proposed an International Finance Corporation (IFC) which would go some way to meet this need. The proposed IFC, with a capital of $100 million contributed by member governments, would finance private ventures by purchasing securities bearing interest only if earned. In that way, it could supply venture capital without itself holding any equity right of control. The IFC would be a kind of investment bank, using public and private funds to finance private international projects.[10]

---

[10] See United States Treasury Department, Press Release, November 11, 1954. The proposed IFC could also purchase debentures convertible into stock if and when sold

Useful as an IFC would be, the Study Group questions whether a new international agency in the venture capital field should be a purely financial institution, precluded from making direct investments on its own account and from exercising promotional and managerial functions. Instead of an International *Finance* Corporation—or perhaps as an addition to it—we believe there should be established an International *Development* Corporation, empowered not only to provide venture capital to private enterprises but also to investigate investment opportunities, set up projects on its own account, and manage them during their initial stages until they could be sold to private investors. Such an institution would both provide a new source of venture capital and open up new opportunities for private investors.

The proposed agency should be provided with a large revolving capital fund—for which it would pay perhaps 3½ or 4 percent interest annually on paid-in subscriptions—to be used to make direct international investments for its own account. Its substantial capital stock should be subscribed by the governments of the industrial nations—principally by the United States. The management of the Corporation should be largely recruited from the same countries. Participation in control should be proportionate to capital subscriptions, as in the IBRD.

In its promotional and investment activities, the proposed International Development Corporation would use private firms as agents. It would be expected and designed to operate at a profit, but whether it did would depend upon the capability of its management. The projects to be undertaken should generally be large and significant, and should be selected in consultation with private firms operating abroad, after careful surveys of possibilities throughout the free world. Care would have to be taken to avoid competing in areas already actively occupied by private capital. Through consultation with experienced private firms, the Corporation would obtain the benefit of familiarity with the technical problems involved, with the basic costs, and with some of the political and social difficulties that should be anticipated. While the Corporation would be justified in taking greater risks than a private business, each project should be undertaken in the expectation that it would eventually become a profitable operation which could be sold to private investors.

Upon construction of a project by a private firm acting as the Cor-

---

by the IFC to private investors. The IFC would be authorized to raise funds in private capital markets by selling its own bonds as well as private securities held by it.

poration's agent on a fee basis, the management of the project would remain with the same firm, or would be assigned to a different private firm, again acting as agent of the Corporation. After a reasonable period of operation—during which a permanent management for the project could be developed—the project would be incorporated as an independent company. The earnings of the project, qualified by its prospects, would be appropriately capitalized in the form of a private company and the securities would be available for sale to private individuals in the various private capital markets of the world. Thus, the proposed International Development Corporation would seek, to the extent possible, to make of its capital a revolving fund re-available from time to time for other investment projects.[11]

The activities of an International Development Corporation of this type—operating perhaps under the auspices, but not administrative control, of the United Nations—should exercise a beneficial influence by impressing upon the governments both of capital-importing and capital-exporting countries some of the policies that each must accept if private international investment is ever to be resumed on a substantial and sustained scale.

United States Government Loans, Grants and Technical Assistance

Even with the stimulus which the measures suggested in the preceding section would provide, private foreign investment will still be on too small a scale to make possible the increases in production and exports of which the underdeveloped areas are capable. Nor is private capital in any event likely to be invested in certain kinds of enterprises which are indispensable preconditions for economic growth—transportation, port and power facilities, water control, public health improvements, etc. Additional investment funds will be needed to supplement private foreign investment and to make possible necessary projects outside the range of private interests. The question is not whether capital transfers from the United States Government to the underdeveloped countries are de-

---

[11] There is no reason why part of the securities of the projects sponsored by the International Development Corporation might not be sold to nationals within the countries in which the investment projects are undertaken, if and when private capital markets begin to develop in those countries. Indeed, it would be an appropriate function of the International Development Corporation to encourage the development of such indigenous capital markets.

sirable or needed, but rather on what scale, in what forms, and through what agencies they should be made.

The United States Government makes loans or grants to other countries because these are effective and morally valid means for the achievement of American foreign policy objectives. Aid which meets these criteria is justified; aid which does not, should not be provided. In Chapter 8, we observed that some forms of United States Government aid to the other industrial countries were losing their effectiveness and validity. These objections do not as yet apply to the underdeveloped areas. For, the latter do not increasingly resent aid relationships which lack mutuality, as does Western Europe. Indeed, the underdeveloped countries tend to regard foreign aid as a "moral obligation" of the West, particularly of the United States. At the same time, their need and desire to obtain foreign assistance makes them less reluctant than they would otherwise be to cooperate with the West in building a more effectively functioning international economy and polity. The administration of financial and technical assistance programs provides the United States Government with opportunities for day-to-day working relationships with levels and branches of the governments of the underdeveloped countries which lie outside the scope of normal diplomatic and consular activities and which are often of crucial importance for the economic and political future of these societies. Thus, the provision by the United States Government of financial and technical assistance is probably still the most effective economic means for the attainment of American foreign policy objectives in the underdeveloped countries.

This justification for American financial and technical assistance programs is so obvious that it should not have to be repeated here. But perhaps its very obviousness has tended to obscure it behind distinctions of dubious validity and irrelevant prejudices which have crept into discussions of foreign aid in recent years.[12] Take, for example, a currently fashionable distinction between loans and grants. Loans are supposed to be good because it is believed that they are used by the recipient countries to finance revenue-producing or self-liquidating projects. In contrast, grants are supposed to be bad because they are "unbusinesslike" and are believed to be used for wasteful purposes. But the economic or political worth of a project or program does not depend upon whether it is self-liquidating or directly produces revenue. For some underde-

---

[12] See above, pp. 315–316.

veloped countries, the earmarking of sizeable amounts of government revenue and dollar exchange to the service of foreign loans is probably not the most economical use of their scarce resources either from their own point of view or from that of American policy. As a practical matter, it would be unwise to deny assistance for purposes important to American policy merely because the aid might have to be given in the form of nonrepayable grants.

If our foreign aid programs are effectively to serve the objectives of American foreign policy, the determination of the amounts and forms of assistance to the underdeveloped countries cannot be premised solely on the strict economic criteria relevant for private banks and business investors. Particularly in the independent underdeveloped countries, the political, military and social returns from United States Government aid programs may be more important than their immediate economic benefits, and may outweigh any violation of "businesslike" criteria. The prevention of actual or prospective communist invasion or insurrection; the alleviation of floods, famines and other natural disasters; the support of long-range development programs and internal social reforms—these, and similar, activities may yield results for American policy which are worthwhile even if the recipient countries cannot repay the aid provided in monetary form. Consistent with the priority of such broader considerations, economic criteria may then be applied. To the maximum practicable extent, the United States should finance only those projects and programs of whose economic necessity and feasibility it is convinced, and the loan form should certainly be used if there is a reasonable prospect of repayment without undue economic strain on the recipient country. But, a high degree of flexibility is also needed in the determination of aid amounts, forms and specific uses. In the long run, foreign assistance programs of a reasonable size and administered with sufficient flexibility will be far less costly of American lives and resources than subordination of the broader objectives of American foreign policy to strictly economic considerations.

The need for greater flexibility than now exists can be seen in the limitations of the agencies through which governmental assistance funds are channeled to the underdeveloped areas. Within the United States Government, the Export-Import Bank can provide loan funds only for projects which it considers economically sound and self-liquidating. The Foreign Operations Administration (FOA) can provide financial grants and technical assistance on a nonrepayable basis. At the international level, the chief assistance agency is the IBRD which obtains its investment funds largely from American sources. The lack of flexibility of these three agencies, and the important gaps not covered by their present restricted operations, have been summarized as follows:

> The most serious limitation in the existing machinery for public investment is its lack of flexibility. The United States Government, and international agencies financed largely by the United States, can make either outright grants or bankable dollar loans repayable in dollars. They cannot, however, provide funds for essential development projects on terms which lie between these two greatly disparate forms of financial assistance. In domestic private finance, many effective and ingenious financial instruments have been devised to cover the middle ground between straight bonds and ordinary equities, but in international public finance there is apparently no stop between pure gifts and strict loans.[13]

Thus, the effectiveness of governmental assistance programs in furthering the objectives of American foreign policy could be substantially increased by expansion of the activities either of the Export-Import Bank or of the FOA to cover this important gap between pure gifts and "bankable" loans. For various reasons, it would probably be advisable to confer these new responsibilities on the FOA (or a successor agency) rather than on the Export-Import Bank. The need—economic or political—on the part of recipient countries for financial assistance lying between pure gifts and bankable loans should be clear in each instance, and there must also be adequate safeguards to ensure that resources thereby made available will be used for specific and intended purposes.

In addition, both the FOA and the Export-Import Bank should be enabled to make loans to underdeveloped countries which would permit the latter to spend the dollars anywhere in the free world and not only in the United States. Such "untied" dollar loans, if undertaken on a significant scale, might contribute to expanding the dollar earnings of the other industrial countries. The Southern-Asian development arrangements recommended in Chapter 7 and other regional development planning organizations suggested below might well be particularly appropriate vehicles for working out triangular transactions of this kind.

It would also be desirable for foreign loans made by United States Government agencies to contain a "waiver clause" which, in the event

---

[13] A Report to the Director of Mutual Security by the Advisory Committee on Underdeveloped Areas, *Economic Strength for the Free World* (Washington, D.C., May, 1953), p. 30.

of another period of severe dollar shortage or of some other kind of political or economic crisis, would permit, not a complete moratorium, but the suspension of payments on the loan in dollars. During the emergency, service on the loan would continue in local currency whose use directly by the United States, or subsequent conversion into dollars, would be covered by the original loan agreement.

Controversy has occasionally arisen in recent years over the possibility of competition between the Export-Import Bank and the IBRD. Competition between the two institutions is now theoretically possible because both seek for the same kind of economically sound, self-liquidating, and relatively short-term investments. As an international organization, the IBRD must be operated along the lines of a prudent investment bank if it is to market its own securities to private investors and retain the confidence of its member governments. In consequence, the IBRD should be given priority in the financing of so-called "bankable" projects except in cases where American foreign policy considerations would strongly dictate use of the Export-Import Bank. As a practical matter, the Export-Import Bank can afford to take greater risks, and to commit its capital for longer periods, than the IBRD since it is not dependent upon private capital markets. However, the Export-Import Bank would be able to liberalize its loan criteria only if the United States Congress agrees.

The necessity for the IBRD to be guided predominantly by sound business standards means, however, that there is not now any international organization which could finance non-self-liquidating projects in the underdeveloped countries. Such projects are often of equal, if not greater, importance than those for which the IBRD can provide funds. If a United States Government agency like the FOA is permitted to expand its activities to cover the gap between bankable loans and outright gifts, the urgency for such additional means of financing at the international level would be correspondingly reduced. Nonetheless, the resources likely to be available from all sources for these purposes will probably continue to be inadequate.

Moreover, there are valid grounds for arguing that some portion of American assistance funds for the underdeveloped areas should be channeled through international agencies. In the preceding chapter, the Study Group took the position that as large a part as possible of our future economic and defense aid to the countries of the Western Community should be provided in the first instance to European and Atlantic institutions rather than directly to national governments. The main reasons for doing so would be to strengthen these regional institutions *vis-à-vis* their member states, and to avoid aggravating the resentments—official and popular—generated on both sides of the Atlantic by bilateral aid relationships. In the case of the underdeveloped countries, the order of priority of the two reasons is reversed and, hence, the proportion of aid channeled through international agencies could be substantially smaller. But, the value of international agencies should not be underestimated, for there are cases in which the objectives of American policy in the underdeveloped countries could be more easily attained by providing resources through the politically neutral medium of an international organization than by direct intergovernmental dealings.

Various proposals have been made for a new international agency to operate in the fields which the IBRD is forbidden to cover. The proposal preferred by the underdeveloped countries, and now under active consideration in the United Nations, involves the creation of a Special United Nations Fund for Economic Development (SUNFED) which would make low interest loans and outright grants for non-self-liquidating and non-revenue-producing projects. The United States Government has officially opposed the SUNFED proposal, and the Study Group must admit to serious doubts of its own, not with respect to the objective of the proposal, but as to its suggested method of operation and control.[14] If, however, its organization and methods of operation and control were to be like those of the IBRD, this proposal might have some merit.

Other proposals for meeting the generally admitted need for international financing of this type have received less attention and their details have not yet been worked out. One suggestion—more consistent with the Study Group's general line of thinking about the problems of the underdeveloped countries and their relations with the West—involves the creation of regional development planning and coordinating bodies. The regional development organization for Southern Asia, proposed in Chapter 7, would be such a body. Regional organizations would have a more homogeneous membership than a single worldwide organization

---

[14] SUNFED would obtain its resources from annual voluntary contributions by member countries and not from fixed assessments. It would be governed by an Executive Board elected from the members which would operate by majority with each director having only a single vote. It would have a full-time Director-General and staff, but to the maximum practicable extent would use technical personnel now employed by other UN agencies. SUNFED would begin operations when at least 30 countries have pledged not less than $250 million for the first two years' budget and have indicated their willingness to make a contribution for at least one additional year.

like the proposed SUNFED and, if successfully operated, could serve as a nucleus for building those patterns of regional cooperation which might lead eventually to true regional integration in the Moslem area, Southern Asia, and Latin America. The United States would have to be the main source of dollar financing for the plans approved by these regional development bodies, but nondollar currencies could be obtained from the other industrial countries of Western Europe and Japan and from the local members.[15] Satisfactory organizational arrangements would, of course, have to be devised for handling the policy-making and planning functions of these regional institutions.

American capital investments in the underdeveloped areas of the types and through the agencies discussed above are now, and should continue to be, accompanied by United States Government technical assistance activities of various kinds. Unfortunately, the technical assistance program is still regarded as a controversial issue and, in recent years, opinions on it have tended to polarize at opposite extremes. Its opponents denounce it as ineffectual "do-goodism" not worth its cost; its most ardent advocates magnify it into a means sufficient in itself to overcome most, if not all, the problems of the free world. Technical assistance yields a greater political return per dollar invested in the underdeveloped areas than any other activity of the United States Government. It is not, however, a panacea, for its economic and social effects are necessarily of limited scope and can produce lasting results only over considerable periods of time.

A danger of technical assistance programs in the underdeveloped areas is that their effect may be transitory. This may happen for several reasons. The duration of an individual project may be too short to ensure a high enough degree of assimilation of the new technique. Or, the people of the recipient country may lack the cultural comprehension, or the motivation, to continue practicing the new methods on their own initiative even if the project has operated for a reasonable time. Technical innovations will persist, and may even stimulate further technological advances, if existing motivations and attitudes are already positive with respect to the new methods, or if they can be modified sufficiently during the course of

---

[15] Another proposal, presenting greater practical and political difficulties, provides for the creation of "regional banks" with financial resources of their own. "Each of these banks would maintain a revolving fund which would be originally established in dollars, but which could be repaid in other currencies and in turn reinvested within the region." *Economic Strength for the Free World, op. cit.*, p. 32.

the project to become positive. Even if basic attitudes are not hostile but are merely indifferent to the new activity or the new way of doing old things, the innovation is likely to disappear—or at least to deteriorate badly—after the completion of the technical assistance project, particularly if the government of the recipient country makes inadequate provision for continuing it. For this reason, long-term direct private investment is often a more satisfactory vehicle for technical assistance than relatively short-term governmental programs.

On the whole, the record of the technical assistance programs has been increasingly good as understanding of the process of social and economic change in the underdeveloped countries has improved, and as greater experience has been gained with particular types of projects and methods. In Latin America, where technical assistance programs have been operating longest, results are already beginning to be apparent on a considerable scale.[16] Even in Southeast Asia, where political difficulties are very great, technical assistance missions have produced some dramatic benefits.

In the circumstances, it would be a pity if the effectiveness of the technical assistance programs were to be unduly restricted by prohibitions against the use of technical assistance funds for capital equipment and operating supplies. There are few technical assistance projects in agriculture, industry, public health or popular education which do not require some capital equipment or operating supplies. If the project itself is worthwhile, there can be no valid reason why the facilities and supplies required should not be financed from the same source as the personnel and other costs, especially when the recipient country has other urgent uses for its own financial resources and other foreign aid funds are not available for these purposes.

The effectiveness of American financial and technical assistance programs could be significantly increased by improvements in the organization and administration of United States Government activities in the underdeveloped countries. A major requirement in this respect is that greater regard be paid to the principles of "jointness" and "continuity." [17] By jointness is meant the carrying on of American operations in ways

---

[16] See, for example, the Reports of the National Planning Association's special project to evaluate the effectiveness of technical assistance in Latin America (TALA).

[17] For an excellent short discussion of the importance of jointness and continuity in United States Government operations see *Economic Strength for the Free World, op. cit.,* pp. 9–11, 36.

which permit full participation by the local population, particularly by members of the social groups to be affected by the activity. Joint operations—such, for example, as the Joint Committees for Rural Reconstruction (JCRR) in Formosa and various current community projects in India—have the merit not only of making Americans better acquainted with the actual needs and aspirations of the local population; they also build those habits of living and working together which, over the long term, can help to create a greater sense of community among the diverse peoples of the free world. Our purposes in the underdeveloped countries are not likely to be achieved by methods which do not involve the active participation of many Americans in day-to-day operations in these areas.

Continuity of policies, operations and personnel is equally necessary in United States Government developmental activities. Since the inception of American assistance programs in the underdeveloped countries only a few years ago, there have been numerous changes in policy and personnel which have made our activities considerably less effective than they might otherwise have been. In part, this lack of sufficient continuity has been the result of inexperience and of a creditable search for better methods and staff. But in part, at least, it reflects the capriciousness of domestic American politics, frequent arbitrary changes of administrators and of agency responsibilities, and lack of incentives for qualified personnel to remain in overseas posts. Overcoming these obstacles to greater continuity should have a high priority in the improvement of our foreign economic operations.

One shift of emphasis in operating methods has recently been made which promises to increase administrative efficiency, to help overcome some of the political and psychological handicaps—at home and abroad —of operations conducted by government agencies, and to influence over the longer term the character of economic and social changes in the underdeveloped countries. This is the practice of appointing private agencies—responsible business firms, non-profit organizations, educational institutions, etc.—to undertake the actual planning and execution of development and technical assistance projects on a fee or cost basis. This practice should be as widely employed as possible, and foreign business firms and non-profit institutions should also be eligible to act as agents either singly or in association with American organizations.

Finally, a word may be said about the cost of development and technical assistance programs in the underdeveloped countries. At bottom, the limiting factor is not the ability of the American economy to supply funds and capital equipment but the capacity of the underdeveloped countries to absorb them. Chapters 4 and 5 have described the various social, economic and technical difficulties which in practice restrict the amount of capital that can be effectively invested in these countries regardless of the magnitudes of their potential development "needs." Moreover, the specific investment purposes for which financial assistance from the United States Government and international organizations is mainly used—transportation, communication and other public utilities, large-scale irrigation and hydro-electric projects, etc.—are particularly susceptible to the effects of these limitations because of their size, long construction periods, and the advanced technology and labor skills required to build and operate them.

While the Study Group cannot, of course, recommend any precise annual figure for American financial and technical assistance programs in the underdeveloped countries, it can nevertheless urge that much greater regard be paid to the broader objectives of American foreign policy when annual appropriations are under consideration. No other aspect of American foreign economic policy is of as much concern to, or as closely watched by, the independent underdeveloped countries as the size of American financial and technical assistance programs. In consequence, their importance to American foreign policy is very great not only for tactical purposes but also as a means for helping to create over time a greater sense of community and common purpose between the West and the underdeveloped countries. The basic issue is whether it will prove less costly to the United States in the long run to underestimate these broad foreign policy considerations than to pay due regard to them now. For this reason, the Study Group believes that annual expenditures on American economic and technical assistance to the underdeveloped areas could and should be increased to at least double, and probably as much as triple, the present size of such programs without exceeding the existing absorptive capacity of these countries.

Commodity Stabilization Measures

The progress of the underdeveloped countries can be fostered not only by supplementing their inadequate indigenous resources of capital and technology. It is also dependent upon the character of their ordinary commercial and financial relationships with the international economy—

in particular, upon the incentives and the disincentives to economic growth which the latter provides. Excessive and prolonged instability in international commodity markets may slow the rates of growth of these countries and, by worsening their balance-of-payments and income problems, may exacerbate social unrest and political weakness. Since the underdeveloped countries participate in the international economy as primary producers, the types of international economic instability which affect them most directly are those in the prices and volumes of foodstuffs and industrial raw and semi-processed materials.

The prices and volumes of internationally traded primary commodities tend to fluctuate widely owing to the economic characteristics of primary commodity markets, and to the many interventions of national governments in these markets. There is now rather widespread agreement that this instability is an important cause of inefficiency in the international economy. The insufficient growth of primary production —especially agricultural production—in much of the free world outside North America is in part the result of this instability. The reluctance of private producers or investors in many countries to expand primary production for export arises in part from their fear that satisfactory prices for their output will be temporary and that prices will fall sharply when new capital has been invested and output grows. Similarly, governments and ruling groups in the primary-producing countries often resist expansion of primary production for export because they are apprehensive—and justifiably so—of the effects on their economies of the violent fluctuations to which international commodity markets are subject.

Thus, greater stability of the prices and volumes of primary products in international trade would contribute materially to the growth potential of the free world's economy. There is, moreover, a convergence of the economic interests—at least of the objective, longer-run interests— of the primary-producing countries and the industrial countries in greater stability. For, the primary-producing countries have, clearly, a long-run interest in a stable, calculable demand for their exports; the present instability is highly disruptive of their domestic monetary stability, of their balances of payments, and of their ability to carry out development programs. Likewise, the industrial countries—especially Western Europe and Japan—have an obvious interest in the long-term expansion of overseas primary production, and in the more rapidly expanding and more calculable overseas demand for their manufactures which would thereby be created.

There is also rather general agreement, at least in principle, that a considerable moderation of this instability is possible without introducing market rigidities whose effects on the economical use of resources and on economic growth would be worse than the instability itself. A recent United Nations report concludes that the prices of internationally traded primary products "could be held within much narrower limits without creating the probability that their long-term allocative function would be frustrated."[18]

Over the past twenty-five years, a great many different suggestions have been made for coping with this problem. Some of them propose to attack it through stabilization of prices; others through stabilization of the volume of trade. These proposals may be grouped into two broad classes—those which would act on each commodity separately, and those which would attempt to stabilize international trade in groups of commodities simultaneously. Let us consider very briefly the kinds of proposals most frequently made under these two headings from the standpoint of their contribution to economic efficiency and their practicability.[19]

The proposals which would deal with each commodity separately fall into four main groups.

(1) *Bilateral intergovernmental purchase contracts* for primary commodities have been used extensively since 1939. They are relatively easy to negotiate, and are well adapted to such commodities as meat and dairy products. These contracts generally guarantee not only a measure of price stability but also the sale of all or part of a country's output of the commodity concerned. They may be particularly effective when expansion of production is an important objective, especially for commodities with a lengthy production period. However, their operation is diffi-

---

[18] *Commodity Trade and Economic Development* (New York: United Nations, Department of Economic Affairs, November, 1953), p. 20.

[19] The criteria of desirability and practicability, suggested by the consensus of expert opinion and in accordance with which various international commodity stabilization techniques may be judged, can be summarized as follows: (a) the suitability of the technique to the peculiarities of the particular commodity market; (b) whether it is desirable to expand or to contract production of the commodity; (c) the ease of negotiation and re-negotiation; (d) whether the technique permits long-run changes in demand or supply conditions to influence the trend of the commodity price—especially whether it permits encouragement of low-cost as against high-cost production (this means, for example, ample opportunity for revision of maximum and minimum prices); and (e) whether importing countries are given a voice equal, if not superior, to that of exporting countries. This criterion is a prerequisite of the preceding one, since price-policy—the crux of all commodity stabilization arrangements—is more likely to be sound if importing countries have the decisive influence.

cult to combine with private trading. Another important disadvantage of this technique is the danger of faulty pricing, especially when there is no longer a reliable free market price for purposes of guidance. The measure of stability such contracts can achieve for the particular trading relationship is usually determined by the duration of the arrangement, and may be limited by the lack of assurance of renegotiation on comparable terms, except where there is so close a relationship between the two governments (as, for example, within the Commonwealth) that neither will attempt to drive too hard a bargain and each can look forward to a satisfactory renegotiation. Furthermore, bilateral intergovernmental purchase contracts, because of their limited coverage, may well increase instability in the noncontract markets, since the effect of variations in supply and demand is perforce concentrated in the latter.

(2) *The Wheat-Agreement type* of commodity arrangement involves a commitment by the major exporters of the commodity to make available specified quantities of the commodity at an "upper price," matched by a commitment by certain importers to buy specified quantities at a "lower price." As long as the free market price stays between the upper and lower prices, the agreement has no effect on prices or trade. It does serve, however, to assure its members a minimum level of demand or supply and a lower or upper limit of price. The effectiveness of this kind of agreement depends on not having the price range too wide, while its negotiability depends on not having the range too narrow. An arrangement of this type is workable only for commodities marketed in a few grades, or whose grades can be related to each other by standard price differentials. Such agreements seem to be very difficult to negotiate and to renegotiate. Only one has been signed and its future existence is in doubt. "The refusal of the major importer, the United Kingdom, to sign the second Wheat Agreement, which runs from 1953 to 1956, is an ominous indication of the tendency of such measures to break down as soon as they fail to serve the immediate national interests of the members." [20]

(3) *International quota agreements* provide for regulation by the governments concerned of the quantities of a commodity which may be produced in, or exported by, their respective countries. The prewar commodity agreements were typically of this type. They were negotiated between producing countries without participation by importing coun-

---

[20] *Ibid.*, p. 43.

tries. Agreements of this kind are akin to private cartel arrangements. As compared with the other types of international commodity arrangements, they are relatively easy to negotiate, but the stability they give is —almost inevitably—bought at the price of freezing an existing pattern of production and obstructing the expansion of output by low-cost producers. Moreover, since they affect only the supply side of the market, they are not very effective in stabilizing prices. They are, in most instances, an undesirable type of arrangement from the standpoint of the longer-run efficiency and growth of the international economy. One such arrangement is now in existence—the International Sugar Agreement, signed in 1953.

(4) *Buffer-stock arrangements* establish an intergovernmental agency, with funds contributed by the participating governments, which keeps the price of an internationally traded commodity within an agreed range by purchasing when demand is weak and selling when it is strong. On economic and technical grounds, the buffer-stock method of commodity stabilization is the least objectionable. It requires no direct interference by governments with the private production, sale and purchase of commodities. If its price stabilization range is not too narrow, and can be readjusted from time to time, it will not interfere with long-run price trends but will moderate violent short-term fluctuations around this trend. However, the difficulties in practice of getting agreement on price ranges and on the provision of the necessary financing by national governments are serious. No international buffer-stock arrangements are in existence today. Prewar experience with them—though admittedly limited—is now generally regarded as having been rather unsatisfactory.

The proposals for stabilizing whole groups of commodities in a single comprehensive arrangement take three main forms. The first would establish an international buffer-stock agency operating with similar techniques in many different commodity markets. The second would have a buffer-stock agency operate on a "commodity bundle" of fixed composition. The third form, usually referred to as "commodity reserve stabilization" or a "commodity currency scheme," would make of the international agency a kind of supranational bank, with power to create credit for the purpose of stabilizing the price of a "commodity bundle." [21]

This brief review of techniques for stabilizing international com-

---

[21] Schemes of these three types are discussed in *Commodity Trade and Economic Development, op. cit.,* pp. 35, 53–66.

modity markets, individually and collectively, raises a major question. Apart from the bilateral intergovernmental contract device (whose contribution to general stability is dubious or even negative) the only existing intergovernmental stabilization arrangements are the International Wheat and Sugar Agreements. But, if the problem of instability of international commodity markets is serious, if both importing and exporting countries have an interest in overcoming it, and if economically sound and technically workable means for attacking it could be devised, why has so little been accomplished?

The reason has already been suggested by the foregoing comments on the various commodity stabilization techniques. The supposed basis for international agreement on commodity stabilization measures is the fact that the objective, long-term interests of exporting and importing countries in the stability and calculability of trade in primary products are, to a degree at least, convergent. But, as this study has stressed, the policies of national governments in foreign economic matters are not typically made in terms of objective, long-run interests. They are normally the resultant of the immediate pressures of claimant groups, or of the state itself, motivated primarily by short-run economic and political considerations. In the words of a United Nations committee of experts:

> The benefits which nations may obtain from commodity agreements are on many different levels, from the most immediate money gains, through the longer-term national advantages of stability, to the broader benefits which may be expected to accrue from world-wide stability. If the eyes of the negotiators are fixed on the narrowest short-run advantages, commodity agreements will be very difficult to reach, especially as they are nowadays expected to include consumers as well as producers; and they will easily collapse. Only by rare coincidence will there be sufficient identity of short-run interest to make agreement possible. But if governments will fix their eyes on the fuller long-run advantages which may accrue to their own countries from world stability (a pre-condition of prosperity), a lasting identity of interest will more easily be perceived and reached. . . . We find little evidence that governments are as yet assigning to stability a high enough value to justify hopes of smooth negotiation and renegotiation of effective agreements. Until there is a change of attitude, [commodity agreements] cannot be expected to contribute materially to stabilization of the world's primary commodity markets.[22]

---

[22] *Ibid.*, pp. 50, 44.

At bottom, the difficulty of setting up multi-national commodity stabilization arrangements—either for single commodities or for groups of them—is the same as besets efforts to establish international monetary and trading arrangements with a wide and heterogeneous membership. Measures to coordinate national economic policies cannot work unless national governments are willing and politically able to put their underlying interest in the calculability and efficiency of the international economy ahead of the immediate interests of claimant groups and of the state itself. As we have seen in other connections, the ability of national governments to consider the efficiency of the international economy in making foreign economic policy is in direct proportion to their ability *to count* on the willingness of other governments to do likewise. As long as governments act on the assumption that each will take advantage of every short-run opportunity to gain at the others' expense, none feels able to relinquish short-term gains for long-term benefits; for the latter are, in these circumstances, theoretical only. The extent to which governments can count on each others' concern for long-term benefits depends on the degree of pre-existing mutual trust arising out of a sense of community. Where important and powerful group interests are affected, it depends also (as we have seen) on a degree of supranational authority. Neither of these prerequisites exist, or are likely to be soon created, between the industrial and underdeveloped countries which would have to participate in multilateral commodity stabilization arrangements.[23]

There are also certain practical difficulties in setting up commodity arrangements which would actually help to stabilize incomes from primary exports and stimulate production increases in more than just a few of the underdeveloped countries. The primary commodities technically most practicable to stabilize—e.g., nonferrous metals, minerals and certain hard fibers—are produced by a relatively small number of underdeveloped countries. But the primary commodities whose long-term growth is of most importance to the other industrial countries of Western Europe and Japan are mainly agricultural products—e.g., breadgrains, feeding stuffs, vegetable oils, meat and dairy products, etc.—which cannot generally be stored for long periods of time. These, too, are produced

---

[23] If this is true with respect to stabilization agreements involving individual commodities, it is true *a fortiori* with respect to the more ambitious proposals for stabilizing whole groups of commodities by a single comprehensive arrangement. Such schemes presuppose a much greater willingness than now exists on the part of politically and culturally heterogeneous groups of states to commit themselves to coordination of their economic policies and to the creation of supranational authority on a worldwide scale.

by only a few underdeveloped countries. Finally, most of the primary commodities imported into the United States in greatest dollar value—e.g., coffee, cocoa, tea, vegetable oils, wool, nonferrous metals, lumber and pulp—either are exported by only a few underdeveloped countries or are relatively unimportant from the standpoint of the economic health of the other industrial countries. This means that a commodity stabilization scheme limited, for example, to such easily stored primary products as copper and tin would help to stabilize the income of only a comparatively few underdeveloped countries—e.g., Malaya, Bolivia, Indonesia, the Belgian Congo, Rhodesia, Chile and South Africa—and the production increases likely to be stimulated over the long term would not be of great importance to the other industrial countries. In contrast, a commodity stabilization scheme covering the major agricultural exports of the underdeveloped areas would make a much greater contribution to a much larger number of underdeveloped countries, as well as to the industrial countries. But, many of these agricultural commodities cannot be stored for very long, and some are not imported by the United States. Indeed, for several of these commodities, the United States would have to participate in any international stabilization scheme as an exporter. Thus, the greater the theoretical benefits of a possible commodity stabilization arrangement for the balance-of-payments, income and growth problems of the free world, the less practicable it would tend to be.

It would nonetheless be *theoretically* possible to devise international commodity stabilization arrangements for several metals and minerals, for hard fibers and perhaps even for some other, less durable, agricultural products which would benefit to a significant extent a sufficiently large number of countries to be worthwhile. Technically sound and economically feasible schemes could no doubt be devised, since a wide variety of devices and techniques are available which could be adapted to the peculiar characteristics of almost any commodity of international commercial importance. But any economically feasible scheme would require high managerial competence. It would also be necessary for members to agree in advance upon some rather specific rules of operation, particularly in a buffer-stock arrangement. In practice, the more discretion and freedom of action the managers possess, the more difficult it would be for them to resist pressure—both from member governments and from private claimant groups—to convert the stabilization scheme into a "rescue operation."

Despite these possibilities, the Study Group doubts that new international commodity stabilization arrangements would be very useful in practice. Accordingly, the principal effort of the United States Government in this field should initially be along unilateral lines, though it might aim at eventual multilateralization. We believe that the most practicable possibility would be a broadened United States Government stockpiling program possessing sufficient financial resources and operational flexibility to moderate fluctuations in American import demand for primary products, particularly in periods of domestic recession. So far as may prove practical, these efforts by the United States should be coordinated with similar efforts by other major importing countries, particularly, of course, the United Kingdom.[24] This approach to international commodity stabilization is analogous to that proposed in Chapter 7 for supplementing Western Europe's dollar reserves and thereby stabilizing to some extent its supply of dollars. To solve the commodity stabilization problem—or the monetary stabilization problem—would require real supranational authority. But the basis for such authority in international community and consensus is now lacking. Hence, in both cases, we must conclude that, as far as American action is concerned, the best that is politically feasible now is for the United States Government, at its own discretion, to cushion the impact of fluctuating American demand on the international economy.

To make possible an American stabilization program of this kind, a substantial enlargement of present stockpiling authority and a change of stockpiling policy would be required. It would be necessary to broaden the purposes for which commodities could be acquired and to increase funds available for stockpiling. The Executive would need authority to acquire stocks of a wider group of commodities and for a broader range of security and foreign policy purposes. To avoid excessive expenditure and the acquisition of unmanageably large stocks, it would be desirable to limit the use of this authority to times and situations of critical need. It should be used only to "cushion" (i.e., to arrest or retard) really major price declines—but it should not be used to attempt continuous price

---

[24] Hitherto, shortage of foreign exchange has prevented most other countries from building up or carrying stocks; and it has occasionally prompted nations like the United Kingdom to dump strategic stocks like lead and zinc. In effect, the free world appears to be willing to allow the United States to become the prime and almost sole possessor of large-scale strategic stockpiles. Perhaps behind this willingness is the comforting assumption that in wartime the United States would again assist its allies with Lend-Lease aid, including drawings on its strategic stocks in the common defense.

stabilization in the usual sense of that term. Used in the former way, it could be justified as an insurance policy against economic catastrophe for our foreign allies and friends. Like the proposed measures to supplement Europe's dollar reserves, this broadened stockpiling policy would substitute for the economic aid which the United States would otherwise be forced, in its own interest, to extend to other countries in periods of domestic American recession—a substitute preferable to aid because the United States would receive tangible wealth in exchange. If "stockpiling" and "avoidance of catastrophe" criteria, rather than a typical "stabilization" rationale, were to guide the operation, there would be no validity to the accusation customarily leveled at American participation in more ambitious multi-national commodity stabilization schemes—namely, that the United States Government was proposing to establish "parity prices" for other countries at the expense of the American taxpayer and American consumers.

Ideally, in order to stabilize markets, the American stockpiling authorities should have the power to dispose of stocks in times of prosperity and rising prices in order to dampen upward price fluctuations and reduce the expenses of the operation. In practice, however, the disposal at home or abroad of stocks of imported commodities would raise serious political problems. This would be particularly true in the case of commodities which are also produced domestically (e.g., wool, synthetic rubber and nonferrous metals). Conceivably, the stockpiling authorities might be empowered to sell from the stockpile only in periods when private inventories in the United States of the commodities in question were rising. It is probably true, however, that domestic political and economic considerations would nullify even this restricted authority, assuming that the necessary legislative authorization of it could be obtained. This limitation on disposal is a major reason why, as a practical matter, purchases for the stockpile would have to be largely confined to really critical situations and could not normally be used for continuous stabilization operations.

Thus, the kind of enlarged United States Government stockpiling program envisaged here would be politically more feasible—and would probably prove in the longer run to be a less objectionable type of market manipulation—to the extent that its stocks were not used as "buffers" but were held as strategic reserves, clearly understood to be insulated from the market except in carefully specified circumstances. Existing legislation does in fact "sterilize" the American stockpile by permitting withdrawals from it only on Presidential authorization in national defense emergencies defined by law and upon recommendation by the Director of Defense Mobilization.

The commodities covered by an enlarged American stockpiling program of this type would have to consist mainly of those important for the security of the United States and capable of being stored indefinitely. Certain non-strategic, but major dollar-earning, agricultural commodities might also be included, if their stocks could be periodically "turned over." Such "mines above ground" may prove more valuable in time of war or national emergency than real ones, which require large labor forces and long development periods. National assets of this character are actually more usable than gold. Nor is there any evidence that most of the metals and minerals concerned would not appreciate in value over the longer term.[25]

The stabilizing effects on international commodity markets of an expanded American stockpiling program could be substantially increased if it were coordinated with those of other major commodity importers— particularly the United Kingdom. Attempts to concert action with other industrial countries would run into some of the same difficulties encountered in attempts to set up fully multilateral international commodity arrangements. But, the difficulties of reaching agreement on price ranges and on amounts would be much reduced if only a few Western importing countries were involved. In a period of declining demand, when a serious dollar scarcity threatened, it should be possible for the United States to exert sufficient leverage on other industrial countries to achieve consistency of import and stockpiling policies with respect to primary commodities—enough, at least, to avoid a catastrophic collapse of prices and of the foreign exchange earnings, dollar and nondollar, of primary-producing countries.

If an economic development policy of the kind sketched in this chapter can be carried out, both the industrial countries and the underdeveloped areas would benefit substantially from it. Western Europe and

---

[25] The cold war may also indicate the importance of considering the stockpiling of materials not now regarded as strategic. An example would be iron ore, which is not now stockpiled by the United States. But, depletion of high-grade domestic ores, and the vulnerability both of domestic and of oceanic transportation, might well argue for some stockpiling of iron ore, or perhaps of pig iron. The desirable size of the strategic stocks of tin, copper and other minerals might also be periodically reviewed in the light of the same considerations.

Japan could expect increases in primary imports from, and manufactured exports to, the underdeveloped countries. The underdeveloped countries would obtain more of the development resources and the technological knowledge which the West, particularly the United States, can supply. More calculable demand for their exports and more ample development resources would also help to overcome the obstacles blocking those internal changes and reforms within the underdeveloped countries which are prerequisites for any acceleration of their economic and political progress.

Important as these benefits would be, however, they would not solve the basic economic problems of the West or of the underdeveloped countries. For the West, improved relations with the underdeveloped areas are a necessary supplement to, but not a substitute for, the organization of the Western Community outlined in Chapters 7 and 8. Nor should the independent underdeveloped nations expect either that the West will supply developmental resources on the scale which they desire, or that such resources as the West is able and willing to provide could be effectively used in the absence of necessary domestic changes and reforms within the recipient countries. Each group of nations must look first to its own efforts.

In theory, so large a degree of self-dependence need not have been inevitable. One of the tragedies of colonialism both for the West and for the underdeveloped countries was its failure to evolve directly into more equitable and mutually beneficial ways of living and working together. Forty or fifty years ago, when it was politically possible to begin the development of such organic relationships, neither the colonial powers nor the people of the underdeveloped areas could have anticipated how valuable such relationships would be today. Now that the need is clear, the political feasibility no longer exists in most countries, nor is it likely to be created anew very soon.

The missed opportunities of prewar colonialism are not, however, completely chimerical even today. In Africa and elsewhere, there are regions with worthwhile development potentialities which are still within the same political sovereignties as the nations of Western Europe. Except in North Africa and Southern Asia, these regions are not likely soon to win —or to be capable of sustaining—complete political independence, and their nationalistic aspirations might be offset by a clear demonstration of the benefits which their peoples could derive from continued close economic and political association with the West. To do so, however, requires changes in the concept of colonial relationships and policies and in the vigor with which political and economic improvements are executed. Granted these changes and reforms, the remaining dependent overseas territories of the West European nations might, in a reasonable time, become expanding sources of supply for primary products, growing markets for European manufactures, and more important dollar earners for the metropolitan industrial countries. This remaining opportunity of the European colonial powers will not be realized, however, unless the mutual benefits of continued political and economic association are clearly demonstrated and unless colonial development programs are larger, better balanced and more vigorously executed than they are today. Kenya, British Guiana, Honduras, and French North Africa have already provided warnings of what may happen if this last opportunity continues to be neglected.[26]

The fact that political independence is not necessarily a prerequisite for economic and social progress is too little appreciated not only in the underdeveloped areas but even in the United States. The Revolution of 1776 is too often seen, both abroad and at home, as a symbol of triumphant nationalism, although the essence of our Bill of Rights is clearly the idea of a specific constitutional declaration of the limits beyond which the national will may not go in its legislative treatment of certain enumerated crucial liberties of the individual and of the mind. In this sense, modern nationalism—with its authoritarian intolerance of diversity and its xenophobia—is the exact opposite of the doctrine of the American Declaration of Independence and the subsequent Bill of Rights. Hence, it is not at all surprising that communist propaganda finds it possible to use such modern nationalist movements as most convenient channels for the achievement of its imperialist purposes. There is sad irony, too, in the thought that Americans, with their commitment to ideals such as human freedom, dignity and community, should in their foreign development activities assume the pre-eminence of economics in the explanation—and of economic change in the solution—of almost every type of

---

[26] In Chapter 7, a suggestion was made for joint development by the European continental countries of their dependent overseas territories. Appropriate arrangements along these lines could substantially accelerate the pace of colonial economic development by making German, Italian and Dutch skills and resources freely available for this work. Participation of the United States and Japan would also be desirable. As far as the British colonies are concerned, the proposed regional development organization for Southern Asia suggested earlier would enable the United States, Japan and other industrial countries to contribute more effectively to economic advancement.

social, cultural or political problem. In contrast, the Soviets—who profess to believe that only a change in the mode of production can bring about social, political and cultural modifications—often ignore economic means in their tactical approach to marginal countries and concentrate instead on seizing both the moral initiative and the political and intellectual instrumentalities by which economic institutions can be overthrown and rebuilt.

The lesson is that in its dealings with the underdeveloped countries— no less than with other peoples—the United States must cease to neglect the moral, ideological and psychological dimensions of society. Not only does this neglect make Western economic policies and programs in the underdeveloped areas much less effective than they might otherwise be; it also deprives the Western countries of means for adequately demonstrating precisely those respects in which Western society is most superior to communist or fascist totalitarianism. Conceivably, the Soviet Union could some day match the productivity and living standards of the West, though it is not likely to want or to be able to do so without considerable modification of its present objectives and methods. But the Soviet Union cannot remain a totalitarian and collectivist state and at the same time expect ever to offer any convincing evidence of a proper regard for individual dignity and worth, for the freedom of thought and speech, or for moral limitations on the means which may be used to achieve desirable goals. In these respects, the West has by the intrinsic nature of its values and institutions a potentially decisive advantage over the communist bloc. Western society has shortcomings, but it can validly claim not simply that it is sincerely striving to achieve freer and more humane forms of living and working together, but also that it is trying to do so in ways that are morally consistent with such goals. When the West has found effective means for demonstrating this fact and its implications for action to the people of Asia, Africa and Latin America, we shall have made a decisive start in the long task of building a new, uncoerced and more enduring sense of community among the many diverse societies on this planet.

10

Administering American Foreign Economic Policy

The measures of primary and supplemental importance discussed in the preceding chapters are all dependent—in one way or another—upon American policies and American actions. Some of them require concrete American support in the form of financial assistance, or of special devices for stimulating economic stability and growth, or of greater and more assured access to domestic American markets and sources of supply. Many of those which consist exclusively of policy changes and actions by other countries are unlikely to be undertaken without strong and continuous American leadership. Hence, the question of whether progress will be made in the next few years toward realizing a constructive program of action for the whole non-Soviet world reduces itself in large part to the question of whether the United States will be capable of making changes in its own policies and of carrying out measures for executing them.

In any period, the structure and capabilities of a nation's economy, the characteristics of its political system, and the motivations and relative power of its major social groups set limits to the possible courses of action which the nation can follow. In turn, the course of events and the broadening or narrowing over time of these social and institutional limits depend upon what choices are made—deliberately or through default—by important groups and individuals, and upon the resolution and skill with which these choices are carried out. In this chapter, we shall outline the social and institutional factors which now seem to fix the limits of the possible for American foreign economic policy, and suggest desirable changes in the processes by which American foreign economic policy is made and administered. In the next chapter, we shall discuss the more fundamental aspects of American leadership which depend upon the character of American motivations and the strength of the will to act on the part of the American people.

The Social and Institutional Limits of American Foreign Economic Policy

Some of the principal ways in which the foreign economic policy of the United States reflects the basic characteristics of the American economy have already been examined in Chapter 1. The fact that the American economy is continental, balanced, dynamic and still relatively free has made it in most respects not basically dependent on the international economy. In consequence, greater integration of the American economy into the international economy has so far not been required for purely domestic economic reasons though, as we have seen, it is desirable for political and strategic ones.

This lack of a major direct economic interest in international integration has been a source both of weakness and of strength for American foreign economic policy. There can be little doubt that it has inhibited the United States Government from taking stronger leadership in international economic relations. At the same time, however, another important consequence of the size, balance and dynamism of the American economy has been that the American people have not generated powerful and pervasive drives for foreign markets, sources of supply, or investments. There have been, of course, some important exceptions to this generalization, such as petroleum, tin, coffee and rubber. But, by and large, American producers, consumers and investors—unlike their counterparts in 19th-century Britain—are still mainly interested in domestic availabilities and opportunities. Politically, this has resulted in the relative absence of private interests seeking to bring strong pressure on the United States Government to pursue an aggressive commercial or financial policy overseas.

Aside from persistent pressures to dispose of agricultural surpluses abroad, it is chiefly with respect to import policy that the influence of domestic interest groups has been active and strong. And because of the balanced character of the American economy, official policy has had to reflect—and attempt to reconcile—the demands for protection of a variety of domestic producers in industry, mining, agriculture and transportation. These demands have been primarily responsible for the more obvious forms of American economic nationalism such as tariffs, import quotas and subsidies. They have also resulted in certain restrictive features of policies and programs designed for quite different purposes, e.g., the agricultural and shipping provisions of the foreign aid programs, or the "Buy American" aspects of military assistance programs. But, in recent years, particularly since World War II, the growing export interests of the United States have to some extent tended to counterbalance the purely protectionist claimants, as evidenced by business support of the recommendations of the Randall Commission and a changed attitude in the most important industrial and banking circles.

At the same time, relative American independence of the international economy has had its own advantages. The United States Government has frequently been able to act—or to refrain from acting—to advance political, strategic and moral purposes without hindrances arising from short-run economic interest. Despite the claims of Marxism, the United States has not behaved as an "imperialist power." A major reason for the prestige the United States enjoyed abroad throughout the late 1930's and the 1940's was foreign recognition of this large element of economic disinterestedness in our relations with other nations.

Popular support for an active and constructive American foreign economic policy has been noticeably stronger on political, strategic and moral grounds than on strictly economic ones. Such broad support has enabled American policy-makers and administrators to achieve the remarkable measure of success attained in the postwar period. But here, too, certain characteristics of our pluralistic society, decentralized political system, tripartite form of government, and heterogeneous political parties have set important limitations on the effectiveness of noneconomic motivations and on the capacity for continuous and strong American leadership in the non-Soviet world.

In most parts of the country, popular interest is mainly oriented toward local, state or functional domestic (e.g., farm, labor, consumer) issues. Although "publics" do exist for foreign policy issues, these are normally concentrated in a few large urban centers, mostly along the Atlantic seaboard. It is possible temporarily to expand these "publics" over much larger portions of the nation if unusually determined efforts are made by the Government and by private groups, as for example in 1947–48 when the Marshall Plan legislation was under consideration. But the effects of these intermittent campaigns soon wear off.

The portion of the public permanently interested in foreign policy is on the whole poorly organized, inadequately financed, and necessarily intellectual in its membership and types of appeals. In contrast, the private interest groups opposed to a more constructive foreign economic policy are well organized, have adequate financial backing and ready access to legislators and administrators. Also, they have a potentially wider appeal because they can rely for support on narrowly conceived self-interest, chauvinistic sentiment, partisan advantage, and the unhappy tendency to search for scapegoats on which to blame the unpleasant problems and heavy responsibilities of the modern world.

The structure of American political institutions and the nature of the party system also help to limit the effectiveness of American leadership in the free world.[1] Constitutional factors are particularly important. Despite the centralizing tendencies in the Federal Government over the past twenty-five years, political authority is still widely dispersed throughout the country in a multitude of local and state political entities. This relatively low political center of gravity has been, of course, a crucial feature of our liberal democracy. But, necessary and beneficial as this decentralization is for the preservation of our free society, it absorbs political energy in state and local matters which might otherwise be available for dealing with national and international problems, particularly economic ones. Sometimes, however, the very lack of local interest permits certain members of Congress a freer hand and a broader attitude.

Paralleling the decentralized constitutional structure, the major American political parties are also not organized in a way that facilitates the development of national leadership, particularly on foreign policy issues. What we call "national political parties" are in many respects not national parties at all, but are rather loose coalitions of state and local party leaders that tend to solidify every four years for the purpose of electing a President, and to a lesser extent for the biennial Congressional elections.

---

[1] While the Study Group has not been guided in its analysis by the findings of the report of the previous group which produced *United States Foreign Policy: Its Organization and Control* (New York: Columbia University Press, 1952) for the Woodrow Wilson Foundation, the reader may find that more extensive analysis useful and interesting—including the more drastic remedies therein suggested.

Between times, the rudimentary central party machinery is notoriously weak. Congressmen—and sometimes top officials of the Executive Branch as well—must look to their home states, if not to purely local party machinery, for political support. Thus, it is ordinarily unrewarding politically for a politician to concern himself primarily with foreign affairs, except perhaps in times of great crisis, or unless such an interest can dramatize his personal abilities without loss of support in his constituency.

The decentralized party structure and absence of strong national party leadership enable each party to contain two or more competing power groups (they are hardly stable enough to be called "blocs"). These groupings are based not merely upon personal rivalries but upon some real differences in sectional, racial or religious attitudes, interests and principles. Except in national emergencies, neither of the major parties is likely to generate a unified and consistent foreign policy, or to support many important aspects of foreign policy with sufficient vigor. Unfortunately, too, in the last few years, highly vocal sections of both parties have been actively concerned with foreign affairs less for the purpose of improving the effectiveness of the United States in the critical world situation than for the narrow purpose of furthering through demagogic appeals their own self-interested ambitions. This tendency is in part responsible for the current struggle over American foreign economic policy and for the recent decline of American prestige in the non-communist world. In the long run, only Soviet imperialism benefits by such activities.

The manner in which responsibility for problems affecting foreign affairs is split between the two Houses of Congress and among their committees also makes it difficult to develop unified and consistent foreign economic policies. Although the two Foreign Affairs Committees have nominal leadership, their influence in economic matters is considerably weaker than in more general political affairs. Even with respect to political foreign policy, the House Committee is weaker than the more powerful, tradition-rich Senate Foreign Relations Committee. There is hardly a committee of the Congress which does not on occasion have some impact on foreign economy policy. The Armed Services Committees make determinations with respect to our military programs which have tremendous impact on the international economy. The Committees on Interstate and Foreign Commerce control our relations with a number of international agencies, such as those dealing with civil aviation, telecommunications, etc. Banking and Currency Committees deal with foreign loans and procurement. The Ways and Means Committee is the primary factor in legislation concerning tariffs and foreign trade, because the tariff is still considered a "revenue" measure. And cutting across the jurisdictions of all are the massive Appropriations Committees which in the last analysis tend to have more influence on certain crucial aspects of foreign economic policy, as reflected in the budget, than do other committees.

Within the federal system, the President is the major stimulator and unifier of popular support on foreign policy issues. The American electoral process and party system inevitably make the President the preeminent national leader. The Constitution makes him the formal Chief of State and endows him with many of the functions and powers necessary for leadership in foreign affairs. In addition to his constitutional responsibilities for legislative leadership, he is required by Acts of Congress to take the initiative and responsibility in many ways that frame our foreign economic policy—the budget, the economic report, and action on tariff changes, to mention only a few. His authority over the Executive Branch provides the President with the information which is the raw material for making policy, and with opportunities for day-to-day coordination and control of the agencies by which it is executed. For leadership and consistency in foreign affairs, we must inevitably look to the President.

However, the system of balances established in the Constitution provides the Congress with checks on the authority and freedom of action of the President which to some extent offset these unifying and leadership influences. Most of these Congressional powers—some exercised by the Senate alone—are well known: confirmation of senior Executive Branch personnel, control of the purse, authority over Executive organization and personnel policies, and the two-thirds vote required to ratify treaties. The general authority to investigate Executive performance, although originally retrospective, has in recent years also had a seriously divisive—or at least disruptive—effect on foreign policy. Recent proposals to amend the treaty-making power so as to restrict further the freedom of the President are, of course, a most serious threat to unified and active foreign policy in any field.

The United States Constitution has a considerable amount of legislative-executive rivalry built into it. This institutional rivalry, aggravated as it frequently is by personal or partisan considerations, produces complex relationships that have important, and often unfortunate, consequences for the making and execution of American foreign policy, particularly in military and economic affairs. Despite the urgent need for coordination, decisiveness and discretion, the Congress—in its anxiety to retain control of policy—has often acted to splinter American foreign policy and to tie or to force the hands of the Executive.

In recent years, as a reluctant Congress has been urged into a more and more active foreign policy, it has expressed its anxiety by attaching all sorts of strings to its grants of authority to the Executive. One simple device is to enact legislation for limited periods only, so as to require the Executive to return frequently—sometimes annually—not only for a new appropriation but also for a policy review and extension of authority. This restriction is important, partly because of the resulting uncertainty of American policy which our allies feel so keenly, partly because of the excessive time it forces Executive officials to spend in justifying themselves "on the Hill," and partly because it extends the authority of individual members of Congressional committees into day-to-day administrative operations. It must also be remembered that even fresh authorizing legislation does not free an Executive agency from the necessity to go before the Appropriations Committees for funds. Thus, officials of foreign aid agencies have had to review their programs with at least four separate committees each year. This, of course, draws out the budgetary process over inordinate periods of time, and increases the opportunities for the insertion of riders and provisos which may have seriously disruptive effects.

A number of other devices are coming into increasing use which bind the Executive closely and are subject to abuse. For example, frequent reporting to particular committees is often now required, and some legislation takes the further (and probably unconstitutional) step of requiring clearance with committees before an executive agency can take certain specified actions. Postwar experiments with a number of devices—some of them sincerely intended to improve Congressional-Executive relations—such as "watchdog" committees, liaison officers, "briefing" sessions, and the like, have on the whole been disappointing.

By no means all of the limitations imposed by our legislative system on the making and administration of American foreign policy arise from Congressional-Executive relationships. An important set of limiting factors is inherent in the organization and administrative practices of the Executive Branch itself. A host of agencies, both permanent and temporary, have responsibilities for, or recognized interests in, some aspect of foreign policy. The economic area of foreign policy especially is badly divided in this fashion.

The economic personnel of the Department of State is ostensibly the principal staff of the Secretary of State and of the President on international economic matters. The State Department, however, is primarily a "policy" rather than an "operating" agency. Economic aid, technical assistance, control of East-West trade, and several other aspects of foreign economy policy have been gathered together in the Foreign Operations Administration, but there are certain key functions still remaining in other agencies. Thus, direct foreign lending by the United States Government is handled by the Export-Import Bank, which lies outside the departmental structure and has a particularly close relationship to the Congress. Furthermore, American policies in the International Bank for Reconstruction and Development and the International Monetary Fund are influenced primarily by the Treasury Department, an agency with an overwhelmingly domestic orientation. United States Government purchases abroad are handled by the Department of Defense, in the case of military items, and by the Office of Defense Mobilization, in the case of strategic materials for the stockpile. Although the Department of State has leadership responsibility for trade and tariff matters, it is often effectively checked by the Tariff Commission and by other departments responsive to domestic interest groups, so that this potentially useful foreign policy tool is today almost neutralized. Other examples could be cited of functions split off from their close relatives or of potentially important policy areas that fall somewhere "between the desks."

The machinery for inter-agency consultation, coordination and clearance which is supposed to knit together all of these dispersed responsibilities for foreign economic policy is at best rigid, cumbersome and slow. It is still difficult to be sure that the various United States foreign programs are having an optimum total effect in a given country, or that they are merely not working at cross purposes. Considering the enormous impact of American policy on the international economy, we are not organized to make the most effective use of our national bargaining power. Moreover, this dispersion of responsibility among Executive Agencies tends to discourage imagination, initiative, decisiveness and vigor —precisely the qualities most necessary for the successful exercise of leadership by the United States. In the postwar period, the most important advances in foreign economic policy have all too frequently depended on the ability of their proponents to bypass or ignore the formally established machinery for inter-agency coordination.

We do not, however, wish to imply that these defects could be easily eliminated by a return to the prewar centralization of foreign economic policy responsibilities (other than military) in the State Department. Coordination and effective articulation of such a vast area of functions would still be a most serious problem even though all the units reported ultimately to the Secretary of State. Moreover, the present dispersion of functions and the existence of temporary agencies has its advantages. The permanent departments are more often plagued with competing internal subdivisions, long-standing vested interests of personnel, and pervasive policy inertia than are smaller and newer—or temporary—agencies.

Another serious impediment to better coordination of foreign economic activities is the lack of a stable, cohesive, respected corps of civil servants of consistently high quality to administer such programs. This is not to disparage the many able and energetic men with whom agencies are now staffed. There has, nevertheless, been an unfortunately high rate of turnover—particularly in the "temporary" economic aid agencies —and the quality of personnel has been uneven. Inter-agency coordination is also not facilitated when "opposite numbers" in the various agencies—and frequently within the same agencies—are recruited, paid and promoted under different personnel systems, have had different types of training, and characteristically have different outlooks, attitudes and expectations. Excessive preoccupation with personnel security has also taken a heavy toll both of the morale and creativity of civil servants, and of public and Congressional confidence in them.

Today, the responsibilities of the President are so numerous and pressing that only a part of his personal attention can be devoted to foreign affairs. This places a heavy burden upon the leadership and coordinating abilities of the Executive Office of the President—notably the National Security Council, the Budget Bureau, and the senior assistants of the other Executive Office staff agencies—in helping the President to ensure that a unified and consistent foreign policy will be devised and carried out by the Executive Branch as a whole. The recent reorganization of the National Security Council should assist this process, particularly in foreign political and military matters, for it is only the President himself, assisted by an adequate personal and institutional staff in the Executive Office, who can offset the inherent weakness of the civilian agencies concerned with foreign affairs *vis-à-vis* the military agencies.

In sum, serious weaknesses—constitutional and administrative—hamper American foreign economic policy-making and execution. But there is evidence of political maturity and of the quality of our national leadership in the fact that, with such a system of built-in difficulties, great national issues have nevertheless been resolved and many constructive policies achieved over the past decade.

Problems of Improving Policy-Making and Administration [2]

An instructive way to sketch the problems of improving foreign policy-making and administration is to review the issues which confronted efforts at improvement since World War II. There have been numerous official studies of the formation, organization and control of foreign policy as a whole (including those of the Hoover Commission), a few special studies of the control and organization of the overseas agencies executing foreign economic policy, and several studies of separate aspects of the relation of foreign economic policy to domestic policy. However, not since the Colmer Committee (the House Special Committee on Postwar Economic Policy and Planning of the 78th and 79th Congresses) has there been a comprehensive effort to relate—structurally as well as substantively—the whole of foreign economic policy to general foreign policy and to domestic economic policy.[3]

In addition to recommendations for strengthening the general control of the Congress and the Executive over national economic policy as a whole, the Colmer Committee specifically noted the need for a "War Resources Board" which would give a more "careful scrutiny of the rela-

---

[2] The remainder of this chapter has been excerpted from an unpublished memorandum prepared by William Y. Elliott for the Randall Commission and is printed here with the Commission's permission.

[3] That Committee had the present Under-Secretary of the Treasury, Mr. Marion Folsom, as its Staff Director. It issued three—out of its total of eleven—reports dealing with the postwar foreign economic policy of the United States. The 6th and 8th Reports set the background for consideration of problems of foreign investment, trade and foreign aid; and the 8th Report made certain recommendations for organizational changes, particularly in relation to foreign aid. It was, however, the 11th Report which contained the main consideration of the problem of the organization of economic policy (including foreign) in the United States Government, both in the Executive and Legislative Branches, in the broadest possible terms. Those reports, along with those of the Select Committee on Foreign Aid of the 80th Congress (Herter Committee)—especially the 8th Preliminary Report and the Final Report, Section III, pp. 599–848—constitute the most comprehensive official study yet undertaken of the problems, political mechanisms and control of our economic foreign policy.

tions of Defense to the total economic interests of the country. The nature of modern war does not permit improvising of Defense programs in
the manner that has been possible to the United States in the past." This
recommendation was implemented in some measure by the National
Security Act of 1947, and its amendments in 1949, which effected a limited
merger of the Armed Services and established the National Security Resources Board, the Central Intelligence Agency, and the top-level National Security Council. Subsequent experience has shown that it was
the National Security Council which, by an inevitable logic, took over
the task of framing, in the broadest terms, the integration of national
security policies with fiscal policy and economic policy, foreign and domestic. It remained for the Eisenhower Administration, however, to accept and implement this centralizing step by requiring a "price tag" for
all security programs through the inclusion of separate financial appen-
dices.

Certain segments of foreign economic policy especially relevant to
general foreign policy were, however, also recognized by the Economic
Cooperation Act of 1948 to be appropriately subject to organization
through a separate administration. The Economic Cooperation Administration was to be subject to the general policy guidance of the State
Department, but to operate independently under an Administrator of
Cabinet rank. Here again, the evolution of policy in this area tended to
bring about a merging of certain related responsibilities for foreign economic operations in the present Foreign Operations Administration—
the successor, once removed, of the Economic Cooperation Administration.

It is significant, though, that large segments of the economic aspect
of foreign policy have remained under the primary leadership of the
State Department, not only for the formation of policy, but for the preparation and presentation of such legislative programs as the Executive has
required to carry out its policies. The Colmer Committee had recommended, and the Congress had accepted in 1946, the creation of an Under-
Secretary of State for Foreign Economic Affairs. By 1948, subsequent
State Department reorganizations and the creation of the Economic
Cooperation Administration down-graded this official to the rank of an
Assistant Secretary of State with responsibility primarily for policy-making and leadership in the field of foreign trade. In particular, control of
the Reciprocal Trade Agreements program remained in the State De-

partment, assisted by the Department of Commerce, and with varying degrees of collaboration from the Departments of Agriculture, Treasury, Labor and Interior. Technical assistance programs also fell to the State Department until 1953.

It should be noted that no changes were made in the Tariff Commission's structure or functions and that the Export-Import Bank continued to flank the International Bank for Reconstruction and Development and the International Monetary Fund. Such coordination of lending policy and international monetary policy as was achieved was brought about through the National Advisory Council on International Financial and Monetary Policy (NAC) under the chairmanship of the Secretary of the Treasury and with representation from all the United States agencies concerned with foreign aid and procurement, as well as from the Federal Reserve Board, the Reconstruction Finance Corporation and the chief American representatives on the IBRD and the IMF.

There was, therefore, no method of bringing together in any one agency or committee the various segments of foreign economic policy represented by the fiscal and monetary agencies; the procurement agencies; the national security agencies, including the National Security Resources Board and, later, the Office of Defense Mobilization; the trade policy and general foreign policy functions vested in the State Department; the large-scale overseas expenditures of the Armed Services and the Occupation Forces; and the foreign aid and technical assistance activities. There was great proliferation of inter-agency committees (with a certain amount of interlocking control inherent in their membership) but no point of general policy resolution or administrative control short of the President himself.

A history of efforts that shows no success in creating a single center of policy integration does not by its mere recital prove the impossibility of success by some as yet untried means. Nevertheless, the record of varying efforts to integrate control of economic policy in general, and of foreign economic policy in particular, probably illustrates the supreme difficulty—and maybe the impossibility—of achieving any control *center* for the various considerations bearing on foreign economic policy. The reason is that foreign economic policy reflects every important aspect of national politics as well as of national policy. To centralize control is, therefore, like centralizing control over all aspects of security policy—it cannot be done by a single agency, or by anyone short of the President.

It is, of course, not to be taken for granted that the fact that agencies have not been brought into a truly integrated and coordinated relationship necessarily means that they should not, or cannot, be brought into such a relationship. But there is strong evidence in the very fact that they have not been, despite numerous recommendations to this effect, that a "one package" integration may be unworkable and indeed unnecessary, even at the Executive level.

Similarly, as already noted, the Congress of the United States has continued to function with a half-dozen, at least, of its major committees all operating in the field of foreign economic policy without any more general integration than the policy committees of the two parties in the Senate (formed for general integration of party programs). The Joint Committee on the Economic Report does attempt a sort of national estimate of the total economic capacities and the nature of tax and fiscal policies, but many Congressional committees continue to have a vital concern and some control over various aspects of foreign economic policy.

Indeed, the only moderating influence on the multiplicity of sources for the origination and modification of foreign economic policy in the legislative bodies has come through the creation of special commissions of inquiry, like the Randall Commission. Some help, too, has come from occasional "farming-out" of projects by the Congress or by committees of the Congress to private research organizations. Finally, some use has been made of the device of special and select committees, like the Colmer Committee and the Herter Committee, both of which made comprehensive reports. In the matter of "follow-up," use has been made of a joint watchdog committee, with representation from the Appropriations Committees of House and Senate and the Foreign Affairs and Foreign Relations Committees, to maintain constant scrutiny of Executive actions under the foreign aid legislation. This experiment of doubtful value lasted only from 1948 to 1950.

Running through the reports of the Colmer Committee and of the Herter Committee was a suggestion which was often repeated by the two Appropriations Committees and others of the standing committees of the Congress. This was a recommendation that the total national bargaining power of the United States should be applied to the promotion of foreign economic policies in a more effective way than through unconditional programs of assistance operated by the various agencies of the Federal Government abroad. In considerable measure, the same theme ran through the preamble to the Economic Cooperation Act and the reports of its originating committees in the House and Senate.[4] Clearly, however, it is most difficult—if not impossible—to use the power of the United States in this way when that power is split up among a host of Executive and independent agencies. This consideration argues for a really serious attempt to concentrate responsibility and power for foreign economic policy in as few agencies as possible. It argues, in particular, for the removal of authority in this field from those agencies which have foreign economic functions that are in reality irrelevant to their main responsibilities. Thus, the Treasury Department has an important—often the controlling—voice in foreign lending policy both directly and through the National Advisory Council, which it dominates. Effective discharge of the Treasury's domestic responsibilities does not require it to have a controlling—or even a very influential—voice in foreign lending or other aspects of foreign economic policy. Hence, these functions should probably be removed from the Treasury, and the National Advisory Council should either be abolished or at least chaired by the top-level foreign economic policy officer, regardless of whether he heads a separate agency or is subordinate to the Secretary of State, as suggested below.

Another essentially domestic agency with important functions in the field of foreign economic policy and operations is the Office of Defense Mobilization. So far, the Foreign Operations Administration appears unable to exercise much leadership in the area of stockpiling, foreign procurement operations, and development of foreign sources of strategic materials. At the same time, the Office of Defense Mobilization—under domestic budgetary and mining pressures—is naturally more concerned with other programs than with foreign development or with the eco-

---

[4] Many individual prescriptions were written into the Act by the Congress, like those which insisted that deliveries of reparations behind the Iron Curtain should be stopped; and that a review of all other reparations should be put into effect through further negotiations with countries receiving foreign aid, with the object of preventing Germany from being stripped of its productive capacities at the same time that the taxpayers of the United States were being asked to make good the capital goods deficiencies which Germany might have supplied. Later the same consideration was applied to Japan. A similar approach was made by the Congress in this Act and its various amendments to the use of "counterpart funds" abroad and, in particular, toward the building up of stockpiles of strategic materials and the development of strategic material resources abroad which would be in the interest of the defense of the United States as well as of the whole free world. In 1946, the Colmer Committee put the matter in general terms by expressing its feeling "that the basic interests of the United States have not been adequately protected by the use of our bargaining position with respect to enforcement of agreements, including equal and protective access for our private trade to the necessary raw materials and commodities." 11th Report, Supplement, Section II, Part A, p. 7.

nomic health of other countries. The State Department has concerned itself with these problems only when it has been necessary to make a series of "crisis decisions," such as have been involved in proposals to continue the purchase of rubber and tin beyond normal stockpile limits (e.g., Bolivia and Indonesia). Unless, as suggested in Chapter 9, the stockpiling mandate is broadened beyond the strictly strategic limits of our own national defense, this unsatisfactory state of affairs is inevitable. Recent legislation permitting exchange of agricultural surpluses for strategic materials, and a broadening of the stockpiling criteria to be followed by the Office of Defense Mobilization are steps in this direction.

The conclusion is that the operations of the stockpile and of the developmental functions of the Office of Defense Mobilization may well require reconsideration and further broadening in the light of the impact of "cease purchase" on the economies of our allies and friends abroad. If it is decided that the strategic stockpile program cannot be broadened under the present legislative mandate along the lines suggested in Chapter 9, serious repercussions—including irresistible pressures to trade with the satellite areas and the Soviet bloc—will be generated in many of these economies. The test of whether or not trade in strategic commodities is going to be freely and openly permitted—in the pious hope of lessening the pressures of the cold war—comes to a focus on this issue. But the issue may well be decided by default in countries like those of Latin America, if our stockpiling purchases come to an abrupt end.

From an organizational point of view, consideration by the National Security Council of the nature of stockpiling in relation to economic aid and international commodity stabilization, and an implementation of the resulting policy by the Office of Defense Mobilization seem to be in order—taking into account the implications of the painful alternatives considered above. Steps in this direction have recently been announced in connection with an expansion of stockpile objectives to include barter of surplus American commodities, and fostering of "long-term" independence of vulnerable foreign sources in the event of war. But, "Buy-American" pressures may undo the results.

Broadly speaking, there are two solutions generally proposed for the problem of excessively dispersed responsibilities for foreign economic policy, which these examples have in part illustrated. One is to have an operating agency separate from the State Department and controlled only in the most general way by the Secretary of State. In practice, this has been—and may continue to be—a more acceptable compromise to the Congress than the second proposal which would, in effect, set up a sort of "Foreign Economic Operations Secretary" as a distinct, but integral, arm of a greatly enlarged State Department to parallel its political arm. Under the latter alternative, the Secretary of State would be in control of both parts by a direct chain of command.

There is a tendency on the part of the Department of State to wish to be free from political pressures by remaining simply a policy agency, and staying "pure" of all operating functions. This pattern has, it may be noted, also been followed in the present organization of the United States Information Administration. The aims of such an arrangement are apparently to achieve a certain presumed operational efficiency by means of a separate organization, and at the same time to "take the heat" of domestic political controversy off the State Department and allow it to assume the roles of policy guide and of mediator in difficulties with other nations. In this way, the State Department argues that it would not be compromised overseas or in the Congress by any antipathy abroad or at home to our foreign economic operations.

This hope of escaping "political heat" may turn out, in fact, to be illusory or dangerous, if thereby the real battles which the State Department must fight to retain control of policy and to get a sufficient means of implementing policy are lost. However, the existing organizational setup is not likely to be reversed at this time unless there is a marked change of attitude towards the problems of foreign assistance and a stronger realization of the need for gearing our foreign economic programs into our total diplomacy, *especially for national bargaining purposes*. The result under the present arrangements is that the State Department still achieves the easier role—but less effective one in terms of protection of national interests—of being the "lawyer," so to speak, with the foreign claimants as its clients. By doing so, however, it weakens its standing with the Congress and lessens its domestic political support. The natural question arises whether the Foreign Operations Administration can exercise much bargaining influence if the State Department's policy—supported by its "immune" and insulated position—continues to impede the use of our total economic strength for national bargaining purposes. Of course, there are many functions, like technical assistance or cultural relations, in which a bargaining attitude may be completely out of place and even self-defeating. It must be acknowledged that the assumption of responsibility for operations by the Secretary of State would force the State Department to operate more obviously and directly in the national interest, and to use all the agencies and channels which can balance the protection of American interests with the promotion of general foreign policy abroad.

The range of experimentation which has been traced in outline in this section indicates that it would probably not be admissible or feasible either in political or organizational terms to have a single coordinator for foreign economic policy on the White House staff. This experiment was tried in 1951 and 1952 when the Director of Mutual Security was given certain coordinating responsibilities with respect to the foreign economic operations of the Departments of State and Defense. At most, however, the Director could be only a mediator and a conciliator. Had he tried to be more—i.e., to become really an "Assistant President"—he would certainly have been confronted with the resignations of the Secretaries of State and Defense. Indeed, the Director's range of authority did not include trade policy, most of the lending policy of the Government abroad, most of the procurement policy of the Government affecting foreign sources, and a wide range of other economic activities rooted in domestic programs which were bound to have foreign implications (such as farm support prices, and the like). In short, the plain fact seems to be that foreign economic policy can, at best, be brought into manageable "chunks" of related functions like those dealing with foreign aid and perhaps military and technical assistance joined with lending functions and with procurement functions. But, it is apparently impossible to give a comprehensive span of policy and administrative control—such as would be involved in the unification of all foreign economic policy—to any person short of the President. Foreign economic policy integration can only be accomplished by broad sectors and in terms of very general policy directives formulated at the top level by the National Security Council.

Changes in Organization and Administration

The following summary conclusions may be reached about the possibilities of improvement in organization for a better foreign economic policy:

For the Executive Branch. Since foreign economic policy is equally linked with security policies and with the total domestic economic and political system:

(a) It is impossible to centralize the control of *all* foreign economic policy at any level short of the President.

(b) Consideration of the broad outlines of general foreign policy can probably not be achieved short of the National Security Council, as advisor to the President.

(c) The organizational segments that deal with foreign aid and lending operations can be joined with "economic warfare" and foreign procurement and, ideally, should be brought under the direct control and responsibility of the Secretary of State through an officer of sub-Cabinet rank heading a separate, but integral, "operations" part of the State Department.

(d) The authority of the Treasury Department over the policy and operations of foreign lending should be abolished, along with its statutory chairmanship of the National Advisory Council.

(e) The distribution of other parts of foreign economic policy (including trade and tariff policies) in the existing organization of the Executive Departments reflects the balance of interests and the effective political pressures within the American political system. But if, in the interest of general foreign policy, it proves feasible to increase the national bargaining effectiveness of our tariff concessions, responsibility for this function should be vested in that agency which brings together as many other aspects of foreign economic policy as possible, namely the Foreign Operations Administration or a suitable successor organized as an economic arm of the Secretary of State. Modification of the "most-favored-nation" clause would be essential, however, to make possible the use of tariff concessions for this purpose.

For the Legislative Branch. The existing committee structure of the Congress probably defies any drastic alteration because of the working logic of our separation of powers, our federal system, and our traditions and resultant political habits.

(a) The strict logic of centralizing responsibility might require a greater concentration of legislative control over trade policies, possible through their allocation to the Foreign Affairs Committees of both Houses for authorizing legislation. But logic is not adequate for politics.

It would seem better in this matter—as in a great many other questions connected with the tariff—not to open Pandora's box by allowing jurisdictional jealousies to confuse substantive issues. The difficulty of ensuring that legislation permitting tariff negotiations would be even reasonably liberal is great enough as matters now stand. If the Foreign Affairs Committees of the House and Senate were given this new jurisdiction, they could probably not be strong enough to withstand the increased pressure on them from claimant groups. Their prestige is not adequate for this additional burden. Moreover, the rest of their legislative calendar would certainly suffer.

(b) Two desirable improvements would be a strengthening of the policy committees of the Senate, and the establishment of a standing foreign economic policy "study" committee for each House (along the lines suggested by the Colmer Committee) to make recommendations for legislation in the same way as the Colmer Committee did.

(c) Short of such a new standing committee arrangment, a periodic assessment by a commission like the Randall Commission, broadly representative of the Executive and Legislative Branches, would perhaps be the next best solution. This device does not, however, provide continuous review, education and guidance for the Congress, but it does for a time get greater attention on foreign economic policy issues both from the Congress and the public. Unfortunately, if the selection of the legislative members is made in order to placate or seduce an expected opposition, past experience with such mixed commissions has proved that they merely serve to equip the opposition with more effective weapons for subsequent resistance to desirable changes.

(d) Just as the National Security Council in the Executive Branch has come to set the major policy outlines of many aspects of foreign policy issues, so the Congress would benefit from the establishment of a select standing committee of both Houses to issue advisory reports to the Congress on all major matters affecting national security policy. Such a joint committee should consist of chairmen or top leaders of both parties from the existing committees dealing with foreign affairs, with the Armed Services, with finance and banking, and with appropriations. Members of other committees could be called in by invitation. This advisory joint committee could assist in breaking down particularistic economic (and other) pressures in the manner that the Colmer Committee succeeded in doing for the House during World War II and the immediate postwar period. Special subcommittees (perhaps drawn from the economic study committees outlined in (b) above) might report on major issues of national security affecting foreign economic policy. It is essential to have in the Congress a means whereby the different aspects of total national security policy can be interrelated in order to emphasize more strongly the broad national interest and the overriding considerations of national security where these conflict with domestic political and economic pressures. Only a very high level committee, really representative of the leadership of both Houses, could achieve this end.

However, in this—as well as in the other—suggestions for Congressional improvements, it must be recognized that there is no magic formula which will change the deep-rooted behavior pattern of the Congress. Perhaps only a deepening crisis of national security could substantially improve Congressional handling of foreign policy. But even a crisis cannot work a miracle contrary to the nature of our political system by the mere mechanics of greater centralization of control, though it may produce the necessarily more basic reforms in other ways.

Much as we recognize the difficulty of changing institutional relationships which reflect the basic pluralism of American life, it seems reasonable on the basis of past experience to find in foreign economic policy a prime example of the need for a higher degree of integration and unified control in our institutional machinery. The Executive, thanks to successive "reorganizations" since 1920, seems to be less "creaky" than the Legislature. But both branches of the Government are still a long way from possessing organizational patterns which would make possible adequate integration and more centralized control of foreign economic policy. This is, indeed, unfortunate, for in the mid-20th century the United States vitally needs a single, unified foreign economic policy rather than many uncoordinated—and occasionally contradictory—policies.

11

Beyond Political Economy

Among the many questions which preceding chapters have raised but left unanswered, there is one subject which cannot be left without a further word. That is the problem of how Americans can summon the will to carry out an effective and morally valid foreign policy. In what mood and spirit, and in terms of what aims, can Americans find the motivation to do what has to be done, and to do it by means which are morally consistent with the goals sought? Should appeal be made primarily to prudent calculations of American national interest? Can the restless energy which characterizes our nation find expression in a will to organize an improved international order? If so, how is that will to be exercised without leading—wittingly or unwittingly—to an intolerable American imperialism? Is the needed energy to be found, as some say, in the dawning sense of a distinctive American "mission" in the international community—a mission which expresses and yet transcends our own national ideals? These are not questions we can pretend to answer; they lead far beyond political economy into more speculative realms where this Study Group has no special competence. But the issues they raise are so crucial to an understanding of the scope and limits of foreign policy that our work would be incomplete without an attempt, in this concluding chapter, to suggest something of the psychological, philosophical, and moral considerations involved in answering them.

National policy, domestic and foreign, is rooted in a nation's basic interest in preserving the continuity of its communal life and safeguarding the possibility of realizing its hopes for the future. For nations as for individuals, the primordial motivation is security—that is, the will to survive and to preserve the material bases of a chosen way of life and direction of growth. In foreign policy, the primacy of security is even more marked than in domestic policy, because the former must cope with an incalculable and often dangerous external environment which obeys no superior law and which the national state cannot simply subject to its own organizing power. American foreign policy, therefore, finds the roots of its motivation and domestic support in this basic communal "instinct" to safeguard our way of life, with its inherent possibilities of future development. If foreign policy gets out of touch with this basic interest, it soon cuts itself off from the nourishing sources of its motivation and support. In such circumstances, foreign policy may become mere foreign meddling without continuity or consistent aim; or sentimental moralism which vainly relies upon unenforcible codes of good international behavior; or abstract idealism projecting utopian schemes for world order without disposing of the energy or the means to realize them. To be successful, foreign policy must be grounded in a conscious concern for the protection of the national security by means actually appropriate for dealing with a dangerous, incalculable and largely uncontrollable external environment. Such means are, in practice, predominantly of a short-term character, seeking prudently to prevent injury to the national interest rather than to achieve new or additional benefits.

Because national security provides the basic motivation for foreign policy, some observers believe that no other element is needed. But this view overlooks the fact that the national security principle is a principle of conservation, while life is characterized not only by conservation but also by creativity. Societies are preserved not simply through continuity but also through novelty which transforms established patterns of action and development when internal or external changes in the conditions of life so require. Without the capacity for transcending their own past, nations and societies, like individuals, would be unable to cope successfully with new problems, or to survive in the face of new and dangerous challenges. Paradoxically, they must break with continuity in order to preserve existence—to transcend their accustomed conception of their national interest in order to go on having a national interest to protect. Security is not achieved in a world of dynamic struggle by mere defense.

A nation or society which lacks the capacity or the willingness for self-transcendence in its foreign policy may survive and prosper according to its accustomed values if its external environment happens to be favorable. Thus, for example, the United States was able successfully to pursue an isolationist policy before World War I because it was protected by the favorable nature of 19th-century world politics. But in the 20th-century environment, an insufficient capacity to transcend an isolationist—or even a merely protective—conception of our national interest could well mean the end of our national existence. Successful protection of the national interest means not simply that the United States must be actively concerned with the security of the rest of the free world as well as with its own. It means also that, given the nature of contemporary problems and values, these protective or preventive objectives are not likely to be realized except as part of a broader concern to create new institutions and relationships in the non-Soviet world capable in time of achieving and maintaining the economic health, political effectiveness and defense capabilities of the other free countries.[1]

Thus, though foreign policy is rooted in the principle of conservation—in the self-interest of basic national security—there is also a second essential element involved. This is the principle of creativity—the transcendence of self-interest in the process by which self-interest is realized. It is the conception of a larger goal or purpose of policy, one that a wider-than-national community can share because it expresses universal human ideals and not simply the particular values of a given historical society.

What can motivate creative foreign policy?

One source of motivation is rational understanding of problems and of the means appropriate for coping with them. Without a rational grasp

---

[1] There is another sense, too, in which it is important today that sufficient regard be paid to the self-transcendent element in foreign policy. An excessive concern with national interest conceived in terms of direct or immediate national benefits may, particularly in democracies, encourage the subordination of these narrow objectives to still narrower considerations of domestic partisan advantage or personal ambition. Already in the United States, the postwar setbacks and disappointments of American foreign policy have been exploited with such partisan bitterness and demagogic obscurantism that vital national security interests have thereby been threatened. This irresponsibility, if long continued, could prove as dangerous to democratic institutions and national independence as, in analogous circumstances, it did in the ancient Greek and medieval Italian city-states.

of changing problems and new possibilities, nations could never over-come the inertia of traditional ways of conceiving and executing foreign policy. The United States today needs to improve its rational under-standing of the nature of 20th-century problems, of relevant goals of policy, and of effective and morally valid means for achieving them. This cannot be done in terms of an obsolescent conceptual framework inherited from the last century. It requires only that we look clearly at present political and economic conditions to see how largely emp-tied of contemporary relevance are the 19th-century meanings still so often attached to such ideas as capitalism, socialism, free trade, com-petition, progress, national sovereignty, international law—even war and peace. If we are to achieve the necessary understanding, we must in-vest these and other ideas with new meanings which express their con-temporary significance and provide the conceptual framework for more relevant policies and actions.

The power of rational understanding alone to arouse our country to accept its historic role should not, however, be exaggerated. It is characteristic of the positivistic strand of modern thought to assume that human beings are nothing more, and nothing less, than rational animals, motivated by a conscious comprehension of their own self-interest. In consequence, there is a tendency to believe that, because a proposed policy can be logically demonstrated to be necessary for American survival or progress, it will surely be adopted, even though it may involve major sacrifices of present interests and radical departures from accustomed practices. But a rational demonstration of self or national interest, though essential, is generally not sufficient by itself to create lasting novelty in society except in conjunction with other, more powerful, forces of human nature and communal life.

One of these forces is the vital energy or egoistic drive which makes nations in some cases rise creatively to new challenges or in other cases seek exuberantly to expand their territory or their economic power. At one stage or another in their history, many political communities have felt the urge to transcend traditional territorial, ethnic, or economic limits in order to exercise their power in a wider field. Generally, how-ever, this urge has been little more than overflowing vitality or will to power, largely devoid of moral purpose. Usually, therefore, it lacks ap-peal to other peoples; it provides no basis for creating wider community among nations, or for the acceptance of one nation's leadership by others. To do so, it must draw upon another force—the power of universal ideals to inform, and of moral values to restrain, the exercise of the will to power.

Great nations which in the past have created widely accepted and enduring "supranational" conceptions of their roles were able to do so because they had two essential qualifications. The first was rational understanding, which made possible the choice of relevant goals and effective means of policy. The second was the enlistment of their expansive vitality in the service of a strong sense of self-transcendent mission, which provided both a moral justification of, and a limitation on, the exercise of their will to power. It was the relevance of their policies and the moral character of their sense of mission which constituted the basis for wide acceptance of their leadership and the "cement" of the new community or system of world order which they created. Other imperial powers have failed to achieve wide or enduring acceptance of their systems of world order because these systems expressed little more than their egoistic will to power disguised in some overmastering myth rather than enobled and disciplined by a genuine sense of moral mission.

Such in our times have been the totalitarian schemes of order which Fascist Italy, Nazi Germany and Imperial Japan have sought to impose by force in the face of overt rejection of their leadership by prospective victims and unwilling subjects. These totalitarian systems failed because they were both irrational and immoral. They were irrational in the sense that their goals and means of policy diverged too sharply from the realities of human conditions, needs, and possibilities; they were immoral because the resulting myths under whose banners they fought were incapable either of transcending or of restraining their will to power. Such, too, is the far more dangerous scheme of world order advanced today by Soviet communism. It is more dangerous because it is less irrational in its appeal than the others and because its intrinsic immorality is artfully concealed in a utopian vision of perfect community and universal plenty. This vision has the power to attract millions of devoted adherents and to sustain them in major hardships precisely because of the element of self-transcendence which it contains. But, at bottom, it too is only a myth, and those who seek to realize it in human history are also victims of a double corruption. The irrationality of their goal of anarchic freedom and perfect plenty—that is, its unattainability—makes it powerless to prevent the diversion of their energizing will to power into the pursuit of narrower and merely self-interested purposes. Their failure of moral judgment, which permits them to choose an irrational goal, is also responsible for their fanatical error of believing that any means may be justified in attempting to achieve their end—even those morally inconsistent with it.

In contrast, the two creative leaders of the Western tradition—Rome and England—have both been distinguished by rational understanding and a genuine self-transcendent sense of mission, though of different content and intensity. The moral content of the Roman world order —summed up in the word *Romanitas* [2]—was most characteristically exemplified in the Roman conception of universal justice under law. The Roman achievement in creating enduring bonds of community among so many diverse peoples and cultures made so profound an impression on human history that it has ever since been looked back upon as the symbol or standard of a more just and rational world order. To this day, the elder branch of the Christian Church still lays claim to the oecumenical prestige of the Roman inheritance. England never felt so grand a sense of mission nor tried to build a world order on so broad and enduring a scale. Nor can it be said that Hindu and West African, Irishman and Boer were won to the *Pax Britannica* to the same extent as their counterparts were to the *Pax Romana*. Nonetheless, for its

---

[2] "[*Romanitas* was] the culmination of . . . the effort to erect a stable and enduring civilization upon the ruins of the discredited and discarded systems of the past. As thus envisaged, it constituted not merely a decisive stage in the life of the Roman people, but a significant point of departure in the evolution of mankind. From this standpoint, the institution of the principate [by Augustus] represented the final triumph of creative politics. For, in solving her own problem, Rome had also solved the problem of the classical commonwealth [i.e., the creative adaptation of the city-state system to the claims and requirements of the times].

"Of this impressive system [*Romanitas*], it may be observed that the dominant conception was novel. Amid the wreckage of empires founded on tyranny and exploitation, it stood alone as the project of a world-community united by ties of the spirit. It went beyond race, beyond colour, and, in all but a few exceptional instances, beyond religion as this was envisaged by antiquity. From this standpoint, it might appear that *Romanitas* transcended all purely 'natural' bonds. This in fact it did, in so far as it denied the possibility of discovering any real basis for concord on the merely affective level of experience. But while transcending, it did not, however, repudiate the human affections, seeking rather to organize them in support of the imperial idea. Under the aegis of Eternal Rome, Greek and Latin, African, Gaul, and Spaniard remained free to lead their own lives and achieve their own destiny; but, while local and racial differences continued to exist, citizens of the empire discovered a bond of community with one another on the plane of natural reason. It was on this account that the Roman order claimed a universality to which alternative systems of life could not pretend." Charles Norris Cochrane, *Christianity and Classical Culture: A Study of Thought and Action from Augustus to Augustine* (London: Oxford University Press, 1944), pp. 27–28, 72–73.

Anglo-Saxon members, the Empire expressed a sense of moral obligation to maintain a just peace among the powers of Europe, and to bring "enlightenment," material progress and eventual self-government to the colonial peoples—a moral content which Paul Tillich ascribes in the main to the large element of Christian humanism in what he calls "England's vocational consciousness" during the 19th century.[3] Britain's concern for the maintenance of the European political balance was not motivated solely by will to power or by prudent, short-run calculations of national interest. It also expressed consciousness of a duty to rationalize and humanize the relations among nations in accordance with those 19th-century liberal ideals whose economic and political expressions were so largely the products of British thought and action. Similarly, though the term "white man's burden" has become one of ridicule and opprobrium in the 20th century, the sense of duty which it expressed was once real enough to evoke a very large measure of sacrifice and devotion from Englishmen of all classes and in all climes.

The purpose of these historical examples is not to suggest that the United States should take Augustan Rome or Victorian England as its models. They are cited only to illustrate the general conclusion that no nation can rise to the tasks of international leadership—such as those which history has thrust upon the United States today—unless it can summon the will to transcend in some degree a foreign policy based on prudent, short-run calculations of its national interest. However abundant its material resources, no nation can become the instrument for creating order and community among peoples unless it has, in addition to a rational grasp of the problems and possibilities of its world situation, two qualities. The first is the reserve of vital energy which can find an outlet in the willingness to organize its international environment; the second is a strong sense of a moral mission to do so, expressed in concepts of justice and welfare which can transcend and control its egoistic will to power and can appeal to men everywhere.

Does the United States have these qualities?

Whatever its rational shortcomings, our postwar internationalism has expressed in some degree both a willingness to use our power to restore a liberal order to the international community and a sense of moral obligation to do so. Without these qualities, we could never have overcome the inertia of the isolationist tradition to the extent that we have.

---

[3] *Love, Power and Justice* (New York: Oxford University Press, 1954), p. 102.

Nevertheless, American thought and traditions still contain important obstacles to a wholehearted commitment to the role of leadership. The danger of a relapse into a foreign policy based on a narrow, overly cautious, and short-sighted conception of our national interest is still very great and would undoubtedly increase with any important setbacks to present policies.

Perhaps the major single obstacle to more effective American leadership is the American attitude toward power. Americans have a deep-rooted antipathy to central political power both in their domestic arrangements and in the international community. Paradoxically, this antipathy is one of our moral qualifications for world leadership and at the same time an important hindrance in exercising that leadership. At home, our suspicion of central organizing power has served as an essential restraint upon the unprecedented expansion of government required by the problems of Western society in the 20th century. Without this restraining influence, the inherent tendency of bureaucracy to grow might well have impaired by now the democratic character of American life. Abroad, we have always regarded ourselves as the natural opponent of any nation which sought to achieve its objectives by the application of political or military power against weaker countries or unwilling subjects. Thus, however much we may admire the positive accomplishments of the Roman or British systems of world order, we are even more impressed by their injustices, which we are apt to attribute too simply to the fact that they were built by power and maintained only through the constant exercise of power. We tend to forget, as Reinhold Niebuhr has observed, that "disavowal of the responsibilities of power can involve an individual or nation in even more grievous guilt" than its exercise. Though American antipathy to central organizing power can be a most important restraint upon any tendency on our part to abuse our power in relations with other countries, the difficulty to be overcome today is American reluctance to exercise power to even the minimum degree necessary to create and support a tolerable political and economic order among the nations of the free world.[4]

---

[4] Reinhold Niebuhr has pointed out that the negative American attitude toward power has its philosophical roots in two sources. One is the conception of human nature in the Judaeo-Christian tradition, which emphasizes realistically the inevitability that men and nations will often abuse their power—that is, will turn it to self-centered purposes—however they may rationalize its use in universal moral terms. The other is the quite inconsistent and optimistic doctrine of liberalism that men's interests are so "naturally" harmonious and their ambitions so inherently ordinate that central organizing power is unnecessary. The former view of human nature does not exclude—as does the pure liberal one—the

We have tried throughout this study to show that, just as order within national communities depends upon the power of national governments, so some kind of central organizing authority is essential both to establish and to maintain political and economic order among nations. An international order—like a national state—also requires power to protect itself from nations which remain outside of it and would weaken or destroy it to serve their own ends. Lasting order without the support and protection of power is, unfortunately, not a possibility of human history. Community among nations, no less than within them, can never be so perfect that the need for central authority will disappear and its structures "wither away." Ultimately, we may dare to hope, this necessary central power will be wielded in the world community by voluntarily created supranational institutions. For the foreseeable future, its functions must be fulfilled to a minimum degree, and its preconditions established, primarily by that nation which has the resources, the rational understanding and creative imagination, and the sense of self-transcendent mission required for effective and morally valid leadership. Thus, the American leadership obligation involves a realistic acceptance of the role which American organizing and protecting power has to play in creating a more just and humane international order.

As we have noted, the liberal internationalism of postwar American policy—despite its inadequacies—was a major step toward that self-transcendence which is among the essentials for successful leadership. True, the sense of mission then achieved has been impaired in the last few years by a resurgence of isolationist sentiment, due in part to frustration of the unrealistic expectations generated by the conceptual errors of liberal political and economic internationalism. Yet the moral content of American internationalism accounted—and still accounts—for much of the domestic support for American participation in the United Nations and the Bretton Woods institutions, and for later and more

---

need for central organizing power to control the self-interested activities of men and nations, even as it insists on the moral ambiguity of power and the necessity to subject it to constitutional and moral restraints. The liberal view expresses a relative truth, but taken as an absolute formula leads to an overly simple and moralistic attitude toward power. Thus, to the extent that the American attitude toward power in the international community is based on the recognition of man's capacity for abuse of power, it is a moral qualification for world leadership. To the extent that it reflects the liberal illusion that there exists a natural harmony among the interests of men and nations which makes central organizing power unnecessary, it is a major obstacle to our willingness to assume that leadership.

realistic policies embodied in the Marshall Plan, the North Atlantic Treaty and the Point IV Program. A corresponding feeling in other countries that these policies were something more than instruments of American national interest has helped undeniably to build community among the nations of the West.

What would now constitute a more adequate expression of the moral content of the American mission?

It is much easier to say what the content of the American mission could *not* be than to describe it in positive terms. Its expression in recent years has generally been too vague to be a compelling source of motivation either for Americans or for other peoples; we must say something much more concrete and evocative than that we are for freedom and democracy and against tyranny. Nor can it be an unperceptive attempt to "sell" existing American institutions and ways of living to nations which, though they may envy our technical accomplishments and even share our ideals, are not attracted to all of the specific values and relationships by which these ideals are expressed in contemporary American society. Indeed, the sooner we cease trying to "export" the *American* standard of living, or the *American* way of life, or the *American* private enterprise system, the more effective our foreign policy can be. For what we can hope to export—what other societies and peoples would be able and willing to receive from us—are the skills and attitudes which make possible, and the essential spirit which animates, these values and institutions, not the specific values and institutions themselves.[5]

Clearly, then, our mission can be no crude or excessively materialistic notion about exporting the American way of life or the American standard of living to other peoples. Those among our self-styled "realists" who have caught something of the necessary sense of mission in

---

[5] Thus, those businessmen, intellectuals and politicians—at home and abroad—who persist in trying to force the realities of contemporary problems into the obsolete 19th-century dichotomy of socialism versus capitalism are hardly likely to devise relevant or practicable solutions. Particularly in the underdeveloped countries, the most difficult issue is not public versus private ownership, but how the large-scale organization and the expanding central bureaucratic control required under either form of ownership for rapid and substantial economic development are going to be reconciled with the decentralization essential for creative initiative, individual responsibility, and personal freedom and dignity. If the process of development increasingly subjects him to gigantic industrial organizations and a massive bureaucracy in New Delhi, it will make little difference to the ordinary Indian worker or farmer whether the means of production are publicly or privately owned.

the phrase "the American century" have unfortunately been vitiating their own concept by their glorification of American productive capacity and resulting level of material consumption. Even the "idealists" have tended in practice to speak of the self-transcending purpose of American policy as though it consisted of the impossible task of raising the rest of the world to the American standard of living. Neither of these two conceptions of the American mission can be sufficient to inspire even the American people with the necessary energy and moral dedication, much less our allies and friends abroad. But then, how does a people so enamoured of its own material progress, and so admiring of its particular brand of private competitive enterprise, talk convincingly to peoples with different value systems and goals? How does a nation which has apparently mastered its major internal economic difficulties by economic expansion find something relevant to say to countries which are unable to solve their economic problems in this way, due to unfavorable historical circumstances?

These are difficult questions, and an attempt to answer them raises other questions even more difficult. At bottom, the task of defining the essence of our self-transcending mission is the same as the more fundamental task of clarifying and reaffirming those qualities and potentialities of American society which engender our love and loyalty to it. These must surely be something more than our material progress which, impressive as it is, may be only one of the fruits—perhaps merely one of the by-products—of the satisfactions Americans derive from the exercise of their unrivaled ability to manipulate and control the material world. A number of other American qualities of particular importance to the purposes discussed in this chapter may be noted here.

One would certainly be our effective freedom of thought—particularly, the pragmatic expression which Americans have given to this ideal through their receptivity to new ideas, in contrast to the more tradition-bound or doctrinaire habits of mind in many other countries. Another is those embodiments of the belief in individual worth and responsibility, and the humble recognition of human evil, which have made possible the largest functioning democracy in history. A third is that strong sense of brotherhood, of friendliness and mutual help, inherited from our pioneering days, which today makes possible social cohesion and voluntary cooperation within a nation whose citizens have such heterogeneous origins. It has also enabled Americans to live and work with the peoples of other cultures in direct human relationships and with little overt concern for status and social position. A fourth is the ways by which Americans have succeeded in reconciling a large measure of private, decentralized decision-making and initiative in virtually all fields of human action with the growing requirements for centralized bureaucratic power and large-scale organization imposed by an increasingly complex and interdependent industrial society, by mass participation in domestic politics, and by heavy political and economic responsibilities abroad. In the conditions of our times, this latter American achievement in making the requirements of power consistent with justice and freedom subsumes all the others, for it both depends upon them and makes them possible.

It is among such attributes of the particular society Americans have built for themselves that we may hope to find clues to any distinctively American contribution to the well-being of human society generally. Americans have, of course, no monopoly of these qualities. But in this century, the particular American combination of them seems to be unique, at least in degree, if not in kind.

To list in this way the merits of American society does not imply any blindness to its defects. Indeed, we have noted American shortcomings throughout this study and we do not minimize their seriousness now. But to be concerned solely with our defects is to take only a partial view of our society. Nor is it necessary to go to the extreme of a cynical moral relativism to recognize the moral ambiguity, inherent in human nature and society, which permits an institution, attitude or action to be simultaneously good and bad. This truism has particular reference to the American qualities under discussion here, which are often cited by critics of the United States as evidence that American society is dominated by crudely materialistic values. It would be foolish to deny that this criticism has a limited validity insofar as our creativity and our joy in work serve no better purpose than to satisfy the artificially stimulated whims of the American people for ever newer models and additional gadgets. But American pragmatism, skill, and productive exuberance have another, and vastly more important, significance for the whole of human society. Today they make the United States the "arsenal of democracy," producing most of the armament which alone protects the free nations from communist imperialism. Tomorrow our willingness to share them freely with others may make their significance even greater. The export of American skills and attitudes may not only be an indispensable means for achieving greater justice and welfare in the international community. If world population growth and consumption expectations both continue their explosive rise, the export of these American qualities may also be essential to enable many countries to provide their hungry peoples with the very bread of life itself.[6]

If, then, we are to rise to the challenges of our times, there can be no more urgent or important task facing the American people today than redefinition and renovation of the living values of our society within the broader context of the universal human ideals they express. The values of our society—which we sum up in the word "freedom"— are preserved by constantly re-expressing them creatively in new and more relevant forms; they can be lost whenever attempts are made to preserve them by a coerced conformity with their existing ideological or institutional expressions, particularly in a critical period when the rapidity of events so soon makes concepts and institutions obsolete. Such enforced conformity preserves only the outward form of these values while it kills their living spirit. Essentially, the task is to find new and more satisfying ways of orchestrating novelty and continuity, cultural diversity and political unity, private decision-making and central organizing power, personal fulfillment and organic community. In America's present situation, one of the main parts of this task is to express creatively and relevantly a new conception of the American mission in the world. In trying to define and to carry out that mission, we may achieve not only a more successful foreign policy; we may also recapture that liberal spirit which is the necessary prerequisite for the

---

[6] In part at least, American shortcomings are products of the restless energy of a young and dynamic people, which can be expressed destructively as well as constructively—and sometimes has to be so expressed if creation is to occur. In this tragic century, the "demonic" capacities inherent in man's human bondage should certainly not surprise us. However, we should also remember that some of the greatest and most fruitful periods in the history of Western culture have been the direct outgrowths of times of trouble and disorder analogous to the present. There is good reason to regard the shock and alarm in other countries at American shortcomings as frequently disproportionate to their cause. No doubt this reflects in some measure the—perhaps unrealistically—high reputation which the United States has enjoyed abroad in the 20th century. But one has only to think of the many millions in Western Europe who, over the past twenty-five years, have succumbed to fascism, communism or neutralism to realize the very much smaller prevalence of similar perverse responses to contemporary problems in the United States. Ironically, too, there is an implied —and doubtless quite unintentional—compliment in the eagerness of so many non-communist European and Asian intellectuals always to believe the worst about the United States and the best about the Soviet Union and Red China. It is as though every American fall from grace, however slight, were an unexpected calamity, and every Communist gesture of good will, however trivial, were a miracle to be received with humble gratitude.

practice of freedom at home. We cannot have one effect without the other; at bottom they are but different faces of the same thing.

These very general comments on the problem of the American will to carry out an effective and morally valid foreign policy may at least serve the purpose of indicating the crucial role such psychological, philosophical and moral considerations will play in influencing the choices and actions of the coming years. For, the outcome of present difficulties and challenges is likely to be significantly different, depending upon whether the United States achieves none, some or all of the three prerequisites for successful and morally valid world leadership —rational understanding, the will to organize, and the sense of moral mission.

One possibility is that the United States would fail to realize any of them, or would be capable of achieving them in too small a degree to be effective. In that event, neither American energies nor American conceptions of the actions required would be adequate to bring about a significant improvement, much less an essential change, in the effectiveness of American foreign policy or in the policies of other leading Western nations. In consequence, Western policy as a whole would not be sufficiently rational, nor would its moral content be inspiring enough, to prevent a steady growth of neutralism, anti-Americanism, neo-fascism and communism in Western Europe, and intensification of isolationism and neurotic and escapist tendencies in the United States. The result could only be continuing drift and disintegration in the West and increasing disorder and communist advance in the underdeveloped countries. In the end, these developments could lead through a series of retreats and appeasements to a third world war, or perhaps even to Soviet attainment of worldwide domination without war. This course of events could well be the outcome of the present predicament of the West unless the United States and its Western allies can combine both the motivation and the means for acting together with greater understanding and vigor in meeting the challenges of our times.

A second possibility is only a somewhat less dismal—and perhaps more likely—variant of the first. It is that the American people would muster sufficient will to organize their external environment more effectively but would fail adequately to understand the kinds of actions capable of meeting contemporary challenges in a positive, creative manner. In the absence of sufficient rational understanding and moral inspiration, a strong upsurge of the American will to power could only take the form of an American imperial "solution." Under this possibility, the American reaction to recurrent economic and political crises in the non-Soviet world and intensified civil strife in the underdeveloped areas—perhaps even in continental Western Europe—could take the form, not of American withdrawal into isolationism, but of direct or indirect assumption by the United States of governmental responsibilities in countries no longer capable of meeting by themselves the minimum requirements for political effectiveness and economic self-support. If the frustrations resulting from continued reliance on obsolete or unrealistic policies do not too seriously impair the American will to organize, the probable outcome would be an American imperium reluctantly and unintentionally brought into being to forestall a universal communist empire.

The third possibility—and the only constructive and desirable one— is that the American people will be capable of the rational understanding and of the energy and moral inspiration necessary for substantial progress to be made in the next few years toward a more effectively organized Western Community and more stable and mutually beneficial relationships between it and the underdeveloped countries. In essence, this third possibility means adoption of policies which more and more consciously seek creative adaptations of the nation-state system. Like all political arrangements, the nation-state system is a means for the realization of human goals; it is not a consummatory value—an end in itself. From its beginnings in the late middle ages through its flowering in the 19th century, this method of political organization contributed to the store of human happiness and achievement. For over four centuries, it progressively met the tests of efficiency and morality which every means must satisfy if it is to foster the satisfaction of humane values. But in this century, the nation-state system has been conspicuously failing to meet these tests for an ever-growing number of countries, some of vital importance to the survival of Western society. For these, the nation-state system is increasingly unable to satisfy their minimum requirements for self-defense, self-support and economic growth, and to achieve a politically acceptable reconciliation of conflicting claims for incomes and opportunities. Were it not for the basic vitality and momentum of Western society—and for the active protection and support provided by certain free nations, particularly the United States, for whom the nation-state is still an efficient and morally valid means—

these countries would now be succumbing in one way or another to totalitarian regimes, communist or fascist.

Specific suggestions for moving toward a more effectively organized Western Community and improved relationships with the underdeveloped countries have been made in the preceding chapters. These proposals are neither as comprehensive nor as detailed as many Americans—with understandable impatience or skepticism—would like them to be. But it is useless to try to give this third possibility a clear-cut definition in institutional terms, for it is essentially a process—a direction of change—rather than a static goal or state. Its institutions would be constantly in evolution, growing out of present Atlantic and European political, military and economic arrangements. Their forms are unpredictable any distance ahead, because they will depend so much on the free evolution of politics and on unforeseeable human decisions and creations.

There is no inescapable determinism in history which compels us to await an inevitable decay of our society, while we try without hope to sustain our morale—like the Romans of the Fall—with the consolations of philosophy. Within the existing limits of the possible, men are always free to choose their fate—or to submit to it if they are unwilling to choose and to act. Though undoubtedly impaired in recent years, Western society still has the vigor and moral inspiration needed to find constructive ways out of its present dangers. Its past is still a moving force in the present that strengthens our actions beyond the power of any current interest or conscious motive. In the course of our efforts, there is bound to be much suffering and many disappointments. Nor can the outcome be "the best," but only "the better." Beyond the present dilemmas of man and society lie other challenges whose nature and magnitude are today inconceivable. But when a people can face the troubles of its own time with energy, intelligence and creative imagination, and in consciousness of the demonic depths and spiritual heights of man's nature, it may be blessed by having the future as its heritage.

Index

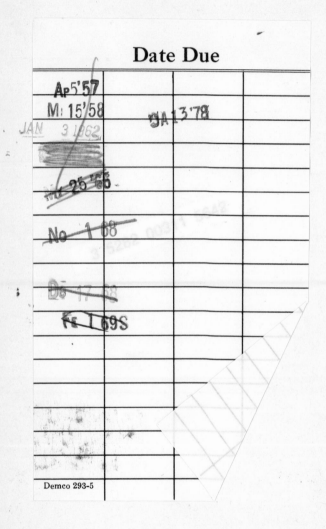